SPAIN

The Gentle Anarchy

BENJAMIN WELLES

SPAIN

The
Gentle
Anarchy

FREDERICK A. PRAEGER, *Publishers*
New York · Washington · London

FREDERICK A. PRAEGER, PUBLISHERS
111 Fourth Avenue, New York 3, N.Y., U.S.A.
77–79 Charlotte Street, London W.1, England

Published in the United States of America in 1965
by Frederick A. Praeger, Inc., Publishers

© 1965 by Frederick A. Praeger, Inc.

Library of Congress Catalog Card Number: 65–18081

Printed in the United States of America

Contents

v

Contents

For "Moses," who taught me to love Spain;
and Mari, who taught me to know it

Acknowledgment

To those friends who have helped me in preparing this book, *"un abrazo."* My colleagues and mentors on *The New York Times,* Theodore M. Bernstein and Drew Middleton, were kind enough to read some early chapters and give me sound advice. Miss Laura Waltz helped with preliminary typing. Mari de Oliva of Madrid and Luís López Ballesteros, Information Councilor of the Spanish Embassy in Washington, assisted me in obtaining photographs and checking last-minute facts and figures, although they bear no responsibility for my conclusions.

To Hanna Gunther, my thanks for her patience and judgment; to Therese E. Nadeau, my thanks for her help in preparing the index. And especially, my appreciation goes to Ann (Mrs. Arden) Peach of Bar Harbor, Maine, without whose unflagging loyalty at the typewriter this book might never have seen the light of day.

BENJAMIN WELLES

Alfaz del Pi, Alicante, Spain
and
West Point, Prettymarsh, Mount
Desert, Maine
June, 1965

SPAIN
The Gentle Anarchy

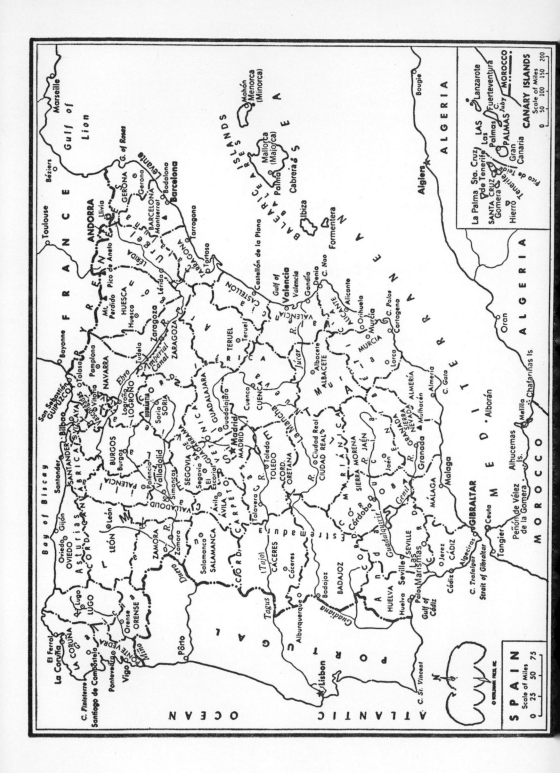

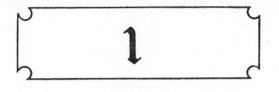

The Gentle Anarchy

Spain, a wise Spaniard once said, is a *dulce anarquia*—a gentle anarchy.

The surface is calm, deceptively calm, like the sea on an August morning. The swells rise and subside, curling occasionally in petticoat foam, then meld back into the great, slow-moving surface of the ocean's face. Heaving, always restless, always heaving, the ocean never sleeps; neither does Spain.

Spain is also a cockpit of conflict. In her blend the Iberian, the sandy-haired Celt, the Phoenician, the Greek trader, the Roman soldier, the blond Goth, the Arab, the hammer-handed Christian knight, the grandee, the booted guerrilla general, the bishop, the banker, and the peasant—always the peasant. If from poverty comes strength, from hardship independence, and from loneliness dignity, then the Spanish peasant is thrice blessed, for he has all three. He is curiously like the peasant of northern China.

His blood, culture, and religion may be very different, but the peasant of Spain and the countryman of northern China have much in common: slow humor, grave courtesy, self-reliance, and the same fatalism acquired through centuries of war, invasion, inclement weather, and long misrule. But while the Chinese has learned to bow to the wind, the Spaniard will bend only so far—

then beware! Then the hand will fly to the knife or gun, and chaos will reign.

No topic exerts a more fatal fascination for the Spaniard than his own national temperament. A foreigner eager to break the ice and launch Spanish friends into animated discourse can do no better than to inquire into the Spanish character. He may then sit back and relax, for the argument will flare up like a fire bursting from cellar to attic. Eyes will flash, voices perorate, hands gesticulate and shoulders shrug, feet stamp, and fingers wave—and the discussion will roar for hours. Time and again in my six years in Spain—from 1956 to 1962—as correspondent for *The New York Times,* I encountered this national characteristic of exuberant self-analysis.

One Spaniard, starting calmly, will explain the need for benevolent dictatorship over so tempestuous a race. Another, cutting in, will add that the underlying sensuality of the Mediterranean peoples requires rigid control over morals and behavior by Church and State. A third will disagree; a fourth will interrupt. The first speaker will ask for attention, be brushed aside, wait his turn, try again, and be interrupted. So it will go on, rising in pitch until it would seem that the Civil War was about to resume.

But it will pass, for this is merely the Spanish method of discussion. With all the fire of his race, the Spaniard puts his soul into declamation. His language is rich, lending itself to dramatic embroidery, and in his every gesture—such as giving a simple direction on a country road, or pointing out a landmark—the Spaniard is an artist. The same volatile courtesy can, however, quickly turn into dogmatic assertiveness when Spaniards debate politics, and from assertiveness the path is short to truculence, to wounded pride, hot rage, and blind destruction.

Blando en acción, duro en reacción: easygoing until pushed too far, is an old Spanish saying, and Spain's history proves it. In the past century and a half, Spain has suffered 109 governments, 24 revolutions, and 3 civil wars.

4

Today, the face of Spain is changing. But whether Spain's soul, too, is changing remains the great unknown. The Spaniards, 31 million strong, still do not have political freedom; but they have greater wealth than ever before, greater even than in their golden sixteenth century. For nearly twenty-seven years, one man, Generalissimo Francisco Franco y Bahamonde, Chief of State, Chief of the Government, Commander in Chief of the Armed Forces, and "by the grace of God Caudillo of Spain," has ruled this turbulent nation with an iron hand that is only now beginning to relax. Discipline and time have been Franco's main allies: discipline to cow the hot-blooded adults into obedience; time to let a disciplined youth emerge. Now, the night of obedience is almost spent, and the streaks of dawn seem to be paling the sky.

What of the new generation? Older Spaniards complain that today's youth is cynical, materialistic, and resentful over propaganda and obscurantism. All that youth in Spain wants now, say the elders, is money, jobs, security, and comfort; and for this situation they blame the regime: the Falange, the generals, the bishops, the bankers, the landowners.

Young Spaniards themselves, rich or poor, privileged or struggling, confirm this. The university students—Spain's elite—are the most frustrated. Most are indifferent to politics, fearful of trouble with the police; but there is also a minority in a state of constant effervescence, and this minority is angry, courageous to the point of foolhardiness, indifferent to arrest or imprisonment, and increasingly drawn by Socialist, Anarchist, and Communist ideas.

"My sons are now in their twenties. They know nothing of life except Franco and the regime, and they regard Franco as Methuselah," confided one of Franco's highest officials not long ago. He paused, reflected, then added, "They are perfectly right."

The restiveness in the state-run universities; the open discontent among the young workers; the steady emigration of young workers to France, West Germany, and Switzerland for better jobs at higher pay; the strikes that break out in Asturian coal

5

mines, are crushed, then break out again: all these bear witness
to an indefinable malaise. Even young country priests are openly
defying hierarchical displeasure by aligning themselves with the
strikers. Even in the army, that bulwark of reaction, young officers are beginning to show signs of impatience. So far, the mood
is unorganized and voiceless, for the habit of discipline is strong;
but it is there.

The casual visitor, however, will see little of this. It is largely
hidden. In 1964 alone, 14 million tourists poured into Spain,
seeking the long, lovely beaches, or camping by the sea in the
colorful camp grounds that dot the coasts. Most came away en-
chanted. The roads of Spain, though bad, are improving; gasoline is abundant; new hotels, villas, and pensions are springing up
everywhere. Suspicion of the foreigner has given way to the jingle
of the cash box, and tourism has become Spain's main industry,
bringing half a billion dollars yearly to the coffers of a nation
that six years ago stood on the brink of bankruptcy.

Go where he will, the tourist will find warmth, friendliness,
and courtesy. The cities are throbbing with new life. In Madrid,
Barcelona, Seville, Zaragoza, and Bilbao, new apartment and
office buildings have risen where sheep used to crop on sandy
lots. Shiny new Spanish-built cars jam the avenues and make the
rush hours a nightmare. Yet until 1953, not a car had been built
in Spain. The cinemas, bars, shops, and the handsome new hotels
are bursting, not only with foreign tourists, but with moneyed
Spaniards. Land speculation is rife in cities and along the coasts,
and although prices are rising, Spain is prospering.

But true to the law of all dictatorships—of left or right—with
better times, the people demand more freedom. This is especially
true of the *pueblo* of Spain. Go into any of Madrid's teeming
tascas, or taverns. You will see well-dressed, well-shod Spaniards
with their womenfolk, downing their two-peseta *pinchos* of local
wine, munching shrimps, sardines, or sausages, and damning the
bureaucracy. Franco's ministers and his policies are openly im-
paled on the stiletto wit that is Madrid's heritage. A decade ago,

the same critics would have spoken softly, glancing warily from side to side.

Spain's newspapers, periodicals, radio, and television remain dull, yoked into plodding conformity by the Ministry of Information and Tourism and by fear of punishment. Despite regime claims of liberalization, the press still censors itself, fearful of fines, dismissals, or loss of government-subsidized newsprint. The press has long lost the habit of thinking for itself, and so speeches or photographs of Franco, of his officials, of his generals, of his bishops, elbow aside the news. There is no real criticism of the regime in the press or on radio or television, for "opposition" is still a penal offense and "illegal propaganda" a one-way ticket to prison.

The regime, rather than Franco, takes the brunt of popular discontent over censorship, political stagnation, lack of trade-union freedom, or the continuing disparity of wealth. Franco has been so long in power that his harsh edges have been sandpapered by time, and he has become an avuncular figure, seen as often in civilian attire bestowing prizes at a football match as in army uniform at a state review. The older generations—the women, especially—still revere him for having "saved Spain from Communism" in the Civil War. Even the new middle class, hypnotized by its new wealth, shrugs indifferently. It knows nothing but Franco and prefers not to think of any alternative. In a free election tomorrow, Franco would win at least 65 per cent of the vote.

But youth and the intellectuals want change—sweeping change —providing it is nonviolent. These groups, still voiceless and unorganized, want land reform, educational reform, higher wages, a curb on monopolies, separation of Church and State, freedom to speak, and freedom to organize. As a typical sign of their new nationalism, they disapprove of the U.S. military bases in Spain: not because of anti-Americanism or an anti-NATO sentiment, but essentially through pride. It matters not that these bases have brought economic benefits, that the average

American airman or sailor is quietly behaved, or that the entire
U.S. military population in Spain totals less than one-twentieth
of one per cent of the population. The U.S. bases are somehow
symbols of "inferiority." Yet, speeding down the road from La
Junquera to the Costa Brava, or over the sierra to Malaga, the
average tourist will never see this. For him, or her, the sun is
shining, the countryside beautiful, the food surprisingly good,
the plumbing improved, the shops well stocked—and while the
villages may have no sidewalks and the pigs may grunt happily
down the streets, nonetheless the Spanish people are better fed
and better clothed today than they have been in more than a
quarter of a century. And without question they are the best-
mannered people in Europe.

Come to Mérida on an autumn afternoon. Here, in the west
of Spain, where Julius Caesar once ruled as governor general,
mile upon mile of rolling, treeless plain separates the little
towns. The mountain border with Portugal looms purple in the
distance, and over the *vega* thin wisps of smoke plume up into
the sky like Indian signals as peasants burn off their scrub. Little
knots of men and women jog softly down the road on burros
laden with wheat bags. Occasionally, a heavy cart will creak past.
A little dog trots under the axle, hiding from the sun, while the
driver sits on the shaft, his arms locked around the neck of his
mule, fast asleep. Nearby, a ragged shepherd boy drives his flock
with a warning stone, while on the highway itself, a soft-eyed
donkey stands dozing, closing its eyes in patient resignation as a
six-ton truck thunders past, missing it by inches. The countryside is at peace, quiet, and hot.

Or come to Aranjuez on a November day. The little palace,
built by Louis XIV's homesick grandson Philip V, first Borbón
King of Spain, still stands, fading like a patch of old velvet. The
green river slides by, coiling around the bridge-piers, while
couples wander arm in arm through the *allées* of sycamore, birch,
and poplar. From the earth rises a cool, clean smell of leaves be-

ginning to moulder. The old guards, in leather bandoliers and wide-brimmed hats, gaze pensively at the river as if it were bearing their lives away.

Young soldiers tease knots of giggling girls in tight skirts and high heels, and four boys in shorts bend over a parapet, trying to spit on a floating leaf. From far down-river comes the hoot of an ancient locomotive, vintage 1850, wearily crossing an iron bridge with its third-class carriages rocking-and-rolling along behind it. This is old, mellow, charming Spain, where nothing will happen this year, or next year, or perhaps any year.

Yet there is also a Spain of noise, of rhythm, song, hand clapping, heels drumming on hard wooden floors: the Spain of flamenco. For this, come to the Feria of Seville in April. Once a cattle fair on the edge of town, the Feria has now become an international event. Here, the day starts with a drink, or several, at noon, in the densely packed bar of the huge, garish, "Euston-Moorish" Alfonso XIII Hotel, the caravansary of Europe's nobility, the Long Island set, India's remaining maharajahs, and an occasional Spanish grandee. From the hotel to the fairground is but a step. The streets are lined with lavishly furnished *casetas,* or open tents, and the parade passes and re-passes throughout the day. Magnificent Anglo-Arab horses bear young Spaniards in leather chaps, white shirts, and flat Cordoban hats, their *novias—* their fiancées—in ruffled dresses riding pillion behind them. Spanking Andalusian mules draw gleaming carriages from which ancient dames gaze haughtily on the crowds. Swarthy Mexican *vaqueros,* crowned by huge straw sombreros, pass by, hands on hips, their silver spurs jingling and their horses proudly curvetting. Periodically, riders stop near the fashionable Club Aereo tent, where photographers and friends cluster around, joshing, laughing, and handing up glasses of ice-cold manzanilla sherry.

By six o'clock, the crowds have moved to the circular bull ring, and now a rich blue cloud of cigar smoke ascends as the aficionados roar out their *"olé"* for a *faena;* or rise, pounding their neighbors' backs in distraught anger, yelling *"¡Mátalo! ¡Mátalo!"*

9

("Kill him! Kill him!") if some nervous matador bungles the kill.

By eight, the bullfight is over and the night descends, warm, soft, and scented. Japanese lanterns flicker in the trees and diners linger at their tables until midnight, one, two, or even later. No one hurries. Movement in the fairgrounds becomes next to impossible as the crowds saunter, eating spun sugar, gazing into the open tents. At every corner, openings have formed, with six, seven, or even eight rows of spectators, to watch a girl, or a couple, break into an impromptu dance. The overhead lights, the wailing music, the hand clapping, the click of castanets, the crying of vendors, the hustle and bustle, even the transistor radios in the crowds—all blend into a magnificent anarchy.

But it is not until three or even four in the morning that the gypsy dancers come into their own. The mood must come on them, slowly, naturally, for their artistry can never be hurried. Suddenly, in the rear of a private *caseta,* one steps forward from a ring of chairs and the rest fall silent. The guitarist strums a few chords. Now, softly, begins the sinuous, pleading, whining quarter-tone trill of the *cantaor,* berating his mistress for her coldness, imploring, pleading for her favors. Magnificent in her somber moodiness, she flaunts her independence, and the Arab heritage of Spain now bursts forth.

The dancer tenses, arms upraised, hands perfectly modeled, a look of savage intensity transfiguring her face. She kicks the train of her dress to one side. Slowly, she begins to move, classic steps at first, then growing faster and more wild as the hand clapping urges her on. Soon, the gypsies behind her are clapping in irresistible rhythm, and now her feet drum a hard staccato on the wooden floor, as her body swirls and her head snaps back and forth, sending the long locks flying. The passion mounts, sensual and wild, until, with a wild twisting of her body and of ruffled skirts, it is over. The dancer is spent. Panting, she retires to her chair as a thunder of applause and shouted *olés* breaks from the audience. The next comes forward. This time it is a man, lithe, booted, his trousers skin-tight. He grips the lower seams of his jacket in one hand as the fingers of the other describe an arabesque in the air. The guitar strums. His feet drum. The wail rises.

On it goes all night, the dancing, the singing, the music—and often the sun has begun gilding the trees before the last of the gypsies has quit and the onlookers have staggered home.

There is still another Spain: a Spain of the snows—Madrid on a midwinter evening. The chestnut vendors huddle over the glowing pans in the arcades of the Plaza Mayor, while out in the Puerta del Sol, blue-coated police snap their arms to keep warm, their breath rising in the icy air. Snow graces the sloping roofs in the old Plaza de Provincias and the turrets of the Palacio Santa Cruz, once a prison for errant nobles but now the Foreign Ministry. With its open patios, its portraits, and its stone balustrades, it is one of the loveliest ministries in Europe.

Students in their traditional slashed black capes run down the steep steps into the Street of the Knifesellers and hurry into crowded restaurants to serenade the customers and pick up enough in tips for a jug of red wine, bread, and cheese. The noise is deafening as families and friends argue, laugh, declaim, sing, and expostulate. Empty wine jugs are held overhead, snatched by passing waiters, and filled in a trice. Long after midnight, the customers begin trudging contentedly home.

In the narrow streets of the old city, soft lanterns throw splashes of light on Gothic or Renaissance walls. Old Álvaro de Bazán, first Marqués de Santa Cruz and a hero of Lepanto, gazes down imperiously in bronze as if daring a passerby to mock the silence, and an old *sereno,* one of Madrid's nocturnal watchmen, stands by a flight of steps murmuring Godspeed to the homeward bound and pocketing small gratuities with no loss of pride. During the Middle Ages, his forebears patroled the streets at night, lulling the citizenry with stentorian calls that all was well—*todo serenoooooooo.* But the *sereno* of today opens apartment-house doors for forgetful night owls and keeps an eye on all that transpires on his beat. He stands, hat on the back of his head, keys stuck in a leather belt, wooden stave of office in his hand. Down the street comes an insistent clapping. Someone wants to be let in.

"Mire usted—look you—we *serenos* know what passes better even than the economists," he tells a passing couple. "We know when things are bad. Our tips go down. Now they are improving. Who knows? In Spain, all things come, all pass. Go with God."

Again comes the clapping, more insistent. He starts, pounds his club on the sidewalk in acknowledgment, and is gone in a flapping of coattails.

There are many other Spains besides the Spain of sunny Mérida, of gentle Aranjuez, of hot-blooded Seville, of chill Madrid. There is the Spain of industrial Bilbao, smoke from a hundred chimneys fouling the bright air, its rivers sour with refuse, its streets potholed, its oyster bars filled with prospering merchants. There is the Spain of broad Barcelona with the stately fountains, the cool, narrow streets of the Gothic quarter, and the flower-banked *ramblas* where the city strolls each evening regarding itself. There is the Spain of little fishing ports such as Suanzes in the north or Andraixt in Mallorca; and there are the faded charms of Sanlúcar de Barrameda, near Cádiz, where the Infante Alfonso d'Orleans y Borbón, one of Spain's great gentlemen and now well in his seventies, still stunts his airplane solo every day.

Then, there is the Spain of the Moors, of Mojáca, near lonely Almería, where the women with their raven-black hair, their green eyes, and their fair skins still wear yellow head veils, holding the ends in their teeth like the Moorish women of Fez or Xauen in Morocco across the Strait.

Finally, there is the Spain of the Balmoral bar in Madrid, the conclave of society, the noon-to-two meeting place for the duquesas and marquesas, the Albas and Eldas, the Medinacellis and Primo de Riveras, for the smart staff captains from the War Ministry resplendent in their blue sashes, for the rich, for the wellborn, for the cognoscenti among Anglo-American tourists.

These are all Spain, but there is a Spain less enticing: a sullen, brooding, explosive Spain. Such as Asturias, where sheep graze on emerald-green hills and men, not many feet below, lie on their backs in dark seams so narrow they can barely move. There they hack at the coal, breathing coal dust, worn out by the time they are forty. By Spanish standards, they earn good money, perhaps three dollars a day, yet they are far from satisfied. The Asturian miners have defied Franco by striking repeatedly in recent years—so far without violence. Will these strikes always be peaceful?

It seems increasingly unlikely, for there is little hope of real freedom in Spain while Franco lives. He detests liberalism, ascribes to it all Spain's past woes, and believes that the West must scrap democracy and adopt something midway between his paternal despotism and De Gaulle's presidential authoritarianism.

"Every day the world sees with greater clarity the inefficiency and futility of *inorganic, formalistic* [e.g., Western] democracy," he told the Spanish people at the end of 1959. "In the political field the solutions and doctrines adopted by the world today *resemble those evolved by us more and more,*" he added in 1964 [italics added]. In Franco's eyes, it is not he who is changing; it is the world that is moving toward him.

Franco's paternalistic despotism is based on the theory that the Spanish masses are too turbulent to rule themselves and are better off with a full belly and a muzzled mouth.

"Welles, Spain is a gentle anarchy." It was one of Franco's cabinet ministers talking, as he pointed to the broad Castellana Avenue. Cars sped through red traffic lights, motorcycles veered in and out of traffic lines like minnows, trucks swerved violently —and in the midst stood a nerveless policeman, yawning, as vehicles almost scraped the puttees from his legs. A few yards farther on, a taxi had halted in the stream of traffic, its driver peering languidly under the hood, as its three male passengers sat comfortably back, smoking their cigars as if in a London club.

"We are a hard people for foreigners to understand," the minister added. "We dislike discipline but we need it. We must have a firm hand."

It is one of the great paradoxes of Spain that 31 million people are aware of the firm hand—but know little of the man who wields it.

Caudillo—By the Grace of God

On a spring evening not long ago, a young Spanish lawyer was called to the Pardo Palace near Madrid for an interview with Franco. After driving through ornate gates past saluting sentries, he continued up the graveled drive to the cream-colored palace and was shown to the gardens, where he found the Caudillo relaxing in his shirt sleeves. Franco was holding a Coca-Cola bottle in each hand, and absorbedly pouring their contents into a tall glass.

"Hola. ¿Qué tal?" Franco greeted his visitor. "How are you?"

Murmuring his respects, the young lawyer asked what Franco was concocting.

"I don't like ice," explained the dictator, "so I always take one cold bottle and one warm one, and mix them until I get just the right temperature."

For nearly three decades, Franco has been tempering the hot Spanish character with his own icy controls. But this political mixmaster of Spain is a man curiously unknown even to his own people. The Spanish sense, rather than know him. His face, his speeches, his audiences, his inspection trips, his hunting and fishing, even his family activities have been reported day after day for nearly three decades in virtually every newspaper in Spain. In general's uniform, Franco is seen receiving the interminable deputations of elderly generals who call periodically to reaffirm their loyalty. In gold trim, as Chief of State, he is shown receiving a South American or Arab ambassador. In a smartly cut gray suit and homburg, he hands a trophy to the Real Madrid soccer team. Gun under arm, he hunts partridge on the moors near Toledo. Occasionally, he is photographed at home with his young grandchildren. Yet the man has long been concealed behind an imperious, arrogant, often testy image. A Spanish general once remarked: *"Valiente, pero poco generoso—*[Franco is] brave, but not overly generous."

For a people famous for warmth, generosity, and dignity, the Spanish are magisterially bad at projecting their best image, and Franco is the worst. This short, portly man with the haughty mien, the dark, liquid eyes, and the high, rapid voice is known to perhaps a dozen persons: his wife, Carmen; his married daughter, Carmencita; his son-in-law, Cristóbal, Marqués de Villaverde; his brother, Nicolás; and his seven little grandchildren. His other intimates include Juan Antonio Suanzes, the industrial empire-builder; Admiral Pedro Nieto Antúnez, the Navy Minister; and the Conde de Argillo, Villaverde's banker father. With the latter, Franco is said occasionally to drive around Madrid, hiding behind dark glasses, relaxing from protocol, and inspecting the capital of the land he rules.

Franco's public image has begun to soften in recent years as the dangers of foreign intervention, Communist subversion, and economic collapse recede. He is less the harsh, arrogant figure of old that shrilled defiance at "foreign incomprehension," and more and more the elder statesman. He can still trot out the old defiant clichés and toss them to cheering crowds whenever Asturian miners strike too boldly or his foreign critics goad him, but even these occasions are increasingly rare.

For twenty-eight years, no enemy, from Stalin down, has broken Franco's grip on power, and the Spanish people have grown so accustomed to his face that few can imagine an alternative. Many, in fact, prefer not to.

Francisco Paulino Hermenegildo Teódulo Franco y Bahamonde Salgado Pardo was born December 4, 1892, at El Ferrol, a small seaport on the Atlantic coast of Galicia, which now styles itself right royally: El Ferrol del Caudillo.

"The inhabitant of a soft, gray land, the Gallegan is of a dreamy disposition," noted Salvador de Madariaga.* A Gallegan himself, Madariaga observed that the Celtic Gallegan is "poetical and imaginative, superstitious, apt to believe in apparitions and to feel the presence of the supernatural world." Galicia, he added, produces "shrewd, intelligent, hardworking, thrifty, physically strong" people who become Spain's lawyers, politicians, stevedores, and policemen. What Professor de Madariaga omitted, perhaps understandably, was that the Gallegans are also notoriously clannish, suspicious, and guileful. In this sense, Franco is a Gallegan to his fingertips.

His forebears, like most Gallegans, followed the sea. His father was a naval paymaster of solid bourgeois stock, while his mother's family, the Bahamondes, were more economically and socially eminent. As one of three sons, Franco was destined for a naval career, but when he was preparing for the naval engineering school, all available places were filled, so he was entered, instead, in the army's Infantry Academy at Toledo.

The small, swarthy, fifteen-year-old cadet who arrived in the *novato del siete*, the novitiate of 1907, with "a trunk, a suitcase, two hats, and a pile of books" was quickly nicknamed Franquito —little Franco. The early photographs show a serious, calm face, a broad forehead, and short dark hair parted in the center. The eyebrows are bushy, the mouth is topped by a military mustache, the chin Gallegan in its stubbornness. The eyes are calm and widely spaced. Reserved and aloof even in his teens, Franco was

* *Spain: A Modern History* (New York: Frederick A. Praeger; London: Jonathan Cape, 1958).

never hail-fellow-well-met in the boisterous Spanish student manner, but short as he was—and his 5 feet 3 inches is still a matter of sensitivity—he was singled out by his more than three hundred fellow cadets for future success.

The army became his passion. In 1898, Spain had been stripped of her last overseas possessions—Cuba, the Philippines, Puerto Rico, and Guam—following the disastrous Spanish-American War, and the army was left to focus its attention on Spanish Morocco, its last fief. There, across the Strait of Gibraltar, Spain in 1912 established a joint protectorate with France, and young Franco, upon receiving his commission, volunteered for duty with the *regulares,* a new native force with Spanish officers. On the blistering sands and rocky slopes of the Rif Mountains, he began to learn the habits of military command and particularly the traditional "carrot-and-stick" techniques of the Arab emirs, which, with his native guile, have characterized his rule over the Spaniards.

"He treats us like Moors," a Spanish official once said. "If we behave, he leaves us in peace but if we make trouble—we get the stick!"

Like most Spanish officers of the day, Franco grew up learning certain fixed dogmas. Great Britain and France, for instance, were Spain's perennial enemies seeking to strip her of her last foothold in Africa. Germany, on the other hand, was the greatest military power in the world, and, being France's enemy, must therefore be Spain's friend. The United States was an uncouth, Protestant braggart, preaching democracy while eyeing territorial spoils in Spanish America. Anglo-Saxon democracy was unsuited to the Spanish temperament and would lead to Anarcho-Sindicalism, revolutionary Socialism—even Communism. It was the army's mission to defend Spain against her foreign foes and even against herself—though it might mean killing her. Such were the doctrines taught young Spanish officers in Morocco prior to World War I, and Franco, by absorbing them, rose rapidly in the estimation of his seniors.

France's crack Foreign Legion had begun attracting the envious interest of the Spanish Army, and Franco now volunteered to help Colonel Millán Astray raise a similar force. By 1923, he succeeded Millán Astray as Commander of the Spanish Foreign Legion and grew to love it. From this period stems a revealing anecdote. One day, while inspecting his legionnaires, Colonel Franco halted before a particularly ugly trouble-maker, a German who had been complaining of the food and other conditions. As Franco listened coldly, the legionnaire, without warning, spat full in Franco's face. Franco moved not a muscle. Slowly, he completed his round of inspection and returned to his office. Then, summoning his adjutant, he wiped his face with a handkerchief and quietly ordered the legionnaire taken out and shot.

In 1925, when Morocco's Rif mountaineers, led by Abd-el-Krim, flared into revolt against their Spanish and French "protectors," Franco's opportunity had come. With characteristic skill, he seized it. At a hastily summoned conference in Paris, Spain and France decided on a joint "pacification," to be commanded by a French general, Pétain, and a Spanish general, Sanjurjo, along plans prepared by a Spanish colonel. The colonel was Franco. Within weeks, Spanish troops covered by French aircraft splashed ashore at Alhucemas Bay on the Moroccan coast, splitting the rebel forces in two and breaking the back of the rebellion. The campaign, one of the first to involve combined air, sea, and land operations in modern war, was successful; and in 1926, at thirty-four, Francisco Franco was promoted to become the youngest general in Europe.

As a general, Franco now joined the power elite of Spain, the praetorian guard of some 200 generals whose main doctrine was opposition to all liberal stirrings. Spanish generals had first started tramping onto the stage of history during Napoleon's invasion, when Spain's fleeing Borbóns had left the nation leaderless. Everywhere, patriotic juntas had sprung up, determined to repulse the invader. Unfortunately, from this moment on, Spain's history has been marked by incessant militaristic intervention in public life, by civil wars, by *pronunciamientos,* by plots, and by administrative chaos. By 1868, the situation had become so desperate that the army even nudged the fat, fair, and amoral Queen Isabella II from her throne. In 1873, the First Republic was established, and when that experiment failed, the army had had no alternative but to call Isabella's son, Alfonso XII, from his cadet training at Sandhurst, and, in league with the Church and the landowners, put him on the throne.

Inexorably, the situation worsened. The humiliating defeat of Spain's armies and fleets in the Spanish-American War and the loss of the colonies unleashed in 1898 a wave of liberal antimilitarism that hardened the army in its truculent contempt for civilians—especially for liberal civilians. To regild its scutcheon, the army began to seek showy victories in Morocco. When Moroccan resistance stiffened and Spanish casualties mounted, Spanish popular resistance to conscription erupted in bloody riots, in 1911, in Barcelona—and in savagely anti-army cartoons in the Catalan press. This was too much for the army's honor. A band of hot-headed officers brutally assaulted the civilian editors, and when King Alfonso XIII's government could not, or would not, bring them to book, the army's domination of Spain became final. From this moment on, the Juntas Defensivas, or secret officers' societies, grew rapidly, finally becoming a state within a state. By 1923, the playboy king, Alfonso XIII, half grudgingly, half gratefully, accepted General Primo de Rivera as his Dictator-Prime Minister. This was the ruling caste into which young General Franco now found himself admitted.

Within six years after assuming power, Primo de Rivera found himself abandoned by his king and scuttled by his enemies. His rise and fall taught Franco a valuable lesson. Primo de Rivera had built good roads and had attracted tourists to Spain, but he had lacked political sagacity. He had fallen to a combination of military and civilian foes whom he had scorned to crush. Franco, observing Primo's fall, learned the first lesson of dictators: Crush or be crushed.

The next lesson followed surprisingly quickly. In April, 1931, King Alfonso XIII himself was abandoned by the army, whose friendship he had so assiduously cultivated. Without a shot being fired, Alfonso took the dusty road to Cartagena and boarded a cruiser for exile, abandoning Spain to the Second Republic, whose unprepared leaders virtually stumbled into power. Franco had taken his oath of loyalty to the Borbóns in 1910, but Alfonso's ineptitude filled him with scorn.

As the Second Republic groped from crisis to crisis, with the moderates paralyzed and the extremists increasingly violent, Franco watched, said nothing, and stayed close to his colleagues in the army high command. The ultraconservative army and the Spanish left-wing Republic were fast falling apart. Then, without warning, Franco's second major opportunity came, and again, with characteristic skill, he seized it.

An armed revolt of the Asturian miners in 1934 brought him national prominence. Assigned to crush the uprising, Franco imported the Legionnaires and Spanish-officered Moors he had trained and led in Morocco, and whose fighting qualities he knew. Within weeks, the *dinamiteros* of Oviedo and other Asturian strong points were crushed and an estimated 2,000 miners were executed on Franco's orders. The story goes that some of the Legion officers, sickening of the butchery, sought to evade their duty, but Franco, alerted by the Guardia Civil, sent word that the executions were to continue or his officers themselves would face condign punishment.

Overnight, Franco had become the darling of the right and the bane of the left. In 1935, Army Minister José María Gil Robles picked him as army chief of staff, but the Republic's suspicion had been aroused; Azaña's popular front government soon dismissed him and sent him to obscurity as Captain General of the Canary Islands. There, he began to be drawn into an army conspiracy, masterminded by General Sanjurjo, in exile in Lisbon, and by Sanjurjo's deputy, General Mola, in Burgos.

At dawn on the morning of July 18, 1936, Franco issued his

now famous *manifiesto* from Las Palmas, capital of the Canaries. Within hours, he had flown to Casablanca, to Tetuan, and thence to Ceuta, in Spanish Morocco, to assume leadership of the rebellion's southern flank. The Spanish Civil War had started.

Luck had always smiled on Franco since that burning day in 1910 when he had knelt by the great equestrian statue of Charles V in Toledo and kissed the flag, swearing to protect the Borbón dynasty and the lawful government. Luck was with him still. Within twenty-four hours, Sanjurjo, leader of the rebellion, was killed in a flying accident en route from Lisbon to assume command. Within ninety days Mola was killed in another mysterious air accident. The leadership of the Civil War now devolved on Franco. On October 1, 1936, by the unanimous vote of the military and civilian rebel leaders, Franco was named Caudillo, or supreme leader, of the national struggle. On that autumn evening in Burgos, few suspected that he would reign as the uncrowned king of Spain for more than a quarter of a century.

Franco probably knows the Spanish character, its strengths and its weaknesses, as well as anyone alive, yet he himself is curiously "un-Spanish."

Where the average Spaniard is headstrong, articulate, and gregarious, Franco is controlled, taciturn, and remote. Unlike his countrymen, whose words and ideas rush out with dizzying brilliance, Franco, as the saying goes, tells "not even the collar of his shirt." Crafty and suspicious, Franco prefers not to act, but to react; and he is a master of letting time work for him. It is said that he has two trays on his vast ormolu desk, one marked "problems that time has solved," the other, "problems that time will solve." The slogan that once graced President Truman's desk—"the buck stops here"—could also grace Franco's, for all major decisions eventually reach his desk.

In his personal life, Franco combines the Spartan and the

royal. He rises around seven, attends private devotions with his chaplain, and is usually at work around nine. His day is long, broken according to Spanish custom by luncheon at three or four, and by dinner as late as ten. His meals are taken with his family or with one or two ranking officials and are of soldierly simplicity. He eats sparingly, seldom takes wine, and refuses flatly to be interrupted at table by telephone calls, no matter who the caller is. He neither smokes nor permits smoking in his presence.

Yet he is punctilious about the deference due him as chief of state, and he lives in royal style. His residence, the handsome little Pardo Palace near Madrid, is surrounded by uniformed guards; he travels in a gleaming Rolls-Royce flanked by motorcycle or cavalry escorts. Foreign ambassadors presenting credentials are brought to another palace, the Palacio del Oriente, in the heart of Madrid, in an eighteenth-century state carriage, drawn by caparisoned horses and attended by liveried servants. Occasionally, Franco even confers titles of nobility on his adherents, but only after corresponding privately with the Pretender, Don Juan.

Longevity runs in Franco's family, and nothing delights him more than to remind visitors that his grandfather lived to be more than a hundred; his father died in his nineties. Except for the effects of a shotgun explosion on Christmas Day, 1961, which seriously injured his left hand, Franco remains in excellent health for a man who was seventy-two years old on December 4, 1964. The only signs of age seems to be an evident listlessness in his expression when he is unaware that he is being seen and a slight slowing down in his reaction to news. His critics complain that he spends at least a hundred days each year hunting or fishing, and there is no doubt that Franco is happiest while casting for salmon in the streams of Asturias, shooting the red-legged partridge around Toledo, or deep-sea fishing with one or two intimates aboard his yacht "Azor," off the coast of his native Galicia.

Reserved and aloof in his official life, Franco is relaxed and affectionate in his family circle. He is a model of the bourgeois paterfamilias, and in a land much given to philandering, his devotion to his wife has become a political asset of the first order, especially with women and the Church. Similarly, for all his royal style and power, Franco has never been accused of the corruption for which some of his subordinates are notorious. His one and only vice is power.

Like most elderly rulers, he finds solace in his grandchildren. Having no son of his own, Franco persuaded his only daughter, Carmencita, and her husband, Cristóbal, Marqués de Villaverde, to name their eldest son, Francisco, after him and to drop the family name Martínez de Bordiú. This unusual procedure was duly ratified by the Cortes. The ties between Franco and his daughter's family are close, and at his insistence the Villaverde children spend much of the year at the Pardo to be near their grandfather. Miss Hibbs, their English nanny, has standing orders to bring the children to the Caudillo every day after lunch and, regardless of the pressures of work, it rarely happens that Franco does not also devote an hour to them before their bedtime.

He idolizes them all but particularly the youngest girl, María del Mar, who is allowed to climb all over him and plump herself down on his lap whenever she chooses. Merry and bright as young jays, the Villaverde children wield a unique power; they alone dictate to the dictator.

Little Francisco has become a television fan. Not long ago, he was heard scolding his grandfather for pre-empting an hour of prime time for his annual state of the nation report to the Spanish people. To Francisco, echoed by his chorusing brother and sisters, this was unforgivable.

Franco himself understands but speaks little English, so he insists that the children learn it and practice every day with Miss Hibbs. Occasionally, when Spain's Real Madrid soccer team humbles a visiting British team, Franco shares a little joke with his grandchildren, asking them in strongly accented English, in front of Miss Hibbs. "Well, children, did Nanny weep?"

Miss Hibbs is one of a vanishing breed of British nannies, very few of whom are still found in aristocratic Spanish homes. Smiling and serene, she remains a pillar of British style and phlegm in the temperamental heart of Spain's ruling family. Franco and his family are devoted to her, and despite lucrative offers, she has steadfastly declined to write her memoirs.

Yet, notwithstanding Franco's insistence that his grandchildren learn English and his predilection for British clothes, automobiles, and ceremony, his family remains Latin and temperamental—as Miss Hibbs has discovered more than once.

On Christmas Day, 1961, a domestic storm arose when young Francisco insisted on being allowed to go shooting with his grandfather. Despite the pleas and cajolery of the Caudillo, of his wife, of Carmencita, of Villaverde, of the children and their friends, Miss Hibbs stood her ground, as unyielding as the Rock of Gibraltar. A firm believer in good works, particularly when rearing privileged children, Miss Hibbs had always taken the Villaverde children to distribute toys on Christmas afternoon to needy orphans, and she was not going to make any exception. She remained smiling but firm in the face of the storm.

Hours later, when Franco's shotgun had exploded, Miss Hibb's stock soared once more, for now everybody realized what might have happened had the child been standing near, or even been holding, his grandfather's gun. The frowns turned to smiles, the tears dried up, and Spanish temperament bowed gracefully to a British nanny's resolve.

Franco will never pardon a slight to his family, although he may retain the offender in high office. In 1950, Foreign Minister Alberto Martín-Artajo, the towering Catholic leader, led a goodwill mission to Egypt, and Franco's high-spirited daughter Carmencita and her husband went along.

For reasons technically correct but politically inept, Artajo placed the Villaverdes at the foot of the list of precedence, and soon Franco and his wife learned of it. The Caudillo said nothing but when the mission returned and Artajo trooped triumphantly off the plane, Franco, at the head of the cabinet, gave him a cool handshake, and Doña Carmen not only cut him dead but refused to speak to him for weeks.

"You were correct. The rules of protocol should not lightly be broken," Franco told Artajo later in the privacy of his office, "but we fathers can also show a little heart!"

Despite the *gaffe,* Artajo remained Foreign Minister for seven years. In 1953, he negotiated not only the Concordat with the Vatican but also the crucial military bases agreements with the United States. Yet in 1959, when Eisenhower paid the first visit ever made by an American President to Spain, Franco coldly struck his former foreign minister's name from the banquet list. He had neither forgotten nor forgiven.

"Tears come easily to Franco," a high Spanish official remarked on another occasion. "Tears are the sign of a cruel man."

Franco's cruelty is not the sadistic cruelty of a Hitler who could order his enemies hung on butcher's hooks, nor the police-type cruelty of a Mussolini with his castor-oil dosing of his opponents, nor the paranoiac cruelty of a Stalin slaughtering subordinates and opposition. Franco's is the soldier's—especially the Spanish soldier's—indifference to life or death, the cruelty of the centurion. His repression of the Asturian miners in 1934, of his beaten Republican foes after the Civil War, of suspected dissidents after World War II are on the record, and no amount of whitewash can efface them. The estimate of the number of people Franco has had shot, jailed, or exiled ranges from a thousand to half a million.

Yet with the passage of time, with improved economic conditions and the waning fear of foreign encirclement, Franco is mellowing. He has granted successive amnesties in recent years, and the jails of Spain are slowly emptying. No more than 1,300 men and women are in jail as "security risks." At a recent cabinet meeting, Franco ordered his Minister of Gobernación [interior] to investigate reports of Guardia Civil brutality to arrested Asturian strikers. Five years ago, Franco would have shrugged off such tales or left the security authorities to behave as they chose.

Occasionally, he displays a wry humor. He once told a cabinet faction urging him to restore the monarchy that he had no intention of playing the role of "Spain's queen mother." Riding with Eisenhower on a chill winter afternoon of 1959, he noticed that the American President seemed genuinely impressed by Madrid's handsome streets and the fervor of the crowds. Turning to Eisenhower's interpreter, the Caudillo murmured, "Tell the President that we haven't paid our people to cheer nor have we brought him into Madrid on the only clean street of the city!"

Franco's early antipathy to the United States has not completely disappeared, but it has been largely mitigated by his gratitude for American help. Whenever requested by the American Embassy, he goes out of his way to receive American visitors such as Senators, Congressmen, officials, or other distinguished citizens. One he sees often is the American Catholic leader James Farley, onetime Postmaster General under Franklin D. Roosevelt and now head of Coca-Cola's international division. Another is Lt. General Leslie Groves, director of America's World War II atomic development, with whom Franco discusses military topics. The Caudillo is becoming more accessible to American journalists, but their questions must still be submitted in advance in writing and they may have to wait two weeks or more before they can be fitted into Franco's crowded schedule.

My own first audience with Franco took place in March, 1957, four months after my arrival as resident correspondent of *The New York Times*. Franco had received my written questions and had answered them in writing, and the exchange had been published. Now, several weeks later, I found myself bidden to the Pardo for personal presentation. I had been told that I could ask Franco any questions I chose, but that his answers could not be directly quoted. Arriving at the Pardo at noon, I waited, with my Foreign Ministry escort, in a long, handsome antechamber hung with fine Goya tapestries and thronged with an assemblage of priests, generals, Falangist officials, civilians, and elderly women in widow's weeds—all, like myself, waiting to be received, and all whispering or speaking in hushed tones. Two hours after the appointed time, my name was finally called by a blue-liveried servitor and, followed closely by my escort, I passed through large double doors into Franco's office.

The Caudillo stood stiffly erect, halfway between his desk and the doors. The spacious office was well lit by the sunlight that poured in from the gardens. The Aubusson carpets, the velvet draperies, and the gilt-inlaid furniture seemed to confer an air of majestic tranquillity. Despite his five feet three inches, Franco, in a general's gold-trimmed uniform, a ceremonial red silk sash around his waist, dominated the room. His face was an immobile mask, his head thrown back slightly, his eyes appraising and cold.

We shook hands, he murmured a few words—more to the Foreign Ministry escort than to me—and then waved us both to two stiff antique chairs placed side by side in front of his desk. He seated himself in another chair, facing us at a distance of five feet, folded his hands in his lap, and waited.

The conversation moved off slowly. Franco, speaking in a high voice, lisping slightly, inquired when I had arrived, whence I had come, and whether I knew anything of Spain. Although he seemed to be speaking to the interpreter, his eyes never left my face. When I began to reply in my rusty Castilian, his face suddenly came alive. Hearing his own tongue, although haltingly spoken, he seemed suddenly refreshed, no longer mentally at arm's length. His whole manner changed.

I had decided this was not the time to cross-question Franco on such well-worn topics as political freedom, censorship, or the monarchist succession. For years, every interviewer had covered these same questions and had received the same contrived, evasive, and inevitably unsatisfactory answers. Instead, I decided to ask him what he thought a newly arrived journalist should look for—expecting him to propose that his Falange propaganda chiefs show me how well loved he and his regime were. To my surprise, he launched into an animated discourse on irrigation, agricultural reform, rural colonization, light and power development, road and harbor improvements, light industry, new housing, and reforestation. The planting of trees over Spain's arid wastes seemed especially close to his heart.

"I have heard that Spain has no forests because the goats eat up the young shoots," I interjected at one point. He smiled.

"The goats are a problem," he admitted. "The peasants are accustomed to letting them graze at will and this is a country of old customs. With the goats, as with everything else, we have to move slowly. But you will see we are moving."

For three-quarters of an hour, he talked of the land and its development, of the people and their slowly rising standard of living. It was propaganda, of course, but it was also fact, as I came to realize during my six-year stay. I noticed how he sat, motionless, every muscle under control, except for the left foot, which pivoted nervously on its heel, twisting right and left.

As a clock struck three, I remembered the priests, the generals, the Falangist bosses, the bankers, and the widows all whispering in the antechamber, awaiting their audiences. Franco would see them all and it would be four or five before he would sit down to lunch. When I got up, he shook my hand and expressed the hope that I would come to know Spain, its problems, and its people. It was a great country, he said, but it required knowing.

I turned at the door and saw him standing where I had first seen him, in the center of the room. His face was again a mask, his head was thrown back to accentuate his height. Cloaked in his dignity, he was awaiting the next in an interminable line of visitors.

"We did not win the regime we have today hypocritically with some votes," Franco reminded the Spanish nation in September, 1962. "We won it at the point of the bayonet and with the blood of our best people!"

After twenty-eight years in power, this is still Franco's creed. He is a soldier, he thinks as a soldier, and he will rule Spain as a soldier until he dies. In his eyes, the Civil War was a mortal struggle against Communism and, even though the rising generations of Spain may not care, even though they may now want political liberties and the freedom to speak or act as they choose, he will continue to use the Civil War as his mandate to rule. The 1936–39 conflict may be a bore to Spain's youth, but to Franco it remains his *raison d'être*. His overriding aim is to preserve law and order, so that the nation's resources may be developed and its geographic and religious unity preserved. If in the process, personal liberties must be suppressed, Franco does not consider this too high a price. How long he can contain the rising flood remains the great question.

Nothing angers Franco more than charges that his is a naked military dictatorship with no freedom. He insists that his system, which he holds up as a model for underdeveloped nations in Latin America, Asia, and Africa, *is* democracy: democracy tailored to special conditions. He calls it "organic" democracy, although his critics call it despotism alleviated by graft.

No one could pretend that Franco Spain is a democracy in the Western concept of the word. Franco still hires and fires all key officials; still muzzles the press; still bans all political opposition; still sets the nation's domestic and foreign policy by intuition rather than by consultation with the people.

Yet no race such as the hot-blooded Spaniards can be ruled for more than a quarter century in total disregard of their desires or in total incomprehension of their needs. Franco has not ruled Spain by ignoring its soul but by adapting—agonizingly slowly —to changing conditions. His regime has been inching closer to the people, just as the people have been inching closer to the regime, and after twenty-eight years, both have learned to accommodate. What emerged from the wreckage of the Civil War as a Fascist dictatorship has become today a more relaxed, competent, and forward-looking administration.

Politically reliable young Spaniards are rising high in the administration, and the average age of Franco's eighteen-man cabinet is now no higher than was that of the late President Kennedy. Foreign Minister Castiella, for instance, is fifty-seven; Commerce Minister Ullastres, fifty; Finance Minister Navarro Rubio, fifty; Minister of Industry López Bravo, forty-one; Minister of Information and Tourism Fraga, forty-two; the new economic planning czar, López Rodó, is forty-four.*

Franco's system has often been called a one-man dictatorship, but this is not wholly true. Franco is an umpire rather than a dictator. From the day of his accession to power in Burgos in September, 1936, Franco has ruled Spain through meticulously hand-picked coalitions. His skill has been in knowing how to balance and reconcile the shifting forces of power. In 1937, while the Civil War was raging, he fused the radical Falange and its "labor" wing, the JONS (Juntas de Ofensiva Nacional-Sindicalista) with the ultrareactionary Carlist Monarchists, thus hamstringing all three. In 1945, when the Western democracies and Soviet Russia were winning the war against the Axis powers, he replaced some Nazi-Falangists with Demo-Christians. In 1951, sensing American interest in a military agreement, he reinforced the business and Monarchist elements of his cabinet. In 1957, anxious to share in Europe's economic boom, he swung further right by including ministers from the economically liberal Catholic movement, Opus Dei.

---

* Franco's latest cabinet reshuffle (July 7, 1965) continued the process of naming younger men to high responsibility. Among the new ministers were Lopez Rodo, named Minister Without Portfolio; Antonio Maria de Oriol, 51, Minister of Justice; Faustino Garcia-Monco, 48, Minister of Commerce, who replaced Ullastres; Adolfo Diaz-Ambrona, 57, Minister of Agriculture; and Federico Silva Muñoz, 41, Minister of Public Works. Ullastres' replacement apparently stemmed from the inflationary rise in food prices, 16 per cent in 1964.

Each cruise of the ship of state has lasted roughly five years, and at each port of call, Franco has replaced his crews with fresh hands, all from the political right: Nazi Falangists, Franco Falangists, Carlist Monarchists, Alfonsine Monarchists, Franco Monarchists, military chieftains, Church delegates, bankers, industrialists, landowners, middle-of-the-road Catholics, and, lately, Opus Dei "technocrats."

Not only does Franco name and dismiss cabinet ministers, he appoints all fifty-odd provincial civil governors, all mayors of large cities; all heads of the twenty-four Sindicates (into which Spain's 8.5 million workers and 3.5 million employers are herded); all army, navy, and air force commanders; and—thanks to his 1953 Concordat with the Vatican—all bishops. His power is immense, for he is subject to neither criticism nor recall. Even the currency proclaims him *Caudillo de España por la gracia de Dios*—Caudillo of Spain by the grace of God.

Still, he insists that he is not a dictator.

"My powers are much more modest and much more limited than . . . in the majority of existing presidential regimes," he told CBS's Walter Cronkite in early 1963. "In all my actions as chief of state I am assisted by a council of eighteen ministers whose agreement is essential for approval of decisions."

Whether "essential" approval would be refused by any cabinet minister is open to question, but Franco's current cabinet is an immense improvement over the quarreling mediocrities of the early days. When troubles beset Spain, Franco ruled as an emir, holding each minister responsible to himself alone and encouraging backbiting and tale-telling. Now that Spain's course is smoother, the trend is toward collective responsibility and greater efficiency. Franco has even been toying with the idea of appointing a prime minister to whom he could turn over routine functions, as De Gaulle did with Debré and Pompidou.

Franco's cabinet serves not only as his executive team, but also as the wellspring of legislation. Laws originate in the cabinet and are sent to a relevant committee of the Cortes for study. Then they are returned, with amendments or suggestions, to the cabinet—that is, to Franco, who not only conceives but also gives final approval to all laws.

Cabinet meetings are held twice monthly on alternate Fridays. On the intervening Fridays, Franco presides over the cabinet's economic subcommittee. Cabinet meetings start at 9:00 A.M. and almost always continue through the night until dawn Saturday. The Spanish penchant for late hours has long been a bane to journalists, who must wait for their predawn briefings from mercurial, cigar-smoking Information Minister Fraga Iribarne.

Franco presides at the head of a long table with his senior minister, Vice President Muñoz Grandes, on his right, Foreign Minister Castiella on his left, and so on down the table. Each minister reports in order of seniority. According to those present, no limit is set on the time consumed by any minister or on the topics he may discuss. The cabinet not only weighs such transcendental issues as renewal of the American military bases agreements or Communist subversion, but even the size of a pension for a rear admiral's widow, or a medal for a deserving railway guard.

Hour after hour, the sessions roll on, and while some ministers occasionally step outside to stretch their legs, Franco himself has never been known to quit a cabinet session. This is how he rules Spain. From start to dawn, he remains imperturbably in his place, attentive, seldom interrupting, unruffled even when his ministers break into angry quarrels. He is the master, and men ten and fifteen years his junior marvel at his fortitude.

He detests paper work. Unlike his friend and fellow dictator, Salazar of Portugal, who isolates himself from his aides and devours sheaves of reports, Franco insists on seeing and hearing his subordinates in person. The desk and table of his study are piled high with tomes, memoranda, reports, illuminated addresses, scrolls, and commemorative editions—all politely accepted and stacked away unread. When young Prince Juan Carlos once asked him how he could possibly read so much, Franco permitted himself one of his rare chuckles. "When the piles become too high, Señor," he replied, "I have everything taken out from the bottom and burned!"

This negligence toward the written word, however, implies no slackening of control. Franco cows his subordinates, whether they are newcomers or old comrades-in-arms, by a combination of reserve and innate leadership. Not more than a dozen men call him by the familiar *tu*. Everyone else addresses him either as Excelencia or Mi General.

His answer to a proposal is hardly ever given at the time it is made. Neither will he argue. He remains chillingly silent and it is obvious that he alone will make the decision in his own good time. Seldom peremptory, never in a rage, he controls his emotions as tightly as he controls the destinies of the men around him and the nation he rules. When subordinates bring him bad news or face him with a distasteful decision, they know better than to press him. They tiptoe away awkwardly.

Like many dominating personalities, however, Franco respects those who stand up to him—or those who can read his mind. He will respect them and use them—although he may keep them at arm's length. The late José Felix de Lequerica was a case in point. No man was more successful in Franco's service than the wily Basque lawyer-businessman-diplomat. As Franco's Ambassador to France in 1940, Lequerica served as go-between in arranging a truce between the conquering Germans and the defeated French. As Franco's agent in Washington from 1948 on, Lequerica restored normal diplomatic relations with the United States. As Ambassador to the United Nations after 1955, he made many friends for Spain. Yet Franco never admitted him to his inner circle—because Lequerica knew too much.

Others who have dared to contradict Franco or to read his mind have encountered similar treatment. A few years ago, several cabinet aides urged a better understanding with Morocco. Relations had reached a low during the Moroccan attack on Spanish Ifni in 1957–58, but the two countries had long been linked by proximity and friendship, argued Franco's ministers;

and if Spain were to take the initiative and invite Moroccan officials to Madrid, existing tensions could be relaxed by returning Ifni and the barren Sahara to Morocco in exchange for clear-cut guarantees to Spain's two city-states, Ceuta and Melilla. Franco turned a deaf ear and refused to consider any cession of Spanish territory or any lowering of Spanish prestige. Cowed, his aides dropped the subject.

One adviser, however, returning from a key post abroad, broached the forbidden topic in his first interview. Franco froze him with a look. "I know the Moroccans well," he snapped. "These gentlemen will come here and ask the jackets and shirts off our backs. Absolutely not. Don't even suggest inviting them."

"True, your Excellency," responded the other suavely. "You are right. They will obviously start off with the most astronomical demands. But, merely for the sake of interest, were they to turn up in Madrid, what would be your way of handling them?"

Franco promptly launched into a detailed analysis of the strategic value of the Spanish territories, of the Moroccan mentality, and of the bargaining tactics that would have to be adopted. He talked for one hour and left his subordinate dumfounded by his exhaustive knowledge of the problem.

"He is a curious man," said the same official some time later. "He will never permit anyone too close to him who disagrees with him or whom he considers controversial or provocative. Yet he will use him. I always tell him what I think, politely and correctly, and he never argues or says yes or no. He will use me so long as it suits his purpose, but I am perfectly reconciled to the fact that he will never promote me."

Franco's claim to constitutional legitimacy rests on his national referendum of July, 1947, which "approved" by an overwhelming majority his designation as lifelong ruler, the abolition of Spain's republican form of government, inherited from 1931, and the restoration of a monarchy—but without a king. Spain, thus, is constitutionally a monarchy, and Franco has not only the power to designate a king to succeed him but to bar any claimant and designate a regent. This is a sword of Damocles held over the heads of his royal rivals.

"Never in the history of Spain has there been a state more legitimate, popular, and representative than ours," he cried to a full-dress session of the Cortes on June 3, 1961. As the *procuradores,* ranging from Falangists in their blue-black shirts to morning-coated Monarchists, sat dutifully attentive, the Caudillo proceeded to inveigh against foreign criticism that labels him a dictator. The Spanish regime, Franco insisted, is an "organic" democracy built on the three main pillars of society: the family, the labor-employer Sindicate, and the municipality.

What Franco failed to point out was that even were this system acceptable in theory—which is doubtful—its popular acceptance would have to be based on free elections and authentic representation. As neither exists in Spain today (though the situation is improving), Franco's system remains artificial and unpopular, and it will almost certainly be swept away after his death.

The only elections permitted are triennial municipal or Sindical elections, and from these emerge not only the local administrators at the local level but also the bulk of the *procuradores* in the Cortes. Every three years, registered electors in Spain's 10,000 municipalities vote to replace half of their municipal councilors. They vote in three blocs: the heads of families; the members of the twenty-four state Sindicates; then, finally, the delegates chosen by the first two in turn select the third bloc, which represents professional-cultural societies such as doctors, lawyers, architects, and so forth. This indirect voting insures that every elector, and every election, is controlled by the regime. Yet Franco proudly announced that a few months earlier, 8,241,303 registered heads of families had elected 9,399 municipal councilors; 8.5 million-odd Sindicate members had elected another 11,616, while these delegates jointly had selected 11,556 more to round out the final third.

The twenty-four state Sindicates also hold complicated triennial elections, in which the workers choose not only 400,000-odd *enlaces,* or shop stewards, but also some 200 *procuradores en Cortes.* These elections are equally controlled in order to weed out suspected leftists. In recent years, since the emergence of a new generation of workers, the pressures for free Sindical elections have grown and now pose perhaps the gravest threat to Franco's tranquillity. The Sindical elections of 1960, for instance, were marked by widespread charges of interference and fraud. In many localities, workers either boycotted the elections or ironically marked their ballots "Fidel Castro" or "Sophia Loren" as a protest.

Spain's economic recovery has released new pressures for genuine representation. Not only are the workers demanding an end to regime interference in elections, but Spain's top administrators, too, are urging Franco to ease his grip in order to improve Spain's image abroad. Franco, however, insists that the political liberalization of the country is continuing—albeit slower than his critics would like.

The Cortes, too, is undergoing a cautious transformation. Created in 1942 on the model of Hitler's Reichstag, it is no longer a mute assemblage of puppets, but is increasingly representative of the new generations. Before the 1958 reforms, membership in the Cortes was a hollow mockery, but lately, young men rising in government, the professions, or business have begun to seek Cortes seats as a forum for constructive legislation. No Pyms, Burkes, Clays, Calhouns, or Websters are heard fulminating against the regime in the Cortes—but in the privacy of its committees, voices are being raised against obscurantism, against censorship, and against the encrusted hesitation of old soldiers, old bishops, and old bankers.

Sensitive to tradition, Franco has abolished the title *diputado* (deputy) from the Second Republic and replaced it with *procurador,* which evokes Spain's past. Each Spanish kingdom in medieval times had its own Cortes, or courts, composed of the rich feudal nobles, local prelates, notaries, advocates, and wealthy merchants. Their power over the purse was great; knowing it, they would assemble before the king, not only hatted but deliberately seated. In a time-honored ritual, their leader would then rise and open the proceedings by informing the often penniless monarch: "We, who individually are as great as you, and collectively greater, recognize you as our king."

It is unlikely that Franco could be addressed thus today, for the Caudillo rules the Cortes with a rod of iron. He usually attends only the plenary session at the beginning of each three-year term, to issue some important proclamation of state. He appoints the Cortes president (who need not be a member), and the president dutifully convokes the assembly, sets its agenda, decides its committees, and adjourns it at will. The present incumbent, the venerable Don Esteban Bilbao, was created a marqués by Franco in 1963 for unswerving political devotion.

The number of *procuradores* fluctuates from 550 to 600. By Franco's law, one-third must represent the economic community —the workers, technicians, and employers grouped into the nation's twenty-four Sindicates. The other two-thirds represent the provinces and municipalities in the peninsula and in Spanish Africa, the universities and cultural bodies, the armed forces, the Church, professional groups, and selected individuals. About 300 *procuradores* are "elected" by their organizations, 193 take their seats "ex officio," and 50 are nominated by Franco personally.

No "opposition" members sit in this carefully selected assemblage, of course, because officially no opposition exists. All *procuradores* are theoretically members of the "Movement," which, Franco insists, embraces all Spaniards of good will and within which, he argues, the nation's conflicting viewpoints can be resolved without a retrocession to political parties. The "Movement" has, in fact, been abandoned in all but name by the Monarchists, by the armed forces, by the Church, by the liberal Catholics, by Opus Dei, and by the other power blocs. The "Movement" is now but a euphemism for the discredited Falange, and while 200 or more *procuradores* may turn up at plenary sessions in gaudy white tunics and blue-black shirts, the bulges around their belted waists indicate how seldom these trappings of the past are removed from the mothballs.

Although the entire assemblage has apparently been carefully selected for its political subservience, the facts are different. Many of the Sindical *procuradores* are suspected of harboring Socialist, Anarchist, even Communist beliefs, and some members of the Falange National Council are fervent Monarchists merely biding their time. A free vote on the succession might easily result in a two-thirds majority for a Socialist republic and a one-third minority for an authoritarian monarchy. Outwardly, however, the Cortes is Franco's obedient instrument.

In the private committee sessions where draft legislation sent down from the cabinet is reviewed, some *procuradores* criticize with mounting vigor the censorship, economic and fiscal policy, road-building, public works, local administration, labor regulations, and other public policies. Criticisms of Franco or of major state policy are still taboo, and any *procurador* imprudent enough to voice his opinions too loudly might find himself under forced residence in a distant province, if not in jail. But there is no doubt that, with each three-year session, newer and younger *procuradores* are pressing for more freedom and for better administration of the nation's resources. In fact, in May, 1965, a huge majority of *procuradores* publicly stamped their feet in an unprecedented display of disapproval after Cirilo Cánovas, Franco's lackluster Minister of Agriculture, had delivered a typically evasive reply to a critical question about Spain's lagging agricultural situation. Shouts could be heard: "¡ *Fuera los todos!* —Out with the whole cabinet!"

A plenary session of the Cortes is a colorful spectacle, for few nations excel the Spanish in pomp and circumstance. From the galleries, a visitor will see a densely packed semicircular chamber. Facing the President, to the left—a position deliberately chosen—sit the Falangist Sindicalists in their white, gold, and

39

blue-black. To their right, prelates in purple or black; generals in gold-trimmed khaki; admirals in navy blue; bankers and businessmen in cutaways or sober gray. The eighteen cabinet ministers, in uniform or cutaway, sit on a blue velvet bench below the presiding officer, facing the *procuradores*. In recent years, colorfully garbed *procuradores* from Spain's African and Saharan provinces have also begun to take their seats, adding black, copper, and the white of flowing robes and turbans to an already multicolored panorama.

As the session comes to order, the buzz of talk and laughter dies away and the white-haired President Bilbao pauses, with an admonitory smile, until silence reigns. Then, for the better part of an hour, the *procuradores,* the cabinet, and the visitors will be treated to a eulogy to some departed member or to some similar expression of the old president's oratorical powers. No presiding officer in the world can match Don Esteban Bilbao for sonorous prolixity. Here, the rich, ripe rhetoric of old Spain achieves its fullest flowering, and Don Esteban's eulogies have become part of the landscape, a holdover from Cervantes or Lope de Vega.

Smoothly, the voice rolls on, rising and falling in Castilian resonance, as the minutes turn to quarter-hours, the quarter-hours to half-hours. To one side, a *procurador* can be seen stifling a yawn, while another settles lower in his seat. Jaws are sagging, eyes close, and soon, throughout the chamber, *procuradores* drift off to sleep, lulled by their president's rolling voice.

The Valley of the Fallen

It is interesting that not a shot, not a bomb has ever been aimed at Franco since he has been dictator. In the last year or so, students and teen-agers have set off crude petards in railway stations or airline offices to frighten away tourists, but these are far from the deadly attempts that have so narrowly missed De Gaulle or the mad act that robbed the world of John F. Kennedy in his prime. Franco continues apparently immune.

His aim is to appear as the national reconciliator, the father-healer of his people; how successful he will be is debatable, for many millions of the voiceless left still regard him as the arch-fiend of reaction. Yet he goes on preaching national unity, national togetherness, and when he dies, his body will almost certainly lie in state—not in the Escorial, the great pantheon of kings built by Philip II—but in the silent magnificence of the mountain crypt Franco has built himself at Cuelgamuros, known as the Valley of the Fallen. Designed to shelter the million or more dead who fell fighting on both sides in the Civil War, the Valley of the Fallen will probably also be Franco's mausoleum.

Carved into a mountain thirty miles from Madrid, this basilica, with its huge granite cross a football field high, lies in granitic hills, wild and lovely in their savagery. At night, floodlights bathe the cross in a glow of light visible for miles, while under it a crypt as long as three football fields drives straight to the mountain's heart. It is forty yards wide, forty-five yards high at the peak of its curving ceiling, and here and there the granite has been softened with plaques of Alicante marble. Every detail is modern, yet in its dignity it is timeless.

In this Valley of the Fallen, one finds the soul of Spain, beautiful and severe. When the great bronze doors—eleven tons each—swing open for state ceremonies, ten thousand worshipers can assemble there at a time. Over the circular marble altar hangs a wooden Christ, carved to life-size in Galicia.

Only Franco and a few intimates know the cost of this monument with its adjacent Benedictine monastery and its lavishly fitted center for social studies. Started in 1942, it was periodically abandoned, then resumed, depending on the availability of funds. Many thousands of Civil War prisoners are said to have labored on the Valley, earning remission of their sentences. It was officially dedicated on April 1, 1959. Falangist veterans bore the coffin of the martyred founder of the Movement, José Antonio Primo de Rivera, from the foot of the main altar at the Escorial, where Franco had had it placed in 1939, and by slow, torch-lit stages carried it on their shoulders ten miles to the Valley of the Fallen, where it rests before the circular altar, marked by a bronze plaque.

Behind the altar stand two gilt-and-scarlet chairs, intended some day for a king and queen. Franco uses one during state ceremonies. At such moments, the lights dim, the congregation hushes, the organ plays softly, and overhead a beam of light picks out the tiny figure of the Cardinal Primate of Spain, Enrique Cardinal Plá y Deniel, Archbishop of Toledo, as he elevates the Host. At that moment many eyes turn to Franco, who kneels, lonely and austere in his gold-trimmed generalissimo's uniform, his aides ranged behind him, his face solemn, his eyes cast down, his hands folded. For a moment, Spain's past and present flash to mind: the Roman grandeur, the Gothic decline, the Arab conquest, the Christian reconquest, the discovery of the New World, the silver mines of Mexico and the gold mines of Peru, the Philippine galleons, Balboa in Panama, De Soto at the Mississippi, Fra Junipero Serra on the California coast, the decadence of the eighteenth century and the Carlist wars of the nineteenth, the Civil War of the twentieth, and Spain's current recovery. All seem to fuse together in that one little man.

The political props that support Franco; the political underground that opposes him; his maneuvers through the mine fields of foreign policy; his country's economic comeback; his relations with the United States and with the Borbóns who hope to succeed him will be examined in detail in the succeeding chapters.

The Armed Forces

The Big Question

Place: Tamariu, a fishing port on the Costa Brava. Time: October.

The tourists have gone and the old women in black sit on the beach, bare-legged, their toes holding taut the fishing nets as their fingers race like busy spiders looking for holes. The sun is setting behind the Pyrenees, and out of the soft darkness comes a "cuff-cuff-cuff" as a fishing boat chugs out of the harbor to the night's fishing. A mile offshore, the great banked stern lights will soon flash on like diamonds on a black baize cloth. I nose a three-peseta brandy, lost in thought, as Manuel, the waiter, stands beside me, idly flicking the tablecloth.

"Manuel, after Franco dies—what will happen in Spain?" Manuel pauses, embarrassed.

"*Pues . . . no se.* I don't know. The generals, I suppose. Who else? Anyway, who cares so long as we have peace."

Place: Madrid's stately Club Nuevo. Time: November. Grandees and young bucks once turned up here each evening in white tie and tails to dine, drink, and gamble until dawn. They are gone now, but the Club Nuevo lingers on—its paneled rooms empty, its marble stairs no longer echoing to footsteps, talk, or laughter. A few elderly retainers in faded blue and silver stand or creak about softly, looking for someone to serve.

My host, the elegant Count Fontanar, Monarchist and patriot, looks grave.

"Paco," I ask him, "what would happen if Franco died tomorrow?"

"God knows. Nothing has been planned. I suppose the army will take over and bring back Don Juan. There is no other solution if we want peace."

Place: Seville. Time: December. The rain pours down from a leaden sky and pedestrians dart across narrow streets, cursing the taxis and motor scooters that snarl past, splashing and drenching them to the skin. Seated in his fire-lit study, Professor Manuel Giménez Fernández, leader of the Demo-Christian left, animatedly discusses his favorite topic: politics.

"What will happen, Don Manolo, when Franco goes?"

"The army," he snaps without hesitation. "The Captains General* will take command, realize they don't know what to do, and bring back the king. They're all very brave and very stupid. Not one of them has any political sense."

Three men of different backgrounds in different places, yet always the same answer: the army. Not three, or three hundred, but perhaps three thousand times have I heard this reply to the question: Who will succeed Franco? No one has the final answer, but everyone has its chief ingredient: the army.

As time passes without any visible guide to the future, key army leaders are beginning to look ahead. But the habit of blind obedience to Franco is hard to overcome.

In February, 1962, a leading Demo-Christian politician was surprised by a telephone call from a ranking army general, an old friend whom he had not seen for many years.

"Come to lunch Thursday," said the general abruptly. He

* The term Captain General connotes both a rank and a temporary designation. Only Franco and Muñoz Grandes hold the rank of Captain General—equivalent to a five-star general in the U.S. Army. The eleven regional commanders, however, hold the courtesy title of Captain General during their appointment.

44

added, as if in afterthought, "We'll take our wives and drive out of town." Puzzled by the summons after years of silence and still more by the un-Spanish suggestion to include wives, the politician duly turned up with his spouse, and the foursome set off, with the general at the wheel. They passed through the majestic stone portals of Toledo, and there, in an inconspicuous restaurant, they relaxed, chatting easily.

The meal was good, the wine excellent, the coffee and cigars superb—but the politician vaguely wondered what was afoot. He sensed that something was coming. After lunch, as the wives walked ahead to the car, the general fell back a few yards, then murmured softly to his old friend, *"Cuando este pase . . .* when Franco dies . . . the army will be unable to rule. There will be divisions among us. I am collecting the private telephone numbers of men we can trust. Give me yours—and tell me who are the men of the left we can talk to."

It might seem odd that in 1962, key Spanish generals would be soliciting telephone numbers from political reliables, and still more odd that after twenty-five years the men of the so-called left might still be unknown to them. Yet this is how Spain runs. Anything smacking of the "left" has been anathema to the army for a quarter century, and none of its chiefs has dared establish "leftist" contacts, fearing not only Franco but ostracism by his own colleagues. The path to success in Spain passes on the right—not the left.

This blind identification with the "right" and lack of contact with even the non-Communist, moderate "left" will prove a grave danger to Spain after Franco. The worker population of Spain is already nearing 9 million—a potent bloc. Nearly 1 million Spanish workers are now working outside Spain in Western Europe, remitting their savings and storing up memories of political, religious, press, and labor freedoms which they will demand in Spain when Franco dies. There has been recent talk of cautious army contacts with Spain's clandestine Socialists, but such tales are often fomented by the Socialists to buck up their own morale. So long as Franco lives, the army chiefs will avoid serious contacts with the left, with whom they will one day have to deal. Still more serious, the army's rigidity has also isolated the Pretender, Don Juan, Count of Barcelona, from worthwhile contacts with Spain's left. So long as Franco watches the army, its hands are tied; so long as the army watches Don Juan, his hands are tied.

"Franco does not believe for a moment that his regime will go on unchanged after his death," a cabinet minister and long-time army colleague of the Caudillo once remarked to me. "What he does believe is that he can make the regime so strong that no successor will be able basically to alter it."

The keystone of the regime is the army.

To cheering reserve officers at a ceremony at Garabitas, near Madrid, on May 17, 1962, Franco declared, "After I go . . . everything will be worked out and guaranteed by . . . Spaniards like yourselves and by our loyal, unbeatable army."

Day in, day out, the newspapers show Franco receiving one after another in the interminable line of *promociónes,* or classes, of infantry, artillery, cavalry, or engineering generals. Drawn to attention, they stand along the edge of the carpet, their caps in white-gloved hands, their boots polished, their swords gleaming. Some are lean, some paunchy, some vigorous, some failing, but all gaze fixedly at the Caudillo as their senior intones the ritual peroration of loyalty.

Franco stands with head slightly thrown back, his sparse gray hair brushed to minimize his baldness. His eye is cold, his stance Napoleonic. But when the photographers have gone, he comes to life. Then the face softens and the dark eyes take on a new warmth. He jokes, or reminisces, *abrazos* are exchanged, and one or two generals—fellow-cadets at the start of the century—may even address him softly with the familiar *tu.*

The Army

For nearly twenty years after the Civil War, Franco maintained an army of eighteen "paper" divisions in the peninsula, special forces in the Balearics, in the Canaries, and upwards of 60,000 men in Spanish Africa. Since 1958, thanks to modern American arms and American advice, he has begun cutting the army down to eleven divisions in the peninsula, although he still has the equivalent of two divisions—including the crack Spanish Foreign Legion—in Africa.

The army's normal peacetime strength now hovers around 180,000 men: 29,000 officers and N.C.O.'s; a hard core of 32,000 volunteers; plus 100,000-odd recruits called up every March for eighteen months' training. Franco controls the army through the Army Minister, always a lieutenant general on active duty, and through the regional commanders or Captains General.

The army has seen little combat since 1939, except for the volunteer Blue Division that fought with Hitler's forces on the Russian front from mid-1941 to late 1943, suffering 5,000 killed and 12,000 casualties from wounds and frostbite. An estimated 45,000 Spanish troops rotated through the Blue Division before it was recalled to Spain.

From then until 1953, the Spanish Army scraped along with obsolete arms plus German and Italian matériel furnished during the Civil War. Then the U.S.–Spanish defense pacts were signed, and ever since, American military aid has been flowing into Spain—reaching an estimated $600 million worth by 1964. Forty per cent of this aid went to the army, the rest was equally divided between the navy and the air force. As a result, American influence has replaced German influence in Spanish military thinking.

The Spanish recruit, for instance, follows a three-month basic training program similar to that of his American counterpart. His training is tough, consisting largely of fieldcraft, close-order drill, weapons training, and personal hygiene. Since most recruits are drawn from the rural classes, illiteracy still runs around 10 per cent, but, at least in theory, no recruit is returned to civilian life until he can read and write. Catholic regimental chaplains play a great part in this cultural rehabilitation.

After his basic training, the recruit is sent to a specialists' school to learn mechanics, electronics, or related skills, and thence to his permanent unit. If he is an infantryman, he will be armed with the Cetme rifle, of a German design improved and manufactured in Spain. The crack units use the Belgian automatic rifle that has also been adopted by the British Army. Armored units are equipped with U.S. M-47 and M-48 tanks, and the artillery with the U.S. 155-millimeter howitzer and with the U.S. 105-millimeter howitzer, now being produced under license in Spanish arsenals.

In 1958, the then Army Minister, Lieutenant General Antonio Barroso, announced a major reform to cut the army's tail and give it more teeth. The eighteen divisions were to be slashed to twelve (eight infantry, two mountain, one horse, one armored), of which five were to become "pentomic" divisions of the type then favored in the Pentagon. The old "triangular" division of three brigades and 20,000 men was to give way to the smaller American formation of 11,000 men divided into five mobile combat groups.

In Spain, however, *"las cosas del palacio van despacio*—affairs of state move slowly." Resistance within the Spanish Army and resistance to foreign aid by the U.S. Congress have combined to delay Barroso's plan. The eighteen paper divisions have now been cut to eleven, but only three have even 80 per cent of their requisite matériel, the other eight not more than about 60 per cent.

Nevertheless, to keep relations friendly and to retain use of the Rota naval base, the United States agreed in September, 1963, to a fresh $150 million "matching" aid program spread over five years. The program provides that by 1968, the United States will have given Spain $50 million in arms, Spain will have bought another $50 million worth with her own funds, after which Washington will add a final $50 million. Spanish officers have already arrived at the Redstone arsenal near Huntsville, Alabama, for training in the American Hawk ground-to-air guided missile, which, with a range of twelve to fifteen miles and a ceiling of twelve miles, is far more effective than a hundred old-style antiaircraft batteries.

Americans who have accompanied Spanish units on maneuvers or in action, have returned impressed. One U.S. assistant military attaché came back from the army's mountain training school at Jaca in the Pyrenees astonished by the physical fitness and morale of the officers and men. Others who have worked with Spanish armored and artillery units or have inspected the paratroop school at Alcalá de Henares have also turned in glowing reports.

"They want to learn. They work. They're damn good," one American officer said admiringly. "If they could only get rid of some of the older officers, they'd be terrific."

The most colorful of all the army units is the Spanish Foreign Legion which, although modeled on the French original, has a distinct character of its own. Most of its 6,000 men are Spanish volunteers, but there are also a few foreigners. The Legion's four *tercios,* or regiments, bear such historic names as "Juan de Austria," "Alfonso Farnese," "El Gran Capitán," and "Duque de Alba." An assignment in the Legion is highly prized because (except in the event of national emergencies) it serves exclusively in Africa, and if fighting is to be found in peacetime, it is more likely to be found there than at home.

Legion officers seem to come straight from the *Desert Song.* Dressed in open-necked gray shirts, gray riding breeches, gleaming black boots, and tasseled forage caps, they carry riding crops and exude a cocky, back-slapping, swaggering good humor that engulfs the chance visitor to one of their desert outposts. To a man, they are gregarious and eager for news. When not on desert patrol in their jeep convoys, they swap tales, play cards, or toss down raw Spanish *coñac* in the fading yellow casinos and barracks that stand on the desert's edge.

In peninsular Spain, the task of training and equipping Franco's five new modern divisions continues with U.S. help. The deployment of these five divisions around Spain is significant. The two light mountain divisions, the 42nd and 62nd, are based respectively at Lérida and Pamplona near the French Pyrenees border; the 31st Infantry is at Valencia on Spain's east coast; the 22nd Infantry at Algeciras in the south (ready to support Spanish forces in Africa), while the highly touted 11th "experimental" armored division is centered on Madrid, strung out in a line running west like an arrow aimed at Portugal. In the case of a left-wing coup d'état against Salazar, this unit could move quickly to the aid of Franco's oldest friend and Iberian fellow-dictator.

The Air Force

The world tends to forget that some of the early "greats" in aviation were Spaniards: Juan de la Cierva, who fathered the Autogiro; Ramón Franco (the Caudillo's late, politically left-wing brother), who was the first man to solo the south Atlantic; the team that first flew Madrid-Manila nonstop in the 1920's. Today, senior American Air Force officers call Spain's first-line jet squadrons "as good as any in the United States." Until U.S. aid began in 1953, however, lack of money had long kept the Spanish Air Force flying obsolete German Heinkel bombers and Messerschmitt propeller fighters.

In the past ten years, Spain's Air Force has been made over into an efficient, modern force. It is now organized into five air regions in the Spanish peninsula plus three air zones covering respectively the Balearics, the Canaries, and Spanish Africa. The Air Minister, always an air force general, has cabinet rank, together with his army and navy colleagues and, according to trustworthy sources, intraservice rivalry, while on a far smaller scale, is no less fierce than in Washington. The Spanish Air Force is still striving for an offensive as well as a defensive role; the Spanish Navy wants a naval air arm plus aircraft carriers of its own, while the army wants its own air force for tactical ground support. In Spain, too, military appetites grow steadily.

Since 1954, more than 400 North American F-86 Sabrejets

have been furnished the Spanish Air Force through U.S. aid, and Spain now boasts seven well-trained front-line squadrons, some equipped with the lethal U.S. Sidewinder missiles, guided by infrared rays. Moreover, Spain has gradually taken over the extensive radar early warning system built as part of the vast U.S. base complex throughout the country. One station alone, atop Puig Mayor Mountain in Mallorca, gives unparalleled coverage of the entire western Mediterranean.

With the current phasing-out of the U.S. SAC bases in Spain, the Spanish Air Force has now assumed responsibility for the defense of its own air space. The U.S. 65th Air Division, whose F-100 and F-101 fighter interceptors once protected the bases, has now gone, its place taken by Spanish fighters. The United States has also furnished Spain with C-54 troop and cargo carriers, T-6 and T-33 jet trainers, and helicopters.

An argument has recently split the top ranks of the Spanish Air Force over plans—allegedly Franco's—to buy from the U.S. a squadron of 21 Lockheed F-104's at an estimated cost of $30 million. After deciding to buy these 1,400-mile-per-hour fighter-interceptors, the Spanish discovered that various "extras" would bring the bill nearer to $40 million, and some Spanish air generals insist that this decision has been forced on them by Franco and his army generals for reasons of prestige rather than necessity. They contended that the Northrop F-5 fighter, though slower (Mach 1.5 instead of the F-104's Mach 2), would be more suitable. They claim that Spain could buy two F-5's for every F-104, and that the F-5, with its two engines, offers a greater safety factor than the single-engine F-104. Moreover, they say, the average rate of aircraft availability in such NATO air forces as Italy's, which has adopted the F-104, is said to be only five airplanes each day per squadron, and that, for an expenditure of $40 million, Spain would be able to count on only five superspeed jets on an average day. In addition, some experts claim that the F-104 is so "hot" that only about 15 per cent of Spain's

51

front-line pilots can fly it—and the accident rate is likely to mount.

From a strategic viewpoint, certain top Spanish pilots challenge the need for the F-104. Although it is now the principal fighter-interceptor for the NATO air forces, Spain is not yet a member of NATO, nor is it likely to be so long as Franco continues in power. Spain most likely enemy is politically left-wing, violently Arab-nationalist Algeria.

The steady buildup of the Algerian forces with Soviet arms has not passed unnoticed in Spain. Yet the Spanish report that the Algerians have received only a dozen or so obsolescent MIG 15 and 17 fighters—which the Northrop F-5 could easily match if the MIG's were laden with bombs. Spain's radar now intercepts at least 85 per cent of all high-altitude flights in the Spanish sector, and if the MIG's flew low to escape the radar, they would be easy prey for F-5's. The F-104's, on the other hand, operate best at a high altitude and would, therefore, be less useful.

At latest report, the Spanish have reached a characteristic compromise: They will have both. Besides the U.S.–furnished F-104's, they will buy with their own funds seventy F-5's, to cost approximately $47 million.

The Navy

The Spanish Navy dates back to the caravels and galleons that took the conquistadores to the New World, brought back the treasures of Mexico and Peru, and later fought a gallant but losing battle in the Channel. Spain's Navy, like Britain's, is the smallest, the proudest, and the most Monarchist of all three services. An old Spanish saying lists only three careers for a gentleman: *"Iglesia, Marina, o Casa Real"* ("Church, navy, or the royal court").

Since 1953, the U.S.–Spanish agreements have brought sweeping changes to the Spanish Navy. More than $100 million in U.S. funds have helped modernize the fleet. From U.S. shipyards have come five destroyers; a training submarine; twelve new, nonmagnetic minesweepers; eighteen auxiliary craft; and, most recently, two 13,000-ton ships to transport amphibious forces and to serve as an electronic floating command post.

The reason for this substantial aid lies in Spain's strategic position astride the entrance to the Mediterranean. More than 400 million tons of world shipping move through the Strait of Gibraltar each year—an obvious hunting ground for Soviet submarines in case of war. And Spain's coast and major ports, such as Cádiz and Barcelona, make the Iberian peninsula increasingly important to American strategists. In any future conflict, Spain could be a vitally important bridgehead for defending Europe.

Steel Pike I, the massive U.S.–Spanish naval maneuvers held in late October, 1964, involved eighty U.S. Navy ships, ten American merchantmen, fourteen Spanish vessels, and a combined landing force of nearly 60,000 U.S. and Spanish sailors and marines. It was the largest amphibious force assembled since Korea —and it revealed the value of Spain's Atlantic beaches for amphibious training. Staged soon after British Labour Premier Harold Wilson had coolly canceled British-Spanish naval maneuvers, Steel Pike I highlighted the growing bond between Washington and Madrid.

Of the 35,000 officers and men of the Spanish Navy, more than 3,000 have been sent to the United States for special training. American influence can also be seen in organization, logistics, and repair arrangements. Until 1953, Spain clung to a time-encrusted three-fleet system, built around an elderly cruiser and four to six destroyers, based respectively at Cádiz, Cartagena, and El Ferrol. That three-fleet system has now been scrapped and Spain is shifting to the U.S. "type authority" organization, under which vessels of a given type—destroyers, frigates, submarines, etc.—are commanded by a "type authority in the Navy Ministry," rather than being parceled out as before among the separate fleets. Spain is developing an antisubmarine warfare "type authority" for her new naval role.

Her navy, at present, comprises the 10,000-ton veteran cruiser

"Canarias," the 4,700-ton light cruiser "Mendez Nuñez," now converted to antisub work; three old 8,000-ton cruisers, of which two have been sent to reserve; twenty-nine destroyers; twenty frigates; a training submarine, and about forty smaller ships. Virtually all Spanish destroyers now carry American sonar, radar, and electronic gunfiring equipment. In addition, the Pentagon has helped Spain to organize a light squadron of nine Bell-47 helicopters for liaison with the Spanish marines and a medium squadron of seven Sikorsky-55's with "dipping" sonar for antisub work.

During the summer of 1964, Spain was negotiating to purchase four British "Leander"-class frigates and British electronic equipment at a reported price of $45 million. However, the anti-Franco statements voiced in the Commons by Labour leaders Harold Wilson and Denis Healey gave Franco an unexpected political boon. He calmly canceled the purchase because of Labour's "unjustified" interference in Spain's affairs, and as Conservative newspapers angrily denounced the loss of the lucrative order to Britain's hard-up naval yards, Madrid quietly announced that it was planning a $100 million, 20-year naval modernization program and would take its custom elsewhere.

Franco now enjoyed the rare spectacle of Britain's Tories springing to his defense in the mother of parliaments where he and his regime had so often been excoriated. With a full purse, Franco now could saunter through the international arms bazaars, as salesmen jostled for his orders.

Salvador de Madariaga once described the Spanish Army as an "utterly useless" public body but at the same time an "indispensable" element in the internal life of Spain. The army, he said, provides that "minimum of outward and mechanical order" without which the country's evolution toward "inner and spiritual order" cannot progress.

Hotheaded and intolerant, the Spaniard nonetheless senses his own need for discipline; he fears that if left alone, he and his countrymen will revert step by step to civil war. The policeman on the beat is thus a *sine qua non* in Spain; not the hated secret police, but the uniformed constable whose mere presence radiates authority. The army under Franco plays a role analogous to the constable's—it is the visible, slow-moving, but ever-present symbol of law and order. And because the army has maintained the peace, it has come to enjoy a grudging public esteem.

There is another reason for this public esteem: the army has repeatedly blocked the Falange. In 1944, when the Falange sought to retain an SS-type armed militia, the army, on Franco's orders, disbanded it, leaving it only enough arms for a ceremonial guard. In 1956, when Falange thugs sought a showdown with liberal university students, it was again the army that warned Franco to bar bloodshed. In 1960, when the burly Falangist ex-militia boss Girón tried to raise a paramilitary legion of Falangist *antiguos combatientes* (Civil War veterans), Franco outmaneuvered him by creating his own picked unit of 15,000 *alféreces provisionales* (ex-reserve officers) under his personal control. The army thus is a mirror of Spain, its good and its bad. The average soldier is a robust country youth in his teens or early twenties, the average officer easygoing rather than severe. Most of the generals have come from the humble or lower-middle classes, although the smart young marquéses in superbly cut uniforms chatting at Madrid's chic Balmoral bar at two o'clock any day of the week are as much a part of the army as the fresh-faced recruits strolling in the Retiro Park in the evening.

The army prides itself on being a patriotic school from which 40,000 men are returned yearly to civilian life with new skills, and in which illiterates are taught to read and write.

Yet to speak politically of the army is to speak of its leaders: the dozen or so Captains General and other regional commanders who control the troops. Without these men, no army rising could succeed, and for this reason each has been hand picked for loyalty. They are now aging men who made their mark in the Civil War and who have come up the long, slow ladder of promotion to enjoy the perquisites of victory.

These perquisites are far from negligible in a country where the average per capita annual income is about $400. Spain still has about 200 generals on the active list, and although a recent bank study disclosed that the country needs only three lieutenant generals, it actually has nineteen. Franco's elderly cronies enjoy dignities and prestige, soldier-chauffeured cars and free homes, and it is customary to "elect" serving senior generals to the boards of banks and industrial empires, where their monthly emoluments may range between $2,000 and $3,000. Since a general's base pay is about $200 monthly, this system puts a premium on conformity.

Time is passing, however, and the old *cabos de guerra* (war lords) are dying off. Only eight of the thirty-one generals and admirals who fought under Franco in the Civil War are left, and all they want now is to float down the stream of time, basking in an aura of fulsome, if harmless, flattery, and garnering a little pelf on the way. As they fade away, seniority is becoming increasingly important, for it is only by seniority that Franco can maintain obedient discipline. After Muñoz Grandes, who will automatically become chief of the government (though not of the state) at Franco's death, the generals in order of seniority include: Camilo Menéndez Tolosa, Army Minister; Rafael García-Valiño, Captain General of Madrid; Alfredo Galera Paniague, Captain General of Seville; Alfredo Erquicia Aranda, commanding Spanish troops in North Africa; Luis Zanón Aldalur, commanding the paramilitary Guardia Civil; Ramón Gotarredona Prats, army chief of staff; Mariano Alonso Alonso, Captain General of Zaragoza; Ramón Robles Pazos, Captain General of Granada; Valero Valderrábano Samitier, Captain General of Valladolid; José Héctor Vázquez, Captain General of the Canaries; and Santiago Mateo Marcos, Captain General of Valencia. Another key general is Lieutenant General Rafael Cavanillas Prosper, who has recently visited the United States as a guest of the Pentagon.

Spain's future will almost certainly be decided by these men. They will take into account the views of other power blocs—the Church, the Falangist-Sindical bureaucracy, the universities and intellectuals, the business and landowning interests—but they will make the final decision themselves.

Muñoz Grandes

The man who, if he lives, will direct the regime after Franco is no Monarchist; if anything, he is a Republican. Calm, grizzled, and experienced, Don Agustín Muñoz Grandes, Captain General and Vice President, has been fighting for nearly fifty years on battlefields ranging from the deserts of Morocco to the steppes of Russia. Now nearly seventy and suffering from old war wounds, he wants only peace, order, and prosperity for Spain; peace, order, and tranquillity for himself. His Spartan simplicity and contempt for intrigue have won him respect in a country addicted to pomp and wracked by intrigue, and in the best sense of the word, Muñoz Grandes is still a peasant—a peasant with the dignity, warmth, and shrewd common sense that have raised Spain's peasants high among the denizens of the earth.

He has been a soldier all his life. Then, in 1926, when Spanish troops splashed ashore under fire at Alhucemas Bay on the Moroccan coast, splitting the Rif rebels, one of the first ashore and one of the first wounded was Major Muñoz Grandes. The colonel commanding the landing was Franco. In 1931, after the fall of the monarchy, Muñoz Grandes' open Republican sympathies brought him to the attention of the Republic, which charged him with organizing and training its Guardias de Asalto, or shock troops. He served the Republic loyally, but his peasant-born conservatism and army training were already turning him against the spreading political chaos. When the Civil War broke out, he offered Franco his services and in three years rose from colonel to army commander.

No breath of scandal has ever touched his name. Despite his high position, he and his wife live in a simple fourth-floor apartment in Madrid's quiet residential section. There, he can occasionally be seen returning in full dress from a ceremony to halt on the sidewalk and banter with a knot of admiring urchins. No gleaming limousine awaits him; merely a small, black, Spanish-built *SEAT* with his pennant on the right front fender.

Although I knew of his reserve toward the press, I was eager to see Muñoz Grandes before leaving Spain. Mutual friends had repeatedly interceded for me, but each time the appointment was mysteriously broken. The Captain General was always leaving on a trip, or he was "ill," or had suddenly been "summoned to the Pardo," his aides would explain. Two days before I was due to catch my ship, I telephoned his office once more, only to be told that he was "out." I learned, however, that he would be dining at nine that night with American officers at the Puerto de Hierro country club on the edge of town.

Surmising that he would be at home to change before dinner, I telephoned his house at seven. A gruff voice inquired who I was. I gave my name and asked who was speaking. It was an "aide," said the voice; the Captain General had left town for the weekend. A sixth sense urged me to persist, and I rang every change on the chimes of disappointment, despair, and disillusion. I said that I was leaving Spain, perhaps not to return for many years. For months, I had sought to pay my respects to the Captain General. Many of my highly placed acquaintances—whose names I reeled off with desperate rapidity—had written letters or had made telephone calls on my behalf: all to no avail. There was a silence. Could I not wait until next week? asked the voice. Alas, no, I replied, I was driving to Gibraltar the next day to catch my ship. It was tonight or never. Another silence.

Playing my last card, I said I had heard that the Captain General would be dining at nine with my American compatriots—perhaps there might be five minutes beforehand in which I could call at his home and pay my farewell respects. A pause—then, somewhat grumpily, the "aide" said he would relay my message. He promised nothing but suggested I come to the house at 8:30 on the faint chance of catching the Captain General in.

At 8:30, I found myself in a small, simply furnished living

room. There were the ritual brown velvet settee and overstuffed chairs, the dark tables and sideboards, the polychromed religious pictures and crucifixes found in all middle-class Spanish homes. The frosted glass doors swung open and Muñoz Grandes, in a well-cut gray business suit, walked in.

He was short and erect, with an unaffected dignity that lent him inches. His hair was still glossy and dark, touched with gray, his eyes were the hooded, half-quizzical eyes of old Spain—eyes that have seen much and have chosen to forget much of what they have seen. He shook my hand warmly and bade me be scated. Neither of us mentioned the gruff "aide" on the telephone.

"Will you take a small glass with me?" he inquired. I thanked him and he poured sherry into two tiny crystal glasses. "To the United States," he said courteously. I raised my glass: "To Spain." He fixed his eyes piercingly on me for a moment. Then we sat down, and he said, "You know, I was brought up to hate the United States. All of my generation were. The defeat of '98, the loss of our colonies, these things left great bitterness among us, particularly in the army. We did not know your nation, and we thought you did not understand us. But I have come to love the United States and I do not use the word love loosely. Do you know why?"

I shook my head, and he went on. In 1958, he recounted, as a guest of the Pentagon he had visited American military installations and had found himself at the Fort Benning Infantry School in Georgia. There, escorted by American generals and aides, he had toured the huge camp, receiving brisk salutes at every turn. As he and his party were returning one evening to their quarters, a file of American soldiers in fatigue uniforms passed by, escorted by a carbine-carrying N.C.O. None of the U.S. soldiers saluted. Muñoz Grandes said nothing, but later an American general explained that the men were soldier-prisoners who had lost the right to salute until their sentences were served.

"This was new to a European, this 'right' to salute," Muñoz

Grandes told me. "The more I thought about the salute as a privilege, as a mark of esteem between officers and men, the more I realized you Americans were right. My feelings about you began to change."

The second incident came some weeks later, when he stood at Pearl Harbor gazing at the hulk of the U.S.S. "Arizona," with its 1,000 American sailors and marines trapped below the waterline, a permanent memorial to the dead of World War II.

"I have seen memorials all over Europe," he said simply, toying with the tiny glass in his hand, "but never have I seen anything more noble, more impressive, than the U.S.S. 'Arizona.' I told myself then that you Americans are a people with heart."

It was late, but he motioned me to stay and refilled my glass. I sat absorbed by this legendary Spaniard whose battle scars, gift of command, and integrity had led Franco to raise him above all others. I asked him about the coming renegotiations of the U.S.– Spanish base agreements. There was talk, I said, that Spain was preparing to ask a high price.

"For us it is more a question of psychology than price," he answered. "Your Admiral Sherman came to Spain in 1951 and gave us his hand when the rest of the world had isolated us. It does not matter that this served America's convenience. What matters is that he extended his hand. We will never forget that. If you Americans help Spain recover you will be helping yourselves. It is no matter whether you offer us $400 million or $40 million if the will to help us is there. With your good will we can solve our problems."

How could America help? I asked. What was the chief problem confronting Spain? He seized a sheet of paper, and with a pencil quickly traced a rough map of Spain and adjacent North Africa. Then he drilled his pencil into a point where the borders of Spanish Sahara, Algeria, Morocco, and Mauretania met. There he scrawled the name Tindouf.*

* French geologists have reported under the desert there an untapped reserve of 1.2 billion tons of 35 per-cent-pure iron; at Fort Gouraud, to the south, an estimated 1 billion tons are believed to be 66 per-cent-pure.

"If ore is ever found there, it will be worth untold wealth," Muñoz Grandes said. "This is a tinderbox where Arabs and Spaniards may clash. But all over North Africa, the West is pulling out and Communism is seeping in. You Americans are due to leave your air bases in Morocco by the end of next year. You must not permit the left to fill that vacuum. We Spaniards have no objections to America giving arms to the Moroccans," he went on, "but for every ten airplanes you give them, you should give Spain forty. Spain is your ally. Never forget what might happen to Spain's cities—or to Lisbon—if the Russians sent five or six submarines to the mouth of the Mediterranean."

Since he was appointed Vice President in Franco's decree of July 11, 1962, Muñoz Grandes automatically will become head of the government in the event of Franco's "vacancy, absence, or illness." A top-ranking Franco official put it this way: If Franco died, Muñoz Grandes would be the "first in line at the airport to greet Don Juan or Prince Juan Carlos—whichever is chosen king."

The future of Spain can only be sensed, not even seen through a glass darkly; but, if he lives, Muñoz Grandes will play a predominant role. And whoever succeeds Franco may need Muñoz Grandes to keep the army in hand. Muñoz Grandes' integrity, his lack of personal ambition, and his sense of duty have already reassured the nation that when Franco dies, law and order will be preserved. For that reason, especially, he is popular.

However, these qualities may also prove defects. He is a soldier, not a politician; a second-in-command, not a national chief. His contempt for politics may lead him to throw up his hands in disgust and leave the politicking to others. So long as law and order are preserved and the army's power safeguarded, Muñoz Grandes may well relegate the task of king-making to less scrupulous hands. Perhaps this will be best for Spain, perhaps not.

Franco's paranoiac jealousy of all possible rivals and his suspicion of intrigue, however, still continues, as was again shown by a recent incident. When autumn floods ravaged industrial

Catalonia in 1963, drowning more than 400 persons and destroying entire textile villages along the coast, Franco was on holiday in Galicia. Muñoz Grandes, hearing of the disaster, convoked an emergency cabinet meeting and flew to Barcelona to supervise relief measures personally. His vigor won the gratitude, not only of the stricken Catalans, but of all Spain, and many privately compared it with Franco's lethargy after the terrible 1957 floods that devastated Valencia. When fresh floods hit Seville three months later, leaving hundreds homeless in the winter cold, Franco himself drove to the Andalusian capital to assume personal command of the situation.

By an apparent "oversight," he failed to notify his Vice President and constitutional successor even of his departure. But there was really no need to notify Muñoz Grandes: he and all Spain understood perfectly.

It is too early to predict what sort of government Spain's generals will choose after Franco dies, although a monarchy seems likely. Franco watches closely all army leaders and the army watches itself—political discussion is not healthy. A few generals have expressed their own personal opinions; for instance, García-Valiño, who favors a monarchy, and Muñoz Grandes, who leans toward a republic, but collectively the leaders blend behind Franco into the great Sphinx. All senior generals, including Franco, swore fealty to the House of Borbón as cadets, and while the years may have clouded their loyalties, there seems to be no alternative to a monarchy. Most of them regard a republic as a breeding ground for subversion. The very term republic evokes memories of disorder, press license, trade union rivalry— all the things they fought against. In their eyes, a republic would be an invitation to civil war. What the generals want is a continuation of the same regime under a different label: an authoritarian monarchy under Don Juan or his son Prince Juan Carlos. Don Juan is mature but liberal, while Juan Carlos is immature, and so the army finds itself in a quandary. It would prefer Don

Juan, but if he and the army cannot come to acceptable terms, it will probably urge him to abdicate in favor of his son.

"If the army hasn't agreed on Don Juan within three or four days of Franco's death, it will compromise on Juan Carlos," predicted a well-placed Spanish observer not long ago. "If it hasn't agreed on Juan Carlos in four months, the monarchy is finished. Spain will again become a republic."

Nose-counting among Spanish officers is of dubious value, but the results of a private poll conducted in early 1962 by members of Opus Dei are interesting: 80 per cent of the generals and colonels were said to favor a Monarchist restoration. Among the lieutenant colonels and majors, those of the elite who had been sent abroad for advanced training were strongly Monarchist; those serving in the provinces and intent mainly on personal security seemed indifferent or even hostile to a monarchy. Almost all the young captains and lieutenants, on the other hand, strongly favored a republic.

In the navy, traditionally a Monarchist bastion, the officers were overwhelmingly pro-Monarchist, while in the air force, the percentage of pro-Monarchist officers was only slightly lower.

The Opus Dei investigators also polled the cabinet and the Consejo del Reino, whose joint decision—theoretically—will determine Franco's successor.

"Out of thirty-one persons questioned, twenty-two said they would favor a monarchy under Don Juan," one of the pollsters revealed. "Seven said they would prefer Muñoz Grandes as a regent. Two refused to reply. None favored the Carlist pretender, and none suggested a republic."

It is not solely self-interest or power-hunger that binds the army to Franco. It is also a common philosophy.

The army chiefs have come up the same arduous path, starting from the military academies of Toledo and Zaragoza, through the formative years of troop duty in Morocco, through the Civil War, then through a quarter century of isolation and foreign rebuke. Franco and his generals have studied together, maneuvered together, plotted together, risked lives and careers together —and, together, have garnered the fruits of victory. Some have pocketed fortunes; some, like Muñoz Grandes, have never stolen a cent. Whatever their ethics, though, one bond links them: their loyalty to Franco and his loyalty to them.

All of them have spent their lives under the influence of two major events: defeat in the Spanish-American War and victory in the Spanish Civil War. The first symbolized the nadir of Spain's prestige after a century of sterile politics and bureaucratic inefficiency; the second, Spain's renascence.

The Civil War has been the other major influence, the re-vindication of Spain's *amour propre*. The story of the Civil War has no place here; it has been brilliantly told by Hugh Thomas* and by others. It is worth pointing out, however, that when it ended in 1939, the Spanish Army for the first time in half a century had a victory to boast, not a defeat to explain away. A new legend arose: the legend of the holy "crusade" against Communism. The flower of Spain—the army, the Church, the Carlists, and the Falange—gave Spain rebirth through fire and sword, the legend runs. It was the doctrine of the Inquisition: salvation of the soul by destruction of tainted flesh. So firmly entrenched is this legend now that no army officer would dare challenge it. It has become an inextricable part of his upbringing, his military ethos, and from this doctrine of the "crusade" against Communism has evolved the plausible theory of the right of the conqueror not only to the spoils of victory but to crush any vestige of the left. Being dogmatists by education and inclination, the anti-Communist Spanish officers extend Marxism to mean liberalism, progressivism, even the burgess Socialism practiced by the British Labour Party. To them, any Spaniard who is not pro-Franco is ipso facto a *rojo,* a Red.

From here, it has been but a short step to blame the West—for

* *The Spanish Civil War* (New York: Harper & Brothers; London: Eyre and Spottiswoode, 1961).

example, the United States—for not having recognized that Franco "saved" Spain and Western Europe in 1936 from Communism. Franco's links with Hitler and Mussolini are justified on these grounds. So is the dispatch of the volunteer Blue Division to the German armies in Russia in 1941. Was not Franco fighting Communism ten years before the United States recognized its true nature? Was not the United States' frantic rearmament after the Korean War and the 1953 defense pact with Spain proof that Franco was right?

The younger colonels and lieutenant colonels, frustrated by slow promotions and low pay, are torn between a grudging appreciation of American aid and a suspicion that Americans will never understand them. Insofar as American arms and military techniques are concerned, the Spanish officer is quick to learn and even to praise, but when it comes to intangibles—spiritual, religious, or historic beliefs—he is far removed from American thinking. Young Spanish officers sent to American army schools for training come home with mixed feelings. They admire the hardware—but not much else. Being ultrasensitive, moreover, they find themselves defending Franco from foreign criticism despite inner doubts.

Most young Spaniards want to change much in Spain, but they close ranks behind Franco in the presence of foreigners. Occasionally, with a trusted foreign friend, the Spanish officer will lash out at Franco's censorship, at police repression, rigged Sindical elections, bureaucratic corruption, or clerical obscurantism, but still he resents the anti-Franco feeling that exists in Europe and in the United States. He imputes it either to incomprehension or to leftist malevolence.

Spain's exclusion from NATO is a case in point. To the Spanish officer, it is not only malicious but strategically senseless. If a dictatorship such as Portugal, or quasi-dictatorships such as Turkey and Greece can be members of NATO, why is Spain still excluded? Why, if the NATO forces are chronically undermanned and the Pyrenees still form a first-rate defense line, is

Spain blackballed by such military pygmies as Denmark, Holland, or Norway?

Despite their desire for closer ties with NATO, there is little evidence that the younger officers want Western-style democracy. They have been conditioned to believe in the alleged evils of party politics, liberal democracy, free speech, free thought, and free trade unions. The need for a hierarchic elite of officers, priests, and civilian conservatives as the only method of controlling Spain's unruly masses has long been drilled into them. They want to get away from the onus of dictatorship but not from its convenience.

De Gaulle has impressed them. His army background, his no-nonsense paternalism, his suppression of parties and parliament, and his nation's economic prosperity have won him almost as much respect as his appeal to old, cultured Europe to free itself from dependence on young, brash America. The United States may be the arsenal of the West but, to many Spaniards, Europe is still the heartland and France the lyric spokesman.

The "Army of Occupation"

While the Spanish Army undoubtedly enjoys prestige among wide segments of the Spanish people, many liberal intellectuals, students, and young workers still see it as an "army of occupation." There is no doubt that the army has closed its eyes to many regime abuses, but with increasing numbers of tourists flocking to Spain and with prosperity easing the pressures for violent change, the army is beginning to divest itself of its more noxious police functions.

The Nazi-inspired 1940 law against "Freemasons and Communists," for instance, has now been scrapped and the army tribunals that used to try Franco's political foes have been replaced by a new three-judge civilian Tribunal of Public Order. The army now confines itself to prosecuting acts of espionage, sabotage, or political violence, yet it remains the iron fist inside Franco's velvet glove.

In a massive report on Spain published in Geneva in 1962,* the International Commission of Jurists declared that "military courts constitute one of the pillars of the existing regime. . . ." This report stung the Spanish Government, but several of the jurists had personally visited Spain and their findings were based on documented observation.

The ICJ report refuted regime claims that Spain was a "state of law" and pointed out, for instance, that the vaguely worded 1945 Charter of the Spaniards (Fuero de los Españoles) had never been followed up by implementing legislation. It noted the predominant role assigned to military law in suppressing offenses against the state and pointed out that as late as 1962, offenders—civilian or military—were still being tried before military courts. No associations (except state-approved bodies) could even be formed, noted the ICJ, without "preliminary authorization by the Ministry of the Interior. . . ."

The jurists traced the history of the regime's repressive legislation. Beginning in 1940 with the Law for the Repression of Freemasonery and Communism, the regime had stocked its legal armory with enough laws, decrees, circulars, and fiats to make the slightest expression of discontent punishable. By 1950, some had fallen into discard, but in 1956, student riots and tension in the Falange led Franco to order a wholesale overhaul of the state's repressive apparatus. Now, fresh decrees followed in quick succession.

On January 24, 1958 (following a Barcelona transport strike and opposition maneuverings), Franco named a retired infantryman, Colonel Enrique Eymar, as "military judge extraordinary for the repression of recently discovered extremist activities" with sweeping police powers throughout Spain. On July 30, 1959, there followed a new Law on Public Order aimed at everything from strikes, shutdowns, lockouts, subversion, and propaganda to "actions that affect, or tend to affect . . . the regu-

* International Commission of Jurists, *Spain and the Rule of Law* (Geneva: International Commission of Jurists, 1962).

larity of supplies or prices." Still another decree followed on September 21, 1960, which defined "military rebellion" as the spreading of "false or tendentious" news; damaging the prestige of the state's "institutions, government, *Army or public authorities,*" and making mutiny, strikes, sabotage, and any similar act rebellion if "inspired by political motives [italics added]."

Not only are so-called offenses against the regime "often vague and imprecise," declared the jurists, but even the laws of Spain are violated by the authorities themselves. Article XVIII of the Spaniards' Charter, for instance, forbids the arrest of any Spaniard except in cases and in the form prescribed by law, and provides that anyone arrested must be freed or turned over to a judge within seventy-two hours. Nevertheless, it found that "this rule is not always respected," and that the police have not hesitated to resort to "threats, acts of violence, bodily injury, etc. in order to extract . . . confessions."

Since 1957, Franco's chief policeman, spy-catcher, and guardian of public order has been Lieutenant General Don Camilo Alonso Vega, Minister of Gobernación (interior). Don Camilo is a crisp, white-haired martinet, whose ruddy complexion and piercing blue eyes reflect physical and mental alertness. Known sometimes as "Don Ca-mulo" (for his mulelike stubbornness), he is respected and even grudgingly admired by members of the political opposition who have been guests in his jails. They agree he is no Himmler; no sadist, but a soldier who rose to prominence in the Civil War, and to whom nothing matters but the maintenance of Franco's peace.

The police and security apparatus under his command are formidable. The Spanish police have gradually divested themselves of their early Nazi taint and now reflect the scientific influence of the French police, with whom they work closely, and of the FBI and CIA, who maintain liaison officers in Madrid. High Spanish police and intelligence officials periodically visit the United States as guests of these federal agencies.

Don Camilo controls the 50-odd civil governors in the peninsular provinces and the 10,000 mayors of all but the two or three largest cities. His eyes and ears in the countryside are the 30,000 ex-army veterans of the Guardia Civil, the paramilitary force that patrols the rural areas in pairs in eighteenth-century patent leather hats and gray cloaks. In the villages, he has the *alguaciles,* or *guardias campestres,* with their distinctive leather bandoliers. In cities of 25,000 or more, Don Camilo controls not only the urban and metropolitan police but a special, highly mobile riot force known as the Policía Armada y de Tráfico (PAT). Even the famous *serenos,* the night watchmen with the flapping coats, wooden clubs, and familiar cry of *"Ya voy . . . I'm coming . . . ,"* serve as his auxiliary eyes and ears. Like Mother Russia, Spain is intensely suspicious and must know not only what the foreigners are doing but what her own children are doing as well.

The most feared force of all, however, is the Brigada Social y Política (BSP), the secret political police whose third-degree methods have damaged Spain's reputation. Spanish students, Catholic laymen, workers, and even foreigners arrested on suspicion of political subversion have often been beaten and tortured.

Despite its grim reputation, the BSP is small: a few hundred agents at most. It is backed, however, by the full apparatus of the state security: the Guardia Civil, the PAT, the urban police, the rural guards, the elderly *serenos,* plus thousands of unpaid spies: chiselers and favor-seekers, dustmen and even duchesses—all who want something from the regime.

Don Camilo, the ruler of this network, is a far cry from the popular image of a hangman. In his tapestried office near the fashionable Jockey restaurant in Madrid, Don Camilo greeted me cordially and talked frankly about the problem of policing what he calls the most unruly people in Europe.

"No Spaniard respects the law in the abstract," he insisted. "He respects only people—not concepts. A policeman who sees a car passing a red light is outraged. This violation must be punished. He whistles the car to a stop. Out comes his notebook. He intends to be very severe. But what happens? The policeman looks into the car, sees a celebrated bullfighter at the wheel, smiles, and apologizes. The bullfighter smiles and apologizes, and soon they are talking about bullfights. They shake hands, and the policeman waves the violator on. This is Spain. It is a country of sweet indiscipline, of gentle anarchy. It is hard for foreigners to understand that Spain can only be ruled by a firm hand."

L'Affaire Grimau

Spain, the wits say, is no longer a *dictadura* (dictatorship) but a *dicta-blanda;* a play on words, meaning a soft dictatorship. The mood of the Spanish people, after twenty-five years, is less turbulent, and Franco, too, is mellowing. Yet his instinct is authoritarian, and when confronted by an emergency, he reverts to type. Then the Moroccan Caid takes over, bellicose and rigid, indifferent to the opinions of others. A case in point was *l'affaire* Grimau.

On November 8, 1962, Spanish plainclothesmen mingling with the crowds in the Madrid suburb of Quatro Caminos saw a thin, balding man alight from a bus. There was nothing particularly striking about him except for the dark, darting eyes. His face was pallid and the reed-slim body in working clothes was like that of any of the tens of thousands of lower-middle-class denizens who enter and leave Madrid daily. Yet the police closed in. At the grim Dirección General de Seguridad in the Puerta del Sol, the arrested man produced an identity card identifying himself as one Emilio Fernández Gil, a commercial traveler of 34 calle Caballeros, in Valencia. The card had been issued on September 10, 1959, and seemed in perfect order.

Within hours, however, "Fernández Gil" had disclosed his real name: Julián Grimau García, born in Madrid on February 18, 1911. Then, with unusual candor, he added: "I declare myself a member of the Spanish Communist Party's Central Committee, here to fulfill my duty as a Communist." A two-year police search had ended, for Grimau was one of three top-ranking Communists known to be operating clandestinely in Spain.

Since entering the country in 1959, he had moved under a variety of disguises in and around Madrid's teeming suburbs.

Five days after his arrest, Grimau—according to the police— jumped from the first floor of the Security Headquarters in a bid to escape. Falling heavily, he fractured his skull, broke both wrists, and was taken under heavy guard to the Madrid penitentiary hospital where he remained until January 19. Then, pronounced sufficiently recovered to stand trial, he was transferred to the suburban prison of Carabanchel.

On April 18, 1963, Grimau's trial opened before a Spanish military court. Foreign correspondents who, with diplomatic and other foreign observers, were permitted to attend, reported that Grimau seemed at ease, smiling and joking with his guards. The military prosecutor demanded death, charging that Grimau, a Communist since early youth, had headed the Criminal Investigation Brigade in Barcelona during the Civil War and had personally directed and taken part in the torture and execution of men and women suspected of pro-Franco sympathies. Furthermore, with his own hands, it was claimed, Grimau had shot captured Francoist army officers. Escaping to Russia at the war's end, he had continued to plot against the regime for twenty-five years and had slipped back in 1959, to organize Communist subversion.

No witnesses were called. All prosecution witnesses had either been killed by Grimau or had subsequently died, the military prosecutor alleged, and under the rules of a Spanish summary military court, defense witnesses were never heard.* As the state charges continued to pile up throughout the day, it was apparent that Grimau stood little chance. The trial ended late in the afternoon and the judges retired to consider their verdict. By nightfall, highly placed Spaniards knew that Grimau had been sentenced to death.

His sentence now passed for review to the cabinet, where, on

---

* These rules have since been eased, following widespread criticism of Grimau's trial.

the following day, Friday, April 19, it produced a heated debate. Foreign Minister Castiella warned that Grimau's execution would lead to world-wide anti-Franco agitation by Communists, Socialists, and liberals. His warning, however, was shouted down by the military ministers, who demanded death for this "Communist murderer and torturer." As Franco gazed coldly down the table, not only the military men but several civilian ministers joined in demanding Grimau's execution.

Now, a dramatic new element obtruded. An aide hurried in with a Reuters flash from Moscow reporting that Khrushchev had personally cabled Franco asking clemency for Grimau. The effect was dramatic. At once the tension rose still higher. This was inadmissible! The head of world Communism personally urging that his agent's life be spared? Unheard of! Clemency would be taken as weakness. The chorus for death redoubled.

Franco and the cabinet now confirmed the death sentence and sent it for action to Lieutenant General Rafael García-Valiño, commander of the Madrid military region and one of the most implacable of the army chiefs. By coincidence, however, it was discovered that high on the cabinet's agenda that day was a decree ending the jurisdiction of army courts over certain political offenses, including "affiliation with Communism." The decree had been in preparation for five months but by chance had only just found its way onto the agenda. Now a fresh debate commenced, for it was obvious that with one and the same breath the regime was confirming Grimau's death sentence and altering the competence of the army tribunal that had sentenced him. What to do? Embarrassed, the cabinet, characteristically, pushed the draft bill under the blotter and turned to less sensitive matters. A few hours later, Grimau was shot by a firing squad in the patio of Carabanchel Prison. The army's honor had been avenged. Spain had "defied" world Communism.

Khrushchev's plea to Franco was kept from the Spanish people for eight days: a strange example of the "truthful, free, and responsible" press Fraga had so glowingly promised. It made no difference to the censors that this was the first tacit recognition of Franco by the head of Soviet Communism. Khrushchev's cable read:

> Your Excellency, I have just received word that Julián Grimau has been sentenced to death in Madrid for acts said to have been committed during the Civil War. This information cannot fail to produce deep anxiety among all men of good will. No reason of state can justify trying a person on the laws of war twenty-five years after the end of the Spanish Civil War. Motivated by sentiments of humanity, I address myself to Your Excellency in the conviction that you will accede to this plea to change the sentence and save Julián Grimau's life. I am profoundly convinced that so humanitarian a gesture on your part would be well received with profound satisfaction in the widest international circles.

The message was dated 11:45 Moscow time, April 19. It was published in Spain on April 27, alongside Franco's reply. To the indignation of Spanish editors, Fraga leaked both cables first to his Ministry's house organ *El Español*.

"*Señor Nikita Khrushchev, Presidente del Consejo de Ministros de la U.R.S.S., Moscu,*" the Caudillo cabled, correctly but coldly. "I regret to inform you of the impossibility of commuting the death sentence passed by a competent tribunal *with full rights of defense* on Julián Grimau García [italics added]. The horrible crimes committed, of which there is overwhelming proof, and his continued subversive activities up to the time of his arrest prohibit the exercise of clemency, particularly since there are many living, including relatives of victims, who recall with horror his tortures and assassinations. You may rest assured that such crimes against humanity will be condemned by the conscience of mankind despite organized propaganda campaigns which seek to mislead public opinion. [Signed] Francisco Franco Bahamonde, Chief of State of Spain."

All over the world, there now arose denunciations of Franco, spurred by the Communists, yet also including liberals and moderates.

In Brussels, foot-high letters were painted on the Spanish Embassy, ungrammatically demanding *"Livertad"* (*sic*), while Spanish exiles burst into the building, breaking windows, insulting Franco, and assaulting the staff. In Paris, police had had to restrain anti-Franco crowds demonstrating outside the Spanish Embassy. In London, Moscow, Prague, Lyon, Bordeaux, Rome, and Copenhagen, anti-Franco riots broke out, spreading to Zurich, Stockholm, Santo Domingo, and even Panama. In Italy —just then preparing for national elections—anti-Franco demonstrations were held at Trieste, Genoa, Milan, Naples, Florence, and Turin.

Even in Spain itself, many officials, prelates, businessmen, and foreign diplomats agreed that the shooting of Grimau was a blunder. The Spanish Church, sensitive to the opinion of the Ecumenical Council in Rome, showed embarrassment, and on May 18, *Ecclesia* editorially urged the regime to curb the use of military tribunals, as a gesture of "civic concord and of full functioning of law and order." The Church's remonstrance was particularly apposite, for at least a hundred progressive Spanish Catholics had been tried and jailed not long before by army courts.

Grimau's execution embarrassed nations normally friendly to Spain. The French Finance Minister, Giscard d'Estaing, who happened to be in Madrid on an official visit, threatened to fly home without seeing Franco rather than risk being labeled a "Fascist sympathizer" by the French left. His threat was averted only at the last moment.

"We're like the Italian religious procession that takes two steps forward and one step back," groaned one of Franco's highest officials. "Every time we begin to move in the right direction, making foreign friends, hoping even to join the Common Market—something like this happens."

Yet even some of the so-called progressives in the cabinet failed to share this viewpoint.

"In 1962, you Americans executed forty-seven persons either in the electric chair, the gas chamber, or by rope," Fraga told an

American reporter a week later. "In Spain, we executed one criminal in 1960, none in 1961, none in 1962, and Grimau in 1963."

He flatly denied rumors that the White House, too, had urged clemency. "The only head of state who protested was Khrushchev," Fraga affirmed. "We will not deal with his own record in the matter of capital punishment. What would the Spanish people have said if we had bowed weakly to him?"

Censorship

No single arm of Franco's dictatorship has done more to blacken Spain's name and to muzzle and hypnotize its people than the censorship. It has manacled the finest minds in the land; it has driven poets, authors, and artists into exile or into silence; and, worst of all, it has so bored the new generation that the Spaniards themselves call their youth *la generación sin fe*—the generation without faith.

Slowly, and superficially, the censorship is beginning to ease. But even in 1962, photographs of society debutantes, the membership of golf clubs, dinner-lists of more than ten guests, advertisements—ranging from those for trusses to those for hamster farms—even notices of Catholic Masses had to be approved before publication. Not even the words of Pope John XXIII were exempt from censorship, for the regime feared that the Pope's stress on social justice and freedom might undermine its rule.

Based on Nazi law, the censorship has continued since 1938, openly violating Franco's Charter of the Spaniards, which guarantees freedom of speech (Article XII). All criticism has been suppressed, while the Civil War has been kept artificially alive. Day after day, the same faces and phrases parade across the pages

77

of the Spanish press. Let a visitor leave and return a year later, and he will find the same venerable generals reaffirming their loyalty; the same prelates blessing dams; the same Falangist speeches; the same soccer teams; the same folklore festivals; the same tourists sunning on the same beaches. The formula remains the same: bread and circuses.

From perusing the press, the visitor might assume that nothing ever went wrong; that no bank ever failed; that no official hand ever slipped into the public till; that no sewers ever broke up because of shoddy contracting; that no juveniles were ever delinquent, no adults put in jail except for "Communism." The picture is one of unmitigated perfection.

Least of all would a reader suspect that any Spaniard had grown weary of the regime. In my own six years in Spain (1956–62) I can recall not a word critical of the government (ruled by Franco); of the armed forces (commanded by Franco); of the Church (protected by Franco); of the Falange-Sindicates (headed by Franco); or of the nation's policies (dictated by Franco). Where criticism is stifled, private gossip, speculation, and calumny flourish. But this matters not to Franco. He regards the press as midway between a harlot paid to lure, and a nursemaid paid to dandle, public opinion.

Censorship in Spain is not new. It dates to the dim reaches of history when everything published was subject to royal approval, the *decreto real*. As early as Pizzaro's conquest of Peru, a soldier-journalist, Pedro Cieza de Leon, was criticizing the censorship that sought to stifle his reports of cruelties to the Indians.

During the nineteenth century, the army, the Church, and the politicians imposed varying degrees of censorship, and even between 1923 and 1929, the Dictator–Prime Minister Primo de Rivera slapped a tight censorship on the press, which he claimed (with some justification) had lost all sense of responsibility.

At the start of the Civil War, Franco contemptuously tossed control of the press to fanatic Falangist disciples of José Antonio Primo de Rivera, such as Dionisio Ridruejo, Antonio Tovar,

and José María Alfaro. Later he began to replace these "orthodox" Falangists with "Franco-Falangists," such as Gabriel Arias
Salgado and Juan Aparicio. Yet while he tossed the censorship
back and forth between various blocs, he never relaxed his hold.
For Franco, the sole purpose of the press has always been to serve
his regime.

In 1936, Franco's political coloration was Nazi-Fascist, so
Franco named his Naziphile brother-in-law Ramón Serrano
Suñer to draft a press law. Serrano has long since been forgotten,
but the shackles he forged in 1938 still bind the nation.* His
1938 Press Law gave Franco the right to:

 a. regulate the distribution and sale of all publications;
 b. control the appointment of editors;
 c. control the profession of journalism;
 d. control the censorship until "such time as it is suppressed . . .";
    and,
 e. exercise all powers of "organization, vigilance, and control" not
    otherwise specified.

It set up a state register of journalists, and gave the regime
powers to punish any person responsible for "anything written
which, directly or indirectly, tends to depreciate the prestige of
the nation, the regime, which slanders the work of the government or of the new state, or which sows pernicious ideas among
the *intellectually feeble* [italics added]."

All managing editors have to be approved, although ownership
and profits have occasionally been left in politically hostile hands
as a bribe for docility. All journalists have to be inscribed in the
Sindicato Vertical del Papel, Prensa y Artes Gráficas, one of
twenty-four State Sindicates; about 1,600 are so inscribed, of
whom about 1,200 are active. The Sindicate also controls the
purchase, import, and distribution of newsprint, ink, and sup-

---

* In May, 1964, the Information and Tourism Minister Fraga de Iribarne announced a new Information Law aimed at replacing the 1938 model while retaining its essential controls.

plies, and a refractory newspaper soon finds its supplies drying up. Such a pillar of the regime as the Falangist mouthpiece *Arriba*, with a circulation of 15,000, receives as much newsprint as that paper's Catholic rivals with 80,000 readers each. *Arriba* sells off its surplus to its rivals at a handsome profit.

The Minister of Information and Tourism can pressure a recalcitrant newspaper in any number of ways. He can slash the proportion of advertising to news by a simple telephone call, confronting the proprietors with economic life or death. In Spain, as elsewhere, newspaper operating costs are rising steadily, and since 1958, some collective bargaining for wages has been allowed. Owners are complaining that the government's fixed 2 pesetas (3.3¢) price per newspaper is 33 per cent too low to cover costs. The regime thus need never resort to threats of imprisonment, and seldom to fines. It has only to delay vital newsprint or warn that advertising must be cut in favor of "news."

The supply of news is tightly controlled. Since 1938, its import and distribution has been the monopoly of the state agency nicknamed EFE (the phonetic pronunciation of the Spanish "F," as in Franco—or even in Falange). For years, EFE has bought the United Press (now UPI) news service for a reported $80,000 yearly, but now it subscribes also to AP, Reuters, and Agence France Presse. It prepares a daily "confidential" file of reports hostile to the regime, which is distributed to 300 key officials. Franco is said to study this confidential file with the care of a field commander examining the enemy's order of battle.

"He is totally indifferent to what his enemies are saying about him," an aide explained. "He is only interested if a pattern is developing, such as an attack on Spain one day in a Milan newspaper, followed by attacks in Moscow, Paris, Bonn, or Buenos Aires. Franco watches the over-all picture, not the details."

A curious side effect of this "confidential" file is a massive Spanish press attack every few weeks on some obscure foreign newspaper. The public remains mystified, but insiders quickly perceive that some minor foreign journal has criticized Franco.

Overnight, canned editorials appear in all Spanish newspapers and honor is saved. The political opposition senses that something is up and hurries to sniff out and disseminate the anti-Franco article. Thus foreign attacks that might have passed unnoticed are spotlighted by the censorship itself, and this solemn farce goes on year after year.

There is something touching about the eagerness with which the Spanish press will reprint foreign news, however obscure, if only it is friendly. Let a gentle housewife in Hove pen a letter to the *Hove Gazette,* praising Spain's sunny beaches, or let a Belgian tourist speak well of Madrid's cafés, and these letters will be widely reprinted in Spain. Decades, even centuries, of foreign criticism have so rubbed the Spanish nerves that it has made the regime hypersensitive to all foreign attention, good or bad.

The New York Times, for instance, which has long been critical of the regime (although not of the Spanish people), is inevitably quoted when anything about Spain appears in its columns. Frequently, the *Times* will be flayed for its "secular hostility" on the same day that it carries a glowing article about Spain's tourist attractions. This sensitivity occasionally gives rise to naïveté. The satirical "Peter Simple" column in the London *Daily Telegraph,* for instance, commented lightly not long ago on a Moscow meeting between Fidel Castro and the Spanish Communist Dolores "La Pasionaria" Ibárruri. The next day, the Spanish press fell over itself, claiming that the "British press" had ranged itself at last with Franco against Communism. The censors had accepted "Peter Simple" as the British equivalent of Arthur Krock, Walter Lippmann, or James Reston.

Spain's hunger for prestige crops out also in reporting of Spanish participation in international affairs. When a Spanish delegate partakes in a U.N. debate—whether on Gibraltar or on seaweed control—the press will dutifully blossom out with such headlines as "Brilliant Spanish Intervention," "Superb Speech by Spanish Delegate," or "Clamorous Applause for Spanish

Viewpoint." These parochial touches contrast with the often excellent reporting of Spain's veteran foreign correspondents: José Luis Massip of *ABC* and Luis Menéndez of *Ya* in Washington; Tristran de la Rosa, Carlos Sentís, Augusto Assis, and Salvador López de la Torre elsewhere. These reporters are intelligent, traveled, and observant and the wonder is that they still manage to break through the insularity of their censors.

There are about 110 newspapers in Spain today, two-thirds privately owned (though, of course, state-controlled) and the remaining one-third published by various organs of the *Movimiento*. Most reflect the views of one of the regime's blocs: Falangist, Carlist, Demo-Christian, Opus Dei, or [Alfonsist] Monarchist. The political opposition is, of course, voiceless, except for occasional copies of the illegal *El Socialista* smuggled in from Toulouse, or for the Communists' well-printed clandestine *Mundo Obrero (Worker's World)*, which circulates with surprising efficiency. Anonymous "opposition" tracts crop up now and then and find their way into foreign correspondents' news offices or mailboxes.

Besides the newspapers, there are 2,427 periodicals devoted to sport, art, religion, culture, women's news, or society. Only one journal in Spain is legally exempt from the Information Ministry's censors: *Ecclesia,* the weekly organ of the Church-backed Catholic Action.

Ecclesia is censored personally by the Cardinal Primate, Dr. Plá y Deniel, whose views it often reflects. Under the Concordat, the Church may "conduct its apostolate"—that is, make its voice heard freely. Nevertheless, Franco has muzzled the Church as ruthlessly as he has the people. *Ecclesia* may not be sold on newsstands. It can only be distributed to subscribers, which sharply cuts its circulation.

Cardinal Plá has kept *Ecclesia* pressing quietly but steadily for those freedoms contained in papal texts and especially in Pope John XXIII's great encyclicals, *Mater et Magistra* and *Pacem in Terris.* Time and again, it has criticized the state's censorship and Franco's repression of other Christian rights, such as his ban on independent trade unions. As the only authoritative dissenting voice in a muzzled land, *Ecclesia* is watched closely by diplomats, by correspondents, and by the political opposition.

What matters in Spain, however, is not what Pope or bishops preach but what Franco wants, and as long as he is alive, his censorship will continue to protect the "intellectually feeble" from harmful doctrines, whether they stem from Moscow, from Washington, or from Rome itself. The result is national apathy.

In 1959, a Madrid newspaper published an illuminating survey on the public influence of Spanish newspapers: 66 per cent of the women readers polled said they never read any newspaper; 12 per cent turned only to curiosities or diversions; 14 per cent read beauty hints; and 8 per cent the "news." Among the men, 24 per cent never opened a newspaper; 52 per cent read only sports; 17 per cent diversions; and 9 per cent "general information."

Instances abound of the lunatic extreme that censorship has reached over twenty-five years. In December, 1960, for example, Madrid's *El Alcázar* ran a small cartoon showing a workman entering his café and asking friends sitting around the corner television set, "Who's winning?" In a soccer-mad nation such as Spain, this might seem inoffensive enough. But the cartoon appeared on the day of the wedding between King Baudouin of the Belgians and the Spanish Doña Fabiola de Mora y Aragón, and all Spain was watching the ceremonies on television. The cartoon must be a veiled attack on authority!

El Alcázar was ordered to halt its presses, while the inch-square cartoon was rushed by motorcyclist to the Pardo, where the cabinet was in session. National problems were now shoved aside as the cabinet pondered whether the tiny drawing was an attack on authority, on royalty, or on Belgium. Tempers flared. One white-haired martinet thundered that the newspaper should be fined 25,000 pesetas ($415). The argument raged until finally it was decided to reprimand the editor. Several hours later, the presses were permitted to roll again—without the cartoon.

Two aspects of this silly incident merit attention. *El Alcázar's* managing editor at the time was Florentino Pérez Embid, a prominent intellectual in Opus Dei (two members of which are cabinet ministers) who himself had once served as Director General of Press. Furthermore, *El Alcázar* is owned by a charitable society, sponsored by the Cardinal Primate. Yet Franco's cabinet found a comic cartoon sufficiently threatening to public order to engage its solemn attention for hours. The mouse indeed was intimidating the elephant.

Although readers are bored, many Spanish newspapers are making money. Franco dictates policy but he also makes newspaper publishing profitable. One example is *La Vanguardia* of Barcelona, a sober newspaper widely known as the "voice of Catalonia," and a gold mine for its owner, Count Godó, a grandson of the founder. *Vanguardia* has a net paid daily circulation of 120,000, a national circulation of 10,000, and a newsstand sale of another 10,000. No paper in Spain carries more advertising. Its annual net profit is estimated at around 36 million pesetas ($600,000), and a few years ago, on the marriage of his daughter, Godó reportedly gave her as a wedding gift the advertising revenues from the back page—$333 (20,000 pesetas) daily—for the rest of her life.

Vanguardia weathered a severe storm in 1960, when its regime-appointed Director, Luis de Galinsoga, was forced out in a wave of regional indignation. The story illustrates how the press is run in Spain.

Galinsoga was a typical Franco henchman. He had been named "Director" of the paper as a payoff when Franco's troops had occupied Barcelona at the end of the Civil War. For twenty-two years he had wrapped himself in the mantle of a pro-consul, seeing himself as a modern Pontius Pilate among the restive, separatist Catalans and ever ready to suppress the least vestige of

Catalan culture. To the Catalans, Galinsoga had come to symbolize the worst of Castilian arrogance.

One Sunday morning, Galinsoga entered a Barcelona parish church and on hearing the service conducted in Catalan—a language spoken by 3 million in and around Barcelona—he publicly interrupted the Mass, noisily abused the priest, and stormed out, threatening punishment. In a heated exchange with outraged worshipers, he was reported to have yelled that all Catalans were *mierda*—an expression ill-suited to holy premises and scarcely calculated to placate the Catalan temper.

That very day, the priest wrote Galinsoga, explaining that of eight Sunday services held in the church, six were conducted in Castilian and only two in Catalan. He pointed out that Catalan is the vernacular of all Barcelona, Franco or no Franco. By now the issue had reached the boiling point and Catalonia decided to oust Galinsoga.

A boycott of *La Vanguardia* began. Youths dashed copies from kiosks onto the streets under the tolerant eye of local Catalan policemen. Anonymous voices telephoned business firms, warning them not to advertise in *Vanguardia*. Sales fell off and revenue tumbled. Six months later, Galinsoga was clinging to his job, but tension was steadily mounting.

Anonymous pamphlets now began to attack not only Galinsoga and *Vanguardia*, but also the regime, and this was a sign of serious trouble. The pamphlets were everywhere; underfoot on the streets, in bars, folded into copies of the paper. By the first week of December, *Vanguardia*'s 10,000 daily kiosk sales had virtually stopped and paid circulation was drastically reduced. Dealers returned unsold copies, and in one climactic week, advertising revenue fell by $10,000. The Christmas advertising was threatened, and Godó now implored the then Information Minister Arias Salgado and Franco to do something.

As Catalan fury against Galinsoga continued, Franco gave in. The cabinet took up the case. Galinsoga spent that whole night in his office with an open telephone line to Madrid, awaiting the verdict. At last his old friend and sponsor Arias Salgado came on the line to tell him he must go. Something would be done to find him another job. Galinsoga hung up the phone, wrote a short note of resignation, and walked out of the office he had ruled with an iron hand for twenty-two years.

The next day, *Vanguardia* merely dropped the words "Director: Luis de Galinsoga" from the masthead. Not another word was said, and peace returned to Catalonia.

Meet the Press

First impressions often afford an insight into national character that neither time nor experience can match. My first insight into the bureaucratic mentality of Spain still delights me as I look back.

On a bright October morning in 1956, I paid my first call on the Information Ministry's then Foreign Press Director, Don José X. I had just arrived in Spain. In accordance with local custom, I had called at the American Embassy and had received a routine letter of presentation. At the Ministry, I was told that Don José was "very busy" but would try to fit me into his crowded schedule at 1:30 the next day. The following day, having arrived with half an hour to spare, I repaired to a nearby café to wait.

It was a typical Madrid *tasca:* the floor tiled, the whitewashed walls covered with mirrors hand-painted with lists of delicacies. Wine vats sat on racks and the zinc bar was lined with *tapas:* anchovies, sardines, hard-boiled eggs, shrimp, and open tins of tuna. Two workmen sauntered in, leaving a trench untended in the street. Three students argued in a corner. At one end of the bar stood a portly individual in a sports jacket, wolfing down a plateful of shrimps. I watched him as he idly tossed the shells in Spanish fashion on the floor to join a heap of bottle caps, toothpicks, molluscs, paper napkins, and cigar butts. Obviously, he was in no hurry. By 1:20, the laborers had sauntered out to their ditch, the students had disappeared, and the portly type, glancing at his watch, bade the barman a casual *"adios."* As he wandered out, he gave me an indifferent glance. A few minutes later, I paid my own bill and left.

At 1:30, I presented myself at the Ministry and was asked to wait, as Don José was still "very busy." I waited fifteen minutes, thirty minutes, forty-five minutes. As I began to wonder what was happening, a secretary appeared and ushered me into the presence. There, to my amusement, stood the portly shrimp-fancier.

No whit embarrassed, Don José greeted me with booming urbanity, waved me to a chair, offered me a cigarette, and pledged himself, his department—the entire Ministry—to my service. Did I need help in securing police permits, language lessons, theater tickets, or the names of good restaurants? I murmured my thanks but said I thought that my only need would be news. Don José allowed the merest shadow of embarrassment to cross his face. Had I had a good ocean crossing? he inquired. I pointed out that I had just come from London and had fortunately been spared the rigors of an Atlantic journey. Ah, yes. He again lapsed into thought. Could he help me find a place to live? I assured him that my hotel was comfortable. Good. I now began to ask him about conditions in Spain, but these routine queries seemed to evoke only bland evasions or ludicrous platitudes, and our conversation soon ground to a halt.

It was now nearly three, and Don José was obviously hungry. I rose and he showed me to the door with vast smiles and professions of dedication to my needs. I departed no wiser than I had entered. I was later to learn that except for me he had seen nobody all morning. It was, however, ritual bureaucracy to keep me cooling my heels for the requisite three-quarters of an hour. It was necessary that I be impressed by the slow majesty of officialdom.

In my six years in Spain, Don José never, so far as I can recall, provided a morsel of news, or even a grain of background guidance. Eventually he disappeared, swallowed up in the huge, trackless jungle of the Information Ministry; but he had given me my first insight into the Spanish bureaucratic mentality in its full flowering.

The Arch-Censor Gabriel

In the history of Spanish censorship, the name of Gabriel Arias Salgado must be accorded a special niche. Censors of many stripes and kinds bedeck Spain's story but in Arias Salgado were combined those special traits that allowed him to swim for twenty-five years in the shark-infested seas of Franco politics: loyalty bordering on servility; an ignorance of the outside world exceeded only by contempt for it; and a guile that smothered both criticism and opposition. He has left a hammerlock on Spain's mind that will take decades to efface.

After Franco, no man bears greater responsibility for the stultification of Spanish culture, for the despair of Spain's intellectuals, for the indifference of Spanish youth, or for Spain's poor image in the world. From 1937 to 1962, Arias Salgado epitomized the intellectual garroting of his countrymen's minds. If the "Black Legend" persists today, he must bear much of the blame.

Arias Salgado was no gaunt Savonarola thundering from a pulpit; no hot-eyed Inquisitor consigning heretics to the flames. No softer, more spuriously amiable little man could have been imagined. The few journalists who ever penetrated his official sanctum found seated before them a tranquil homunculus in his early fifties, rapt—or pretending to be rapt—in contemplation of some weighty tome on "information policy." The smooth, sallow face tended to fleshiness, the nose was sensitive and slightly disdainful, the mouth weak. In repose, the face seemed to carry the empty gravity of a Roman senator's during Rome's decline.

The visitor would stand patiently, not wishing to disturb the Minister-Censor's deep brooding. Suddenly, the Minister would look up, the eyebrows rising in feigned surprise, and with a warm, soft voice bid one be seated. Everything around him seemed sweet, cloying, immobile, from the noise-muffling carpets, the heavy draperies, the religious paintings, and the crucifixes to the massed books written by Arias himself. They stood foot-high on tables and desks, shutting out the world behind words.

After a momentary pause, the floodgates would open and soon logic, reason, and intelligence were inundated. Arias would brook no interruption. For an hour, he would drone on—prolix, tedious, and interminable. Out poured all the tired excuses for censorship: the Red atrocities in the Civil War, the dangers of Communism, the stupidity of the West, and the treason of the regime's critics, be they Christian Democrats, Socialists, Republicans, Monarchists, or merely "liberals."

For Arias Salgado, time had stood still since 1936. Nothing had happened in the world or in Spain in the intervening years. The Civil War was still raging: the Red hordes were still at the gates, Spain was still in peril, but Franco—praise God—was still in command. Anyone who dared murmur against Franco was guilty of defeatism, treason, and heresy.

The gilt clocks on the tables would chime the quarter-hours, but the monologue never varied until, at last, glassy-eyed, the visitor would rise: none the wiser, his questions unanswered, his mind bludgeoned, his soul depressed. For those who loved Spain and admired its people, a meeting with Arias Salgado was saddening.

Yet no servant of Franco's sniffed the political winds more keenly. He not only ingratiated himself with Doña Carmen, Franco's influential wife, but even copied the Caudillo to the point of distributing directorates in his Ministry in the exact political proportion of Franco's cabinet. The Direction General of Tourism, for instance, was given to an amiable duke whose workday occasionally exceeded three hours. The Director General of Cinema was close to the army. The Secretary General had a Jesuit background, like Arias himself. Opus Dei was represented through the Director General of Books, while the smiling little Director General of Press was a fanatic Falangist who spent most of his time away from Madrid, lecturing on religious themes and leaving the day-to-day censorship of Spain's 110 newspapers to a bureaucratic hack in his early thirties with no knowledge of journalism, and less of the world.

Arias Salgado's background was undistinguished. His and Franco's families were distantly connected. The story goes that as a young cadet, Franco used to take little Gabriel by the hand to watch parades. Arias Salgado had studied for fourteen years to become a Jesuit priest but failed, and this bitter frustration marked him all his life.

The outbreak of the Civil War found him traveling as an electric light bulb salesman. He managed to reach Franco's headquarters, where his fanatic loyalty brought him quickly to Franco's attention. He was a perfect doormat. Never was he heard to utter a reproach or criticize Franco. He was certain that God had chosen Franco (and Franco had chosen him) to safeguard Spain from Communism, Socialism, Republicanism, Protestantism, Masonry, pornography, and "liberalism." He knew nothing of the outside world. In early 1960, he blandly advised the then Spanish Ambassador to Washington that a Republican victory would be best for Spain because "Nixon is a Catholic." The envoy was aghast at such ignorance but knew it was useless to argue.

Like Franco, Arias Salgado never gave precise orders, and this enabled him to shuffle off criticism onto his subordinates.

"Play this up," he would tell an aide, or, "Play that down." That was all. Then the all-powerful Minister's dictum would seep down through the vast flaccid bureaucracy of the Information Ministry, oozing out as either a mammoth campaign for or a flat ban against the original topic.

News about the monarchy was a case in point. Arias, who loathed the Monarchists, would order some trivial aspect of Prince Juan Carlos' military education "played down." By the time the order reached the censors, this had become magnified into a total ban on any mention of Juan Carlos, of Don Juan, of the Spanish royal family, of Queen Mother Eugenia Victoria, or even of the Monarchist cause. The censors—unemployed journalists, Falange scribblers, an occasional priest—preferred to red-pencil everything rather than to risk their 1,500 pesetas ($25) in monthly fees.

A consummate politician, Arias also used the press to harass his rivals. In 1959, shortly before sweeping economic reforms, he deliberately leaked news that the peseta would be devalued, to embarrass Commerce Minister Ullastres, a member of Opus Dei, the Falange's chief critic. The resulting run on Spain's low reserves troubled him not. His morbid jealousy of Foreign Minister Castiella was also proverbial. Foreign press criticism of Spain was culled by Arias' minions and rushed daily to Franco to demonstrate the alleged incompetence of Castiella's diplomats.

Arias' value lay in the fact that he never complained, never argued, never fought for an idea unless it was Franco's. The effect on Spain was disastrous, for in time the censorship became universally convenient.

"Cabinet ministers, generals, bishops—even some foreign diplomats—would be on the phone day after day, asking him to censor this or play down that," said an official. "Everyone wanted something suppressed, and Arias enjoyed it."

This tremendous power of "No" became almost a fixation, for Arias had come to envision himself as a St. George, as Gabriel, the arch-guardian of the nation's morality.

"You are doing well, my boy," he told a young Ministry official one day. "But I am not satisfied with the music on Madrid radio at night. There's too much," he groped for words, "cha cha cha and boom boom boom. We need something more decorous."

Puzzled, the young subordinate asked what the Minister would suggest.

"I don't know," snapped Arias Salgado impatiently. "Something that won't overexcite married couples when they retire for the night."

The Foreign Press

Most Spaniards believe that the foreign press is Spain's enemy, and Franco has shrewdly exploited this phobia.

"No event takes place in our country, however minuscule it may be," he complained on May 27, 1962, "that is not blown up and trumpeted abroad if in any way it can harm or undermine us." The 15,000 Spanish reserve officers listening to him in the hot sun at Garabitas, near Madrid, cheered him to the echo.

It is hard to persuade the average Spaniard that the foreign press devotes perhaps one-tenth of one per cent of its news space to Spain. Spain is still not really "news." However, interest is growing. The Associated Press, United Press International, Reuters, and Agence France Presse now maintain bureaus in Spain, while *The New York Times, The Times* of London, *Le Monde, Neue Zürcher Zeitung,* Radiodiffusion Television Française, West German State Radio-Television, and other news organizations maintain full-time correspondents. *Time, Life, Newsweek,* the Sunday *Observer, Guardian, The Washington Post,* and many European, Latin American, African, and Asian news agencies have part-time correspondents in Spain. In all, approximately 300 foreign correspondents have been accredited by the Information Ministry, yet for the average news editor, Spain only becomes "news" when the regime is menaced by strikes, by political disorders, by natural disasters, or by rumors of Franco's ill health.

This is manifestly unfair in the eyes of the average Spaniard, to whom Spain is the center of the world, and he takes a masochistic delight in imagining himself, sword in hand, defending his country and its culture equally from Russian Marxism and American materialism. This old suspicion is beginning to ease, but it has by no means died away.

If the Franco regime has suffered international ill will, however, it has itself chiefly to blame. No Western European nation (except Portugal) has so flaunted its indifference to foreign opinion or done less to understand its neighbors. In no country of Western Europe is the task of the foreign reporter more frustrating. Paradoxically, the foreign correspondent is free of censorship. In my six years' experience, not a word I wrote was subject to censorship nor was I once summoned to the Foreign, the Information, or any other ministry to be upbraided, threatened, or pressured. Occasionally, friends in official positions remonstrated over a dispatch or volunteered information to expand my knowledge—but there were neither warnings nor blandishments. Yet Spain is no sinecure for an active journalist.

When, occasionally, Franco wants to help the foreign press for his own purposes, he does so extremely well. In 1959, when President Eisenhower paused overnight in Madrid at the end of a world tour, several dozen American correspondents were traveling with him, and at least a hundred American, European, African, and Asian reporters arrived to cover the visit. To everyone's surprise, the regime organized press facilities with remarkable efficiency. Two press officials, Luis Ballesteros of the Information Ministry and Adolfo Martín Gamero of the Foreign Ministry were given full authority. A press room was set up in the Castellana Hilton hotel, extra telex and telephone links specially installed. Typewriters, paper, and desks were provided, press stickers for correspondents' automobiles printed. Eisenhower's quarters at the Moncloa Palace were opened for inspection; even television and newsreel trucks were included for the arrival. Every facility that the press might need was there.

The next day, Eisenhower flew away and the honeymoon was over. The facilities ended and the press was back where it started. The Spanish performance had been brilliant—for one day.

By 1959, the swell of discontent over Arias Salgado's censorship could no longer be ignored. The army, the intellectuals, the Monarchists, and the Church—each for its own reasons—began maneuvering to dislodge the censor. Franco, sensing the trend, bided his time, but the Information Minister, sensing it too, essayed a counterattack.

At the National Press Congress in Salamanca that same spring, in the course of a three-hour speech on "information policy," Arias Salgado announced the creation of a national committee to "weigh"—not a new press law, but merely the "bases" for a new press law.

A forty-member National Committee, packed, as expected, with ministerial reliables, was constituted on June 23, 1959. To lend it prestige, Arias named three prelates: the Bishop of Malaga, the Bishop of Ciudad Real, and the auxiliary Bishop of Lugo. On July 27, the committee assembled in the Valley of the Fallen, posed for the photographers, shuffled its papers, and adjourned for the summer. From its birth until Arias Salgado's dismissal three years later, it met infrequently, received reports from thirty consultative bodies, and eventually disappeared, strangled in its own wordage. The equivocal role of the Bishop of Malaga caused deep soul-searching among his admirers. To many, Dr. Angel Herrera was one of the few champions of liberty left in Spain. In pre-Civil War days, he had been a renowned liberal as editor of *El Debate*. As a bishop, in 1954, he had publicly disputed with Arias Salgado over the censorship. Then his luster had begun to dim. By 1958, when, with Franco's approval, he was named head of the powerful Catholic-financed *Editorial Católica,* many began to regard his role as more expedient than independent. His participation in Arias Salgado's committee dismayed his admirers only slightly less than two of his subsequent pronouncements.

The first of these came in November, when in a special tribute penned for the twenty-fifth anniversary of the sober *Diario Vasco* of San Sebastián he announced that "the country is not ready to do without prior censorship."

The second was even more disheartening. In December, he and his two fellow prelates handed Arias a confidential minority report that soon became widely distributed. Part I consisted of a draft "Fundamental Law" for the press, liberally quoting Pontifical texts on press freedom. Part II, to everyone's astonishment, expressed the "profound gratitude" of Dr. Herrera and his fellow bishops for the "incalculable good" that, they said, Franco had done in suppressing "unbridled license" in the news. "The rectitude of the regime's censorship," they asserted, "cannot permit it to be termed arbitrary."

The incredulity that arose in all quarters was soon followed, as always in Spain, by cynicism. Church spokesmen hurried to insist that Dr. Herrera and his colleagues were speaking only for themselves, but confusion and dissension increased. Arias' maneuver to split his foes had succeeded brilliantly, but the situation grew steadily worse.

By 1960, the censorship had become so stifling that 227 of the nation's leading intellectuals addressed a withering letter of protest to the Minister.

"The intolerance, confusion, and vagueness . . . of the censorship," they protested, "is stultifying the development of our work. A text may be approved for magazines but barred for books, theaters, or films, or it may be approved today and banned tomorrow. . . . Spanish culture now presents a precarious spectacle to the outside world. The Spanish writer or scientist is virtually forced to produce in exile . . . only for foreign-language publications. . . . [This is having a] deplorable effect on the formation and information of the average Spanish reader." The intellectuals also cited the "mutilation that constantly takes place in foreign texts, plays, films . . . shown in Spain."

Among the signatories were such internationally known figures as Ramón Menéndez Pidal, President of Spain's Royal Academy; José María Pemán; Pedro Laín Entralgo, Julián Marías, Ramón Pérez de Ayala, José Luis Aranguren, Alfonso Sastre, Camilo José Cela, Dionisio Ridruejo, Joaquín Calvo-Sotelo, Alfonso Paso, Enrique Tierno Galvan, Jesús Prados Arrarte, Ana María Matute, José María Pi Suñer, Juan Ramón Mas Oliver, Juan Goytisolo, Carlos Barral, Edgar Neville, Lili Álvarez, Antonio Mingote, and many others. Newspapers in New York, London, Paris, Rome, and other world capitals published the protest, but in Spain, of course, it was suppressed.

Gabriel's Fall from Grace

For Spain, 1962 was a fateful year: the year the pressures burst out. First came the Asturian strikes, next the Munich incident, and then as the people and the Monarchists jointly seethed against Arias' policies, Franco realized that some change was unavoidable.

For three weeks, Arias Salgado permitted not a word about the strikes in the newspapers, on the radio, or on television. At the same time, and for seven hours daily, Radio Moscow and Radio Prague were broadcasting accurate, up-to-the-minute news of the Asturian strikes into Spanish homes.

On May 4, Franco, in a curt four-line communiqué, suspended his own *Fuero de Trabajo* (Labor Charter) in the strike-bound provinces, thus tacitly admitting an emergency which by then had become the talk of the nation.

As the walkouts continued, *Ecclesia* on May 12 openly challenged the regime by declaring that strikes were "licit weapons" when negotiations failed.

"Just as a war is the final argument when one group finds its views trampled upon," proclaimed *Ecclesia*, "so is the strike the final means available to a working group when it finds its own rights ignored."

At long last, Arias sent a hireling reporter north, to tell the "truth." His glowing reports were dutifully published a few days later. Arias' envoy waxed lyrical over the beauty of Asturias in spring, its happy, industrious people, its tranquillity, even the number of television sets per capita. By some curious oversight, he failed to note that 80,000 miners and workers were defying Franco by striking. Arias was still determined to "protect" the Spanish people from noxious ideas.

June 8 brought a second crisis. Before a gathering of West European statesmen in Munich, Franco's political foes demanded that Spain be barred from the Common Market until democratic reforms had been introduced. The cabinet raged and the press, on Arias' orders, imputed blame for the incident to the Monarchists and to Don Juan, whom it labeled ingrates and traitors. It was now the Monarchists' turn to seethe and Franco realized that a crisis was at hand. At last, he moved. On July 11, 1962, he abruptly dismissed seven ministers including Gabriel Arias Salgado. After a quarter of a century, the archangel of reaction had finally fallen from grace.

The denouement had a touch of Greek tragedy. Two weeks later, Arias expired of a heart attack. The press, radio, and television were ordered to observe national mourning, and eulogies filled the newspapers. One, penned by Arias' Director General of Press, Adolfo Muñoz Alonso, epitomized the rest.

"He was faithful to God, to Spain, and to Franco," intoned Muñoz Alonso. "He had his own alphabet in which the word 'truth' was never absent. He carried out the policy of truth as a norm, as a criterion, as a faith. . . . Throughout his life he bore the moral responsibility for 30 million Spaniards entrusted to his zealous . . . care. Perhaps the seeds he has sown will grow into light and stars. . . ."

The appointment of forty-one-year-old Manuel Fraga Iribarne as the new Minister of Information and Tourism gave rise to hopes of more press freedom and a better foreign image for Spain. These hopes, however, have only been partially fulfilled.

In America, Fraga would be called a "whiz kid." Seventeen when the Spanish Civil War ended, he had been too young to participate actively. He was a gifted scholar and had won law and diplomatic degrees with honors, had become a university lecturer, a prolific writer on economics, law, and politics, a legal advisor to the Cortes, a member of the Royal Academy of Moral and Political Sciences, an official of the Institute of Hispanic Culture, and Director of the regime's Institute of Political Sciences. His political background was unassailable. No one could accuse him of Communism, Anarchism, Socialism, or Freemasonry. He was a right-wing progressive.

Fraga was typical of the wheeler-dealer generation raised under Franco. He knew intimately the regime's weaknesses, its cynicism, its corruption, and its reaction. He also knew its strength. Like many young Spaniards, he was cynical. He was an *accidentalista*, who could swim in any water.

Fraga had risen in Franco's service because he was quicker of eye, smoother of tongue, and faster of foot than the others. He was unusually articulate in a land where talk counts, a hard worker, and a man who lived the "good life" and had a fondness for the rich food of Madrid's great restaurants exceeded only by his love for politics. Many believed that Fraga was the white hope who would restore Spain's voice and regild her image, but they overlooked one vital point. Franco changes his ministers—the ministers do not change Franco. Since Fraga's appointment, the worst aspects of Arias Salgado's mindless censorship have been eliminated, but the iron hand still rules.

Fraga entered upon his new duties with a blast of trumpets. Arias Salgado's entire staff was dismissed, with the exception of the able Luis López Ballesteros, who was sent to Washington as press attaché. To the astonishment of the many foreign journalists whom Arias had shunned, Fraga invited them to a lavish reception.

"We respect the information you send to your newspapers . . . ," he told them. "We believe that you will be able to report objectively what the Movement has done, is doing, and hopes to do."

During Fraga's first months, foreign correspondents flocked to Spain to report glowingly on the new "liberalization," but although Fraga exuded good will, experienced observers remained wary.

Fraga lifted prior censorship for all newspapers except the most important—those of Madrid and Barcelona. Everywhere else, editors themselves would decide what to print, he decreed. There was nothing particularly new in this. Even under Arias, the press in forty-two out of fifty provinces had censored itself, although this was due more to ministerial laziness than to policy. In any case, vital topics remained off bounds: the Chief of State, the armed forces, the Church, the constitution, and all judicial sentences. Fraga timed his degree for midsummer, when most editors were away on holiday and their ill-paid deputies would refuse to take risks.

Everywhere, fresh paint was slapped on the rusting machinery. The censorship bureau became a "consultation" bureau—but the editors in Madrid and Barcelona were reminded to consult it daily. State radio announcers, who for over twenty years had barked "*¡Viva Franco! ¡Arriba España!*" at the midnight sign-off were replaced by dulcet feminine voices cooing "*Buenos noches, señoras, señores.*"

Ten months after taking office, Fraga told visitors that he had authorized 315 new magazines, most of them, of course, of a religious, scientific, sporting, or otherwise nonpolitical nature. He was relaxing censorship on plays, but in some theaters the claques had begun loudly stamping their feet to signify disapproval of his liberalization.

Censorship of books remained strict, and Carlos Barral, a leading young Barcelona publisher, told CBS in an interview in November, 1962, that "nothing has changed. . . . The mechanics of censorship are still the same." Sixty-five per cent of the books he had submitted during the previous two years had been banned, he revealed.

Political discussion also remains tightly muzzled. Early in 1963, for instance, Fraga banned from *ABC* an article by the Opus Dei intellectual Rafael Calvo Serer, on the role of a "loyal opposition" in a democracy. But he astonished Madrid by telephoning Calvo personally to explain.

"Under Arias, I never would even have been notified," marveled Calvo. "The censorship is as rigid as ever but now it's more polite."

Fraga assured the American Club in the presence of Robert F. Woodward, the then Ambassador, that he would soon announce the long-awaited new press law. It might be an "experiment," but Spain would have a "truthful, free, and responsible press," and more liberty for what he euphemistically termed "differentiations." To puzzled reporters, this seemed to mean that for the first time in twenty-five years, Spain's newspapers might be permitted to report the endless tossing and heaving under the surface.

Meanwhile, the vested interests—all opposed to any easing of the censorship—were biding their time, waiting for the new minister to trip. Paradoxically, the newspaper strikes in New York and Cleveland in 1962 provided Fraga's critics with ammunition.

"As [Franco's] supporters see it," Richard Scott Mowrer reported from Madrid, "the plight of America without newspapers, and newspaper employees without work, is an object lesson for those Spaniards who complain of lack of freedom here."

Even these timid moves of Fraga rang the alarm for everyone who had anything to hide or who, like the Church, sought to control censorship itself. They closed ranks.

Fraga let *ABC* publish a sharp protest by Madrid's City Hall against the Housing Ministry's practice of speedily constructing low-cost housing in the suburbs and winning national acclaim, then walking off, leaving sewers, water, light, transport, and other essentials to the overstrained city budget. Workers were bitterly criticizing the city fathers, and the situation was a scandal. Never had such open criticism of one public authority by another been tolerated in Franco Spain. A storm broke loose.

The Housing Minister, a vainglorious Falangist, fumed at a cabinet meeting that Fraga's relaxation of censorship was unpardonable! Public criticism of "authority" was tantamount to Communism. Other cabinet ministers took up the cry and soon a flood of recrimination arose. Everyone had a complaint: there was too much sex in plays and moving pictures, too much "differentiation" in newspapers and periodicals. It must stop.

Franco, at the head of the cabinet table, sensed the tide. He gave orders. Fraga's "reforms" were postponed; criticism virtually ceased; and the dream of a "truthful, free, and responsible" press ended.

The summer of 1963 brought Fraga into open conflict with

two persistent critics of Franco, each with high-level Church contacts. One was Dom Aurelio Escarre, Benedictine Abbot of Montserrat and a revered figure in Catalonia, whom Fraga (on Franco's orders) forbade to broadcast in Catalan over the Barcelona radio. After writing a strong protest to Fraga, the Abbot told three thousand worshipers that the regime had given Spain progress in "propaganda and dazzle" but had conspicuously failed to give it similar progress in "liberty and justice." Later, the Abbot reiterated his charges in an interview with *Le Monde* of Paris.

Next, Fraga found himself embroiled with the nation's intellectuals. One hundred two well-known names in university, literary, and artistic circles were signed to an "open" protest alleging police torture of miners arrested during sporadic summer strikes in Asturias. Fraga publicly ridiculed the charges; but when 188 intellectuals soon after demanded an "independent" investigation by the Madrid College of Lawyers, he angrily replied. The government's promise of liberty, he warned, was meant for "creation, not destruction."

Fraga is still young and energetic, and the first three years in office have taught him the penalties of going too fast in a reactionary regime. The knee-and-groin infighting remains a wondrous thing in Spain, and Fraga is up against men who learned intrigue when he was cutting his milk teeth. They are waiting to move in for the kill—as they did with Arias Salgado.

His problem is how to permit "differentiation," how to accustom the public to the forgotten spectacle of debate, without exposing himself to charges of endangering public order. His staff says that he is now being realistic; his critics say that he has abandoned any hope of real press freedom, and is merely using his position for post-Franco era political ambitions.

Fraga insists that Franco's government, while not perfect, is the first that has worked in modern memory, and that all others—ranging from liberal democracies to absolute monarchies—have failed. He attributes this to special social, economic, and climatic conditions in Spain, and to the Spanish "national temperament."

Spaniards are "hopelessly bad at propaganda," and for a quarter of a century have been forced to "duck as the barrage from the massed typewriters of the world whistled about our ears," he once said. However, Spain is now seeking a political framework that will give "expression" to the social and economic forces of the land.

"My job is to gather and give expression to the feeling of the youth of our country who took no part in the Civil War—among whom I include myself," he said recently. "My approach has been cautiously pragmatic and, after sounding out all sectors of national life, I believe . . . that Spanish public opinion remains firmly in the middle between the principles of liberty and authority. . . ."*

Fraga, however, has begun inviting cabinet colleagues and high officials to be interviewed on the state television by selected Spanish journalists. Even the latest Asturian strikes were recently discussed before an audience of ten million televiewers. There have been improvements, unquestionably, since the days of Arias Salgado, but there have also been blatant attempts to harass the correspondent. There is still some validity to the old quip: "Spain's censorship is like a switchboard in a cheap hotel: it either refuses to answer or it gives you the wrong number."

* Quoted from a speech given at Chatham House, London, in the summer of 1963.

5

The Falange

On a windy March day in 1963, 160 bosses of the Spanish Falange (the National Movement) assembled in a Madrid sports arena for their first working session in nineteen years. Not since 1944, at the imminent collapse of the Axis, had Franco called them together, and expectation ran high.

Urbane and sleek in their gold-trimmed white tunics and blue shirts, the political bosses of Spain reflected years of good living. They greeted each other effusively with hearty *abrazos* and cries of "*¡Hombre! ¿Qué hay?*" ("What's new?"), as the buzz of speculation rose and fell. Obviously, Franco had summoned them for some plum—perhaps to grant the Falange a permanent role in the country's future.

Few, however, even suspected what lay in Franco's mind. He had not the least intention of giving the tarnished, unpopular Falange control over Spain's future—the other regime blocs would violently oppose it. His purpose was far more subtle. Ostensibly, he was convoking the Falange chiefs to draft political "reforms," but actually he was buying time. By launching the 160-man National Council into the trackless jungles of political discussion, he would give the nation—and the world—the impression that liberalization of the regime was under way. The majority of lazy Falangist bosses would be flattered with a sense of their own importance, and the power-greedy hard core would be stymied.

Meanwhile, Franco would be weakening the Falange's death grip on the aimless, amorphous Movement. For years, the other regime blocs—the army, the Monarchists, the Carlists, the liberal Catholics, the Opus Dei technocrats, and the moneyed interests—had shunned the Movement because of its Falangist coloration. Now, with a restive new generation arising and demanding greater political freedom, Franco either had to open up his Movement to other groups standing sullenly on the sidelines or would risk seeing the Spanish people turn again to the banned political parties, which he and his army both feared and hated. The Falange must be called together, flattered with words, bribed with a "task"—and reminded of Franco's authority.

For more than twenty-five years, the Falange had elbowed all rivals from the political trough. Frequently, Franco had appointed non-Falangists to his cabinet but down at the grass roots, in the 8.5-million-strong Sindicates, in the municipal and provincial councils, wherever the jobs and the lucrative contracts were to be found—there the Falange was to be found too. Confident of Franco's protection, cynical and arrogant, the Falange had degenerated into an Iberian Tammany—a fraternity of graft. Its appeal to youth was gone and it had split into factions: some ambitious, others supine; some progressive, others regressive; some eyeing power after Franco, others content to suckle while he lived.

Most of the 160 National Councilors wanted only comfort, but the veteran hard core, the Old Shirts (Camisas Viejas)—Arrese, Girón, Herrero Tejedor, Fernández Cuesta, Solís, Salas Pombo, and others—wanted power. For years, they had been pressing Franco to "institutionalize" the Falange; to give it a permanent constitutional role in Spain. The Old Shirts feared that Franco would either dissolve the Falange by a pen stroke during his lifetime or leave it to the mercy of its enemies—the army, the Church, and the Monarchists—on his death. They wanted legal equality with the Cortes and the Consejo del Reino. In short, they wanted Franco to make the National Council a type of senate. As the Falange congress droned through three days of speeches, all minds were focused on Franco's wind-up speech. This speech would spell out defeat or victory.

At last Franco addressed them, not in the attire of a Falangist chief, but in the gold-trimmed khaki of the army. No one missed the point. Moreover, in an hour-long speech, Franco never once mentioned the Falange by name, only the National Movement. As the Old Shirts stirred sullenly in their seats through the familiar platitudes about Communism, foreign incomprehension, and the glories of Franco's rule, there ran a somber note of warning.

"Our satisfaction," shrilled Franco, "cannot excuse us from perfecting those instruments of state which, conceived a quarter of a century ago, may have lost some of their effectiveness."

If there was one instrument that had lost effectiveness it was the Falange—and everyone knew it. This was the key to the meeting. The strikes the preceding year had exposed the incompetence of the Falange's Sindical machinery, just as the nationwide support for the strikers had laid bare the failure of Falangist propaganda. Young workers were emigrating in steadily increasing numbers for better jobs and freedom abroad, while at home, able young regime officials were quitting in disgust. One of them, Francisco Jiménez Torres, the deputy chief of the Sindicates, had recently resigned because Franco had refused urgent Sindical reforms.

In concluding his address, Franco cited the device of the national referendum, which he had used only once, in 1947, when he had transformed Spain into a monarchy. The implication was clear: When the time came, the Spanish people would decide their future by a national referendum without any intermediary —even the Falange.

Franco stepped down to weak, dutiful applause and then,

flanked by generals and bishops, moved to his waiting Rolls-Royce and drove away. The bell had tolled for the Falange.

Hours later, a secret thirty-nine-page report on university student opinion leaked out of the congress, where it had earlier provoked a violent dispute between those Falangists who favored reform for the sake of appearance, and those who opposed all change whatsoever. Its findings were sobering: 77 per cent of the students polled had no interest in politics, which, as the report drily observed, could mean either satisfaction with Franco's rule, or boredom; 82 per cent had derided Spain's information media as "inadequate" to express views on public affairs; 50 per cent had complained that they had no means of influencing Spanish legislation.

Citing the "climate of drift" in universities, "paternalism," and "excessive dogmatism, too much monologue," the report pointed out that "exchange of opinions and the airing of positive and responsible crticism are essential. These entail risks . . . but only by facing up to these risks can . . . vitality be assured."

"It might appear less risky," it concluded, "to stick to toned-down, somnolent routine but in the long run this engenders . . . political atrophy and . . . loss of influence over the younger generation in whose hands the future lies."*

The word "Falange"—Phalanx—conjures up visions of jack-booted Spaniards marching by, their arms raised in stiff Nazi salutes, their faces sullen, their eyes fanatical. One sees torchlight rallies and hears bull-throated orators denouncing Jews, ranting about imperial glory, and chorusing: *"¡Franco! ¡Franco! ¡FRANCO! ¡Arriba España! ¡Una, Grande, Libre!"* Fortunately, this nightmare no longer threatens. The original Falange has long since been interred.

The Falange of today is an aging bureaucracy with four sources

* The report was attributed to Francisco Gómez Arboleya, who, before his death in 1959, had been a member of Madrid University's faculty of political science.

of power: the labor-employer Sindicates, censorship and propaganda, a few scattered youth groups, and a women's organization. Although there is no formal membership, it claims about one million members. Only the women's branch, headed by Pilar Primo de Rivera (sister of the Falangist martyr, José Antonio), has served the nation selflessly. Under her supervision, more than 800,000 young Spanish women have served an obligatory six months in social service, and at present, at least a million Spanish girls are being taught by 24,000 women teachers of the Sección Feminina. Otherwise, the Falange's influence on youth today is negligible.

Spain's 63,000 university students must all still join the official Falangist student union (SEU), and the Falange still exercises thought control over all teachers, hounding from their jobs those suspected of liberalism. Its control over the national censorship, too, has allowed it to stifle political criticism or fresh ideas, while at the same time filling the void with obsequious flattery of Franco and itself.

No other agency in Spain today bears so much responsibility for the stagnation of Spanish political life.

To understand the Falange, one must go back over the winding path of memory.

Europe in the early 1930's lay gravely ill. The Wall Street crash had rocked the old continent. Business was stagnant, capital frozen, fear and unemployment were spreading. Everywhere "strong men" were hawking strong-arm solutions from balcony and cellar. Italy had its Mussolini; Portugal its Salazar; Austria Dollfus; Germany Hitler; and even France had its Fascist Cagoule. Europe's youth, angry and bitter over the failure of its elders to solve the problems of jobs and food, turned to the new nostrums. Youth wanted a drastic solution, and while many in Spain turned to Marxism, many others, restrained perhaps by their traditional Catholicism, turned to the alternative—Fascism.

Fascism in the early 1930's had a multiple appeal for many Spaniards. Its stress on patriotic mobocracy and "sacred violence" excited youth, while "corporate" control over restless labor soothed the frightened middle classes, the Church, the army, and the financial interests. From 1930 on, the old order slowly disintegrated, as economic conditions worsened and parliamentary reforms died smothered in words. The left and the right each began arming in "self-defense," and the leaderless masses of the center sank into the bog of indecision. From this welter, Spanish Fascism was born in 1931.

In April of that year, King Alfonso XIII had slipped out of Spain, preferring to leave the tiller of state swinging rather than to risk bloodshed. The Second Republic had virtually stumbled into power with neither program, nor capable leaders, nor tested political parties. It had prestigious intellectuals: Ortega y Gasset, Marañón, Pérez de Ayala, but its politicians—Lerroux, Azaña, Largo Caballero, Gil Robles, Ángel Herrera, Prieto, Casares Quiroga, Alcalá Zamora, and Maura—proved so fractious or incompetent that the public administration lurched from crisis to crisis, and even public order became a mockery. It is not surprising that in such conditions a Falange should emerge. What is surprising is that it was merely the fifth in a list of Fascist splinter parties arming to do battle with the left.

The credit for Falangism must go to a penniless postal clerk named Ramiro Ledesma Ramos, who gathered around him in Madrid during 1930–31 a dozen fellow fanatics groping for the formula for Spain's renascence. Mussolini's and Hitler's ideas for rekindling patriotism and crushing Marxism attracted them, and soon the Ledesma group began to introduce Fascist "corporate" principles into their program. They began airing their ideas that autumn in a pallid little weekly, *La Conquista del Estado (The Conquest of the State)*.

Gradually, Ledesma and his disciples evolved a sound-and-fury program tacked together from nationalism, Spanish imperial revival, and expropriation of land from the rich. At the same time, they proposed state control over both labor and management through vertical Sindicates. These ideas became the genesis of the National Sindicalism whose tattered banner still hangs limply over Franco's regime.

Violence dominated their thinking. These reforms, Ledesma warned, could not be achieved by the old, corrupt, bourgeois political parties but solely by a tight, disciplined "elite" using "sacred violence." From Ledesma's heated brain emerged such slogans as *"¡Arriba España! ¡España: Una, Grande, Libre!"*

Meanwhile, in Valladolid, another young rabble-rouser, Onésimo Redondo, was becoming autointoxicated, too, with the need for a "Spanish frenzy" to rip out the twin cancers killing Spain: bourgeois complacency and right-wing intrigues. Tossing a dose of clerical reaction into his broth, Redondo began to call for "social justice," "national unity," and the revival of what he vaguely called Spain's "eternal values." Gradually, bored and restive Spanish youths began drifting to his banner.

A merger of the two splinter groups was decided in October, 1931, largely for self-protection. There was little to link them other than their mutual hatred of Marxism, their contempt for bourgeois liberalism, and their poverty. Yet, characteristically, they permitted themselves the luxury of a grandiloquent title: National Sindicalist Action Groups or JONS (Juntas de Ofensiva Nacional-Sindicalista). That, plus their restlessness, was virtually all they had.

For three years, 1931–34, the JONS struggled for survival, Ledesma and Redondo each ruling his own followers, with little political coordination and little popular support. Money was short, for the Bilbao bankers (traditional paymasters of right-wing subversion) were frightened by the JONS's radicalism; the left was angered by its arrant nationalism. Thus, ground between the two millstones, the JONS slowly starved. Then, suddenly, fortune smiled.

In 1933, another Fascist-oriented movement of very different hue was founded by a rich young lawyer-politician named José Antonio Primo de Rivera. This was the Falange Española, or

Spanish Phalanx, an amalgam of country-club patriots and wealthy authoritarians.

By early 1933, as Dr. Stanley G. Payne has ably explained,* José Antonio Primo de Rivera's political ideas had begun crystallizing into "a plan for leading an audacious minority which would inaugurate radical political and economic reforms by authoritarian means, employing the ideological framework of nationalism to enlist the moral enthusiasm of the young." If successful, such a movement would not only save the "political integrity" of Spain but would raise Spain to a more prominent position in the new nationalist European order. This, says Payne, was "Spanish Fascism."

José Antonio was a striking contrast to the embittered lower-middle-class Ledesma and the peasant-born Redondo. A son of General Primo de Rivera, Alfonso XIII's Dictator–Prime Minister, José Antonio came from the minor Andalusian nobility. He had been reared in wealth, had learned languages from foreign governesses and tutors, and had traveled. He had finished his university education, and after taking a law degree, he had become mesmerized by the dynamism of Mussolini and Hitler, and by the mounting threat of Socialism, Anarchism, and Communism.

Like other young Spaniards of his class, José Antonio needed an outlet for his energy and found it in politics. Politics gave him not only a personal platform, but also an arena where he could vindicate his father's "sacred" memory. His father's fall from power in 1929 haunted and goaded him as he grew up. Until his death, he harbored a bitter antipathy toward King Alfonso XIII and the Monarchists, whom he accused of having abandoned and betrayed his father. Some of the doctrinaire hatred of Don Juan, King Alfonso's son, still found among Falangists, stems from this distant emotional spring.

As the Republic reeled and street fighting intensified between

* In *Falange: A History of Spanish Fascism* (Stanford, California: Stanford University Press, 1961; London: Oxford University Press, 1962).

Socialist and Fascist *pistoleros,* Spain's right wing turned increasingly to José Antonio. Funds poured in and ardent university students, discontented officers, and patriotic intellectuals began hurrying to enlist in his cause.

On October 29, 1933, José Antonio and two friends, Julio Ruiz de Alda and Alfonso García Valdecasas, gathered 2,000 supporters into La Comedia theater in Madrid, and officially founded the Falange Española. José Antonio's inaugural speech exposed the truculent ideological isolation into which Falangism was born.

The "liberal" state, declared José Antonio, offered "economic slavery." Socialism was no panacea, for it not only preached a "materialistic" interpretation of history, but worse, demanded class warfare. Spain needed neither class warfare nor even political parties: it needed unity; and this could only be achieved by regrouping the nation into "organic" or natural channels. No one was "born" into a political party, José Antonio said; "we are all born members of a family; we are all neighbors in a municipality; we all labor in the exercise of a profession." These were the natural "organic" channels for popular participation in political life: family, municipality, Sindicate. Political parties must be banned.

Spain, he continued in his inaugural speech, needed "less liberal word-mongering" and more "authority, hierarchy, and order." There was to be no "shrinking from violence" but the "dialect of fists and pistols" to preserve justice and to protect the *patria*. Parliamentary democracy was a failure, and the "new" Spain would never emerge from the Cortes, where, as he put it, the atmosphere was "tired and murky, like a tavern at the end of a night of dissipation." The proper place for Falangists, he insisted, was "outside . . . in the fresh air, under the cloudless heaven, weapons in our hands."

Then, well aware of left-wing charges that he and his followers were *señoritos* (lordlings) of the moneyed classes, José Antonio declared:

"I should like . . . my voice to carry into every last working-class home. . . . We come to fight so that hard and just sacrifices may be imposed on many of our own class. . . . We come to struggle for a totalitarian state that can *reach the humble* as well as the powerful with its benefits [italics added]." The great power of the moneyed classes under Franco and the continuing disparity of wealth have been criticized by the original Falangists as betrayals of José Antonio's inaugural pledge.

For some time, desultory negotiations had been carried on between the Ledesma-Redondo JONS and José Antonio's circle, and now, with the official founding of the Falange, a merger was the obvious course. The university students originally attracted to the demagogy of the JONS were beginning to switch en masse to José Antonio; but more important, the Falange was more expert at extracting funds from bankers and other Spanish reactionaries. The merger took place in February, 1934, and the new political hybrid assumed a still more mouth-filling title: Falange Española de las Juntas de Ofensiva Nacional-Sindicalista. It adopted the JONS symbols, the yoked arrows evocative of the glory of Isabel and Ferdinand, and the red-and-black colors of Anarchism (to show how radical it was). After considerable discussion, it was agreed that a triumvirate of Ledesma, José Antonio, and Ruiz de Alda would run the organization and set policy. Soon it became clear, however, that while the new FE-JONS was short on program, it was long on intrigue. Redondo remained in Valladolid, where he continued to run his local JONS more or less as a feudal fief, while trouble simmered in Madrid. Within a year—by early 1935—José Antonio expelled Ledesma for conspiracy.

Now the Falange-JONS was José Antonio's; he was the *caudillo* —medieval chieftain—of a mixed bag of student fanatics, poetasters, left-wing National Sindicalists, and right-wing Fascists, numbering a few thousands in all of Spain. Within two years, José Antonio, Ledesma, and Redondo would all fall before Republican bullets, and the Falange, tossing its horns and snorting fire, would end up in Franco's corral.

Franco, at the outbreak of the Spanish Civil War, was no political theorist: he was a military conspirator. Franco had belatedly joined the conspiracy, with little more than an average Spanish general's knapsack of maxims: unity, patriotism, obedience, order, authority. Franco had no political philosophy except to win; he knew only that the left had to be crushed.

Having suppressed the left-wing Asturian miners' revolt in 1934 with a savagery so merciless that it assured his promotion, Franco had been named head of the general staff in 1935 by Gil Robles, then Army Minister. As political conditions worsened, repeated efforts had been made to lure Franco into various anti-Republican plots, but he had preferred to wait. He knew of the noisy FE-JONS but thought little of it and had in fact even vetoed a harebrained scheme of José Antonio's for an antigovernment coup in 1935. Distrust between José Antonio and Franco might have hardened but for a political twist of fate.

National elections in February, 1936, gave the left a narrow victory over the right, and the reinvigorated popular front government now began cracking down on its foes. José Antonio and his Falangist followers were jailed by the hundreds, and even Franco was ousted as chief of staff for his right-wing leanings. He was posted as Captain General to the distant Canary Islands, where, with poetic justice, he now exiles his own enemies. Street fighting increased; a wave of strikes crippled trade and industry; and meanwhile in Lisbon, General Sanjurjo, exiled leader of the abortive 1932 army rebellion, was busily planning a fresh army rising with the Carlists. From his prison cell in Alicante, José Antonio sent word to General Emilio Mola, Sanjurjo's deputy in Pamplona, offering his Falangist militiamen for the plot. The offer was accepted, for many of the army chiefs were still hedging, and every armed man would be needed.

When, on July 17, 1936, the rebellion commenced, the Falange's 4,000 ill-trained but ardent militiamen were rushed piecemeal into the front lines, but within a few months, the Falange's independence was gone. Franco, shouldering Mola and other rivals from power, seized the *caudillaje* of the war on October 1, 1936, and the dictatorship had begun.

Franco's takeover of the Falange was but a question of time, and the manner of its execution explains many seeming anomalies: why the Falange still has its hands in the public till though not on power; why it is split; why the original Old Shirts detest Franco, and why the late-comers cling to him as to a life raft.

In that chaotic summer of 1936, Franco found himself faced by an estimated 5-to-1 Republican military superiority, and critically short of troops, weapons, ammunition, supplies, and food. The solution was obvious: totalitarian organization of the civilian population behind the Nationalist lines, conscription, and propaganda. The Falange was the obvious instrument. The movement had a rudimentary national organization, a Fascist ideology, fanaticism—and manpower. Moreover, José Antonio and other high Falangist leaders were in Republican prisons. The Falange fell into Franco's lap.

In the first war months, Spaniards of all ages, classes, and views —including Republicans, Anarchists, Socialists, and Communists caught in Nationalist lines and anxious to save their lives— poured into the Falangist militia. Few army officers or noncoms could be spared, but somehow the militiamen were trained in basic drill and rushed to the front lines, often stiffened by Franco's Foreign Legion or Moorish detachments. More Falangists were used to police the rear areas. Student volunteers were given a rapid thirty-day course and became the *alféreces provisionales* who still parade before Franco every year, slightly larger of girth and somewhat slower of movement, but no less ardently pro-Franco. Behind the front, meanwhile, the rival Falangist-JONS cliques maneuvered for leadership, as Franco looked on with growing distaste. Two developments brought matters to a head.

In March, 1937, Ramón Serrano Suñer escaped from the Republican zone and made his way to Franco's headquarters in Salamanca. The two men were closely bound, not only because they had married sisters, but still more by common political sympathies. Serrano had been a prominent lawyer and politician linked to Gil Robles' monarchist Demo-Christian CEDA and had, in fact, organized and led its Fascist youth branch, the green-shirted JAP (Juventudes de Acción Popular). He was widely acquainted with the political right. He knew many Carlists and had collaborated closely with José Antonio, but, still more important, he brought Franco something that no one at headquarters had—least of all Franco: a burning ideology. Serrano was a Fascist, an admirer of Hitler and Mussolini, an inveterate foe of Communism. He could give the rebellion an ethos, a political cloak of respectability; and Franco, who trusted no one, at least could trust him. Serrano became Franco's director for the civilian war effort.

The next development was characteristically Spanish. By April, 1937, Manuel Hedilla, a Falangist provincial boss from Santander, had gathered around him a group of conspirators; he was planning to succeed the martyred José Antonio as national chieftain, and take over the entire movement under Franco's nose. Spurred by Serrano, Franco moved quickly. On April 19, 1937, the Falange and the Carlists, the two main civilian movements in the uprising, were forced to the altar at the point of Franco's shotgun, with some small splinter groups such as Acción Española and Renovación Española shoved in as bridesmaids. That the Falange and the Carlists were diametrically opposed in their composition and aims and had nothing in common but a mutual hatred of the Republic mattered not a whit. Franco had a war to win and wanted no further intriguing.

With Serrano as his political chief of staff, Franco now decreed "total" discipline: totalitarianism. The new merger was christened the Falange Española Tradicional y de las JONS, and it remains the cornerstone of Franco's National Movement. It was brazenly, defiantly Fascist. Political parties were outlawed, as was universal suffrage, and in their place emerged the "organic" state, with participation in government theoretically limited to three channels: family, municipality, and the worker-employer Sindicates. To the new FET y JONS, moreover, Franco turned over censorship and propaganda.

Next, Franco assumed the right to appoint the members of the Falange's National Council, or ruling body; to control the party's rank and file, he decreed that army officers and N.C.O.'s were automatically members. So were all who had ever been imprisoned by the Republic.

Ruthlessly, Franco was isolating the Old Shirts on an atoll of orthodoxy in a sea of opportunism. As Dr. Payne has pointed out, the composition of Franco's first National Council showed what was going on. Of 50 National Councilors, 20 were "legitimate" followers of José Antonio, while the rest, named by Franco or Serrano, comprised 8 Carlists, 5 Army generals, and 17 vari-colored "Monarchists, conservatives, and opportunists."

"The Falange," Payne wrote, "far from controlling the state was no more than an instrument for holding the state together."

With Franco's Civil War victory in 1939, the corruption of the Falange began in earnest. Tens of thousands of patriotic Spaniards who had joined for the duration quit to remake their homes and their lives. Other thousands—covert leftists or careerists—began shifting laterally into the new Sindical organization where jobs, and, most important, political security were to be found. Kangaroo courts and firing squads were still the law of the land and many thousands of Republicans who had fought and lost were still being driven across the Pyrenees or hunted down. Many found safety by infiltrating the winning side. With a curious irony, the Falange now began to fill the vacuum created when Franco destroyed the "left."

For Franco, this was a grim moment. The land lay wrecked, its farms neglected, its industries ruined, its coffers empty. The clouds of World War II were gathering, and within six months Hitler's armies would sweep through France to the very borders of Spain.

The effect of the Nazi victories on the Falangists now was electric. Already intoxicated by their Civil War victory, they began to dream of imperial glory and a new place in the sun—on the Nazi coattails. Intrigue and plotting grew, abetted by German and Italian agents, but Franco once again played his trumps: the stick and the carrot—the army and graft.

He named the trusted Muñoz Grandes to head (and disarm) the Falange, while he assigned Pedro Gamero del Castillo, an early *Joséantonista* of Monarchist leanings, to steer the Falange's appetite safely into the channels of bureaucracy. The scramble for spoils now increased. Where the nation hungered, the Falangists fed. Where gasoline was unavailable, Falangists' cars ran. Where there were jobs, the Falangists could be found at the head of the queue.

The first serious check to Axis fortunes, the U.S.–British landings in North Africa in late 1942, marked the Falange's political watershed. Until then, Franco had given the Falangists considerable rope, but now that Hitler's fortunes were declining, he began to hedge.* With 100,000 troops in Spanish Morocco, he remained neutral, allowing the raw, untested Americans to stream past, supplied by a single narrow-gauge railway. Many believe that it was Salazar who warned Franco to stay on the sidelines; but whatever the facts, with each successive Axis defeat, Franco hedged further. He needed wheat and oil to prevent riots in Spain and, thanks to wise heads in Washington and London, limited supplies were permitted to reach him through the Allied naval blockade—thus foiling his dependence on Hitler. By now, as the prospect of Allied victory heightened, pro-Allied Spanish generals around Franco began growing openly restive.

Most were Monarchists who had joined the 1936 uprising to

---

* As Franco's ambassador in Paris at the time, the late José Felix de Lequerica, told his American counterpart Robert Murphy: "If the Germans had been aggressive Spain would not have resisted them. We had nothing with which to resist ten German divisions but we kept them out by diplomacy." Robert Murphy, *Diplomat Among Warriors* (Garden City, N.Y.: Doubleday and Co.; London: William Collins Sons & Co., 1964), p. 69.

replace the Republic with a monarchy, but not with a Franco dictatorship. During the early Axis victories, they had remained silent, but as the Allied strength increased, their disenchantment with Franco grew. If Spain was to be spared Allied retribution after victory, Franco would have to go—but who would dare to be the first to move against him?

Gradually, starting in 1943 and continuing into 1944, a group of Army Monarchists, headed by the late Lieutenant General Alfredo Kindelán, a tall, graceful aristocrat who had headed Franco's air force during the Civil War, began to plot. Slowly, they were joined by increasing numbers of civilians, even prominent early Falangists such as Gamero del Castillo and Alfonso García Valdecasas, who were convinced that the restoration of the monarchy alone would save Spain from Allied retribution. Franco caught wind of the maneuver and bided his time, until in early 1945, as the Allied and Soviet armies poured headlong into Germany, he cracked down.

The signal was Don Juan's Lausanne *manifiesto* of March 19, calling on Franco to resign and urging the Monarchists to desert him. The world scarcely heeded the Spanish Pretender, piping defiance from the shores of Lake Leman; but in Madrid, Franco heard him and struck back with characteristic ruthlessness. The Falange, bitter enemy of the monarchy, was unleashed and began a wholesale purge. Through 1945 and well into 1946, Falangists hunted down their enemies by the thousands. Monarchists, Socialists, Anarchists, Communists, trade unionists, liberals, Republicans, intellectuals, and students were arrested, jailed, and many were shot.

Falange propaganda outdid itself in vituperation, and the hapless Don Juan, who had moved from Switzerland to Portugal in 1946 to be near when Franco fell, became the target of abusive hysteria. He was labeled a traitor, a plotter, a revolutionary, a subversive, a Freemason, and an "Englishman." Spain's musty claims to Gibraltar were trotted out to highlight the "English" background of the Pretender, a grandson of Queen Victoria, and arouse Spanish xenophobia.

It was an ugly moment, responsible perhaps for much of the anti-Franco feeling left in the United States and Europe. Yet when it ended, Franco was master of Spain; his foreign enemies were defied and his domestic enemies in jail or in tombs. A year later, by mid-1947, secure in his fief, Franco could redress the political balance, cut the raucous Falangists down to size, and turn cautiously to the Monarchists for a simple reason: he needed them. The army still insisted on some political formula other than a naked Franco-Falangist dictatorship. Franco's answer was the Law of Succession. Spain would become a monarchy—but without a king.

So it came about that on July 26, 1947, a bankrupt and politically isolated Spain approved Franco's newly decreed Law of Succession by an 82 per cent majority, in the only national referendum held to date. The nation's 17 million voters, men and women over twenty-one, were not offered a choice of candidates but merely of alternatives: yes or no. For the Spanish nation, it was Franco or the unknown; and no one wanted the unknown. Now, having used the Falange to cow his enemies, Franco rechained it. Spain needed credits, foreign aid, and respectability and the Falange could provide none of the three. With ice-cold realism, Franco turned to the moderates, the liberal Catholics, and the bankers with international contacts.

Between 1945 and 1950, Soviet aggression saved Franco. The years tell the tale. 1946: Soviet occupation of northern Iran and Churchill's Fulton, Missouri, "Iron Curtain" warning. 1947: threats to Greece and Turkey and Truman's dispatch of the Sixth Fleet to the Mediterranean. 1948: the rape of Czechoslovakia. 1949: the Berlin blockade and Communism's seizure of China. 1950: Korea. When, a year later, the United States dispatched Admiral Forrest Sherman to ask Franco for military bases, the Falange was mired down in corruption, its revolutionary dynamism extinguished, and its membership nominal. The hard core, though bitter, was powerless—for Franco needed Wall Street credits far more than stiff-arm salutes. In 1956, the hard core came briefly to life, but by then it was too late.

The Waves of Liberalism

Franco's reign has been characterized by five-year cycles of rising pressures for reform, last-minute cabinet reshuffles to avert a crisis, then another long period of torpor. Wary, and loath to change men or policies, he has made a fetish of "continuity," or, as his critics call it, immobilism. Each cabinet reshuffle has been preceded by an exhaustive analysis of the competing political forces inside Spain and of shifting conditions abroad.

After 1945, the overt Falange influence in the cabinet was subordinated to that of the Demo-Christian Catholics, personified by the new Foreign Minister, Alberto Martín-Artajo, who, Franco believed, could "dialogue" with the new Demo-Christian leaders in Europe: de Gasperi in Italy, Bidault in France, Adenauer in West Germany. After his 1953 defense pact with the United States and his Concordat with the Vatican, Franco decided that now he could edge the Falange further into the shadows and begin collaborating with the "safe" Monarchists. This policy was to produce a violent Falangist reaction.

By 1955, a fresh current of liberalism was beginning to invade Spain. The United States, Britain, France, Holland, and Italy had by now all returned to Madrid the ambassadors they had so haughtily withdrawn in 1946. Moreover, the U.S. Congress had approved the U.S.–Spanish defense pacts and the start of major aid. Monarchist bankers, such as the late, respected Count Fontanar, had persuaded American financial houses to invest in Spain, and tourists were once again beginning to visit the land, delighting in its beaches, its mountains, its cathedrals, and the dignified warmth of its people.

Spaniards, too, were beginning to journey abroad again and discover, despite the xenophobic propaganda of the Falangist censors, that the outside world was not "hostile" to Spain or to its people, but critical of Franco. Tourism, books, periodicals, moving pictures, and commerce were all beginning to open Spain to fresh ideas, and nowhere was the ferment more marked than in the universities.

The Falange was not only aware of Franco's Monarchist dabblings but still more aware of the effervescence in the universities, which was taking on an openly anti-Falange and anti-authoritarian cast. The more these trends developed, the uglier became the Falangist die-hards. Franco's interview of February 27, 1955, in *Arriba* warned the Falange that his patience had limits.

Deliberately choosing the Falangist mouthpiece, Franco made two significant points. He made his first public distinction in twenty years between the Falange and the National Movement; then went out of his way to praise the late King Alfonso XIII and to criticize the Falange's "revolutionary" mumblings. A few weeks later, Franco tartly reminded the Falange's Vieja Guardia (Old Guard) that he was the leader, not just of the Falange, but of "all Spaniards."

The rebukes infuriated the hard core as it delighted its enemies, and soon clashes broke out between the Falangists and their rivals, the Monarchists and liberal Catholics. Meanwhile, Old Guard hostility to Franco increased, culminating in an unprecedented hostile demonstration by Falangist die-hards during ceremonies for José Antonio at the Escorial. Two more incidents late in 1955 showed how far the liberal tides had penetrated the younger generations, and how low the Falange's prestige had fallen. During funeral services for the renowned liberal philosopher Ortega y Gasset, Franco's Education Minister, Joaquín Ruiz-Giménez, and the Rector of Madrid University, Pedro Laín Entralgo, liberal Catholics both, openly implied the need for further liberalization of political thought in Spain. Wildly enthusiastic, more than a thousand students followed the philosopher's coffin through the streets, arousing not only the alarm of the generals and other reactionaries but the fury of the Fa-

lange. The second incident was even more devastating to the
Falange's pride.

A confidential poll of student sentiment in Madrid University
found its way into the hands of the opposition. Entitled "On the
Spiritual Situation of the University Youth," the poll had been
prepared under the supervision of Laín Entralgo. As reported by
Herbert Matthews in his penetrating *The Yoke and the Arrows,**
the poll showed that "75 per cent of the students considered the
government to be incompetent and that 85 per cent accused the
ruling classes of immorality. Ninety per cent thought the military hierarchy ignorant, bureaucratic, and worthless; 48 per cent
accused the military of being brutal libertines and heavy drink-
ers. Fifty-two per cent of the students even considered the
ecclesiastical hierarchy to be immoral, ostentatious, and ambitious."

The students' indictment was disclosed to the world by the
able late Camille N. Cianfarra, correspondent of *The New York
Times,* who was to perish a few months later in the sinking of the
"Andrea Doria." Overnight, it became world news, and with the
feeling of foreign support behind them, the students now increased their agitation for an end to the Falangist student union
(SEU) and for freedom to elect their own representatives.

As 1956 dawned, Franco's police began seeking political agitators in the student body and soon found them. Months before,
the Falangist renegade, Dionisio Ridruejo, had organized his
Nuevo Tiempo (New Time) clandestine political club and had
gathered into it a heterogenous mixture of young Communists,
Socialists, Liberal Catholics, and left-wing Falangists, whose only
bond was anti-Francoism. They intended, through student unrest, to embarrass the regime, but the knowledge that Ridruejo
was in the background was enough to convince the Falangist
hard core that serious subversion was afoot. Tension mounted
until even the sight of Falangist officials in the University provoked catcalls, booing, and abuse. This proved too much for the

* New York: George Braziller; London: William Heinemann, 1957.

Frente de Juventudes (Falange Youth Militia). Throwing caution aside, it decided to crack the skulls of its student enemies.

Many believe the Falange fell into a trap. Secretary General Raimundo Fernández Cuesta was away on a trip when the riots started, and his deputy Tomás Romojaro took it upon himself to order goon squads into action. Two hundred Falangist hoodlums invaded Madrid University buildings in the narrow swarming streets of old Madrid early in February. Fighting began, and in the fray a shot was fired. One Falangist youth fell, gravely wounded. As he hovered between life and death, tension rose further. Armed Falangist "centuries" now began preparing for a massive invasion of the University, but before they could move, the army interposed itself.

The generals warned Franco to rein in the Falange and prevent a blood bath whose outcome no one could foresee. The nation and the world were watching, and moreover, the students were drawn almost entirely from the social classes whose support Franco needed. He yielded. The Falange goons were disarmed and sent to their barracks to dream of revenge.

His own nerves strained, Franco now characteristically set about chastising all who had disturbed his peace. Fernández Cuesta was fired. Laín Entralgo was fired. Students were arrested, student publications suppressed, and Franco's "constitution" suspended as police swarmed over the University for weeks.

Franco next toured Spain, uttering menaces which, according to those who heard them, smacked more of Axis hysteria in 1940 than of Europe in 1956. He threatened blood baths and purges, and the country shrank back into its accustomed apathy.

For months, workmen labored day and night to rush the completion of the half-built University City on the outskirts of Madrid. Franco wanted no more rebellious students milling about in the city's teeming heart, infecting the citizenry with their liberal ideas. On the edge of Madrid, where the fresh winds blow in from the Sierra de Guadarrama, these young minds could be isolated and protected from liberal thoughts. Out there, those foolish enough to be dissatisfied with the regime could tell their troubles to the wind.

The 1956 Wage Increases

The Falange now began to perceive that its strong-arm days were over. Neither Franco nor the army would tolerate violence. It was obvious, moreover, that the army was steadily closing ranks with the Monarchists, the Catholic groups, the bankers, and the bourgeoisie against the Falange. The Falange now needed something better attuned to the middle 1950's. The answer was wage increases. This had the twin allure of buying popular support and hitting the Falange's conservative enemies in the pocketbook.

The Falange had paid lip service to wage increases over the years, but its pleas had always died away down the stony corridors of bureaucratic indifference. Since 1939, when the Falange had first created Sindicates, its aim had been to regiment labor; to keep it obedient and mute. Falangist labor policy was supremely simple: "no strikes, no lockouts, no dismissals; obedient stagnation." Pay, working conditions, hours, holidays, overtime, safety, health, and social security benefits were all decreed by the Falangist Labor Ministry and the Falangist-run Sindicates. The workers had nothing to say. Moreover, management found the Sindical system ideal for keeping wages low. So long as it could not dismiss labor, or boost individual productivity, it could not be expected by the regime to pay higher wages. Wages, thus, had long remained frozen, and slowly the workers' purchasing power had eroded.

But with the onset of the Korean War and the prospect of Western help, industrial and labor conditions in Spain began to change. Spanish uranium, copper, zinc, lead, and mercury became valuable as the West again started stockpiling strategic minerals. Meanwhile, Franco's crony, the astute naval engineer Juan Antonio Suanzes, had persuaded the Caudillo that Spain must build an industrial base of her own, even at the risk of inflation. Franco enthusiastically agreed, so a wave of industrial expansion had begun to spread across the face of Spain, as treasury presses churned out money to erect lavish new plants, such as the vast Aviles steel works near Oviedo. Prices shot up, and by 1955 labor had begun to protest openly in the industrial north, in Bilbao and Barcelona. The regime met the issue by police and censorship, but even the most sanguine Falangists grew alarmed.

So it happened that in April, 1956, the burly, high-living Labor Minister, José Antonio Girón, and his Falangist colleagues sought to convince Franco that worker standards in Spain were "dangerously" low and public order was in peril. Moreover, there was criticism of the wealth rapidly being acquired by highly placed speculators—some in Franco's own cabinet.

Normally, Franco turned a deaf ear to economic advice that bored him, but this was different: public security was a matter close to his heart. He was a despot, but a benevolent despot. He wanted peace, order, and prosperity for everyone, and he believed that prices were as susceptible to military discipline as recruits on the drill grounds. He listened to Girón, to Agriculture Minister Cavestany, and to the other Falangists who assured him there was no risk of inflation—then gave his approval. The result was disaster.

During the year, two successive national wage decrees raised the basic wages of Spain's 8.5 million workers by 25 per cent in April; by 15 per cent more in October, with no compensating rise in output or productivity. By year's end, the flood of new currency had set the feeble economy on an inflationary waltz that, by mid-1959, whirled Spain to the abyss of bankruptcy.

The Arrese Crisis

By 1956, Franco had a fresh political crisis on his hands, instigated again by Falangist Old Shirts. This time, the Old Shirts, headed by José Luis Arrese, made a bid for power.

Their plan was simple. Under Arrese's leadership, the hard

core would prepare three draft Fundamental Laws,* which the 160-member National Council would then rubber-stamp and pass to Franco, and which—it was hoped—Franco would approve. With Franco's approval assured, acceptance by the coalition cabinet and the timorous Cortes would be a formality—or so the hard core believed. The three draft laws would have reinvigorated the Falange's moribund machinery, broadened its powers as the sole electoral machinery in Spain, and turned it into a permanent constitutional watchdog after Franco's death. It would "guide" the post-Franco era in Falangist orthodoxy.

Arrese is a tense Catholic architect from Malaga, whose Falangism is exceeded only by his loyalty to Franco. Franco discovered him in 1941, and used him to succeed Serrano Suñer when his brother-in-law's pro-Axis sympathies ended his political value. Arrese had done well. In 1943, when Hitler was making a final desperate bid to persuade Franco to join him, Franco had sent Arrese to Berlin to stall; the moody fanatic had so inundated the Führer with sophistry about the "unbridgeable gap" between Nazi atheism and Spanish piety that Hitler had given up. Arrese had become Franco's star performer, shifted from the front to the rear row of the chorus when it became necessary to play down the regime's totalitarian trappings, but always in reserve. His loyalty to Franco never wavered, yet his Falangist zeal had retained for him the trust of the old guard. If anyone could win Franco's blessing for the Falange's power grab, it was Arrese.

Arrese proposed to retain Franco's Monarchist succession plan while making the Falange the "constitutional" power behind the throne. To sugar the pill, the Falangists proposed to allow Franco's successor—for example, a king—to name his own prime minister for a five-year term *after consultation with the Secretary General of the Movement.* In effect, the Falange would have a veto. Real power would thus remain in the Falange's National

* The Principles of the Movement, the Organic Law of the Movement, and the Structure of State.

Council, which, purged of such outside elements as the army, the Church, and variegated "opportunists," would again become Spain's "elite." When Arrese's political "take-over" bid became known, it caused consternation.

The army, the Carlists, the Church, and the pro-Monarchist economic groups fell on the scheme with indignation. Between the National Council's meeting in Salamanca in September and its final meeting in Madrid on December 29, 1956, protests poured in on Franco.

As 1956 drew to its close, Franco summoned Arrese to the Pardo, told him of the opposition, reminded him of the 1947 Law of Succession, and observed that any "tutelage" over the future reposed by law in the hands of the thirteen-man Consejo del Reino. The Falange's bid had failed—this time permanently.

Angry and bitter, Arrese threatened to resign as Secretary General of the Falange, but Franco wanted no martyrs. No one resigned in Spain except on his orders. On February 27, 1957, Franco reshuffled his cabinet in the most sweeping shift since 1951. Arrese was kept chained to Franco's chariot as Housing Minister, a post that gave his training and social zeal full scope while keeping him muzzled, and in his place as Secretary General, Franco now named a loquacious and politically light-weight Andalusian, José Solís, a veteran Sindicalist who had been visiting American trade-union leaders, trying to break down their prejudices against Franco's labor laws. Solís had one immense asset: he would do what Franco told him, and no more.

Franco named Solís not only Falange chief but also head of the Sindicates—the first time that the two offices had ever been held by one man. It was obvious that Franco was determined to steer the hungry Falange away from political pastures into the trackless swamps of labor legislation, social security, and social justice. There it could push for true labor reforms, higher wages, better conditions for the workers. And if the Sindical tail henceforth wagged the Falange dog—so much the better.

Having caught the Old Shirts at the river's edge, Franco now proceeded to filch their ideological garments. Within a year and a half of rejecting Arrese's draft Principle of the Movement, Franco had issued his own Twelve Principles, to rank henceforth as the first of the nation's Fundamental Laws. On May 17, 1958, in full-dress army uniform, he proclaimed his new constitutional mishmash to a Plenary Session of the Cortes, and while few understood its meaning, one thing was clear: henceforth, any successor to Franco—be he king, president, or regent—would have to kneel and swear to observe the so-called Principles. It was all a sop to the embittered Old Shirts.

Spain would remain a "traditional Catholic, social and representative monarchy . . ." but, added Franco, the monarchy would function "within the immutable Principles of the National Movement." Now the Monarchists in the Cortes were seen to slump dejectedly as the Falangists ironically cheered.

There was little, in fact, for any faction to cheer about, for Franco's Twelve Principles changed nothing. They were but a mantilla of words. The Falangists wanted doctrinal continuity and the Monarchists a monarchy—and each had it. Franco still had power.

The Asturian Strikes

Four years later, in 1962, the Falange's Sindical machine suffered its most serious loss of prestige. Strikes flaring up in the Asturian coal mines showed the workers' contempt for the state-run Sindicates and the need for rapid labor reforms throughout Spain.

The Asturian miner, like all miners, lives in discomfort and danger. He lies on his back six and seven hours daily in seams so narrow and crooked that they defy mechanization. Dust fills his lungs, and soot begrimes his face, yet he is proud of his ugly, dangerous calling. He has always been the aristocrat of Spain's workers and, until recently, the highest paid. Father-and-son teams bring home 10,000 to 12,000 pesetas ($166 to $200) a month—compared with the 1500 pesetas of a civil servant in Madrid. The miners' *economatos* (commissaries) in such towns as Mieres, Nalon, and Turon sell television sets—even imported champagne.

But in 1962, whereas the mine face-workers earned high wages through overtime and bonuses, the 40,000 or more "peons" who ran the shaft elevators, handled the heavy wagons, and performed nonskilled jobs, earned only 60 pesetas ($1) per day. Married men found it impossible to live on such wages. Their bitterness had been aggravated by the 100-per-cent wage increases granted a few months earlier to thousands of steelworkers at the government's Aviles plant down the coast. The miners decided that if the regime could double salaries, the mine owners could too. In theory, by April, 1962, the mine owners had already accepted wage demands for a 160-peseta ($2.66) daily minimum but, in accordance with the law, had passed them first to the Sindical organization for approval. The Sindical headquarters had passed them on to the Ministry of Labor. The Ministry of Labor had "consulted" the Ministry of Commerce, the Ministry of Finance, and even the nationalized railways (RENFE), which use coal. RENFE had consulted the Ministry of Interior, which had passed the buck back to the Sindicates. Committees had met, subcommittees had met, ministers had sent more experts to investigate—until Franco's bloated Sindical bureaucracy had ground to a halt.

Paradoxically, there had been some improvement just before the strikes started. The government had conceded part of the miners' claims, and the cabinet had even authorized the mine owners to charge the government $1.00 more per ton to cover the higher wages, when seven miners were fired on disciplinary charges at the privately owned La Nicolasa mine at Mieres on April 7. This was the last straw. A week later, sympathy strikes had spread all down the coast, bringing out workers in Madrid, Valencia—even as far away as the Rio Tinto mines at Huelva. It was clear that only years of starvation wages, total indifference from the Sindicates, and general disgust over management could have spurred 80,000 to 100,000 men to defy the law and strike. The regime, true to form, blamed Communist agitation.

"Italian and other foreign agitators came into Spain equipped with funds," Franco told me in the summer of 1962, "but they got away before our police could put their hands on them." This was partly true. As soon as the strikes began, French and Belgian Socialists slipped into Spain to subsidize and encourage the strike leaders. The Communists also moved in, and strike funds were plentiful. Even AFL-CIO strike funds were widely reported circulating in the strike areas. Franco ordered the *economatos* to continue giving miners credit for foodstuffs to allay hardship to their families, but even so, the miners seemed surprisingly well supplied.

Marcos Peña Royo, the young civil governor of Asturias, told me that summer that not only foreign agitators but even Basque priests and militants of the Catholic Workers' Brotherhood (HOAC) had openly defied Franco by furnishing the strikers aid and support. Yet despite the large numbers on strike, one thing above all had surprised observers: both the strikers and Franco abstained from violence.

The Sindicates

Franco's sindical machine has a total monopoly over labor and, theoretically, over management. Of the 12 million active working population of Spain, about 8.5 million workers (3 million industrial, 5.5 million either agricultural or self-employed) must by law belong to one of 24 vertical Sindicates, as must also the nation's 3.5 million employers. The Sindicates collect dues from both. Strikes, lockouts, labor dismissals, and independent unions are all illegal.

Under the Sindical system, delegates of the workers and of the employers are grouped, respectively, into "social" and "economic" cells, starting from the factory level and continuing up through local, provincial, and national levels, culminating, like a pyramid, in the person of Solís, Minister Secretary General of the Falange and National Delegate of the Sindicates. At each level—factory, local, provincial, and national—state control is preserved with Falangist (Sindicalist) officials presiding by law over labor-management relations. Of all labor's complaints, the bitterest has been that the Sindical bosses have too long sided with management.

Theoretically, the huge Sindical bureaucracy has been "elected" in triennial elections ever since 1944. In fact, it was not until 1956 that Franco even grudgingly recognized the rising anger of Spain's workers and the need for token authenticity. This issue of Sindical authenticity has become the burning topic in Spain today, with Franco insisting that authenticity already exists and the workers indignantly retorting that the Sindical elections are a farce.

In the 1957 Sindical elections, approximately 70 per cent of the 350,000 shop stewards elected throughout Spain were newcomers. About half were men in their mid-twenties, while the rest were older workers with a background of trade unionism in the old Anarcho-Sindicalist CNT and Socialist UGT.

This left-wing voting pattern was again reflected in the 1960 Sindical elections, which were marred by regime interference and by a high proportion of blank or protest ballots. Of the 400,-000 worker delegates chosen, at least 2,000, according to Francisco Jiménez Torres, Solís' able young ex-deputy, were "known Communists."

"We know who they are and have already removed about 500 from positions of leadership," he said candidly in an interview at the time. "We don't jail them or expel them from their jobs, but we try to isolate them from control of other workers. Gradually, we'll screen out the remaining 1,500 but there will always be clandestine Communists, Anarchists, and Socialists in Sindical circles."

Throughout the country, there are approximately 14,000 Sindical officials organized in hierarchic fashion, with Solís at the peak, but workers contradict the regime's contention that the triennial elections give them freedom of choice. "Solís claims that out of 13,000 or 14,000 elected officials, only 30 or 40 are named directly by him," commented a young official of the HOAC. "Who runs an army? The noncoms or the generals?"

According to official statistics, 2,465 new wage agreements have been negotiated since 1958, affecting 840,559 firms and 4,334,166 (roughly half) of Spain's workers. Basic wages were raised from 15 per cent to as much as 100 per cent of their former levels, on the understanding that prices would not be raised, yet individual productivity would be improved.* It was also largely Solís' doing that caused Franco to announce, at the start of 1963, a new national minimum wage, increased from 36 to 60 pesetas ($1) daily. The increase affected only the worst-paid 15 per cent of the national labor force, but it was a step in the right direction.

A more important political weapon for the future is the Sindicates' vast social security program. With their 8 to 12 per cent rake-off on every payroll in Spain, the Sindicates now dispose of an estimated $130 million per year, to be paid out in benefits; a powerful slush fund in a land where the average annual income is still under $500.

There can be no denying that the Spanish worker today is better protected by the state than ever before in history. He has no right to strike—but if any regime hopes to follow Franco successfully, it will have to conserve and even expand the social legislation of the past twenty-five years. This legislation comprises old age and sickness insurance, annual cash grants to large families, industrial accident insurance, maternity insurance, retirement insurance, and a social security plan recently extended to domestic servants. The land once famed as a source of servants now faces a growing shortage, as light industries and shops lure girls from the broom and duster.

* While these wages might appear low by American standards, they are substantial in Spain, where basic wages have always been kept down to avoid the social security charges that sometimes add 125 per cent to the wage itself. In recent years, management has had to retain skilled labor with "blue envelopes" (under-the-table bonuses), doubling the take-home pay. Such payments, however, benefit only the skilled minority.

In addition to social security, Solís' Sindical machine also manages the Obras Sindicales, which include rest, cultural, and sporting centers in seaside and mountain resorts; guided tours, theaters, and sports arenas such as the Parque Sindical outside Madrid, with room for 30,000 workers, their wives and children; and a swimming pool—the largest in Europe, with a capacity of 9,000. Other Obras include the construction of 200,000 low-cost workers' homes—approximately 100,000 built in a year; rural colonies to bring low-cost power, irrigation, and light industry to poor agricultural regions; the creation of 10,000 workers' cooperatives; stimulation of craftsmanship through 18 artisans' markets; the building of four immense and lavish labor universities at Gijón, Tarragona, Seville, and Córdoba, plus 117 industrial craft schools elsewhere; and, finally, the establishment of at least 40 sanitariums to provide supplementary sickness, maternity, or accident care for workers and their families.

Further, Solís has done much in recent years to ease repression and to moderate police brutality. He has intervened repeatedly with his cabinet colleague Interior Minister Don Camilo Alonso Vega to release workers arrested for "strike propaganda" or held on charges of "rebellion." The young Basque lawyer Antonio Amat, seized in 1958 as the Socialist underground's liaison with the exiles in Toulouse, was released from Burgos Prison after three years, thanks chiefly to Solís' solicitations. Again, after the 1962 Asturian strikes, Solís won freedom for arrested miners and the right of others to return to their homes.

Solís now travels extensively throughout Western Europe, visiting government and labor leaders in an effort to dispel the popular caricature of Spain as a dungeon. Some suspect that his trips have been planned with an eye to the post-Franco future, yet back-slapping and glad-handing have helped Spain join eighteen international labor organizations.

Solís' wiles, though, have still not managed to overcome the opposition of the three great free-world labor organizations, the AFL-CIO in the United States, the ICFTU (International Confederation of Free Trade Unions), and the IFCTU (International Federation of Christian Trade Unions) in Europe. They regard Franco's Sindicates as captives, and there is every indication that they will continue to do so until Franco grants the workers freedom to elect their own leaders and the right to strike.

"The strike is an antiquated weapon," Solis once told me. "The day is coming when there will be no strikes and no lock-outs. In the American West, there used to be vigilante law—the law of the six-gun—until the sheriff came along and established law and order. That is what the Sindicates have done; they are our sheriff."

But the right to strike, I insisted, has not only been accepted throughout the civilized world, it has been sanctioned repeatedly in the Papal encyclicals. How could Spain, an allegedly super-Catholic state, continue to refuse what has been set forth by Pope John XXIII in his celebrated encyclicals?

"Strikes," said Solís, shaking his head patiently, "are merely a struggle to see which side is the strongest—with the public paying in the long run and the public interest trampled on. Rich countries can afford such a death struggle—but not Spain. Our laws protect both labor and management, each against excesses by the other. That is our Sindical concept."

Still in his early fifties, alert, with a bald bullet head and a sturdy thickset frame, Solís personifies the type of word-spinner Franco has recruited more and more to improve the regime's image. There is nothing of the Fascist storm-trooper about Solís; quite the contrary. If anything, with his Andalusian accent and his cocksure volubility, he is the small-town demagogue. He is Franco's creature, torn between building a labor machine and keeping Franco's confidence. Clichés protect him from probing questions.

Why, I asked, if the Sindicates had eliminated the need for strikes, did 80,000 Asturian miners strike openly during 1962?

"Foreign Communists," answered Solís without blinking an eye. "Foreign Communists with funds moved in from France and exploited grievances just as we were reaching agreement."

There it was again; the convenient explanation of "Communism" so beloved in Franco Spain when anything goes wrong. Perhaps Solís himself believed it, for he spoke with all the fervor of a medicine man. The afternoon sun poured in through the long French windows and glinted off Franco's stern features gazing down in bronze. Whenever Solís' eye would alight on the Caudillo's graven image, the prose flowed in a richer stream.

In early 1963, Falangist splinter groups were being allowed for the first time to form "doctrinal clubs" under the cabinet's plan of permitting greater diversity inside the National Movement, and Don Camilo was also allowing Monarchist groups to organize harmless Círculos Vasquez de Mella, Círculos Balmes, and Amigos de Maeztu so that his informers could more easily eavesdrop.

Among the new Falangist clubs that sprang most quickly to public attention was the Círculo Doctrinal José Antonio, founded by one of the most vocal Falangist left-wing chiefs, Dr. Luis González Vicén, a one-time militia leader and unrepentant Franco critic. In a new monthly bulletin titled *Es Así* (*This Is It,* or *Get This*), Vicén warned in 1963 that the Falange would oppose any constitutional formula that might lead to "capricious or personal" government—for example, a monarchy. He not only challenged Franco's 1947 Law of Succession, but declared that if a monarchy did return, "rebellion would be permissible," should it alter existing legislation. Having laid down the rules, Vicén next proposed that Spain recognize Soviet Russia and buy Soviet oil to free herself from "Western interference." The Falange was still anti-Communist, he averred, but this did not require Spain to deny Russia's "diplomatic existence."

González Vicén condemned the European Common Market (which Franco had applied to join) as a "maneuver of international capitalism" and charged that the Franco regime was increasingly threatened by "liberal capitalist deviation."

"We fought the Civil War for justice in the land and to set up

a national Sindicalist state," he cried. "If the regime now trans-
forms it into a liberal-capitalist state . . . not to protest and oppose it would be a betrayal!"

Despite such outbursts from the Falange's extreme left, however, the bulk of the party was still clinging tightly to Franco. On
February 12, 1963, for example, *Arriba* outdid itself in adulation
by naming Franco, with Charles V and Napoleon, as among the
"great leaders of Europe" who were "masters of events."

In April, 1964, the National Council met again in Madrid,
heard Solís proclaim that "now while Franco is still with us . . .
is the moment to solve our problems," and duly presented Franco
an eight-point political plan calling for the Holy Grail of "institutionalization," for a new Fundamental Law to give the Falange
permanent status and thus complete the "open" constitution,
and for Falange membership in the Consejo del Reino. But
again, as in 1963, Franco's closing speech failed even to hint at
permanent constitutional status for the Consejo Nacional. "The
Movement needs renovation," he repeated. "An important part
of [political] representation rightly belongs to it but *another
part must be opened to minorities with popular support* [italics
added]."

Where the Falange will go from here, what the future holds,
none can tell. But the Falange's domination of the Movement
seems doomed. If it is not, the Movement itself is doomed.
Franco wants no political parties; he wants varying political
viewpoints within the Movement, and to encourage this, he has
to end the Falange's long monopoly.

For nine years, the students remained mute, although increasingly discontent. In early 1965, however, their long dissatisfaction with Falangist obscurantism broke into the open, publicly
supported by several of Spain's leading university professors.
Student demonstrations erupted first in the University City,
finally spilling over into the heart of Madrid, where estimated
crowds of three to four thousand students paraded noisily near
Falange headquarters. As usual, student leaders were seized for

interrogation, while massed police charged the others, keeping them split and ineffective.

Three university movements were credited with staging the demonstrations: The MRU (Movimiento de Reforma Universitaria) founded in 1962 by professors José Luis Aranguren and Mariano Aguilar Navarro of Madrid, J. L. Sureda and A. Latorre of Barcelona, and Enrique Tierno Galvan of Salamanca. This faculty movement is reportedly in close touch with such exiles as De Madariaga, Julián Gorkin, Ramón Sender, Federico de Onís, Bosch Gimpera, Ferrater Mora, and Sánchez Albornoz.

The two other organizing factions are both student-run: The FUDE (Federación Universitaria Democrática Española) which is allegedly Communist-dominated, and the UED (Unión de Estudiantes Demócratas) under Demo-Christian Catholic influence.

Although Aranguren, Navarro, Tierno Galvan, and other faculty demonstrators were suspended, their pay continued and repressive measures in general were far lighter than usual. By early April, the regime had even conceded the students' demand to elect their own Sindical delegates up to the highest national level. How wholeheartedly the regime will carry out its pledges remains to be seen, but the extent and success of the student demonstrations attracted attention far beyond Spain's borders. Many now expect increasing agitation in the universities in the years ahead.

The best recent analysis of the Falange's decomposition has come from Dionisio Ridruejo, *l'enfant terrible* of Spanish politics. Since 1936, only Franco has held power, he avers. The army might have swung power to someone else, but it has been too neutral, too supine, and never pro-Falange. With no power base of its own, the Falange thus has had to seek power through fidelity and, as Ridruejo says, "It has exercised fidelity to the point of self-annulment."

Ridruejo has pointed out that no fresh initiative is coming from Solís' bureaucratic command post; that whatever fresh thinking there is seems to be coming exclusively from González Vicén's extremist wing or from Emilio Romero, editor of the Sindicalist newspaper *Pueblo*. Falangists such as González Vicén or Romero, he says, would like to differentiate between the "official" Falange of the dictatorship and the "authentic" Falange, which seeks internal pluralism of ideas, more democratic voting freedom in the municipalities and Sindicates, and a presidential succession instead of Franco's tailored monarchy. But so long as Franco rules, he will go on turning to the right, and there will be no role in his regime for the Falange.

"If the Falangists . . . really want to do justice to . . . their ideological inquietude," he wrote not long ago, "they have no other collective road than that of self-dissolution; no other individual road than that of self-criticism; no other practical course but to prepare the way for the genuine democratic left which . . . the nation needs."*

* *España 1963: Examen de una Situación* (Paris: Centro de Documentación y de Estudios, 1964).

The Church

Holy Week in Seville: carnival and Christ; God and Billy Rose.

Every spring, the twin natures of Spain, the carnal and the ascetic, reach their flowering during Holy Week—but where one begins and the other stops is hard to say. The annual reawakening begins in the towns and fishing villages, progresses through the land, then bursts in a spasm of piety in the great cities: Madrid, Barcelona, Bilbao and Burgos, Valladolid and Valencia—then dies away until the following year. Nowhere, though, does it reach quite the peak of Seville, the pagan-Arab capital of southern Spain, where hot blood and holy austerity wrestle for supremacy.

Religious processions wend through the streets of Seville all week, as the city fills to bursting with Spaniards from all over the country and with tourists: Christian, Moslem, Jew, Buddhist, or pagan. Some come to pray; the majority to watch. The high point comes at midnight on Holy Thursday, when the great *pasos,* or floats, with their marvelous life-sized images of Christ, the Virgin Mary, and other actors in the Passion are borne forth in splendor from local parish churches and paraded until dawn.

By sundown, the streets, balconies, windows, and even the roofs swarm with people. Youths shinny up lampposts for a better look, while down on the sidewalks, tots scamper through on-lookers' legs, chivvied back gently by patient policemen, until exasperated parents pick up their protesting offspring and sling them onto their shoulders. A bugle cleaves the soft air, and suddenly there is a hush.

Now comes a file of Roman soldiers, preceded by a centurion in plumed helmet, marching to the thud of a muffled drum. Behind them, in parallel lines, come silent figures in white or black robes, their feet naked, their identities concealed by towering conical hoods pierced only by eye-slits. They bear lighted tapers. Some drag ankle chains, and one or two stagger past under a cross. These are the Nazarenos, the penitents who belong to local religious confraternities and who expiate in Holy Week the sins of the previous year. Often, as they file by, the onlookers fall to their knees, crossing themselves devoutly. From above, the rising and falling looks like a field of wheat ruffled by a passing wind.

At last come the floats, borne by as many as a hundred volunteers. They are steered by walking guides who must halt for breath every hundred yards or so, leaving their floats propped on wooden blocks as they emerge, shining with sweat, to relieve aching muscles and quaff wine handed them by joshing friends in the crowd. The pause is brief. Soon comes a word of command. The bearers duck back. Another command, the huge floats rise, and off they move in short, jerky, rhythmic steps, their legs in the gloom making them look like giant centipedes.

Each parish has its own float and the carven images of the Virgin rival each other in the splendor of their gold-trimmed silk or velvet robes and the priceless jewels loaned year after year by the Albas, the Medinacellis, the Osunas, or other great families of the region. Occasionally, a jewel will jiggle loose and fall but never, according to legend, has one been lost or stolen. Always, there are reverent hands to find and hand it back.

Hours before midnight, the plaza before the Church of the Macarena, the bullfighters' quarter, fills to overflowing. The masses stand packed patiently in the moonlight, while from a balcony or roof breaks forth a *saeta*, the wailing Arab-type trill to the beauty of this or that parish Virgin. She is the purest; the most holy; the most beautiful—more beautiful by far than that of any other parish! Midnight strikes, and now the doors of the church swing open.

The crowds murmur as the lovely float bearing the Virgin de la Macarena emerges, bathed in light. Now comes the pushing, the shoving, the end of waiting, the excitement. Wine jugs pass from hand to hand and the raw animal excitement of the Arab-Andalusian surges up, profaning what had begun as a religious observance. Women, foreign women especially, are trapped by the crowds like helpless fishes in a net of sensuality, of bold glances and sly words and caresses; and the boundary posts between piety and libido are trampled down in the rush. Christ and carnival are truly rolled into one.

Holy Week reveals the celebrated religious passion of the Spaniards: dramatic as the Spanish nature, beautiful as the Spanish heritage. But this fervid mood flowers once, twice, three times a year—the rest of the year it lies fallow. All over Spain, on the three occasions of birth, baptism, and burial, the people turn automatically to the Church. Spain's docile, semieducated peasantry—especially the older women and men—still cling to the faith of their fathers, but the industrial classes and the younger generations are restless. They criticize the Church's inflexibility and its docile subservience to Franco.

In a world where men in their late thirties and early forties are presidents and prime ministers, where ability and vigor are the key to success, where new nations and leaders emerge overnight, the youth of Spain is understandably cynical. It feels chained by old age, by fear of change, by corruption and decadence. Not all Spanish youth is anti-Franco, but all know that Franco is over seventy. Not all Spanish youth is anticlerical, but all know that the Cardinal Primate, the head of their Church, is close to ninety.

Inside the Spanish Church, there are stirrings. A new generation of priests has grown up whose feelings few know. Like the rest of Spain's youth—outwardly submissive, mechanically obedient—it is a force that may rise one day and help topple the idols: Franco, the generals, the bishops. Yet so long as free speech, free thought, and freedom of association remain forbidden, this new generation cannot find itself or communicate with its elders. It is isolated.

The Church is worried by this restiveness among young workers, university students, and young country priests. Sensing the public's mood, leading prelates are beginning to challenge the repression of trade unions, of speech, thought, and peaceful assembly. The Church has not yet moved away from Franco but it is eyeing possible alternatives, such as a monarchy. And Rome is pressing discreetly.

In 1962, Paul Hofmann, of *The New York Times,* reported that the Spanish Church had begun "reassessing its role and tightening its organization." Within the Church, he wrote, were elements for and against collaboration with the Franco regime, while a new outside pressure was becoming evident: an "attempt by the Vatican to bring about Catholic unity in Spain." Hofmann emphasized the personality of Pope John XXIII, whose opposition to the Church's "over-close involvement" in politics was repeatedly being stressed. He also noted the Spanish Church's own realization of its "immense responsibility" during the transition from Franco to the Spain of the future.

Since then, Madrid and Barcelona, the two most populous sees, have been raised to archdioceses, ending the anomaly that had prevented their spiritual leaders from even attending the annual conclave of *metropolitanos* (archbishops). Dr. Eijo Gáray, the fanatically Falangist "blue bishop" of Madrid-Alcala, who died in 1963, has been succeeded by the liberal Dr. Casimiro Morcillo, former Archbishop of Zaragoza, and it is considered very likely that when the eighty-nine-year-old Primate, Enrique Cardinal Plá, Archbishop of Toledo, dies, the primatial see will be transferred from Toledo to the capital. Another liberal, Dr.

Vicente Enrique Tarancón, Bishop of Solsona and former Undersecretary of the Ecumenical Council, has been named Coadjutor to the Archbishop of Oviedo, capital of strike-wracked and politically explosive Asturias.

Whether these new appointments really reflect a new liberalization in the Spanish Church remains to be seen. It may be significant, however, that on April 15, 1964, the respected *Vanguardia* of Barcelona, reporting on a Madrid meeting of Spain's bishops, called it the "most important . . . in many centuries" and the "first mature fruit of the Second Vatican Council."

"Spain's ecclesiastic structures," said *Vanguardia,* "need . . . reform."

Officially, 99.9 per cent of Spain's population are Catholic; but religious observance varies greatly. "All Spaniards are Catholics. We are all baptized," the Abbot of Montserrat told a CBS reporter in 1962. "But regarding the faith of Spaniards inside the Church, we should not be so optimistic. A great part of the people . . . has left us. I don't know why this is so . . . internal motivations, motivations from abroad, lack of justice, and lack of freedom. Above all, a lack of being civilized. When the people don't have enough to live on, it is very difficult to speak to them about religion."

Others note the sharp contrast in church attendance in the country and in the cities. In rural Castile, half the male and three-quarters of the female population regularly attend church. In the Basque provinces, at least half the population go to Mass on Sundays. In the big cities, even one-fifth of the bourgeoisie attend Sunday services out of habit. But in the industrial suburbs around the big cities, only 5 to 10 per cent of the workers worship regularly.

Anticlericalism stems partly from the Spanish character, alternating between apathy and violence, and partly from long identification of the Church with privilege and reaction. Nineteenth-century Spain was torn by a struggle of liberalism versus clericalism, with clericalism hand-in-glove with the crown, the army, and the rich. The Church, recruited preponderantly from the poor rural class, has long viewed the proletarian masses as a breeding ground of discontent, atheistic and heretical discontent. This doctrine has naturally provoked resentment amongst workers, intellectuals, and students.

Yet the caricature of Spain as a priest-ridden land is no longer just. Not only has the number of priests been reduced, but the type of priest is changing. Statistics furnished by Dr. William Ebenstein in his *Church and State in Franco Spain** show that Spain today ranks eighth in proportion of priests to the Catholic population among European countries (outside the Iron Curtain) predominantly Catholic, or with large Catholic minorities. In 1957, Spain had one priest for every 1,264 Catholic inhabitants—a smaller proportion than in Switzerland, England, Belgium, Ireland, France, Italy, or Holland. Spain's average was about the same as the European average: 1 per 1,250 Catholics, and less than the United States' average: 1 priest per 1,150 Catholics.

For two hundred years, the proportion of priests to laity has been dropping, Dr. Ebenstein reveals, and during the tumultuous 1930–40 decade, it fell precipitately. Franco's "Crusade" gave the priesthood a momentary spur, but today recruiting has leveled off. There are approximately 25,000 ordained priests in Spain; 8,000 studying for the priesthood; and 18,000 Spanish priests in Latin America. Moreover, the social background of priests is changing. In 1934, according to Dr. Ebenstein, nearly 60 per cent of Spain's priests came from agricultural families, 24 per cent from commerce and industry, and 13.2 per cent from the professional middle classes. By 1947, the agricultural element had fallen to 52 per cent, the industry-commerce proportion had remained the same, while the middle-class bloc had risen to 19.6 per cent. Only 1 to 2 per cent of the priesthood derives from wealthy or aristocratic families.

* Princeton, N.J.: Center of International Studies, Woodrow Wilson School of Public and International Affairs, Princeton University, 1960.

"Among the younger priests *today*," wrote Dr. Ebenstein, "the middle-class and enlightened outlook is much more strongly represented than among the clergy of only a generation ago."

The Concordat

The Church's privileged position derives from the Concordat signed on August 27, 1963, one month before the defense treaties with the United States. Eager as he was for U.S. recognition and aid, Franco was careful to placate his clergy, alarmed by the prospect of a "Protestant invasion."

The Concordat changed little in the Church-State relations; it merely formalized them. Since Franco's 1939 victory, the Church had been—next to the army—the most powerful prop under the regime, and Franco had bound it to himself by manacles of silk and gold. He had restored the Church's privileges, its control over morals and education, its voice in the censorship, its participation in every agency of state, its properties, and its subsidies.*

Soon after World War II, negotiations for a Concordat had begun, but neither Franco nor the Vatican was in a hurry. Not until the outbreak of the Korean War did the issue come to a head. With the long-awaited break between the Western Allies and Soviet Russia, a new world lineup was looming, and Spain could expect eventually to be readmitted to the Western family— albeit at the foot of the table—her pro-Axis sins forgiven. Now a Concordat would have some meaning.

Of all the provisions of the Concordat, Article VII has been hailed as a tribute to Franco's skill. It confirms Franco's right to choose his own bishops and gives him virtual domination over the Spanish hierarchy. It sanctifies the historic "right of patron-

---

* Franco's annual subsidy to the Church is disguised and difficult to ascertain. The Directorate General of Ecclesiastical Affairs reports an annual $12 million, which seems a drop in the bucket. In October, 1961, for instance, at Burgos, Franco disclosed that in twenty-five years the regime had rebuilt sixty-six seminaries in Spain's sixty-four dioceses at a cost of $50 million; no trivial sum for a nation then emerging from insolvency.

age" enjoyed through centuries by Spanish monarchs and continued in the 1941 *modus vivendi* between Spain and the Vatican. When a Spanish see falls vacant, the Apostolic Nuncio in Madrid begins confidential negotiations with the regime. The regime proposes six names, which are transmitted by the Nuncio to the Vatican, and from which the Pope selects three. These are reported back to Madrid, and within thirty days Franco must notify the Vatican of his choice. Provided the Vatican has no objection, Franco's nominee becomes the next bishop. If, on the other hand, the Pope approves none of the original six, he may propose three names of his own. If none of these is acceptable to Madrid, confidential negotiations continue for as long as necessary.

The late Camille Cianfarra once wrote: "There is no question but that . . . the Franco regime enjoys a privileged position in regard to the appointment of bishops. Its advantage over the Vatican consists mainly in that it can veto the appointment of bishops whom it does not consider politically acceptable, whereas the Vatican is given no right to interfere with the appointment, say, of civil governors or Captains General, even though they may be notoriously anticlerical."

The Vatican, by waiving part of Article 329 of the Canon Code, which provides that bishops are "freely appointed by the Pope," has, in effect, conferred most-favored treatment on Franco —a privilege not granted to the chiefs of state of such other predominantly Catholic nations as France, Italy, Portugal, or Austria. Yet Spain's privilege dates from the seventh century and was confirmed in the Concordat of 1753, and again in that of 1851.

There is no sign that the Vatican has ever seriously opposed any of Franco's episcopal nominations. It certainly made no objections in 1941, when, after the signing of the *modus vivendi,* Franco selected his friend Dr. Enrique Plá y Deniel, Archbishop of Salamanca, to be the next Archbishop of Toledo and Primate of Spain. Cardinal Plá remains a stalwart supporter of the regime, although in recent years he has frequently and publicly reproved Falange officials for harassing his HOAC (Catholic Workers' Brotherhoods).

No intellectual like his predecessor, the late Cardinal Segura, who used to thunder against tourists' brief bathing costumes or the "immorality" of young couples walking hand in hand, Dr. Plá has nonetheless worked inside the regime to improve the lot of the underprivileged, particularly Spain's workers. He is known as a man of few words, and this contrast with the majority of high Spanish officials has endeared him to Franco, too.

The Catholic Church's monopoly over religion is also formally guaranteed under the Concordat. Article I provides that the "Catholic, Apostolic, and Roman" religion will be the "only" religion in Spain. "No one is to be molested on account of his cult," adds Article VI, but all other ceremonies and "external" manifestations are rigorously banned.

Other articles exempt the clergy and members of religious orders from military service and Church properties from taxation, and establish state subsidies for the Church and all its members. Article XXIII recognizes only canon law for marriages, a provision that has created untold problems for Protestants.

The Church's control over education stems from Articles XXVI–XXXI, which make instruction in the Catholic faith obligatory in all schools and place responsibility for religious instruction (in all but primary schools) in the hands of the clergy. The Church must teach Catholic dogma and morals and must block the dissemination of "heretical" views—giving it a veto over educational curricula and over teachers. Its participation in the censorship is guaranteed by Article XXIX, which gives it power to guard over religious "truth" in public information: books, radio, press, television, and theater.

One final clause—Article XXXIV—is vitally important and highly controversial. It gives the Church the right to conduct its "apostolate" through Catholic Action (Acción Católica), a lay organization regarded by many as a latent Demo-Christian party.

This clause above all others has led to protracted tension behind the scenes between Church and State. Cardinal Plá's HOAC workers' brotherhoods, for instance, are an arm of Acción Católica and—theoretically—exempt from regime harassment. Yet time and again, their leaders have been arrested and fined for "illegal" propaganda, and during Sindical elections, HOAC candidates have been flattened by the Falangist steamroller.

The Concordat provides that Acción Católica's "apostolic" activities shall be supervised by the bishop of each diocese, but to prevent a Demo-Christian party from organizing under cover of the Church, Franco has also insisted that "nonapostolic" activities remain under state control. What is, and what is not, "apostolic" activity has been the core of Church-State tension for many years, and as Franco grows older, the Church is becoming more militant.

Nothing worries the Spanish hierarchy more than the specter of "progressivism," for progressivism can mean many things in Spain: materialism of the type associated with the United States; "leftist" ideas on social reform; public protests over lack of human liberties—even regional demands for autonomy.

It is one thing for the Cardinal Primate to complain about persecution of the HOAC brotherhoods, or for senior hierarchs such as the Bishop of Bilbao or the Bishop of Malaga to hint that the regime is depriving the faithful of their rights. But it is quite another thing when individual priests, especially those from the Basque provinces, Catalonia, or Galicia, express open discontent. Then the regime cries "politics" and demands ecclesiastical discipline to muzzle the offenders. Discipline in the Spanish Church is severe.

In May, 1957, the Cardinal Primate ordered a rigid tightening up of discipline among the nation's 25,000 priests. They were forbidden to smoke in public, to attend soccer games, bullfights, moving pictures, theaters, and other "modern spectacles." The wearing of the cassock was made mandatory when traveling.

All priests were to be tonsured. The growing use of motor scooters—especially among country priests obliged to conduct as many as three services in outlying areas each Sunday—was to be strictly regulated by the local bishops. Priests might wear a beret or crash helmet instead of the traditional wide-brimmed hat, but they were not to "ride about too much," and, above all, no women were to be transported. The rhythm of modern life and the temptations of modern spectacles, the Primate warned, were tending to lead the clergy into an "unedifying" display.

Yet a more serious sign of a deep dissatisfaction has been the widening gap between the younger clergy, who share the problems and vexations of their flocks, and the aging hierarchy. A Basque priest, interviewed by the Columbia Broadcasting System in 1962, put this dissatisfaction into words: "The future of the Spanish Church does not seem very auspicious," he confessed. "We are greatly concerned with the obstinacy of the Church [leadership] in giving unconditional support to a totalitarian regime . . . which violates many postulates of natural law, as is logical in any totalitarian state."

Discontent is not limited to the Basque region. Three years earlier, in Madrid, a National Union of the Spanish Clergy, an anonymous group of progressive priests, circulated a pamphlet denouncing the hierarchy's "slavish identification" with the regime. It contrasted the scant attendance of Spanish hierarchs at the coronation of Pope John XXIII with the appearance of virtually every Spanish prelate at the dedication of Franco's Valley of the Fallen. It assailed the regime's "glorification" of the Civil War and the reduction of Spain's masses to "forced silence." It complained that the Pope's views on press freedom had been suppressed by Franco's censors and asked why, if Latin American bishops dared speak out against local tyrants, Franco's bishops remained mute.

Regime and Church spokesmen angrily denounced the attack as the work of crypto-Communists, free-thinkers, and "progressives," but it did attract attention because of the very rarity of open discontent in a muzzled Church. The leadership insists that all is under control, but individual clerics refute this claim.

One who has repeatedly raised his voice to denounce repression of human rights is Dom Aurelio María Escarré, the fifty-five-year-old Abbot of Montserrat in Catalonia. "There are two trends in the Spanish Church," he told an interviewer in 1962. "The progressive—vital and open to the world, full of life and youth; and the other—traditionally limited and narrow-minded."

His views were challenged by the Bishop of Malaga, Dr. Ángel Herrera (now Cardinal Herrera). "We cannot speak of two trends within the Church," he retorted in a separate interview. "In Spain, as in all other countries, there is a group of priests, generally very intelligent men . . . who might embrace some of the ideas that nowadays are called 'progressive.' . . . But they are good priests in the final analysis. . . . They may have some inner conflicts; they may need discipline. But our clergy are docile and obedient. . . . I see no problem."

Here were conflicting views, expressed by two leading prelates. One insists that there is a distinct gap between the "progressives" and the "traditionalists." The other admits that progressive ideas may be held by some priests but is convinced that they are nonetheless "good priests in the final analysis." The Bishop of Malaga is certain that "docility and obedience" will eventually overcome progressivism.

In May, 1960, 335 Basque priests signed and handed to the bishops of the four Basque provinces (Álava, Guipúzcoa, Vizcaya, and Navarra) a circular letter denouncing police brutality and the continuing suppression of human rights. "An abyss is opening between us and the souls entrusted to our care and guidance," they warned. "The accusations being leveled against us of complicity with the regime constitute a veritable clamor." The priests urged their bishops to press the regime for an "effective, calm formula to restore the people to their lost peace." Their petition, however, was suppressed by Franco's censorship, and the ringleaders were punished by their ecclesiastical superiors.

In Barcelona, meanwhile, another incident showed the courage of a few militant churchmen. Franco had spent a month in the Catalan capital to soothe local susceptibilities and to persuade the Catalans of the growing moderation of his regime.

On May 19, 1960, the cream of Catalan society gathered in the Palace of Music for a concert by the Orfeo Catalan choral group to commemorate the hundredth anniversary of the Catalan poet Juan Maragall. A few evenings earlier, Franco had presided over an official act honoring Maragall. The Catalans were exuberant. Franco was not at the concert, although he was still in Barcelona. Word had gone out that for the first time since 1939, he had approved the playing of the banned "Hymn to the Catalan Flag," with Maragall's lyrics.

At the last minute, however, and without warning, Franco's shambling old Civil Governor, General Felipe Acedo Colunga ordered the hymn omitted. The audience's hopes were dashed, and anger mounted. Some booed, others defiantly began chanting the hymn. Suddenly, police and plainclothesmen swarmed into the crowded hall shoving, clubbing, and hauling away protesters. Among those dragged to the police stations and brutally beaten was Dr. Jordi Pujol, thirty-one-year-old member of the Archdiocesan Catholic Institute for Social Studies.

For four nights, Pujol and approximately twenty other young Catalans were held incommunicado in police cells. Then, on Monday, May 23, a crowd of 600 to 1,000 parents, relatives, and friends gathered before the palace of the Archbishop of the Bishopric of Barcelona, Dr. Gregorio Modrego Casaus, to ask his intercession. After much delay, Dr. Modrego reluctantly consented to receive a delegation, including youths who showed him the marks of police mistreatment on their bodies. This was too much for the timid Archbishop. The next day, the gates to the palace were bolted and the Archbishop became "unavailable." But for nights thereafter, crowds gathered, kneeling on the sidewalk to pray silently for Modrego's intercession with Franco. It never came.

Dom Escarré, however, was made of sterner stuff. He had been host to Franco at the great Benedictine Monastery only a few days before the concert, but now he refused to join local authorities in bidding Franco farewell at the Barcelona railway station.

"Profoundly regret repression and tortures inflicted on young Catholics arrested during Orfeo Catalan concert," he telegraphed the departing Caudillo. "Lamentable epilogue to your government's stay in Catalonia."

The Abbot has continued to voice his protests. In November, 1963, he told the Paris newspaper *Le Monde* that "Spain remains divided in two. We have not had twenty-five years of peace but twenty-five years of victory." And, charging the regime with having ignored the doctrines of political freedom promulgated in the Papal encyclical *Pacem in Terris,* he added, "The people should be able to choose their government and change it when they wish; that is liberty."

In early 1965, Franco finally succeeded in silencing the courageous prelate's protests. Dom Escarré came under Vatican, rather than Spanish, hierarchic authority, and the Holy See was finally persuaded to transfer him abroad for "temporary studies."

The Church and Education

Spain's cultural stagnation since the Civil War has given Franco's critics a powerful weapon. The Church must share the blame. It is now beginning to raise its voice to demand more schools and more teachers but whether its voice will be as effectively raised for a liberalization of the curricula remains to be seen. Many Spaniards assail the Church's role in education quantitatively and qualitatively.

They deplore the catechism* still being taught children, which lists "modern errors" in this order: Materialism, Darwinism, Atheism, Pantheism, Deism, Rationalism, Protestantism, Socialism, Communism, Sindicalism, Liberalism, Modernism, and Masonry. One can envisage tiny schoolchildren in smocks dutifully intoning such passages as these with their religious teacher:

* *Nuevo Ripalda* (Barcelona: Editorial José Vilamala, 1946).

On Reading Newspapers

Q. Does he who subscribes to liberal newspapers sin *gravely?*
A. Yes, sir.
Q. Why?
A. Because he puts his money to bad use, puts his faith in danger, and gives others a bad example.
Q. Could it be even a *mild* sin to read the liberal press occasionally?
A. Yes; if news or mildly dangerous articles are read now and then.
Q. Could the reading of a liberal newspaper cause serious consequences?
A. Rare; but possible.
Q. How can one avoid erring?
A. Ask advice from a wise and prudent director.

At this point, there follows in brackets a note of confidential advice to the religious instructors: "Advise the pupils that if there *is* a good reason to read a liberal newspaper—*for example, the rise and fall of the stock market*—there is no reason to read the rest [italics added]."

This delightful *sotto voce* remark about stock market averages in a child's catechism is followed by another example of the Church's fiduciary conservatism: "Socialism," warns the catechism, must be shunned because it teaches that the state "can dispose of private property, which is the fount of wealth, and distribute it among workers as it chooses. A system absurd, and, above all, unjust . . . because it violates private property *which is sacred* [italics added]."

Apart from such tenets of the feudal age still being pumped into young minds, many Spaniards blame the Church for ignoring the education of the masses and concentrating on teaching only the "elite." Among Spain's 3 million primary school students, for instance, only 24 per cent can afford to attend the Church-run schools, which normally charge fees. The remaining 76 per cent receive only a state education, which is often inadequate.

On the other hand, of Spain's 580,000 secondary students, 84 per cent attend Church schools and only 16 per cent the state-run schools—evidence that the Church concentrates on the children of the better-off.

Church spokesmen deny such charges. They contend that, had it not been for the Church, the standards of education would be still lower than they are. There are now nearly 700,000 students studying in the Church-run elementary schools (60 per cent of them free), they claim; 300,000 in the Church's secondary schools (27 per cent of them free); 8,000 being trained at Church expense in religious universities, chaplaincies, residences, and other institutes of higher learning. Moreover, all five of the regime's Labor Universities are staffed by teachers from the Jesuit, Dominican, Salesian, and Augustinian orders, and the secular clergy.

Church spokesmen say that throughout Spain the Church maintains more than 20 schools for women social workers; staffs more than 70 agencies to help young emigrants find well-paying jobs abroad; runs nearly 800 occupational training centers and more than 1,500 charitable institutions.

In many dioceses, efforts are being made to close the cultural gap. In Malaga, where a few years ago 10,000 children had no hope of even a primary education, Dr. Herrera has prevailed on the regime to agree to build 250 special "chapel-schools" (school and chapel in one building) within 3 years and to recruit 250 teachers. Under his guidance, lay teachers have begun to cut down illiteracy in the rural areas, teach modern farming methods, and recruit teams of seminarists to guide the peasants.

Finally, there is the educational work being performed by the army chaplains, who are helping to eliminate illiteracy among the young Spanish recruits called up every year for military service.

Opus Dei

What is Opus Dei? Is it a Catholic "white Masonry?" A religious octopus whose tentacles reach into government, banking, education, public relations, commerce, real estate, newspapers, and radio? A Catholic secret society preparing to rule Spain through a military-clerical monarchy after Franco? Or is it merely a Vatican-approved secular institute, a voluntary body of Catholics seeking to emulate Christ's teaching in their everyday lives, not only in Spain but in fifty other countries, including the United States?

Nothing in recent Spanish history has caused more controversy than the spectacular rise of the Sociedad Sacerdotal de la Santa Cruz y Opus Dei, known as Opus Dei, or God's Work. Some claim that the organization is saintly, others that it is cynical; many Spaniards believe it is both.

"The basic split between my supporters," the Pretender Don Juan once told a friend, "lies between those for and those against Opus Dei." The leaders of Opus Dei know this and they have few illusions as to who their real enemies are.

"Our true enemies are in the Church," a ranking Opus Dei member once told me. "What irritates them is not so much our clandestinity—discretion would be the correct word—but our efficiency."

Efficiency is always suspect in Spain. It smacks of subversion, of secrecy, of the occult. Opus Dei's efficiency, together with its passion for anonymity, has aroused powerful enemies among the Jesuits, the Falangists, and, of course, the liberal intellectuals. The Jesuits resent Opus Dei's growing influence on education, which the Jesuits have for centuries regarded as their own preserve. The Falange detests Opus Dei mainly as a rival whose leaders are unassailable in their Catholic orthodoxy, personally honest, and high in Franco's favor. The intellectuals distrust its slick unctuousness and its quasi-totalitarian methods.

"What surprises Spaniards," wrote the Falange-Sindicalist newspaper *Pueblo,* on February 5, 1964, "is the sudden emergence of Opus Dei in cultural bodies, business and banking groups, and in high administration posts. . . . How have they reached these posts without some controlling apparatus? . . .

These new men have appeared on the scene overnight without any political background, most of them without having rendered any service in the Civil War."

"Opus Dei has very intelligent men," added an anti-Franco intellectual, "but it is doomed—corrupted by money."

The Priestly Society of the Holy Cross and of God's Work was founded in Madrid on October 2, 1928, by a twenty-six-year-old priest of well-to-do parentage, José María Escrivá de Balaguer. A former lawyer and teacher at Zaragoza University, Escrivá, like many militant Catholics, had become increasingly disturbed by the antireligious, antimilitarist, and antimonarchical ferment widely prevalent in the universities during the 1920's. After long deliberation, he decided to take holy orders and was ordained in 1925. He and a small band of followers then organized a counterattack in the form of Opus Dei, a secular institute whose members would spread Christ's doctrine in the course of their workaday lives.

The early years showed slow progress. Gradually, however, adherents began rallying to the cause, and by 1935, the first "residence" was founded, with contributions from students, families, and friends. The outbreak of the Civil War a year later interrupted the work. Fearing Republican persecution, Escrivá and his followers fled across the Pyrenees to France, then gradually re-entered Spain, one by one, and found their way to the Nationalist zone, where they re-formed and took up their work once more. By 1939, Opus Dei had won the approval of Franco and of the Church and became a recognized Church agency. With the publication of his book of maxims, *Camino* (*The Way*),* that year, Father Escrivá personally came to the attention of the Holy See. Promotion followed with dramatic speed.

On March 10, 1941, Opus Dei was recognized by the Bishop of Madrid-Alcala as a *Pia Unión* (Saintly Union) and two and a half years later, it was raised by the Vatican to the status of a diocesan activity without vows.

---

* More than 1.2 million copies of *Camino* have been published in thirty languages, including Arabic and Japanese. It continues to be a bestseller.

The Vatican had begun to plan for the post-World War II period, but the prospects were somber. Western Europe's economy was shattered; Soviet armies were overrunning central and eastern Europe; Communist influence was spreading in Europe and Asia, and Stalin unquestionably would have a seat at the peace table. The Vatican now developed the concept of secular institutes, elite Catholic groups tailored to fill the gap between the old religious orders, isolated from everyday life, and the mass organizations such as Catholic Action, whose very size often robbed them of efficiency. Escrivá's plan won Papal support. This was not to be a worker-priest organization but a tightly knit body of lawyers, doctors, architects, bankers, economists, and professional men united by a common belief and responding to a common discipline. In 1946, Escrivá was summoned to Rome, named by Pope Pius XII President General of Opus Dei, and authorized to develop his idea throughout the world. Opus Dei's star was in the ascendant.

On February 2, 1947, the Pontiff promulgated the Apostolic Constitution *Provida Mater Ecclesia,* which established the norms for secular institutes, and twenty-two days later he conferred on Opus Dei provisional approbation as Primum Institutum, making it the first secular institution ever recognized. Three and a half years later, on June 19, 1950, Opus Dei was granted final approval as Primum Inter Instituta. It became also the first Catholic association authorized by the Holy See to "cooperate" with non-Catholics—even with non-Christians. Moslems, Buddhists, and pagan African students now attend its schools.

Never in the modern history of the Church had any organization risen so fast. To jealous rivals it became known as the Vatican's nuclear-age answer to Marxism—a modern successor to the old Spanish legions of the faith, the Dominicans and the Jesuits.

In *Camino,* Escrivá's personality emerges with fascinating clarity. "Underrate yourself? You? You were born to be *caudillo!* Among us there is no room for the faint-hearted." (P. 16.) "Keep going in *holy shamelessness* without stopping until you have reached the summit in the fulfillment of your duty." (P. 44.)

He stresses discipline.

Maxim 625: "Your obedience is not worthy of the name unless you are ready to abandon your most flourishing personal work whenever someone with authority so commands." Maxim 624: "Hierarchy: every piece in its place." Maxim 619: "Never forget you are only an agent."

He also demands silence.

Maxim 627: "Yours should be a silent obedience: that tongue!" Maxim 639: "Remain silent and you will never regret it: speak and you often will." Maxim 840: "May your state in life pass unnoticed, as that of Jesus did for thirty years."

Secrecy is intended to avoid "misunderstanding." Maxim 839: "Never go into details of your apostolate unless it be for someone else's benefit." Maxim 643: "Be slow to reveal the intimate details of your apostolate; don't you see that the world in its selfishness will fail to understand?"

But Maxim 838 could serve as a guide for all politicians, whatever their race, tongue, or party: "Have no enemies: Have only friends—friends on the Right, if they have done, or have wished to do you good; and on the Left, if they have harmed, or tried to harm you."

The membership of Opus Dei is secret, but well-informed Spaniards believe the number of members fluctuates between three and ten thousand, apart from large numbers of contributing "sympathizers." The head of Opus Dei in Spain is Father Antonio Pérez Fernández, who resides at the Estudio General de Navarra, the Opus Dei university in Pamplona. His orders come from the President General, Monsignor Escrivá, at the Vatican.

Opus Dei is divided into four categories. The highest category, the "numeraries," have normally taken at least two years of philosophy, four years of theology, and the three vows of obedience, poverty, and chastity. Some are ordained priests but the majority are civil servants, bankers, lawyers, engineers, architects, doctors, and other laymen who contribute as much of their salaries or other earnings as they can spare. Numeraries do not wear clerical garb, nor do they lead a common "canonic" existence, although in some cases they live together in residences.

The three other categories include "oblates," or beginners; unmarried men who live with their families; and married "supernumeraries" who assist Opus Dei financially but without taking vows. Supervision of these three categories falls to the bishop of each diocese. The vow of chastity, taken only by the highest category, is one of the reasons for the organization's emphasis on clandestinity. "It is difficult for a Spanish male to accept taunts on this intensely private subject," a member once explained. "This is one reason why we prefer not to discuss the intimate details of our dedication."

Proselytizing, or the steady recruitment of the nation's best young brains, has long provoked the jealousy of the Jesuits and other established orders, for Opus Dei finances the education of its needy young members. Aspirants undergo a period of probation and training, after which they take temporary vows. These vows are repeated annually, for members are considered in constant training for Christ's work. From the start, three maxims are drilled into them: good humor, humility, and discretion.

"Opus Dei has something of the worker-priest movement—but none of its disadvantages," wrote Hugh Kay, a British Catholic journalist, in the *Catholic Herald* in December, 1962. Like others, he noted that there was an aura of "jobs for the boys" about the institute. On the other hand, Julián Herranz, an Opus Dei priest, has publicly insisted that "Opus Dei cannot be identified in any country with any type of political movement."

Opus Dei is "above class or parties or political doctrine," said Herranz, and its members enjoy "total political liberty." They can belong to "any party, group, or movement not opposed to the Christian outlook on life." Throughout fifty nations, Herranz added, Opus Dei includes "republicans and democrats, conservatives and labor, Demo-Christians, liberals, and Monarchists. . . . The movement respects the liberty God has given to every man to think, speak, write, or act in accordance with the dictates of his own conscience . . . ," he insisted. "Only the Church, through the hierarchy, can decide . . . under extraordinary circumstances of public life . . . when the formation of a single front of Catholics shall be necessary."*

Other leading Opus Dei intellectuals, such as Rafael Calvo Serer, Florentino Pérez Embid, Ismael Sánchez Bella, Alberto Ullastres, Laureano López Rodó, and Antonio Fontán, have also repeatedly insisted that there is no such thing as an Opus Dei "political party."

"Ullastres and I are both members of Opus Dei," noted Pérez Embid, "but we do not hold the same views. I believe firmly in the monarchy. Ullastres does not. We both have absolute freedom to think as we please—so long as it does not contravene religious principles."

Opus Dei's chief pride is its lavish new university, the Estudio General de Navarra, at Pamplona, which has faculties of law, medicine, philosophy and letters, physical sciences, chemistry and mathematics, an institute of journalism, and graduate business and engineering schools. Founded in 1952, with private subscriptions and funds from the province of Navarra, the university was reported to have received a 100 million peseta ($1.67 million) grant from the Franco regime in 1963. Its total cost, however, has never been disclosed.

Pamplona university was officially recognized by Franco in the spring of 1962, after protracted opposition by the Falange and its entrenched university professors. The battle centered ostensibly around Opus Dei's demand that the regime recognize Pamplona's degrees as equivalent to those of the twelve state universities. In fact, it was a Church victory over the Falange's twenty-five-year stranglehold on university education. Until then, only two universities had been built in the course of this century: one in Murcia in 1910, and one in the Canary Islands

* "Opus Dei and Politics," published in *Nuestro Tiempo* (Pamplona, 1957) and in the Opus Dei–controlled Madrid newspaper *Alcázar* (July, 1962).

in 1925. Apart from five garish "labor" universities, not one state university had been built.

University degrees are the keys to jobs in Spain and they had long been the monopoly of the tight-knit, self-perpetuating corps of university professors—almost all of them Falangist appointees who are legally irremovable once they have passed their exams. For years, Opus Dei has been working to penetrate this clique, placing its own members on the university examining boards whenever possible, and helping to promote their talented students. This campaign has had some success, and Opus Dei is now said to control about 40 per cent of the professorships, including several influential chairs of history and law.

The Church's struggle to gain a foothold in university life has been long and difficult. Its right to run universities was recognized in the 1941 *modus vivendi,* and again in a 1943 law drafted by Education Minister Ibáñez Martín and confirmed in the 1953 Concordat. However, Article XXXI of the Concordat stipulates that a separate *convenio* must be negotiated to work out details, and for years Franco has ignored Vatican suggestions that the time had come to implement the *convenio.*

Franco has feared any outside influence in the Spanish universities—even the Vatican's. His ideas of education are the army's: respect for authority, discipline, and law and order. The Spanish Army has always considered the universities hotbeds of antimilitarism, anticlericalism, and agitation. Franco has not forgotten the key role the students played in the fall of another dictator, Primo de Rivera, in 1929.

For twenty-five years, debate, free speech, free discussion of liberal or nonorthodox views have remained strictly forbidden. Conformity has been the rule. The Falange has policed the student body through its Sindicato Estudiantil Universitario (SEU), which all students must join.

However, in April, 1962, Franco finally capitulated to Vatican pressure and the *convenio* was published in the *Boletín Oficial del Estado.* Opus leaders hailed it as the first break in the state's monopoly in a quarter century.* "Spain now has two systems of higher education," explained an Opus leader. "The state will continue to examine students in the twelve official universities but in Pamplona it will examine only the teachers."

Opus members are also prominently placed in public affairs and seem to be extending their influence. The 1957 cabinet reshuffle promoted to power two Opus adherents, Alberto Ullastres and Mariano Navarro Rubio, as Commerce and Finance ministers respectively, and moved to a key post Professor López Rodó, one of Opus' highest ranking members. Some call him the most powerful man in Spain after Franco. López Rodó is a Catalan educator in his late forties who has risen from virtual obscurity to become Technical Secretary General—or number two man—in Franco's Presidencia, the Prime Minister's office. He has also been named commissioner of Spain's Four-Year Economic Plan—the Jean Monnet of Spain.

Quietly and cautiously, López Rodó has started a long-overdue reform of Spain's archaic bureaucracy with its 300,000 low-paid job-holders, and power seems to have concentrated in his office. Like Franco, he is a master of the empirical step-at-a-time technique. Since 1956–57, when he joined the Presidencia, his acquisition of power has been impressive.

First the *Boletín Oficial*, which announces all laws and decrees, came under his control. Next the Presidencia began quietly assuming responsibility for loose ends such as new foreign industrial or oil concessions. In the cabinet changes of July, 1962, the quiet Opus chieftain became the boss of the Economic Development Program, and any doubts over Opus Dei's control of Spain's economy were dissolved when the thirty-nine-year-old Gregorio López Bravo—another Opus protégé—became Minister of Industry. By the middle of summer in 1962, the four men controlling Spain's economy were members, or adherents, of Opus Dei.

* The Vatican also recognized the Jesuit universities of Deusto and Salamanca as "Universities of the Church" on August 19, 1963, granting them equal status with the Opus Dei university at Pamplona, a decision ratified by the Spanish Cabinet on September 6, 1963.

Where is Opus Dei going? What are its goals?

The answer is political stability and economic development. Opus wants no left-wing revival. It wants a modernization of Spain's economy and cautious integration into Western Europe. It has begun sweeping reforms: a slash in the swollen bureaucracy; a cutback in deficit spending; fairer taxation; a revamping of the obsolete transportation system; development of irrigation, forestation, and agriculture; promotion of exports; a healthy climate for foreign investment; and the development of tourism. Modernization is Opus' basic aim and to accomplish it, Opus insists that the country must be kept politically tranquil. On this, Opus and Franco agree.

This insistence on political "tranquillity" guarantees that Franco will back Opus as long as he lives. Opus is, first and foremost, an instrument of the Vatican, and the Vatican recommends obedience to the regime in power. The problem confronting Opus is the succession. After Franco, what? Opus has never taken, and will never take, a formal position on Franco's successor, but many signs point to its support for a Monarchist restoration under Don Juan.

The late Conde de Ruiseñada, a Catalan industrialist and Opus backer, was the man who first forged the link between the Monarchists and Opus Dei, by creating the Amigos de Maeztu. This ultra-right-wing club tried to bring Franco and Don Juan together but failed. Since Ruiseñada's death in 1958, other Opus members have taken over the tortuous negotiations and have persuaded the Monarchists to give up their ineffective opposition to Franco in favor of a policy of patient waiting. This, of course, suits Franco very well. He is indifferent to Don Juan's smiles or frowns, but in any event he prefers Opus' moderating influence to agitation.

Although many Opus members are not Monarchists (Commerce Minister Alberto Ullastres, for instance, is decidedly cool toward the monarchy), the influence of Opus on Don Juan and his entourage is impressive. The publicist Rafael Calvo Serer has been a personal friend of Don Juan since their World War II days in Lausanne. Tireless, urbane, discreet, he shuttles between Madrid and Estoril and usually bobs up wherever Don Juan happens to be: England, Switzerland, Athens—even the United States. Calvo Serer was even named "secretary" and escort to young Prince Juan Carlos and Princess Sophie on their global honeymoon trip in the summer of 1962. Early in 1963, he was back in New York and Washington, sounding out influential figures in Wall Street and in the Kennedy Administration.

If the monarchy is restored, Opus Dei may be expected to play a powerfully conservative role.

"The monarchy can neither be absolute, nor a nineteenth-century type monarchy based on parliamentary maneuvering and courtiers," Pérez Embid wrote recently. "The future monarchy must be . . . based on two fundamental principles: Catholic unity and social justice. The volatile, violent, arbitrary Spanish nature cannot support political parties . . . the monarchy, therefore, must correct what the Franco regime has failed to correct. . . . It must restore basic Christian liberties such as freedom of the press, freedom of association, and so forth. But political parties do not suit Spain."

Opus is playing the Monarchist game but should Franco (or the army) one day switch to a military regency or a De Gaulle-type presidency, Opus would switch, too. Rightly or wrongly, it regards itself as the Vatican's agent for maintaining political tranquillity and blocking a left-wing coup. It cares far more for real power than for its façade. Its techniques may not be to everyone's liking, but as Vicente Marrero, one of its leading publicists, recently put it, "Opus members have at their disposal contacts, means, instruments that make it possible to place themselves in society, in intellectual, economic, and political spheres in a singularly effective way, unknown before now in Spanish Catholicism. . . ." No one knows this better than such bitter rivals as the Jesuits or the Falange.

Hermandades Obrera de Acción Católica
(Catholic Workers' Brotherhoods)

The Spanish Church is painfully aware of the little time left to rebuild its image before Franco dies. Some prelates have begun urging reforms in education, censorship, agriculture—but particularly in labor. Labor reforms are vital, for whoever controls Spain's 8.5 million workers after Franco may well control Spain. It is no secret that the Church has begun to show a new interest in the Catholic Workers' Brotherhoods, or HOAC.

The Brotherhoods were formed by Cardinal Plá in 1947, when the Vatican and the Spanish Church both sensed the rising force of labor in postwar Europe. The hierarchy was worried by labor's traditional contempt for the old Catholic Sindicates, which were regarded as boss-run, or "yellow," unions. If the Church could not provide an alternative, the workers might revert to Marxism or to the old Socialist UGT and the Anarchist CNT. The HOAC was meant to be that alternative, but it never was.

Every move was blocked by the Falange's Sindicates, resentful of this foray into their domain, and by placid bishops, alarmed over anything that might disturb good relations with local Falangist bosses and fearful that HOAC might become a breeding ground for "progressives." It made no difference that Cardinal Plá had placed control over HOAC's activities in the hands of the bishops in each of Spain's sixty-four dioceses. Plá's prestige was great, but his authority was limited. The Brotherhoods remained Plá's creation, but their freedom to operate depended on each bishop's personal good will. Except for the operations of the Primate and a handful of prelates in industrialized areas, the Brotherhoods were resented and suppressed.

As late as 1960, HOAC had only 10,000 militants in all of Spain, with perhaps twice or three times as many sympathizers; one HOAC bulletin, for instance, claimed a circulation of 17,000, and the bulletin of its youth branch JOC (Juventud Obrera Católica), 25,000.

The 1960 Sindical elections brought the HOAC-Falange struggle into the open. HOAC candidates were openly intimidated and harassed, and the Falange steamroller crushed all opposition. In a blistering, 2,500-word "private" letter, the Primate of Spain accused Solís of totalitarian methods. "In Spain, one of the few confessional states with a model Concordat," he wrote, "the Brotherhoods are ignored; they are labeled subversive in government documents; their leaders are harassed by the police; they are fined for what they say—or even for what they do not say—and sometimes in the very presence of their bishops."

Pointing out that HOAC leaders had lately been invited to visit the United States, the Cardinal pointed out that this recognition was in "sad contrast" to HOAC's repression in Spain. "You cannot behave in 1960 as you did in 1940," he said, in a biting allusion to the Falange's Nazi origins.

His voice was ignored. Six weeks later, Franco blandly praised the "rule of law" that existed in Spain. The "authenticity" of Spain's Sindicates, he coolly insisted in a national broadcast, gives the "lie" to those who "question our system."

The persecution continued. In May, 1962, Franco's police arrested the national president of HOAC, Teofilo Pérez Rey, as well as the president and vice president of JOC, and drove the three Catholic leaders to the Dirección General de Seguridad, where they were interrogated like felons and fined 50,000 pesetas ($830) each for having permitted the HOAC bulletin to support the Asturian miners and to criticize Franco's labor laws.

Soon after, an angry confrontation between Franco and Cardinal Plá took place at the Pardo. Also present were Foreign Minister Castiella, Justice Minister Iturmendi, and the Papal Nuncio Monsignor Antoniutti. As his glasses slipped angrily down his nose, the bantam-cock Primate inveighed against the persecution of the HOAC leaders on charges of "subversion." Franco icily retorted that strikes were illegal and that anyone who supported them, however prestigious his backers, would be punished.

Since the Asturian strikes of April, 1962, HOAC's prestige has grown, and HOAC brotherhoods have begun springing up where they never existed before. The Church, too, has grown much bolder in its criticism of Franco's labor policy. In September, 1962, for instance, *Ya* declared that it was neither "justified, nor politically wise" to ignore the fact that "there is something in Asturias and in other labor areas that must be corrected." This was blunt talk for the normally obedient Catholic Action newspaper. Shortly after that, *Ecclesia* retorted to an attack by the Sindical newspaper *Pueblo* on "extralegal Catholic labor unions" by asserting that the Church, far from reining in HOAC, would continue to protect and stimulate it.

In Rome, meanwhile, Archbishop Morcillo of Zaragoza, serving as Undersecretary of the Ecumenical Council, conceded frankly to reporters that "a new form of civilization has appeared in the world: labor." With an oblique reference to Franco's labor policies in Asturias, he added, "It has been necessary for workers to raise up their threatening fists to make men understand the justice of their rights."

Frente de Liberación Popular (Popular Liberation Front)

One of the most troublesome problems for the Spanish Church today is the emergence of a strongly left-wing, Marxist-inclined group of young Catholics. They berate the Church for its close ties with Franco and claim that only "Castroist" Marxism can really reform Spain. Such a movement is the Frente de Liberación Popular (Popular Liberation Front).

Founded in 1955–56 by a young lawyer-diplomat, Julio Cerón Ayuso, the FLP (or "Felipe") has adopted a militant program that throbs with the violent, revolutionary, and confused aims typical of frustrated young Spanish Catholics under the dictatorship. Article 1, for instance, urges "revolution," which it defines as the "violent seizure of power by the working classes, the liquidation of the capitalist system of production, the suppression of private ownership of means of production, and the creation of a classless society." Article 2 affirms that the FLP wants the "social-

167

ization of . . . production; socialist planning of the economy . . . radical agricultural reforms . . . nationalization of banks; organization of all consumption through cooperatives; education for all; and the . . . replacement of the Army by popular militias including all the people." Article 3 lists as the Front's goal the establishment of a "true democracy of the workers" via their natural niches in society, the communities in which they live, and the Sindicates in which they work.

The emergence of strongly left-wing Catholics of the Cerón-FLP brand has given the Church concern. Although only a small minority today, they might become the core of a full-fledged Castroist movement in the post-Franco era. The Spanish Church fears Castroism almost more than Marxism, for Castroism appeals especially to Spain's hot-tempered, dynamic, and politically immature youth.

Dionisio Ridruejo told *L'Express* of Paris not long ago that the FLP could be found on the "extreme left" of the Spanish opposition to Franco, along with the delegates of the Basque government-in-exile and of the Catalan nationalists. He described it as a movement of Castroist inspiration, unimportant numerically, which nonetheless had played an active role—and had considerably reinforced its prestige—during the Asturian strikes. Not as a movement but as a symbol of left-wing Catholic discontent, it bears watching.

The Protestants

It is a Sunday morning in 1961, and on a drill ground near Melilla, a Spanish city-fort in Morocco, a Spanish infantry regiment kneels in the open air at morning Mass. Only one private, head reverently bowed, stands erect, despite the angry commands of his officers. He is Private Jenaro Redero Prieto, a Spanish Protestant whose conscience will not permit him to participate in a Catholic ceremony. As a consequence, he will serve eighteen months in prison for "disobedience."

Private Redero has since been forgotten, except as a symbol: a symbol of the "second-class" minority of Protestants in a nation of 31 million Catholics. For years, this one-tenth of one per cent of Spain's population has suffered contempt and discrimination in questions of marriage, burial, education, careers—even the simple right to worship without fear. Now, at long last, the situation is slowly improving. Thanks mainly to one man, the liberal-minded Foreign Minister Castiella, Franco has agreed to redress the plight of non-Catholics. After five centuries of hostile neglect, legal recognition—that is, protection—of Spain's non-Catholic minorities is in sight.

Spain's religious intolerance stems from centuries of historic struggle. One can trace it to 1492, when Isabella the Catholic and her stern councilor Cardinal Cisneros expelled Spain's 200,000 Jews immediately after crushing the final remnant of the Arab occupation. To maintain religious unity—the only unity possible in medieval Spain—it was deemed necessary to root out any trace of heresy, and, incidentally, to placate the Christian nobles with the Jews' possessions. The Arabs and the Jews both were cast out, whatever treasure they owned seized. The resulting loss of Jewish financiers, advocates, mathematicians, poets, physicians, merchants, agronomists, and craftsmen has retarded Spain ever since.

Self-mortification is, however, a Spanish characteristic; and because religious zeal once provided Spain and its Church with a dynamic force, the Church has always kept the issue of religious unity alive. The Inquisition, so loathsome to the Protestant world, was to the Spaniards a holy battle to preserve the true faith.

Political rivalry has also played its part. Protestantism has been historically linked with England, the chief Anglo-Saxon rival, and with the Netherlands, the rebellious colony, and with the United States. Spanish lands discovered and explored by De Soto, Ponce de Leon, Cabeza de Vaca, Narvaez, and others were successively wrenched away by land-hungry Anglo-Saxon Protestants. After the Spanish defeat of 1898, the process continued with Cuba, the Philippines, Guam, and Puerto Rico. Always, it seemed that the Protestants were behind Spain's decline.

The end of the Spanish Civil War saw the nadir of Protestant fortunes. Not only were the Protestants identified with Great Britain and the United States, whose governments had denounced Franco, but also with Freemasonry—a movement regarded as tantamount to Communism. Franco cloaked his rising with the mantle of a Catholic crusade against heresy, and on March 22, 1938—shortly before his Civil War victory—he returned to the Catholic Church control over baptism, education, morals, marriage, and burial, and ever since, the Protestants have remained an underprivileged minority. A petition to Franco in 1961 listed their complaints.

1. Protestants had not been recognized by the state; they had been "tolerated" and subjected to chronic harassment by regional or local officials, without legal redress.

2. Marriage by a Protestant minister still was not officially recognized, and Protestant couples had found themselves forced by clerical or administrative hostility into "common law" marriages.

3. The children of these "illicit" unions had undergone hardship and humiliation throughout their lives. Their parents had been forced either to send them to State or Church schools to be reared as Catholics or else to shoulder the heavy burden of private education.

4. Burial for Protestants was still difficult in large towns and virtually impossible in rural communities except in abandoned plots reserved for suicides, criminals, paupers, and the insane.

5. Posts in the government, in the Cortes, in provincial or even local assemblies were still barred to Protestants. No Protestant could become an army officer (although in 1955 Franco named Lieutenant General Mizzian, a Moslem born in Spanish Morocco, Captain General of Asturias). Protestant girls were still barred from nursing in Spanish hospitals or teaching in Spanish schools.

6. The importation or printing of Protestant literature—the Bible, liturgy, and catechism—was forbidden.

7. Protestant places of worship had been legally viewed as "foreign-owned businesses," and Protestant youth camps and charity organizations had been banned.

At the end of World War II, Franco, conscious of world opinion, announced his Charter of the Spaniards, which guaranteed religious "liberty."

"No one will be molested for his religious beliefs or in the private exercise of his cult," he proclaimed in Article VI of the new Charter. The next sentence effectively negated this pledge. No "ceremonies or external manifestations," he warned, would be permitted, except those of the Catholic religion. Above all, proselytism would be banned.

This wording gave the Catholic authorities absolute power. Any meeting of Protestants that the authorities chose to oppose became a "ceremony." "Private" worship could only be permitted in a *recinto consagrado,* an enclosure legally "consecrated" for religious use; worship in private homes was forbidden. A Protestant pastor who said grace at meals in a private home was breaking Spanish law. Prohibited "external manifestations" included the cross, the ringing of church bells, even the shape of a building that might indicate its holy nature. Protestant schools or seminaries, the distribution of charitable gifts, recreational centers—even summer camps for Protestant children—became forms of "proselytism."

Repression grew worse in 1948. Secret orders went out from the Ministry of Interior to civil governors and police authorities ordering them *paulatinamente* (cautiously, or warily) to start closing any remaining Protestant chapels not officially licensed. This was a hard blow, for, even during the relatively tolerant Second Republic, only 40 out of some 300 Protestant meeting places had ever been officially licensed; the rest had been quietly tolerated. The spur behind the campaign was political. In 1948, Franco's regime was isolated and bankrupt, and to rally Spanish opinion, Franco needed "enemies." The Protestants served his purpose.

The regime's repression of the Protestants was especially cynical, given their small numbers. The hard core was (and still is) calculated at 12,000 adults and 20,000 children, plus a few thousand foreign Protestants: Portuguese, Germans, Swiss, Swedes, Dutch, Danes, Norwegians, British—and about 200 Americans. In addition, there are some 90,000 Spanish *simpatizantes*—Catholics who attended Protestant services more or less regularly, although they were not prepared to risk official and ecclesiastical censure by abandoning the Catholic faith.

Protestant chapels or meeting places in Spain have always been clustered along the coasts, where foreign commercial colonies are strong. Most chapels are still shabby cellars, inconspicuous in back alleys, without cross or bulletin board or any other outward indication that they are places of worship.

There are still some 150 to 200 "leaders," or pastors, with varying degrees of theological training. Fifteen to twenty are foreigners—Americans, British, Swiss, German, or Dutch—but the rest are Spaniards prepared to risk jobs, security, and even their physical safety for their Protestant faith.

The Protestant churches and sects included the Plymouth Brethren, the Spanish Baptist Evangelical Union, the Spanish Evangelical Church, the Seventh-day Adventists, the Federation of Independent Evangelical Churches in Spain, Jehovah's Witnesses, the Spanish Christian Mission, the Spanish Reformed Episcopal Church, the Pentecostalists, the Quakers, and other smaller congregations. The largest groups—the Plymouth Brethren, the Reformed Church, the Evangelical Church, and the Baptist Evangelical Union—each numbered between three and four thousand; the rest, a few hundred.

The 1948 repression drove the Protestant minority underground but many liberal Spanish officials, to their credit, closed their eyes. Often, official reaction varied, depending on the community. In seaports with a history of foreign trade, such as Barcelona, the Protestants fared best. Valencia, Malaga, and Bilbao were also areas of relative tolerance, and along the Atlantic Coast north of Portugal the Plymouth Brethren, long established through old trade ties with England, were almost unmolested. In such rural areas as Navarra, Old Castile, León, Estremadura, and Murcia, however, the flames of fanaticism flickered high. Protestants were hounded, their chapels sealed, they were refused permission to wed except as Catholics, and their children were denounced as the "fruit of sin." Even deceased Protestants were denied burial, except in the local potter's field.

With the signing of the U.S.–Spanish defense treaties in 1953, the situation took a turn for the better, and three years later, on June 8, 1956, a three-man Defense Committee representing the national Protestant leadership addressed Franco with a fifteen-point plea requesting not equality with Catholics, but merely legal recognition and a definition of their responsibilities and rights. The timing was deliberate, for six weeks earlier, Spanish police, led by a fanatic Jesuit priest* had invaded both the Protestant Theological Seminary in Madrid and the premises of the British and Foreign Bible Society, a venerable institution not only sponsored by the British Embassy but actually licensed by the Spanish Government since 1912! Indifferent to the international repercussions of this raid, the police carted off 35,000 Bibles (in Spanish) belonging to the Society and sealed its premises.

The Protestant Defense Committee's plea was ignored by Franco, but the British Government's angry protest was not. The raid on the Bible Society was an affront to a world power whose trade, tourists, and good will Franco needed. The British Ambassador, Sir Ivo Mallet, handled the situation with aplomb. Neither threatening nor pleading, he told his friends in the Spanish Gov-

* Father Ramón Sánchez de León, Superior of the Jesuit Order of Spain and head of the Commission for the Defense of the Catholic Faith, which maintains a card file on 30,000 Protestants. On January 22, 1959, in a public ceremony in the Madrid Chamber of Commerce, attended by high officials, prelates, and financial and social leaders, he branded Spain's Protestant bishops and pastors as "subversive, Masonic, immoral, and mentally unbalanced."

ernment that the regime was behaving idiotically; and to his surprise, many agreed. Yet in self-justification, they stressed two aspects of Franco's hostility toward the Protestants.

First, nine out of ten Spaniards had never given the Protestant "problem" a thought: they ignored the Protestants' existence. If the average Catholic thought at all about his Protestant compatriot, it was more with curiosity than contempt. The Spanish masses were not hostile to Protestants. It was the Catholic hierarchy, fearful of apostasy, and the regime functionaries, fearful of political subversion, who were behind the persecution.

Second, officials charged that some Protestant sects, notably those financed from the United States, had repeatedly maneuvered to dramatize their mistreatment in order to gain world attention. It was not the Spanish Protestants but the aggressive dollar-rich foreigners who were exacerbating the situation, insisted Spanish officials.

In the last two years, the Protestants' lot has begun to improve, and credit is due Fernando María Castiella, Foreign Minister since 1957. One of the first tasks Castiella set himself on taking office was to repair Spain's world image by improving the lot of the Protestants. It was to take him seven years of uphill struggle, but by 1964 success was in sight.

Eisenhower's overnight visit to Madrid on December 21, 1959, aided Castiella's policy because it brought home sharply to Franco the damage his policy was doing Spain abroad.

As a shrewd politician, Franco wanted domestic peace, but at his elbow stood the formidable phalanx of fifteen elderly archbishops plus sixty bishops. No greater monolith of anti-Protestant reaction existed in the world, and in Franco's view, repression of a tenth of one per cent of the population was a small price to pay for the good will of this august bloc. Now, however, here was the President of the United States in Spain as Franco's guest. As Eisenhower expressed to Franco his feelings about the Protestant and other issues, twisting his syntax but getting his meaning across, Franco listened gravely. The U.S. public and Congressional opinion were deeply resentful, Eisenhower said, and the Protestant issue was causing an unnecessary strain in U.S.– Spanish relations. Many Protestant American tourists returned from Spain genuinely shocked by the "second-class" status of their Spanish coreligionaries, by the shabby chapels, the back-street meeting places, and the general air of persecution. Religious tolerance was not only just—it was essential if Spain wished to resume her role in the Western world.

Other statesmen had previously voiced similar warnings: John Foster Dulles, Selwyn Lloyd, Douglas Home, Couve de Murville —not to mention the ambassadors of West Germany, Holland, Denmark, Norway, Sweden, and other nations. With Eisenhower's visit, however, the ice began to crack, and not long after it, Castiella named a special Foreign Ministry committee, headed by a bright young diplomatic aide, Fernando Olivié, to sort out the tangled skeins of the Protestant puzzle. After several centuries, the problem was coming into focus.

Meanwhile, in October, 1961, more than 150 Protestant pastors from all over Spain met secretly in Madrid for their first congress since the Civil War. In isolated chapels and private rooms, they formed six discussion groups to work out a common position on the major aspects of their struggle: the legal situation of believers and of the evangelical churches; the problem of evangelization (use of churches); evangelical literature; the position of the Spanish Government toward evangelical believers and the Church; and, finally, the possibility of cooperation among the various evangelical churches themselves. After four days, they prepared yet another appeal for legal recognition and sent it to Franco. Again it was ignored. By now, however, the Vatican had launched its own appeal for ecumenical unity under the inspiration of Pope John XXIII. When Castiella, heading a Spanish mission to celebrate John XXIII's birthday in 1962, was received in private audience, he outlined to the Pontiff his ideas on Protestant reform. John XXIII listened with obvious approval, then, half rising in his seat, his face wreathed in smiles and his arms thrown wide as in benediction, he exclaimed, "If our Lord has told us to love our enemies, how much more fitting is it for us to love our brothers in the Christian faith!" This was the vital Papal approval Castiella needed to push ahead.

As word of the Pope's stand spread in Spain, help began to reach Castiella from unexpected ecclesiastic sources. The Primate, Cardinal Plá, now pledged his support—provided, however, that the Protestants would still not be permitted to celebrate services in public. He was for religious tolerance, but not proselytism. Two other influential prelates, José María Cardinal Bueno Monreal, Archbishop of Seville, and Dr. Ángel Herrera, also promised help. Others, recognizing the trend of the times, gradually fell in behind the Foreign Minister, but a powerful Church bloc still blindly opposed all reform.

"For twenty-five years, there has been no burning of Catholic churches, no murder of priests and nuns," wrote a dour old metropolitan of Basque extraction to Castiella. "Now, with your ideas on religious liberty, you will again unleash the flames of religious war in the streets of Spain!"

Despite the entrenched opposition, Castiella, with Franco's approval, is steadily pursuing his campaign. His draft law, based on a massive study of the history of religious minorities and legislation in other Catholic and non-Catholic countries, has been approved by the Vatican. Early in 1963, it was examined by the Spanish metropolitans (the fifteen archbishops, three of whom were cardinals) at their annual Madrid conclave, and approved in principle with recommendations for minor changes. It is still being blocked in the cabinet by the ultraconservatives headed by Admiral Carrero Blanco, but in time it is certain to pass.

Meanwhile, Protestant chapels are quietly being allowed to reopen, and Information and Tourism Minister Fraga has authorized hotels and pensions to post names of local Protestant chapels and their hours of services for the convenience of tourists. In an unprecedented step, the Spanish Supreme Court in early 1964 even reversed the Ministry of Interior and authorized the opening of a Protestant chapel in Valencia.

Yet many still grumble and still predict religious warfare. "If we open the doors—where do we stop?" a Spanish priest recently wrote in the Sindical newspaper *Pueblo*. "The Protestants may come, armed with dollars, and the poor may let themselves be suborned. . . . Our knowledge of the Gospel is weak and we are not ready for the struggle." And Dr. Pedro Cantero, Bishop of Huelva, warned not long ago that "Spain is neither mentally, nor psychologically, nor socially prepared for the exercise of religious freedom in a way that, in other countries, is normal and even indispensable."

If and when Castiella's reform plan is finally passed by the cabinet and goes to the Cortes for ritual approval, Protestants and other religious minorities will probably have legal protection, including the right to own property; to print and distribute evangelical material, Bibles, liturgies, and catechisms; to open and run schools and seminaries; to celebrate civil weddings; to operate hospitals, charitable institutions, youth camps, and cemeteries; and to hold any public or military office—except that of Chief of State. However, "public" worship outside licensed premises, the use of "external" symbols, such as crosses or church bells, and, above all, proselytism will continue to be banned. Among Spanish Protestant leaders there is no tendency to gloat, but rather a sense of awe mingled with trepidation.

"Moderation, tact, caution must be our watchwords," said Bishop Santos Molina. "Blatant publicity or open defiance of Spanish customs not only harms our cause but saddens the hearts of many Protestants and also Catholics who might eventually join us. We owe it to ourselves to move with decency and circumspection."

The Jews

On October 2, 1959, 200 Jewish residents of Madrid met in a former ducal palace at 19 calle Pizarro to dedicate their first synagogue in 467 years. The edict that expelled the Jews on August 2, 1492, still stands on the lawbooks—but it is now only a historic anachronism.

"The dedication of this Jewish Community Center and Synagogue," said Louis A. Blitz, president of the community, "gives evidence of the tolerant and benevolent attitude of the Spanish Government toward the practice of our religion." Blitz drew attention to the imminent opening of the World Sephardic Bibliographical Exposition, which the Spanish Government had agreed to sponsor and for which it had made available space in Madrid's National Library.

Why this "tolerant and benevolent" attitude toward the Jews in contrast to the churlish intolerance of Protestants? The answer —like everything in Spain—is steeped in history. Spain's tiny community of about 8,000 Jews (3,000 in Madrid and 5,000 in Barcelona) seeks no converts, and thus poses no threat—real or imaginary—to Catholic unity. Besides, the Jews, unlike the Protestants, have never been associated with a foreign rival. Dispersed over many lands, repeatedly persecuted, they have never presented a visible political threat. And, in fact, before their expulsion the Jews flourished in Spain.

The Gothic kings, who seized Spain from Rome in 409 and ruled it until the Arab invasion of 711, employed Jews as counselors, administrators, even as tutors for kings and nobles. The Arabs, far from eliminating the Jews, made full use of them. Spanish historians sometimes accuse the medieval Jews of having aided the Arab conquest.

"Nowhere had the medieval Jews so prospered as in Spain," wrote Hugh Trevor-Roper. "There, outside Galicia and Catalonia, all commerce seems to have gravitated into their hands; they were the intermediaries between Moslem and Christian rulers; physicians, literati, diplomatists, financiers, they formed almost the official class, chancellors and treasurers, sometimes even (if converted) archbishops and Inquisitors of Castilian kings. To Erasmus the whole [Iberian] peninsula seemed to have become a Jewish colony."*

* *Men and Events* (New York: Harper & Bros., 1958). Published in England as *Historical Essays* (London: Macmillan, 1957).

The ancient Jews called Spain "Sefarad," from which sprang the term Sephardim to distinguish the communities of the Iberian peninsula from their coreligionaries, the Ashkenazim, of Germany and central Europe. Unlike the Ashkenazim, who were subject to repeated persecutions and thus forced to concentrate inwardly on the Talmud and the Bible, the Sephardic Jews were free to develop their intellectual capacities. Sephardic grammar, Scriptural explanation, jurisprudence, theology, history, mathematics, astronomy, cartography, medicine, and poetry came to rival anything in the civilized world. Moslem rule in Spain owed much of its brilliance to the Jews, while the Jews' freedom to develop owed much to Moslem tolerance.

In 1492, however, the iron curtain of Catholic intolerance clanked down. Half of Spain's Jews fled to Portugal, whence, at Spain's insistence, they were to be expelled four years later, while the remaining 100,000 scattered in little knots throughout North Africa, Italy, France, Holland, England, the Balkans, Turkey, and the Near East—particularly Palestine. Wherever they went, they cherished their Spanish heritage. The scattered Sephardic communities carried on the Spanish language, the prayers, synagogue rites, folklore and popular literature, music, food, Spanish names. They even preserved the keys to their homes in Spain. To this day, Sephardic communities in Odessa, Salonika, Cairo, Alexandria, Tripoli, Oran, and Tangier speak Gidio, or medieval Spanish, in their homes, Ladino in their temples. They remain so Spanish at heart that they are still split into rival blocs: Castilian, Aragonese, Sevillian.

After the expulsion, for four and a half centuries, there was no Jewish presence in Spain. Then, toward the end of the nineteenth century, under the tolerant Alfonso XII, Jews began filtering back. Slowly their numbers grew. The Civil War forced many to leave again, and only twelve Jewish families stayed on in Madrid throughout the conflict.

Paradoxically, it was Hitler's persecution and the outbreak of World War II that gave birth to a new Jewish community in

Spain. At least 30,000 Jews fled across the Pyrenees to find temporary—in some cases permanent—haven. Despite the presence of ten German divisions on his border, Franco resisted Hitler's pressure to impose the brutal Nuremberg racial laws in Spain. In fact, Franco ordered Spanish diplomats in the Balkans and in other Nazi-occupied areas to issue Spanish visas that saved an estimated 10,000 Jews from concentration camps and death. Many Jewish refugees paused in Spain or Portugal long enough to gain passage to North or South America, but the elderly, the ill, and the indigent stayed on, cared for by the American Joint Distribution Committee—which today still provides for about 100 impoverished coreligionaries.

By 1949, the Jewish community in Madrid had again grown large enough to hold regular religious services. A local resident placed two basement rooms at the disposal of his fellow Jews and eventually, with the arrival of more and more Jewish tourists, the rites marking the High Holy Days were transferred (in 1954) to the Castellana Hilton Hotel.

Finally, after lengthy discussion with Franco's Government, Spain's Jewish leaders received oral permission to open a synagogue. Funds were obtained from the American Joint Distribution Committee, from the Conference on Jewish Material Claims Against Germany, and from local subscriptions. Two apartments were purchased on the second floor of 19 calle Pizarro—and Madrid had its first synagogue in nearly five centuries.

All the furnishings were made in Spain: the ceremonial candelabra, the Ark for the Sacred Scrolls, the eternal light, and the Hebrew lettering that forms a decorative frieze. The Sacred Scrolls, for example, originally the property of the Spanish synagogue of Baghdad, were donated by the Haam Gaon, the chief rabbi of the Spanish community of Great Britain.

In marked contrast to their disdain for Spain's Protestants, high regime officials attended the opening of the first Sephardic Bibliographic Exposition in Madrid on December 18, 1959. More than $1 million worth of cultural treasures from thirteen nations—including the Vatican—were displayed in six tapestry-hung salons of the National Library, and among the dignitaries who came to honor the Jewish community were Dr. Jesús Rubio, Minister of Education; Dr. Cesáreo Goicoechea, Director of the National Library; and Dr. Ramón Menéndez Pidal, President of the Royal Spanish Academy. In six weeks, the exhibition drew 12,000 Spanish visitors, including large numbers of Catholic schoolchildren on sponsored tours.

Officially, the Jewish community is still not recognized and cannot purchase property, but unofficially there is no interference with Jewish religious, or corporate, life. Franco shows tolerance and even good will. A Jewish-Christian Friendship Society (Amistad Judeo-Cristiana) was authorized in 1961. In early 1963, Label A. Katz, President of B'nai B'rith, and Saul E. Joftes, Secretary of the Jewish organization's international council, called on Franco to arrange an exhibition of Sephardic treasures in the United States, to thank him for Spain's "good treatment of European Jews, especially during those difficult moments in World War II, and for the Spanish Government's defense of Jewish interest in those other countries where they were persecuted," and to help get recognition for the Spanish Jewish community.

Few outside the regime and the Jewish community are aware that in the past two years more than 50,000 Jews driven from Morocco have been permitted to enter Spain via Gibraltar without question or formality and to continue their journey to Israel after a period of rest and recuperation.

In the spring of 1964, the historic Levi Synagogue in Toledo was declared a national monument, and Franco appointed to its board "The President of the Jewish Community of Madrid"—thus conferring on the community tacit recognition. The Jewish communities of Madrid, Barcelona, Ceuta, and Melilla have been permitted to form a Council of Jewish Communities in Spain and to apply to join the World Jewish Congress. And in January, 1965, Franco received at the Pardo Palace Max Mazin and Alberto Levi, the heads of the Jewish communities of Madrid and Barcelona, respectively, and promised to examine their request for legal recognition of these communities. Later, government spokesmen described the meeting as probably the first between a Spanish head of state and local Jewish leaders since King Ferdinand rejected the protests of Rabbi Isaac Abravanel, his Portuguese-born former aide, over the expulsion edict in 1492.

So far, Franco has withheld diplomatic recognition from Israel, chiefly to avoid friction with the Arabs. He likes to boast of Spain's role as a "bridge" between Christianity and Islam, but although he invites Arab potentates to visit Spain and subsidizes exhibitions of Spanish-Arab culture, it is probably a matter of time until Spain recognizes Israel.

There is one personal factor also to be considered here: Franco's blood heritage. Many Spanish families boast Arab and Jewish blood as a legacy of their country's history, and Franco almost certainly has Jewish blood in his veins. Devout Catholic though he is, his cast of countenance, his surname, and even his mother's name—Bahamonde—are characteristic of Spanish Sephardic families.

The Church is clearing its desk for the post-Franco struggle, for the 1962 strikes opened its eyes. It is no coincidence that in the course of 1962, the Church began a sweeping reorganization, "approved, and probably urged, by the Vatican," as Paul Hofmann reported to *The New York Times*. Fourteen bishops' committees were set up, giving the Church its own central "government" for the first time in centuries. *Ya* even compared these committees to cabinet ministries in a national administration.

The most important, the Committee on Social and Workers' Affairs, was entrusted to José María Cardinal Bueno Monreal, Archbishop of Seville, a possible future Primate of Spain, who had won national attention by denouncing as "scandalous" the low wages paid by Spanish landowners to their agricultural workers.

Generalissimo Francisco Franco y Bahamonde, Chief of State, Chief of the Government, Commander in Chief of the Armed Forces, and "by the grace of God, Caudillo of Spain."

Franco's Minister of Foreign Affairs, Fernando María Castiella.

José Solís Ruiz, Secretary General of the Movement (Falange) and National Delegate of the Sindicates.

Don Esteban (Marqués de) Bilbao, President of the Cortes.

The late Gabriel Arias Salgado, Minister of Information from 1937 to 1962.

Alberto Ullastres Calvo, a former professor of economics, a member of Opus Dei, and ex-Minister of Commerce.

Mariano Navarro Rubio, a former director of the Opus Dei Banco Popular, and Minister of Finance.

Rafael Calvo Serer, a professor at Madrid University and a member of Opus Dei, who serves as an adviser to Don Juan.

Laureano López Rodó, Minister Without Portfolio, commissioner of El Plan, and a member of Opus Dei.

The Church, in all likelihood, will not break openly with Franco, despite its growing concern, but behind the scenes it is pressing for at least four major reforms. It wants:

1. "Authentic" representation in the Cortes and in the Sindicates.

2. "Institutionalization" of the regime—the appointment of a prime minister and the separation of the powers long concentrated in Franco's hands.

3. "Social justice"—fairer distribution of the national wealth.

4. "Pacification of spirits"—an end to the Falange's raucous trumpeting about the Civil War and the continuing division of Spain into "victors" and "vanquished."

The Spanish Church quite obviously foresees the dangers of Castroism or other extremisms when Franco dies. Like a man awakening from a protracted sleep, however, its brain and its limbs are not yet fully coordinated. The steps are still slightly unsteady and the speech still slightly slurred.

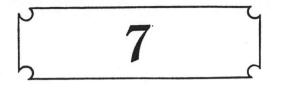

The Opposition

No aspect of contemporary Spain is more confusing than the political "opposition" to Franco.

Legally, no opposition exists. Political activity of any kind is banned—except through the hardening arteries of the Falange. There are no opposition newspapers, no opposition *procuradores* in the Cortes, no opposition meetings. Theoretically there *is* no opposition, yet, in fact, the opposition permeates Spain.

There are cabinet members who proudly insist that they are in the opposition; bishops, bankers, and generals who flirt discreetly with the opposition; and policemen who will courteously direct foreign journalists to the homes of rich or prominent opposition figures. Why has Franco not flung these enemies into jail?

In many cases, he has. Those who act, rather than talk, end up in his jails. But the problem is no longer one merely of cowing or stifling the discontented. Much of the youth of Spain today is discontented, the intellectuals are discontented, and even in the sacred tabernacles of the regime, there are signs of restiveness. More and more Spaniards want the windows flung open, the beds aired, and the Civil War quietly forgotten. There are compelling reasons for Franco's new mildness.

Franco is being forced to heed and placate foreign opinion, scorn it though he may. A new generation is emerging in Spain less prone to violence than its parents. Then, too, the opposition is split between those who want cautious evolution (but not revolution) and those who insist on throwing out the baby with the bath water. Francoism must be uprooted and burned, the latter insist, but since few among them agree on how to fill the vacuum, Franco quietly continues to rule.

Ivreach MacDonald, the able foreign editor of the *Times* of London, once divided the Spanish opposition into the "clandestines," who slip pamphlets under doors at night, and the "intellectuals," who send florid protests to Franco, knowing he will ignore them. A Spanish observer more cynically divided his country's opposition into the "gallant" and the "comfortable." Both descriptions have merit.

Franco tolerates a surprising amount of grumbling. Any visitor with a grasp of Castilian can hear it in the *tascas*, where the chatter and the arguments resound, while the shrimp shells, toothpicks, cigarette boxes, and paper napkins pile up on the sawdust floors. In offices, homes, restaurants, even in government ministries, a visitor will hear people grumbling about the nuts and bolts of daily life: the rise in food prices, the cost of housing, the lack of schools, the bad roads, and corruption—municipal, provincial, and national corruption. The regime is damned and individual cabinet ministers are openly denounced as knaves—but the flood stops short of Franco. Seldom, in my six years in Spain, did I hear Franco personally abused: his satraps take the beating.

Equipped with a quick mind, an impulsive tongue, and courage, the Spaniard is a rebel by nature. He knows what windmill he wants to topple, but seldom what to erect in its place. He wants to mount, and sally forth against the foe; but position warfare bores him.

When confronted by an immovable force, or when he acquires a job, wife, and children, he begins, however, to accommodate himself to his situation—still grumbling. In time, this accommodation becomes his way of life. This is what is happening in Spain today. Spain has been slowly accommodating itself to Franco. It does not necessarily like Franco—it is merely making the best of Franco.

The national vigor is beginning to reassert itself through new industries, new businesses, new shops, new garages, new houses and apartment buildings, through the booming tourist industry, through engineering, shipbuilding, banking, roads, export-import. Spain is becoming more conservative as Spaniards are acquiring more to conserve.

Franco, too, is changing. He has become less militaristic, less cold, less aloof. He has invited Spain's exiles to return, and has promised them peace, provided they leave him in peace. He is beginning to reshape his image, appearing in public less in khaki and more in the sober garb of the man of affairs: the well-cut gray suit, the homburg, the shepherd's-check tie. Now usually accompanied by his wife, daughter, and grandchildren, he beams amiably and accepts floral tributes from well-scrubbed tots. Basking in the mellowness of his evening, Franco allows opposition mice to scurry until the squeaks become too loud. Then out flicks a paw and—silence.

"It is hardly possible," reported the International Commission of Jurists in its 1962 survey, "to find [in Spain] a single form of opposition activity that is not threatened by legal sanctions."

This is the opposition's problem: It can talk to itself but not act. "None is condemned for his political beliefs," Franco's Justice Minister Antonio Iturmendi reminded the Cortes in November, 1963. He failed, of course, to add that any attempt to propagate such beliefs leads to prison.

Yet the picture of Spain as a political dungeon is a caricature. World protests erupt when Franco's political prisoners are jailed or—less frequently—executed, but it would be a mockery to claim that the jails are still filled with gaunt, silent creatures eking out lives behind bars for Civil War crimes. When the war ended, at least 300,000 Republican prisoners were herded into concentration camps, and as many fled to France, Mexico, or elsewhere. In recent years, thousands have returned, taking advantage of Franco's amnesties provided they eschew politics. Spain's entire penal population, as of January 1, 1964, was officially reported as 11,395. Those imprisoned for "crimes against the security of the state" numbered 355 men and 10 women; for "banditry and treason," 155 men.

Spanish statistics are always dubious, especially those concerning political prisoners, but reliable non-Spanish sources not long ago revealed that no more than 1,300 Spaniards are still held as "political" prisoners. There is little reason to believe that the numbers have increased since. Of these, 800 were listed as "subversives" (organizers of underground cells, and the like); another 400 were reported to be in jail for sabotage, bomb-planting, and similar offenses; the remaining 100 or so were probably being held unjustifiedly.

To rebut the International Commission of Jurists, Franco's Ministers of Justice and Information called a joint press conference in Madrid in December, 1962, and announced that exactly 611 persons were then in jail for "crimes against the security of the state." The government insists that Spain's penal population is the lowest in Western Europe—excepting only Holland.

Franco's nine successive amnesties—each carefully timed for maximum political effect—have helped empty the prisons. The first came on October 9, 1945, to herald the close of World War II. Others followed on July 17, 1947 (to celebrate the Monarchist Law of Succession); on December 9, 1949 (Holy Year); on May 1, 1952 (Eucharistic Congress in Barcelona); on July 25, 1954 (to celebrate the Marian Year); on October 31, 1958 (Pope John XXIII's coronation); on October 11, 1961 (Franco's twenty-fifth year in power); on June 24, 1963 (the accession of Pope Paul VI); and the latest on April 1, 1964, to highlight Franco's "Twenty-five Years of Peace."

Not only has the number of political prisoners decreased but, according to prisoners freed from Carabanchel, Ocaña, Burgos, and other prisons, their treatment has improved. The worst brutalities of the old days appear to be over, though exceptions periodically come to light.* The old Spanish police technique of mass roundups attracts world attention and has helped to perpetuate the bad odor that clings to the regime. Innocent friends, relatives, business contacts, even chance acquaintances whose names are found in the address book of a suspect are indiscriminately rounded up and held for questioning. After two or three days of confinement, the majority are set free with orders to stay within reach. The technique is grimly effective: it cows the masses and sometimes unearths information, but it also blackens Spain's name. The third-degree treatment of prisoners usually comes during this initial roundup period, when the police are frenziedly following every lead. Confronted by defiance, the harassed Spanish policeman hits first and thinks afterward.

Deliberate sadism, however, is decreasing. The Spanish authorities have begun to open the prisons to inspection by international experts. In November, 1963, *The Times* of London reported that sixteen political prisoners at Burgos had delivered to the Minister of Information and Tourism through the prison governor a protest alleging police torture to extract confessions. Several weeks earlier, 102 Spanish intellectuals, including Pedro Laín Entralgo, former Rector of Madrid University, José López Aranguren, Professor of Ethics at Madrid University, and Enrique Tierno Galvan, Professor of Political Law at Salamanca University, had publicly protested to Fraga about indignities, tortures, and even a killing allegedly inflicted on striking Asturian miners during the summer. Fraga pooh-poohed the charges, although he blandly conceded that miners' wives had had their heads shaved by police for their "provocatory attitude."

---

* In recent months, high Church prelates have interceded with Franco on behalf of prisoners at Burgos Prison who have gone on hunger strikes to protest alleged mistreatment.

Make-up of the Opposition

To a political scientist, the opposition seems like amoebae under a microscope. Colorless, shapeless, melding and untangling, the translucent forms squiggle across the lens in a fury of activity or else drowse in deep torpor. How to classify or evaluate these bloodless bodies is a task best left to the scientist; but since the modern world likes classification, the opposition spectrum looks something like this:

Starting at the extreme left, there are the Communists; the Castroist Catholics of Julio Cerón's FLP; the Anarchists (with their trade union branch, CNT); the Socialists (with their trade union branch, UGT); Dionisio Ridruejo's little Partido Social de Acción Demócrata; and Giménez Fernández' left-wing Demo-Christians. These groups, of varying origins, size, and impact, broadly make up the left.

Moving from the center to the right, one finds Gil Robles' Demo-Christians, the DSC (Democracia Social Cristiana), and the liberal Monarchist Unión Española headed by the fire-eating young Basque millionaire Joaquín Satrustegui. These two compose the moderate right. Further to the right are the collaborationist Carlists (Tradición Española) and the ultrareactionary Monarchist Acción Española.

The Carlists, who want a monarchy without Don Juan and whose feudal doctrines are more religious than political, still claim 100,000 followers, mainly in Navarra. They are, however, increasingly split and increasingly disillusioned with Franco. They rallied to Franco at the start of the Civil War and for a quarter of a century have shared such spoils as the Falange has allowed them, but as their power wanes, they are becoming increasingly disgruntled.

The opposition spectrum is complicated because even such regime agencies as the Falange and its Sindicates have been progressively infiltrated by Communists, Anarchists, and Socialists.

There are also various exile factions with scattered pockets of support inside Spain; regional blocs of separatist Basques and Catalans; young anti-Franco Catholics operating under the cover of the HOAC (Catholic Workers' Brotherhoods) and the JOC. Finally, there is the younger rural clergy, especially in the Basque country, which frequently defies both Franco and the Church.

The main weakness of the opposition lies in the struggle between the "exterior" and "interior" opposition: the Socialist (Republican) exiles who fled abroad in 1939 with the aura of legitimacy and with funds; and the new young leaders, unknown and untested, arising inside Spain. The former have long insisted on total adherence to their policies under the threat of withholding funds or expelling the insubordinates from the party's ranks, whereas the young leaders of the "interior," daily risking detection, imprisonment, and even their lives, argue that they know the nation's mood and the realities of underground activity. For twenty years, for instance, the late Socialist leader, Indalecio Prieto, tried to run the Socialist underground in Spain from Mexico—only to see it penetrated and smashed by Franco's police at least seven times. Still the wrangling continues.

Other exiled leaders, too, have tried to direct the anti-Franco underground: Martínez Barrio, the late President of the government-in-exile; Rodolfo Llopis, Prieto's successor as Secretary General of the Socialist Party (PSOE); his colleague, Pascual Tomás; Salvador de Madariaga, former Republican Ambassador, who has been writing and teaching at Oxford for many years; Alvarez del Vayo, the Communist fellow traveler, and—before their deaths—Luis Araquistain, the Socialist, and José María Aguirre, former President of the so-called Basque Republic. All have failed because they have underestimated Franco's grip, the revulsion of the Spanish people against renewed violence, and the emergence of a new "a-political" younger generation. Old men and old slogans no longer stir Spain's heart.

A further feud has split the nation's two largest potential parties: the non-Communist left led by the Socialists, and the non-Fascist right, grouped in a loose Demo-Christian movement. The Socialists and Demo-Christians will be numerically the most important blocs in Spain when Franco dies but, while both exist in theory, neither yet exists in leadership, organization, or even settled doctrine. Like the armies of South America, each produces more rival generals than shock troops. Repeated efforts to bridge the gaps have failed: never over common hostility to Franco; always over how to replace him. The Socialist-Republican exiles, clinging forlornly to dreams of regaining power, have persistently refused a compromise formula for a constitutional monarchy led by Don Juan, the Count of Barcelona, or by his son Prince Juan Carlos. To them, a monarchy would merely be Francoism under a new name.

Yet Demo-Christian and other opposition leaders sense the repugnance still felt in many parts of the nation toward another Republican experiment. For twenty-five years, Franco's propaganda has warned that Republicanism is tantamount to chaos, to Communism or Anarchism. It has revived memories of strikes, of assassinations, and of church-burning, and millions of ordinary Spanish citizens now believe this. Knowing this, and that the terms "Socialist" or "Republican" alarm the power blocs—the army, the Church, and the financiers—the interior opposition leaders have long sought to persuade the exiles to compromise, to agree in advance on a constitutional monarchy in which all non-totalitarian political parties would become legal. They have argued that constitutionally, Spain is already a monarchy; that the legitimate Pretender, Don Juan, is waiting in nearby Portugal; that he is a liberal by inclination; that the army, the Church, and other conservatives will probably install a monarchy anyway, once Franco is gone; and that, therefore, it would be wise to plan realistically rather than bay for the moon. These pleas have fallen on deaf ears, year after year.

In 1946, when Franco's prestige was at its lowest ebb, efforts to conclude a pact between Gil Robles and Prieto foundered on the monarchy vs. republic issue. Eleven years later, in 1957, efforts to reach a similar agreement again failed. The Socialist and Republican exiles still insist on a prior national plebiscite to choose between monarchy and republic, while the interior leaders fear that any delay will encourage extremism—left-wing or right-wing.

Time, nonetheless, is having its effect. The mass of exiles have become slowly *aburguesado* (bourgeoisized). Tens of thousands have remade their lives, and some their fortunes, abroad; and while many still profess hatred for Franco, many more have watched Spain's economic recovery with pride, and have come home under amnesty. The exiles have seen Communism at work around the globe for twenty-five years and their illusions are gone. Even the old clenched-fist militants, prating that "the left can talk to the left," now know better.

Since the recent death of Prieto, an imperceptible spirit of compromise seems to have grown among the exiled leaders. They have by no means agreed to a constitutional monarchy, but they no longer blindly exclude it. They realize that with every year their influence is diminishing and this, no doubt, has led to recent efforts to consolidate the scattered legions of the left.

In May, 1961, a potentially important coalescing took place in Toulouse, traditional foreign headquarters of the Spanish exiled left. There, delegates of the old banned trade unions UGT and CNT met to forge an "Alianza Laboral" to subordinate past rivalries and to prepare plans to take over Spanish labor from the Sindicates when Franco dies.

Simultaneously, the political groups of the non-Communist left were drawing up an eight-point program. Besides the dominant Socialists (both of exterior and interior), there were present Professor Giménez Fernández' IDC (Izquierda Demócrata Cristiana) or left-wing Demo-Christians; the regionalist Partido Nacionalista Vasco, and five little Republican exile splinter groups calling themselves the ARD (Acción Republicana Demócrata) and led by Fernando Valera, "Foreign Minister" of the government-in-exile.

The program for this new Unión de Fuerzas Demócratas, as

the organizers called themselves, included: "total" opposition to the Franco regime; a provisional government after Franco "of no defined institutional form," to hold elections to decide on a monarchy or republic; no cooperation with Communism or Fascism; a foreign policy based on solidarity with all free peoples, especially in Europe and Hispano-America; respect for the rights of various regions in Spain, and the opening of a "channel for their aspirations toward autonomy."

The cosignatories agreed, while preserving their respective programs, to bar "unapproved marginal alliances" and to work together "at least until the dictatorship has been overthrown." Other opposition groups "manifestly and unequivocally democratic" that would accept these provisions might, they concluded, be allowed to join—as might individuals fulfilling the same conditions.

Since then, little has been heard of the Unión de Fuerzas Demócratas, but its spokesmen insist that it is merely biding its time. They stress that its creation marked the first step in twenty-five years to unite the non-Communist left, thus paving the way for eventual collaboration with the moderate anti-Franco right.

"It was the bitter hatred between Gil Robles' CEDA and Prieto's Socialists that led step by step toward the Civil War," a veteran opposition leader once told me. "The middle-of-the-road groups remained paralyzed and the extremists took over. This must never happen again."

THE CHRISTIAN DEMOCRATS. This conservative element is a mood rather than a political party, yet, although divided and vague in its aims, it remains the most important potential political force in Spain. Its most distinct wing is led by José María Gil Robles, a lawyer, orator, parliamentarian, and veteran of thirty-five years in Spanish politics.

In a nation lacking in "names," Gil Robles' pre-Civil War leadership of the Demo-Christian CEDA, his ties with the Church, his long intimacy with the Pretender, Don Juan, and his persistent opposition to Franco all lend him a prestige no other opposition chief can boast. His is a lusty voice in a weak choir.

Yet to many Spaniards, Gil Robles is an "expert in chaos," a dabbler in muddy waters, at home more in intrigue than in statesmanship. They hold him largely to blame for the events leading to the Civil War. The army chiefs, for instance, have never forgiven him his refusal to "rise" against the Republic when he was Army Minister in 1935; many oppositionists still criticize him for having repeatedly bungled, or scuttled, efforts to create an anti-Franco front after World War II. Thanks to his right-wing Catholic coloration, he has been exiled but not jailed by Franco, and, in fact, Franco does not really take him seriously. Gil Robles' forte is maneuver, not revolution.

In 1957, after years of exile, he made peace with Franco and was allowed to return to Madrid where, though watched, he began slowly to reweave the threads of his Demo-Christian network. He traveled around Spain, using his lucrative law practice as a cover. The police followed him, mechanically, but this veteran politician knew the police as well as he knew their fathers before them. He is an institution rather than a revolutionary.

His forensic skill has been brilliantly demonstrated, as it was in 1959, when he defended the young diplomat Julio Cerón Ayuso, founder of the Castroist FLP (Frente de Liberación Popular). Cerón had been a delegate to UNESCO in Geneva, whence he was recalled on a pretext to Madrid and arrested. Gil Robles used the military court so skillfully as a platform that it left the army prosecutors speechless. Cerón received a savage eight-year sentence for "military rebellion"* but Gil Robles' reputation soared.

Occasionally, like many old men in a hurry, Gil Robles overreaches himself. Though an avowed Monarchist and charter member of Don Juan's Consejo Privado del Rey, he has long decried what he considers the Pretender's excessive caution and

* Cerón was finally released from Valladolid Prison in 1962, after serving three years and three months of his sentence.

the fecklessness of his aristocratic advisers. Don Juan has repeatedly insisted to Gil Robles that no histrionics, no flamboyant
appeals to the masses will bring him an inch nearer to the Spanish throne and that, conversely, the sort of fanfaronade Gil
Robles urges on him will axiomatically scare off the army. As a
result, the two men have split.

The break with Don Juan followed the 1962 Munich rally of
Franco's enemies, which Gil Robles secretly helped organize,
without informing the Pretender. At Munich, Gil Robles and
Rodolfo Llopis, the Socialist, publicly clasped hands to sym-
bolize the reconciliation of the right and the left against Franco.
To no one's surprise, Gil Robles was arrested on his return to
Madrid and given his choice of confinement in the distant
Canary Islands or exile.

The old veteran once again packed his bags and retired to a
comfortable exile in Switzerland where, among his other pur-
suits, he was reported to have been a consultant to a syndicate
of Barcelona bankers interested in the funds of the late Generalissimo Trujillo of San Domingo. He was permitted to return
and resume his law practice in Madrid in July, 1964, after two
years' punishment in exile.

Unlike other Spanish opposition leaders who bask in publicity, Gil Robles normally ducks the press, but when tracked to
his book-lined lair in a quiet Madrid apartment, he can be
cordial and even engaging. Of middle height, now in his late
sixties, he has a massive forehead, a small chin, and the bright
little gimlet eyes of a forest elf.

In personal conversation, he is an old-style word-spinner. He
talks at length in bland generalizations: Franco is a knave; the
cabinet are fools; most officials are dishonest; reforms are needed;
civil liberty and parliamentary democracy must be restored to
the people; and so on. But how, when, by whom, at what speed,
and to what extent—for example, the detailed blueprints for
transforming an old dictatorship into a new democracy—these
are conspicuously lacking. One senses the veteran demagogue of
the 1930's, not the leader of an awakening nation.

Gil Robles' platform offers something for everybody. He urges a restoration of the monarchy under Don Juan; free enterprise and a "transformation" of Spanish capitalism both to "facilitate the harmonization" of capital and labor and to ensure "just" distribution of the national income. He proposes a ban on all totalitarianism, especially Communism; national unity, yet with regional freedom; free education at all levels; recognition of the Church's right to educate but also of the state's right to "inspect"; and he suggests "dual" suffrage for Spanish citizens, based on their capacity both as individuals and as members of "organizations and natural societies." He calls, finally, for judicial independence, international and European cooperation, and Spain's integration into European common associations.

Not even Franco could find fault with this program, which, as one cynical Spaniard remarked, is probably the reason why it has had virtually no impact in Spain.

A second wing of the Demo-Christians, further to the left than Gil Robles is the IDC (Izquierda Democrata Cristiana), captained by the grizzled, fiery Professor Manuel Giménez Fernández, teacher of canon law at Seville University and long an idol of reform-minded university students. The IDC's Catholic coloration is virtually all that differentiates it from Socialism.

Like Gil Robles, Giménez Fernández is a veteran of the political wars, a one-time Agriculture Minister in the Republic, whose land reform projects aroused the undying enmity of the landed interests, who effectively blocked them. He has remained so impenitently and openly anti-Franco that the army, the Church, and the vested interests all suspect him and will probably never yield him any real influence in political life. He remains a Don Quixote tilting at windmills.

"Spain is not just a dictatorship!" he likes to bark scornfully in his cool, dark study in Seville. "Spain is a bureaucratic, praetorian, clerical, plutocratic regime—worse than a dictatorship!"

He is scathing about the regime's corruption, nepotism, and

maladministration, and insists that after Franco "the robbers must be prosecuted and forced to hand back their loot." Yet, paradoxically, he is almost benign about Franco.

"Franco is the most intelligent and the least bad of the Franquistas," he maintains.

I have often visited Don "Manolo" in his whitewashed home on the narrow calle Galdós in Seville, and each time I have come away stimulated. Taxis, trucks, and motor scooters grumble by outside, while inside, a trim little maid shows the visitor through a marble patio to Don Manuel's office. Books crowd the room, and the heavy furniture, the soft lamplight, the deep chairs add their touch of serenity. His tall, vigorous body strains forward as the ideas pour out like bright daggers. Unlike Gil Robles, he does not hide behind words: he is blunt, even harsh, the censor Cato reborn, yet with a mocking, sardonic humor. He has facts, figures, statistics of graft, details of scandals at his fingertips.

He revels in pseudo-dramatic conspiracy. The telephone jangles. He lurches from his chair, seizes it, and barks a salutation, annoyed at being interrupted. After a moment, he hangs up. "One of my friends says a detective is now across the street watching the house," he snorts. "Bah! Who cares?"

Occasionally, Giménez Fernández joins in a public protest to Franco over censorship or police brutality, but not too often. His eminence in canon law and his ties with the Church help protect him and, while he makes no secret of his views, he is publicly cautious. He declined, for instance, to attend the 1962 Munich meeting for fear of being refused readmission to Spain. He also cultivates an air of persecution in his talk with foreigners. Should he ever be found by the side of a road in a car "accident," he told me once, it would be no accident.*

---

* In early 1965, Giménez Fernández' left-wing Demo-Christians met openly at a state-run inn in Gredos, near Madrid, to form a Democratic Christian Union and draw up a fourteen-point program rejecting any collaboration with Franco's regime, demanding an a-confessional state and a future federal constitution. In due course, the organizers were called in by the political police for extensive questioning.

The third, and potentially largest, block of Demo-Christians, however, looks neither to Gil Robles nor to Giménez Fernández but rather to the Church for leadership. This waiting mass is likely, when Franco goes, to organize rapidly under the leadership of *Acción Católica*. Already, there are signs that the groundwork has been prepared with the discreet approval of the Vatican.

The first sign came early in 1958, with the sweeping reorganization of Editorial Católica, the Spanish Church's publishing and propaganda network. Editorial Católica today controls not only *Ya,* one of the two most important Madrid morning newspapers, but also papers in Granada, Logroño, Badajoz, and Murcia, plus many magazines, periodicals, and radio stations. *Ya* has recently installed high-speed rotary color presses, paid for by subscriptions from wealthy Spaniards abroad.

Politically, the reorganization was significant. Francisco de Luis, the respected Demo-Christian who had been editor of *Ya* for seventeen years and an indomitable critic of the regime, was dropped, and control passed to a board comprising Franco's former Foreign Minister Alberto Martín-Artajo, his brother Javier, and Dr. Ángel Herrera.

Herrera's presence on the new board was also significant, for, as one well-informed Spaniard observed, "Dr. Herrera is the only Spanish bishop *en diálogo* [in real contact] with Franco." This former editor of the liberal *El Debate,* Spain's greatest pre-Civil War newspaper, probably has forgotten more about politics than most Spaniards have ever learned. Before taking holy orders in 1940, he was a power behind the scenes in Gil Robles' CEDA, but he has moved steadily closer to Franco, and in 1965 received a cardinal's hat. If any Catholic can outmaneuver Gil Robles among Spain's Catholics, it is the Cardinal Bishop of Malaga. The rivalry will be interesting.

"Many members of the Church are convinced that what Spain needs . . . is a strong Catholic party backed by, but not identified with, the clergy," noted Paul Hofmann in *The New York Times* in mid-1963. Franco still bars all Demo-Christian political organizing, but he occasionally lets "safe" Catholics air demands for reform, as a safety valve.

Joaquín Ruiz-Giménez is an apt example. A former Education Minister and former Ambassador to the Vatican, this fifty-two-year-old liberal Catholic was named an official observer to the Second Ecumenical Council by Pope Paul VI. Many in Spain regard Ruiz-Giménez as a potential Demo-Christian prime minister of the future. Nevertheless, when, in 1964, he openly opposed Franco's new Law of Associations as overly restrictive, and announced his intention to resign from the Cortes in protest, he was summoned to Franco's office.

"I have no objection to your opposition activity, but I want it continued *inside* the Cortes," Franco told him. Then, cutting off all further discussion, the Caudillo blandly inquired, "How is your wife?"

THE SOCIALISTS. In a country that is 99.9 per cent Catholic, it might seem logical that after Franco the Demo-Christians would monopolize Spanish politics. Yet from every indication, Catholic Spain—like France, Italy, and Austria—will give birth to a powerful Socialist party: reformist, antimilitary, anticlerical, and certainly aimed at youth. The Socialists may rival the more populous but divided Demo-Christians, for after twenty-five years of Francoism, Spain is swinging left. The young Socialist leaders seem less demagogic and more technologically minded than their predecessors. Although they number perhaps 2,000 militants in the whole country, they continue to live a hound-and-hare existence, harassed by police and periodically jailed. Their minds, however, are less focused on subversion than on overhauling Spain's backward industries, her transportation system, and her agriculture; on reforming education, on nationalizing banks, and on producing a "great leap forward" without the cruelty of Stalin or of the Chinese Communists.

The danger facing the Socialists is, as always in Spain, fragmentation, for already there are at least three rival factions: (1)

doctrinaire Marxist, (2) economically Marxist but with democratic safeguards, and (3) old-style, horny-handed, anti-Communist trade unionist. Which of these three will win is hard to say. What seems most likely to emerge after Franco is something between the hair-shirt Socialism of British Labour in 1945 and the pin-stripe Socialism of Guy Mollet's France in 1955.

Spain's young Socialists claim that they reject dictatorship of either right or left. Their first aim, they say, will be to restore Spain's lost freedoms of the press, of political association, and of trade-union activity, and they contend that they want to cooperate with the free world; but whether they will favor the continued presence of U.S. military bases seems doubtful.

Socialism in Spain has passed through many mutations between its birth in 1879 and its apogee during the Civil War under the leadership of Largo Caballero, the ex-plasterer nicknamed the "Spanish Lenin." At the turn of the century, it was branded by the "haves" as an armed mob of "have-nots," bent on seizing private property and ready to bomb or shoot anyone in the way. At the time of World War I, Socialism had earned the army's loathing for opposing conscription; the Church's loathing for its anticlericalism; and the landowners' loathing for its designs on their lands.

As the "people's party" in 1931, the Socialists swept into power at the fall of the monarchy, lost to the right in 1933, and won parliamentary domination again just before the outbreak of the Civil War; but internecine quarrels with the Communists and Anarcho-Sindicalists, plus the confusion and incompetence of the Socialist leaders, soon tarnished the party's image. As the Civil War got under way, the Kremlin's growing hold over such Socialist bosses as Largo Caballero, Negrín, and Álvarez del Vayo became clear.

With the end of the civil conflict and the collapse of the Republic, the Socialist Party dissolved, its members fleeing abroad by the thousands or ending up in Franco's concentration camps and prisons. Between 1939 and 1951, the party palpitated ineffectively. Inexperienced, rudderless, hounded by Franco's police, the Socialists floundered. Yet somehow they went on. By 1951, new leaders were trying amateurishly to reconstruct a national network under Franco's nose and establish links with the "exterior" in Toulouse and Paris.

The risks were appalling. Seven times between 1951 and 1953, for instance, ferrets of Franco's Brigada Social y Politica penetrated the secret Comités Ejecutivos. Socialist leaders disappeared into jail, some never to be seen again. Tomas Centéño, a forty-year-old architect's draftsman, was arrested in 1953 and found under interrogation to be the general secretary of the illegal Socialist UGT. After third-degree questioning in the Dirección General de Seguridad, he died, and the police announced he had committed suicide with the steel bars taken from his bedsprings. Ex-prisoners, who know Dirección General de Seguridad cells well, claim that they never saw mattresses there, let alone beds with springs.

After Centéño's death, direction of the Socialist underground was shifted to a twelve-man directorate in France, two of whose members represented the "interior." (This "directorate" still exists in France, now with three delegates of the "interior.") Little by little, a new professionalism was beginning to replace the hit-or-miss methods of the past.

Between 1953 and 1958, the PSOE (Socialist Party) slowly rebuilt its organization inside Spain, recruiting mainly from two groups: young workers and students. This policy paid off, for as inflation soared and purchasing power fell, membership steadily rose. By 1956, the Socialists (and other opposition groups) were ready for two test operations.

The first was the Madrid University student riot of February, 1956, which marked a turning point in the history of the Spanish underground. Before this, the opposition had been defeatist, but as a result of the riots and the regime's hysterical reaction, it became suddenly clear that a new spirit of resistance was awaking among young Spaniards.

The second operation was a boycott of public transport—buses, subways, and tramways—carried out with moderate success in Barcelona in January, 1957, and once more in March, 1958. In each instance, foreign observers were struck by the sight of orderly masses of Barcelona metal and textile workers leaving home at five or six in the morning to walk to work, then trudging silently home again at the day's end. No violence took place. Not a bus was overturned, not a driver or conductor molested. Not even a stone was thrown, but the public demonstrated its feelings with silent, impressive unanimity.

Disaster again struck the Socialists, however, on November 6, 1958, when the police laid hands finally on Antonio Amat, chief Socialist organizer in Spain, whom they had long been hunting.

For months, the Socialist high command had known that police were on Amat's trail. Amat was a thirty-nine-year-old left-wing lawyer born into a wealthy family in Vitoria, capital of one of the Basque provinces. As one of the "interior" delegates to the Socialist leadership-in-exile, his duty had been to pass secretly in and out of France and to return with instructions. He had also served as a roving delegate inside Spain, using his legal practice as cover. His code name was Guridi and for months the police had been interrogating prisoners as to Guridi's identity.

How Amat was betrayed remains a secret, but some suspect that his growing prestige led to his betrayal by exiles unwilling to relinquish control. Whatever the facts, more than 500 suspected Socialists were arrested in one of the largest roundups ever conducted by Franco's police. Within a week, all but a hundred had been released. Fifty-six were brought to trial and of these, according to prime Socialist sources, only three or four were key leaders. Even their loss, though, dealt the party a blow.

Amat was not tortured, but he was severely interrogated. Lights were kept blazing in his eyes at night to prevent him from sleeping and weaken his resistance, but he was spared the beatings that had killed Centéño, possibly because of his family's influence and his membership in Spain's legal fraternity. Questioned for months on end, he was held in Burgos Prison without trial for two and a half years.

In the spring of 1961, he was quietly released and allowed to return to his home. His release is known to have been due largely to Solís, boss of the Falange and the Sindicates, who sees Socialism re-emerging and, like many Franco officials, is insuring himself against the day when Franco is gone.*

The 1958 arrest of Amat and the subsequent roundup of such Socialist leaders as Professor Juan Raventós of Barcelona University and Antonio Villar Masso, a young lawyer in the office of Antonio Garrigues (former Spanish Ambassador in Washington), had three serious effects. It frustrated plans for a series of nonviolent strikes in concert with militants of HOAC to demonstrate strength and test techniques. It wrecked the party's national network again. Finally, it torpedoed plans for a "common front" with other anti-Franco groups (excepting the Communists), for all contact between opposition blocs now perforce ceased, and the country lay quiet.

By January, 1959, the Socialists were again cautiously lifting their heads. Plans were resumed for a nationwide strike on July 18, the anniversary of the rising and Franco's national holiday, and all through the winter, meetings were held among the Socialists, Ridruejo's Partido Social de Acción Democratica, Cerón's left-wing Catholics of the Frente de Liberación Popular, and Giménez Fernández's Demo-Christian Left. The goal was to persuade the pleasure-loving Spanish masses to abstain from football, bullfights, and movies as a nonviolent but dramatic show of strength, and the holiday was chosen to deprive Franco of any excuse to arrest workers for "striking." This was to be a national gesture of reproof—but it was stillborn.

The Communists, hoping to profit if the strike succeeded, in-

* In February, 1964, eleven of thirty-three Socialists arrested during 1958 and later charged with reviving the illegal Socialist party and UGT were imprisoned or fined. The rest were acquitted. Amat was given the stiffest sentence—five years and a 50,000 peseta ($835) fine—although it was said that his time in jail would be taken into account.

sisted on joining in, but the common front broke up, frightened by the specter of Communist collaboration. First, Giménez Fernández' IDC pulled out, then the Socialists, and soon Franco's police knew everything. Regime propaganda now swung into action, warning the nation against "blindly" playing the Communist game, and police reinforcements were ostentatiously massed. July 18 came and went, and from one corner of Spain to the other, not a sign of protest could be seen. By the hundreds of thousands, Spaniards packed football games, bullfights, cinemas, and theaters, indifferent to—or ignorant of—the opposition's abortive ploy. The masses relaxed over bread and circuses and the regime boasted that national support had frustrated the "Communist" maneuverings.

In the last two years, Franco has shown signs of easing up on the Socialists—owing partly to foreign disapproval, partly to his desire to join the Common Market, for each Common Market country has a strong Socialist party. On November 3, 1962, for instance, *The New York Times* reported that a scheduled trial of fifty-four Socialist "lawyers, students, and other intellectuals" in Madrid would be postponed "indefinitely." This mildness, coming on the heels of the Cuban crisis, was attributed to the regime's desire to show "strength and confidence." Yet despite this recent tolerance, the Socialists are still far from being a cohesive party with recognized leadership and a clear program. Any overt sign of activity still brings Franco's police in on the run, and the Socialists are still deeply divided over such key points as whether or not to cooperate with the Communists in fighting Franco and what sort of government must follow him.

"We're *accidentalistas* about the monarchy," a young national leader said recently. "We don't care whether Spain is a monarchy or a republic, provided the Socialist party can function. We would prefer a republic, but we won't fight a monarchy if the people approve it by a referendum."

The nearest to a Socialist policy line in Spain was published in October, 1964, by Professor Enrique Tierno Galvan, instructor in law at Salamanca University and generally considered the chief Socialist theoretician. Tierno, though repeatedly harassed and fined by the regime, has refused to be silenced and his prestige with students and intellectuals is growing.

"The principle that popular sovereignty resides in the people is the basic principle of the Socialist party," he wrote in a leaflet entitled *Analysis of a Situation*. "The Spanish Socialist party accepts any form of government that is authentically democratic in origin and practice . . . democratically established, and that includes in its Constitution the principles and governmental institutions of a democratic country."

Were all Spaniards, or even all Spanish Socialists, agreed on the meaning of the word "democratic," there would be little to fear for the future of Spain. Even among the Socialists, however, there is a veritable spectrum of political opinion, ranging from those who regard the Communists as totalitarians worse even than Franco to those who regard them as patriots who must be enlisted in the common struggle to replace Franco with "democracy."

THE COMMUNISTS. "When we leave or enter Spain, we must go like smugglers through the Pyrenees," confessed a young Socialist organizer. "The Communists have false passports, airplane reservations, and even hotel rooms booked for them."

Making due allowance for hyperbole, an observer still can have no doubt that the Spanish Communist Party is the best organized opposition party in Spain. As one prominent opposition figure once told me, it is "the only movement with a true national organization of its own."

The current strength of the PCE (Partido Comunista Español) ranges somewhere between the 350,000 "adherents" estimated by a certain European intelligence service and the tally of a Spanish expert who numbers it at "between 2,000 and 5,000 hard-core members."

Regardless of its size, most observers would agree that the PCE has successfully penetrated both the Falange and the Sindicate leadership. Juan Antonio G. P., a top Falangist official in San Sebastián, and Enrique M. H., a prominent Basque lawyer with close regime contacts, for instance, were both recently discovered and arrested as senior Communist agents. There are also well-founded reports that the Church-backed HOAC itself recently uncovered a Communist high in its ranks—an alleged Catholic convert. In 1964, a Communist courier seized with incriminating documents and funds turned out to be the twenty-four-year-old son of Franco's Minister of Air, Lieutenant General José Lacalle Larraga.

Patience and burrowing are still the hallmarks of Communist technique in Spain, and the regime has repeatedly turned up agents who had been sent into Spain from abroad and told to lie low, blend into the background, and wait. In 1958, the French police uncovered one such agent visiting Paris. He had been sent to Spain in 1956, and told that he would not be needed until 1960 *at the earliest*. Once every year, he would report to a Metro station in Paris for orders, carrying in approved spy-thriller fashion a copy of *France-Soir* under his left arm. The French were not unduly surprised when his control turned out to be a woman officer of the Soviet Embassy.

Inside Spain, the growing migration of ill-paid agricultural workers to industrial areas—Madrid, Barcelona, and Bilbao—has been stimulating Communist recruitment, especially around Madrid. However, in the two other cities, the Communists are finding more competition. In Bilbao, the labor Sindicates still have a strong Basque Demo-Christian flavor; in Barcelona, they are dominated by Catalan Anarcho-Sindicalism. In Madrid, on the other hand, the labor Sindicates have shallower roots and the Communists have recently become so influential there that many regard Madrid's suburbs as Communism's chief bastion in Spain. The PCE also has members dotted throughout the land, of course.

"In one of our factories in northern Spain," confided a French manufacturer three years ago, "five of our nine senior workers were Communists. The police were aware of this, but these men were highly respected by the other workers and competent, so what could we do?"

Founded in 1921 by a motley collection of Anarchists and rebel Socialists, the PCE has pursued ever since a course as sinuous as a ferret's. Despite repeated setbacks, savage in-fighting, schisms, the crushing defeat of the Civil War, and Franco's persecution, the Party still hangs on, waiting for his death. Given popular revulsion against Communism as a result of the Civil War, there is little likelihood that the Communist Party can seize power at Franco's death.

On the other hand, should Franco's death leave a protracted power vacuum, should the generals and politicians prolong their squabbles, or should a king be enthroned and then fumble badly —in any one of those events, the Communists will increase their hold rapidly. The Spaniards, like their French and Italian cousins, are emotionally antigovernment, and with the demise of the old Anarchist movement in Spain, Communism will give millions of discontented Spaniards a vehicle for a protest vote.

A glance at the Party's history is revealing. In the 1920's, it was ignored by Moscow, absorbed in its own Stalin-Trotsky-Zinoviev power struggle, but even so, the mere suspicion of "foreign" direction made it repugnant to the xenophobic Spaniards. By 1931, its membership still hovered around 1,200. Stalin's gradual decision, however, that the PCE could help his projected *cordon sanitaire* around Hitler gave the Party its first real momentum, and by 1933 its membership had grown to 16,000. Now, under Moscow's guidance, it abandoned its old fire-breathing posturings for a more subtle, more successful popular-front approach, which attracted large numbers of militant Socialists, Anarchists, and Republicans.

By 1936, on the eve of the Civil War, the PCE could boast 30,000 members. In the Cortes, 16 out of 269 deputies were Communists—including the celebrated Dolores "La Pasionaria" Ibárruri, the Basque ex-sardine seller with what Hugh Thomas describes as the "grave but fanatical" face. Still active today in Moscow and Prague, La Pasionaria is still the official head of the PCE-in-exile and has lately been cultivating Fidel Castro on Moscow's behalf.

With the outbreak of the Civil War, Soviet arms, plus the Communist-led International Brigades, made the PCE the most powerful political force in the Republic. But with the Republican collapse of 1939, it dissolved. Its leaders fled to Moscow to be swallowed up behind the curtain of secrecy, and there they remained through World War II.

In 1944 and 1945, they moved west again, establishing themselves after Germany's collapse in Czechoslovakia and especially in France, where they operated with complete freedom, for this period marked De Gaulle's trial honeymoon with Moscow. In southern France, for example, the PCE attempted its first—and only—"direct" action against Franco, sending 3,000 Spanish Communist guerrillas, veterans of the Maquis, on an armed raid through the Valle de Aran in the Pyrenees. The raid was a disaster. The Communists were met by Spanish troops and by the Guardia Civil and slaughtered. For the next five years, until 1950, the Party reverted to subversion, espionage, and recruitment.

By 1950, the French Government had resumed normal diplomatic relations with Spain, and the outbreak of the Korean War had provoked widespread European distrust of Communism. The presence of Communist *agrupaciones de guerrilleros españoles* on French territory was increasingly embarrassing to Paris, and soon the PCE found its anti-Franco operations prohibited. Forced to go underground, it recalled its guerrillas from the border area, settled them around Toulouse, and began an exhaustive self-criticism. The outbreak of the Korean War had also aroused anti-Communist opinion in Spain and was reviving the international prestige of Franco, Europe's original "anti-Communist." There were signs, moreover, of U.S. interest in acquiring military bases in Spain, and from many points of view, the Communist leaders decided, a radical new approach was indicated.

After prolonged and often acerb discussion for a period lasting three years, a new "conciliatory" policy was gradually adopted, aimed at substituting for nonproductive violence a new technique of reconciling all anti-Franco forces, regardless of coloration. The signing of the U.S.–Spanish defense agreements in September, 1953, gave this new tactic a sharp spur, for the PCE calculated that Spanish public opinion would turn against Franco. The PCE was wrong. Franco, not for the first time, had gauged the national mood far better than the exiled Communists, and no such change occurred. The popular-front technique, which La Pasionaria had long advocated, nonetheless now replaced the pistol-packing tactics of earlier days. In August, 1956, it was adopted formally as Party policy at the Second Plenary meeting of the PCE's Central Committee under Dolores Ibárruri's leadership in Prague.

The Hungarian uprising in 1956 temporarily stalled the "reconciliation" tactic for many Spanish Communists and fellow travelers turned against Moscow, but it remained the Party line. During the Central Committee plenum in Prague (December 7–9, 1956), for instance, Vicente Sainz, a Committee member, called for national reconciliation plus increased recruiting among exiles in France for infiltration and propaganda work inside Spain. Sainz's plan was approved, training was stepped up, and by summer, 1957, roving Communist agents were once more penetrating as far as Madrid and even to southern Spanish cities. In time, their movements were detected by Franco's police, however, and it became apparent that key PCE leaders must now settle down in Spain and direct Party organization on the spot.

Since 1957, the PCE's emphasis has been on penetration of Franco's bureaucracy, particularly his labor Sindicates, youth, and intellectual circles. Even the Spanish police concede that the PCE has had considerable success.

According to trustworthy sources, the Communists have a

three-stage program. Stage A, the penetration stage, seeks to exploit the malaise among workers by electing Communist sympathizers to positions of responsibility in the Sindicates and Falange wherever possible. In 1961, Francisco Jiménez Torres, then deputy Sindical chief, conceded that at least 2,000 known Communists had been elected out of a total of 400,000 shop stewards during the national elections the previous year. Of all Spanish workers over forty (those with some recollection of pre-Franco Spain), he estimated that 60 per cent were probably still loyal to the Anarchist CNT, 30 per cent to the Socialist UGT, and the remaining 10 per cent to the Communist Party. The preferences of those workers under forty, however, no one could tell, he said.

Once the Communist leadership feels that Stage A has been sufficiently developed, the next steps involve Stage B, a merger of all discontented elements in Spain behind a "Day of National Reconciliation," and Stage C, mass demonstrations against Franco.

The Communists' national reconciliation policy has failed so far to attract other opposition groups, but in the process, one important development has taken place: the Communists have recognized that no one in Spain now wants violence. This is a cardinal political fact. "Violence is fatal to our hopes," a Communist sympathizer told me in Madrid. "Violence makes the Spaniards draw more closely around Franco."

Sensing the antiviolence mood current in Spain today, the Communists are bending every effort to soften their grim image and promote the national reconciliation line; they seek to lure other anti-Franco groups into alliance and eventually dominate the common front. The other groups, however, sense the apathy of the Spanish masses, their disinterest in politics, their preoccupation with security and comfort, the rise of an apolitical generation, and the taint that the word Communism still bears. The non-Communist opposition groups deeply mistrust the Communists.

In 1959, for instance, the Spanish Communists caught wind of a new united opposition approach to Don Juan. The plan was to secure in advance Don Juan's agreement to a two-year "take-over" government to take power after Franco and to be headed by General of the Air Force Infante Alfonso de Orléans y de Borbón, Don Juan's cousin. Don Juan flatly refused to bind himself in advance, but in the midst of the maneuverings, a courier from Dolores Ibárruri arrived at the home of a key opposition leader in southern Spain. La Pasionaria offered to broadcast over Moscow and Prague radio Communist recognition of the "legality" of the proposed provisional regime and even publicly to commit the Spanish Communist Party to abstain from violence during the succession—provided the Communists be allowed to participate. The Communist offer was refused; but it was typical of the PCE's determination to penetrate, dominate, or sabotage rival political combinations.

The Spanish Communist emphasis inside Spain is on nonviolence, yet two of Fidel Castro's chief sabotage, espionage, and subversion instructors in Cuba are Spanish Communists: Enrique Lister, who commanded the Republican V Corps during the Civil War, and Alberto Bayo, who led an unsuccessful Republican attack on Majorca. Among the twenty-four desperadoes, led by the Portuguese Henrique Galvao, who highjacked the Portuguese luxury liner "Santa María" in 1961, a half dozen were Spaniards, some of them known Communists. Galvao told Max Frankel, of *The New York Times,* in Recife, that the Spaniards in his Directorio Revolucionario Iberico de Liberación had demanded he sail to Spain's African colony Fernando Poo, to raise the anti-Franco flag before going on to "liberate" Portuguese Angola.

Franco has, in fact, long been so concerned with the possibility of a revolution in Portugal that on learning of the Galvao highjacking, he sent staff officers to Lisbon to confer with their Portuguese colleagues, and at Salazar's request sent the venerable cruiser "Canarias" scouring the south Atlantic on a wild-goose chase to find Galvao and his "pirate" crew.

"A revolution in Portugal would infect Spain in twenty-four hours," a Franco official conceded at the time.

THE HOUSE DIVIDED. In the past three years, the split between Moscow and Peking has riven the Spanish Communist Party into factions: pro-Soviet Russia, pro-Communist China, and even pro-Castro Cuba. A clandestine meeting of Communist leaders in Spain early in 1964, for example, ended in a violent dispute, and ever since, the Communist newssheet *Mundo Obrero* has violently attacked the pro-Moscow leadership of Dolores Ibárruri and Santiago Carrillo. The pro-Chinese wing had seized power.

One issue of *Mundo Obrero* printed a photograph of Grimau with the caption: "Who are the real murderers of Grimau? Who sent him, a 'marked' man, into Spain? Why? His comrades will unmask those responsible when the time comes!"

Another, dispensing the pro-Chinese line, complained bitterly. "For years, our party's directive from Moscow has been to 'keep silent and obey.' Nothing was gained by that. We lost the Civil War and have spent twenty-four years losing the postwar period against Franco."

The Communist paper contrasted the 1963 renewal of the U.S.–bases agreements plus growing foreign aid for Spain's Economic Development Plan with the impotence of the 1962 Asturian strikes. And it asked: "What interests does the present political leadership of the Spanish Communist Party serve? The Spanish revolution or the economic interests of the U.S.S.R.?"

It is possible, of course, that such issues of *Mundo Obrero* have been faked by Franco's police to further divide the Communists. Nonetheless, there is ample evidence that the Spanish Communists are quarreling, and this plays into Franco's hands. In June, 1964, his police rounded up at least a hundred men and women—some of them foreigners—belonging to what was officially described as a "vast clandestine organization of Communist ideology."

At the same time, Franco's relations with the Soviet Union are improving. For years, Moscow has been seeking a foothold in Spain. In 1958, Foreign Minister Castiella told me that he had had at least fifty approaches that year from Moscow for closer contacts, ranging from an exchange of soccer teams and dancers to bunkering facilities for Soviet whaling fleets in the Canary Islands. Spain's trade with the Iron Curtain countries has been slowly growing, and in Paris, at the start of 1964, Spain's astute envoy, José María Count Motrico and his Soviet colleague, the urbane Vinogradoff, attracted widespread attention by toasting the eventual resumption of Russo-Spanish diplomatic relations, terminated in 1936.

There is no likelihood that these ties will be resumed until Moscow ceases its subversion in Spain and returns 513 tons of gold sent to Russia by the Republican government in 1936. However, Moscow is dangling the gold under Spain's nose and has begun treating Franco more politely. It is not impossible that Moscow might quietly help Franco crush the pro-Peking "deviationist" Communists in the Peninsula, leaving long-range Madrid-Moscow relations for later.

Franco appears increasingly untroubled by the specter of Communism, which he has been brandishing before the Spanish people for a quarter of a century. In July, 1964, after two years of negotiations, the Spanish public was treated to the spectacle of a Soviet soccer team playing in the vast Bernabeu Stadium in Madrid. As Franco entered his box in a gray suit and homburg, a roar of approval rose from the crowd of a hundred thousand. In 1936, Franco's armies were fighting Communists; in 1964, his soccer stars were playing Communist athletes. In each case, Franco's team won.

"I've been waiting twenty-five years for the Communists to get here," muttered a left-wing Spanish fan, "and now all they do is play football!"

RADIO ESPAÑA INDEPENDIENTE. "We Socialists see more clearly than any other opposition group the steady growth of Communist

(Top) Joaquín Satrustegui, a lawyer, who is the founder of Unión Española and an *active opposition figure.* (*Bottom*) Dionisio Ridruejo, the organizer of the Partido Social de Acción Demócrata.

Cifra

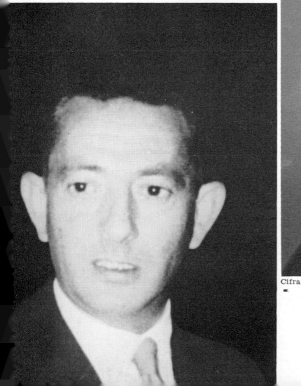

Cifra

Serrano

(Top) José María Gil Robles, a Madrid lawyer and former member of Don Juan's Consejo Privado del Rey, a leading opposition figure. (Bottom) Professor José Luis López Aranguren of Madrid University, a founder of the Movimiento de Reforma Universitaria.

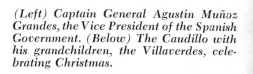

(Left) Captain General Agustín Muñoz Grandes, the Vice President of the Spanish Government. (Below) The Caudillo with his grandchildren, the Villaverdes, celebrating Christmas.

Cifra

Wide World Photos

(Left) Don Juan, Count of Barcelona, Pretender to the Spanish throne. (Below) Princess Sophie holding Princess Cristina and Prince Juan Carlos holding Princess Elena. The photograph was taken in June, 1965.

Jaime Pato

President Eisenhower takes leave of Generalissimo Franco with a hearty Spanish abrazo at the end of his December, 1959, visit to Spain.

influence on the workers. Much of it is due to the clandestine Communist Radio España Independiente, which the workers hear night after night." The speaker was a young Socialist organizer in Madrid.

In 1960–61, the Communist bloc was broadcasting a total of 116 hours weekly to Spain in Castilian and Catalan. Of this, Radio Moscow contributed 19¼ hours; the European satellites 36¼ hours; radio Peking 7 hours (Peking's output has since increased); and REI, the voice of the exiled PCE in Prague, the remaining 53½ hours.*

Each weekday morning, REI reaches Spanish homes between 7:00 and 7:30 A.M. and resumes with news, liberally larded with propaganda, from 5:30 until after midnight. On Sundays, there is a one-hour newscast from 1:30 to 2:30 P.M.

A sampling of typical REI programs in 1961, for example, showed a clear anti-American line, criticizing the U.S. bases and Spain's vulnerability to Soviet nuclear retaliation. Santiago Carillo, Secretary General of the PCE, broadcast from Prague to Spanish Army officers ("you who have suffered the stupid and arrogant ignorance of the Yankee commanders"), urging them to *"dialogar"* with Communism while time remained. The U.S. defense treaties had made Spain a "bridgehead" aimed at the U.S.S.R. and at Socialist countries, which "by legitimate right" would bomb the American bases in the event of war.

"Spain would be left partly destroyed and partly infected by radioactivity," continued La Pasionaria's deputy. "Isn't it preferable to talk now while there is still time? The bases could be *occupied* by the Spanish Army, the 1953 pact annulled, and U.S. soldiers and technicians evacuated *with all courtesy* [italics added]. If you don't do it," he warned the Spanish officer corps, "it will have to be done over your heads by the noncommissioned officers, the soldiers, and the people."

There is no evidence that Communist propaganda has had

---

* By contrast, the Voice of America, owing to budgetary cuts, ended broadcasting to Spain in late 1959. Even before this, however, VOA's appeal to the Spaniards had been negligible because of Washington's ban on all criticism of Franco—which, in contrast to REI, made it seem bland and pallid.

much effect on army officers or troops, but its influence on the nation's workers has been much greater. Day after day, the broadcasts continue, hammering implacably at the "bases" issue, and it would be unwise to underestimate the effect of propaganda, spiced with tidbits of news. Americans in their own country, swamped as they are by the deluge of words pouring daily from newspapers, radio, television, movies, books, magazines, and lecture halls, can scarcely realize what it means to live in a land where all news is officially slanted, where the truth circulates only by word of mouth, and then usually mixed with rumor. It is little wonder that even non-Communist Spaniards become REI listeners—if only to hear criticism of the regime.

During the Asturian strikes in 1962, REI amazed foreign newsmen with the speed and accuracy of its reporting. Thousands of "nonpolitical" Spaniards, indifferent to Communism, began listening to Communist broadcasts, thus absorbing the propaganda along with the news.

"Communist propaganda is bound in time to affect more and more Spanish workers," said an independent Spaniard. "Intellectuals can see that the United States supports Franco for strategic reasons. But the Spanish worker, at the end of the day, tired, underpaid, and discontented, neither understands nor wants to understand."

DIONISIO RIDRUEJO: L'ENFANT TERRIBLE. If any opposition figure in Spain knows the Communist strength, it is Dionisio Ridruejo, a rumpled, boyish-looking poet over fifty. Once a fanatic Falangist with all the ardor of his Castilian nature, Ridruejo is now Franco's bitterest critic. Once Franco's Director General of Propaganda and author of the Falangist hymn "Cara al Sol" ("Face to the Sun"), Ridruejo today is *the* disenchanted Falangist.

An early friend and disciple of the Falangist founder, José Antonio Primo de Rivera, Ridruejo's reformist zeal carried him high in the party. At twenty-three, he fought for Franco in the Civil War. Soon after José Antonio's execution, he became an

aide to Ramón Serrano Suñer. For many young Spaniards, this
was a period of political intoxication and Ridruejo grew slightly
addled on Hitler's theories.

By 1940, with the Civil War won and the Falange growing increasingly arrogant and corrupt, Ridruejo's disillusion began to
set in. The reforms so passionately envisaged by the little band of
original *Joséantonistas* were being cynically pigeonholed as the
grab for spoils progressed. Embittered and disgusted, Ridruejo
resigned his Falange appointments and, in 1941, volunteered for
the Blue Division then being recruited to join Hitler's armies
on the Russian front. "Many men found in volunteering to fight
in Russia a solution to vital conflicts caused by maladjustment to
everyday life," he later wrote.

One fellow volunteer now high in the regime recalls the night
the train bearing the Blue Division rolled north across the Bidas-
soa River into France. To a man, the Spaniards leaving their
country—some forever—knelt in silent prayer, but one voice
broke the silence. *"¡Qué muera Francia!* Death to France!" It
was Ridruejo. France lay defeated and half occupied, her name
tarnished and her power gone, but hatred for the "decadent"
democracy still welled in his heart.

On his return from the Blue Division in 1942, Ridruejo broke
openly with Franco and was banished first to an isolated Andalusian town, and later to a Catalan village, where he spent six
years under surveillance, writing poetry and nursing his disillu-
sionment. After his release in 1948, he moved to Rome. He returned to Spain in 1951, and continued his opposition with a
reckless disregard for his own safety. He helped mastermind the
student uprising at Madrid University in 1956, and in the following year began organizing his small intellectual splinter
group: Partido Social de Acción Demócrata.

He is the regime's most open, most implacable, but not necessarily most effective, foe. Franco and many officials remember
Ridruejo's early services and concede his moral integrity. They
grudgingly admire this thorn in their flesh, but he worries them

not. He is a firebrand, an idealist, and a publicist, dispensing anti-Franco interviews at home and abroad and accepting fines or brief jail sentences indifferently.

He slipped out of Spain in June, 1962, to attend the Munich meeting, characteristically defying the regime, which had confiscated his passport, and counting on highly placed ex-Blue Division friends to protect him. They either demurred or failed, and he remained in exile for two more years, alternating among Paris, Geneva, London, and Rome; writing and conspiring; boyish and engaging; invariably late for appointments.

In early 1964, after months of quiet negotiations had failed to get his passport returned, he decided to go back to Spain anyway, openly defying the authorities. A dramatist to his fingertips, he crossed the French-Spanish border in disguise in a car with Spanish friends, was quickly intercepted by a Spanish police patrol, driven to a mountainous area, dumped out, and obliged to walk several hours to the nearest French village. Many would have returned to Paris—but not Ridruejo. Reckoning that the Spanish police would now be relaxing, he slipped across the border once more, and turned up hours later in Madrid to surrender in—of all places—the home of his former Blue Division commander, Vice President Muñoz Grandes.

After a dressing down and several days in jail, he was freed under promise of good behavior. He is at liberty now; but if anything is certain in Spain, Ridruejo will spend his life conspiring openly against Franco—for such a nature is not repressible in jail or out.

Some months ago, I sat with him in his cluttered study in the calle Ibiza, discussing Spanish politics. The bookshelves were filled and the floors piled high with paperback copies of his prose and poetry, the works of other authors, newspapers, magazines, and half-finished articles. Down the hall, the telephone rang incessantly in the pantry, and every few minutes a timid maid would tiptoe in with messages. Smoking in chain fashion, running his fingers through his tousled brown hair, Ridruejo was undistracted, lucid, and blunt in evaluating the Communist strength in Spain.

"The PCE is expanding faster than any other party," he said. "In any future regime, they will have third place in the country —after the Demo-Christians and Socialists." They were persistently penetrating the Falange, the Sindicates, the cinema, the press, the arts, and trying—although not too successfully—to infiltrate the lower ranks of the army, the N.C.O.'s and soldiers, he admitted.

"Get a copy of the Falangist youth publication *Acento,*" he suggested. "It's 50 per cent pure Communist propaganda." Marxism was attracting Spain's university youth, he went on. In recent months, half the Party's recruits had been drawn from the sons and daughters of the *burguesia o alta burguesia*—the middle or upper middle classes. "Communist influence is increasing among the workers, too," he added. "Everyone knows what Communism is, its methods and aims, but few workers have any true idea about Socialism, still less about Christian Democracy."

THE ANARCHISTS. Anarchism, Spain's powerful working-class movement, which had 2 million members at the start of the century, now holds little appeal except for older workers. Among men who remember pre-Franco Spain—those of forty or older— 60 per cent are said still to cherish the banned Anarchist CNT as *their* trade union, but the young workers have little interest in such Anarchist shibboleths as the abolition of the state, of parliament, of the army and the police, and their replacement by a society based on "open discussion" among communities and trade groups. In the twentieth century, such ideas seem impractical nonsense, yet only thirty years ago, they appealed far more to the Spaniard's rebellious emotionalism than either Communism or Socialism.

Anarchism's birth, growth, and decline are all studded with violence. From the first congress of the Confederación Nacional de Trabajadores in Barcelona in 1881, the movement adopted

bomb-throwing and public outrages in a campaign to inter organized society and raise the curtain on the Anarchist millen-
nium. But even Spain wearied of bloodshed.

By the 1920's, the gradual "bourgeoisization" of the CNT
and its tendency to compromise with its rival, Socialism, led to
an inner split. A militant wing, the FAI (Federación Anarquista
Iberica) broke away in 1925, demanding more, not less, terrorism; or "propaganda by deed." That terrorism had always proved
counterproductive in Spain, had always provoked more violence
than obedience, troubled them not. During the Civil War, the
FAI was responsible for mass executions of suspected rivals—
Socialists and Communists included—in Republican territory,
and at the war's end, thousands of its gunmen fled to France,
settling around Toulouse, where many nourish dreams of revenge to this day.

In recent years, some have died, other have mellowed or
moved away, yet there are enough of the second generation,
brought up hating Franco, to provide recruits for amateur terror
missions into Spain. For this, they have formed their own organization, the FIJL (Federación Ibérica de Juventudes Liber-
tarias, or Federation of Libertarian Iberian Youth). Some recruits
are Spaniards born or reared in France; some are Algerian re-
patriates of Spanish origin; others are young French fanatics. In
1963, after a series of plastic bomb explosions in or near Spanish
tourist offices, Franco's police arrested two FIJL agents, Delgado
and Granados. They were tried and executed by the medieval
practice of garroting.

That autumn, at Spanish request, the French authorities
rounded up Spanish Anarchists in Paris and in the provinces,
after they had been making further attempts all summer to scare
tourists away from Spain by planting bombs in Spanish airline
and tourist offices.

Not all the ineffective current terrorism seems to be Anarchist, however. In June, 1964, Franco's Brigada Social seized one
Andres Ruiz Marqués, a forty-six-year-old ex-army officer who,

by using his uniform as cover, had successfully planted no fewer than sixty-eight small bombs in various public places of Madrid. Under the pseudonym "Colonel Montenegro," he had even sent pamphlets boasting of his coups to foreign diplomats and correspondents.

During his court-martial, it was brought out that he had been recruited at a recent Socialist congress in Toulouse by Julio Ávarez del Vayo, the veteran left-wing Socialist known during the Civil War as the "man of Moscow." According to the court, Álvarez del Vayo had organized, in early 1964, in Geneva, a Frente Española de Liberación Nacional to carry out sabotage against Franco and his regime in Spain. This network, said the prosecutor, was linked with another, styling itself the "Third Republic," based in Algiers under the patronage of Ben Bella. How effective was the Algiers group has not been stated, but it seemed evident that it was far-flung. One of its leaders, the prosecutor said, was Eduardo Ortega y Gasset, a kinsman of the late Republican intellectual, then living in exile in Venezuela.

The Munich Manifesto

The much-publicized 1962 Munich meeting gives an interesting insight into the opposition's idealism, techniques, and persistence—and why Franco has repeatedly outmaneuvered it. Munich has become a symbol of the futility of fighting Franco on foreign battlefields.

In June, 1962, Franco faced serious problems. The Asturian strikes, the Church's maneuverings, the hostile world press, the incompetence of the Sindical machinery, cabinet wrangling, and the loss of sleep because of an injured hand had taxed even the Caudillo's *sang-froid*. Rumors of his failing grip were spreading.

On Friday, June 8, during a cabinet meeting, Castiella was called to the long-distance phone. He returned, his face grim. Two hours earlier, 118 anti-regime Spaniards had issued a manifesto at Munich, calling on the Common Market countries to bar Spain's admission until democratic reforms had been introduced.

Castiella's news produced an uproar as ministers now vied with each other to demand punishment for the "traitors."

Of the 118 Spaniards who had met at Munich, 80 had come from Spain with passports obtained on a variety of pretexts; 38 were Socialist exiles living in France. The former group, Demo-Christians and Monarchists, was led by Gil Robles; the latter by Rodolfo Llopis, a former Republican Minister of Education. The cover for the meeting was a congress of the European Movement, a private body formed after World War II by Churchill, De Gasperi, Spaak, Léon Blum, and others, to promote European unity. Its Spanish representative was Franco's implacable foe, Salvador de Madariaga.

Madariaga was the mastermind behind the Munich rally. He had long refused to return to Spain despite several offers of amnesty. From Oxford, he had continued his long campaign to unseat Franco, using his international prestige and his post in the European Movement for the task. In Robert van Schendel, the Dutch Secretary General of the Movement, he had a firm ally.

Madariaga's plan to reconcile the quarreling elements of the anti-Franco opposition had taken years of patient negotiation, for the Catholic Gil Robles and the anticlerical Llopis had been bitter enemies. Yet Madariaga knew that if a solid anti-Franco front was ever to be formed, these two men had to subordinate their dislike. Franco's shotgun accident the previous Christmas had highlighted the need for haste.

After two years of persuasion, Gil Robles and Llopis had agreed to be "reconciled." To win world publicity, a suitable international forum now had to be found. The Fourth Congress of the European Movement scheduled to be held at Munich on June 7–8, 1962, seemed ideal. Its officials were drawn from the top political strata of their respective countries, and the slap at Franco would be world news.

By chance, some months earlier, Franco's police had seized plans for the meeting sent by the exiled Socialists in Paris to their colleagues in Mexico. The Paris group had urged its Mexican counterpart to back Madariaga's project.

The police coup had come about in an extraordinary way. A Mexican postman had handed a top-secret letter addressed to the Spanish exile organization to Franco's agent in Mexico City! Some said it was a mistake. Others detected the telltale glint of gold. Be that as it may, Franco and his police knew what Madariaga was planning. Nevertheless, they granted passports to Gil Robles, to Joaquín Satrustegui, chief of the liberal Monarchists, and to other opposition figures, and planted their police spies among the delegates.

By agreement among Gil Robles, Madariaga, and Llopis, neither Communists nor Anarchists were invited to Munich. The usual Spanish wrangling soon broke out, nonetheless. The Demo-Christians and Monarchists, for instance, refused to sit in the same room with the Socialists. Madariaga broke the deadlock by proposing that two non-ideological committees be created: Committee A under Gil Robles, Committee B under himself. This salved everyone's conscience, for the delegates now could join whichever committee they preferred.

The goal of the four-day meeting, held in Munich's Hotel Regina, was a petition to the European Movement from all democratic anti-Franco Spaniards, right and left, interior and exterior. Madariaga had agreed to moderate his bitterness and to persuade the other delegates to foreswear polemics, but a quarter century of enmity between the left and right was not easily overcome. The arguments were long and heated.

In Madrid, meanwhile, Castiella was trying to foil the activity in Munich. Hour after hour, by phone, he implored friends in Paris, Bonn, and elsewhere to block the expected anti-Franco resolution. The West German delegate, Von Merkatz, did his best to help. His efforts came near succeeding—infuriating Madariaga—but ultimately they failed.

After four days of impassioned discussion and maneuvering, the 118 Spaniards finally agreed on a draft. The hour was late;

it was already noon of June 8, and the resolution had to be presented before adjournment that afternoon. Just before the deadline, Madariaga handed it to his friend Van Schendel, administrative chief of the Congress. Then, as Maurice Faure of France presided over the closing session, Madariaga ascended the rostrum and proudly announced that Spanish delegates representing both the "interior" and "exterior" opposition to Franco were agreed that democracy should be restored in Spain before Franco's regime was accepted in the Common Market.

For Madariaga, this was a moment of triumph after two years of intense work. The resolution won international publicity. But it did nothing to weaken Franco. When Franco's axe finally fell, however, it fell not on Madariaga's neck, but on the necks of Gil Robles, of Dr. Jesús Prados Arrarte, of Satrustegui, and of many of the other eighty delegates who had returned to Spain.

The anti-Franco resolution was mild by any standards, but to Franco it was a public affront from Spaniards who had traveled on passports granted by the regime and who were "washing Spain's dirty linen" before all the world.

It urged:

1. "Authentically" representative and democratic institutions, and government based on the "consent of the governed."

2. All the rights of the human being, especially personal freedom and freedom of expression, and the lifting of censorship.

3. Recognition of the "personality" of different communities [e.g., Basques, Catalans, etc.].

4. Trade-union freedoms and the right to strike.

5. The organizing of currents of opinion, political parties, and "recognition of the rights of the opposition."

It declared that such an evolution would permit Spain's incorporation into Europe, and significantly concluded by asserting that the "immense" majority of Spaniards wanted democratic evolution carried out with "prudence" and would forgo all "active or passive violence before, during, and after the evolutive process."

This would hardly have caused a quickened pulse-beat in the European democracies, but when Castiella reported it to Franco's cabinet, the ministers exploded with a violence rare even in Spain.

The Falangist Arias Salgado gloated as he fumed, for he knew that Gil Robles was a member of Don Juan's council, and here was an excuse to attack the Monarchists. Army Minister Barroso and Public Works Minister Vigón (both Monarchists), fearing to be outflanked, outdid Arias in demanding punishment for the Munich "traitors." Solís, the Falange boss, needed a whipping boy after the strikes and he, too, joined the chorus. Conscious of Franco's cold stare, minister after minister outbid one another in lofty patriotism. Only Castiella sat silent. Cooler and more levelheaded than the rest, the Foreign Minister warned that reprisals would only publicize the Munich *manifiesto* to the world and add fuel to the flames. But he was drowned out.

"What do we care about the foreign press?" cried one angry minister. "It always blackens Spain anyway!"

In the evening of the following day, Saturday, June 9, a small, nervous man with a domelike forehead disembarked in Madrid at Barajas Airport. Spanish plainclothesmen standing unobtrusively on one side of the teeming arrival hall approached him, spoke a few words, and he followed them quietly to a side office. It was Gil Robles.

As the night wore on and more planes landed, other delegates returning to Spanish soil also found themselves taken into custody. Dr. Jesús Prados Arrarte, chief of economic studies at the powerful Banco Central, and the Monarchists Joaquín Satrustegui and Fernándo Álvarez de Miranda were arrested. Some of the returning minor fry were allowed to slip through to their homes, but the ringleaders were all seized. A few—notably Dionisio Ridruejo—prudently stayed out of Spain.

Gil Robles was held all night in a back room at Barajas Airport, protesting his patriotism. His arguments availed him nothing. Offered the choice of forced residence in the Canaries or foreign exile, he chose exile. Someone brought him a toothbrush and a suitcase with clothes, and when daylight came, he was marched to the first aircraft departing for Paris. Dr. Prados Arrarte was given the same choice. Prados had already spent seventeen years of his life in self-imposed exile in South America but he, too, chose exile again.

Others opted for the Canary Islands. Satrustegui and Alvarez de Miranda, accompanied by plainclothesmen, sat out the five-hour flight to the Canaries amidst holiday-bound passengers carrying spear guns and snorkel gear, who probably never noticed the grim-faced men in the rear of the plane.

Now the Falange press obediently exploded in denunciations of the "traitors." With Arias Salgado holding down the throttle, the newspapers, radio, and television shrieked "treason." Don Juan's haughty Consejo Privado met, re-met, wringing its hands and wondering what to do. Don Juan had been on his yacht returning from his son's wedding in Greece at the time of the Munich affair and had known nothing about it, yet he was being blamed by the Falangists.

Soon Gil Robles had become the Monarchists' prime whipping boy. The grandees, the landowners, and the wealthy distrusted Gil Robles. He was no aristocrat; he was even suspected of favoring liberal reforms. Angry and scared, the Carlists tore into Gil Robles. Demands arose for his expulsion from the forty-three-member Consejo Privado del Rey. Gil Robles, they thundered, had "betrayed" Spain and the Monarchist cause by his role at Munich.

As the storm raged, two Monarchist emissaries drove to Cartagena to brief Don Juan, who had by now touched in on his yacht for supplies while en route home to Portugal. They reported the mounting Monarchist demand for Gil Robles' head. Don Juan sighed: another schism was looming. But there was no alternative. On June 17, Gil Robles' resignation lay on Don

Juan's desk at Estoril. Don Juan's most militant advisor had, through his own scheming, been forced out.

As if the Munich affair were not enough to plague Franco, a few small bombs now exploded harmlessly in Madrid. No culprits were seized, but this time Arias Salgado pinned responsibility on the left-wing Frente de Liberación Popular. FLP members had also attended the Munich meeting.

Franco now decided on a triumphal tour to dissipate rumors of his ill health and failing grasp. He would use Munich to promote national enthusiasm—and the Black Legend of foreign hostility would come in handy.

The tour revived him. As he gazed down into a sea of 50,000 shouting, enthusiastic faces in the central square of Valencia on this June 16, 1962, his spirits began to rise. In the crowd were thousands of young workers in overalls with their fresh-faced wives and their black-eyed children, most of them carrying tiny Spanish flags. Under the balcony at the ornate *Ayuntamiento* (City Hall) were massed Falangist militia veterans, recognizable by their blue shirts and hard-faced authority. The crowds shoved good-naturedly as a line of gleaming Rolls Royces drove up and aides rushed about, helping Franco and his suite, including Doña Carmen, her ladies-in-waiting, and several cabinet wives, emerge. Up the marble staircase they moved, royally, graciously, while cameramen ran around them and radio announcers chattered into microphones. In their midst, imperturbable, smiling gently, was the small figure of Franco.

Then he appeared on the balcony and the crowd roared. Modestly he waved his hand. Gradually, the noise died down.

"Spaniards," he began in his high, lisping, rapid voice. "I would like the foreigners to see you here! When they ask where are my legitimate powers—here are my powers!"

The old political craftsman had plucked exactly the right chord and the roars went up again. Give it to them, General! To hell with the foreigners! To hell with the Munich traitors! Tell them, General, tell them! In the dense throng, Falangist militants began the familiar chant, "Fran-CO! Fran-CO! Fran-CO!!!"

He had them in his hands now. The foreign press came in for the usual sarcasm. "The freedom of the press is already a myth, passing into history," proclaimed the Caudillo, who has proved it so in Spain, at least. "The press is controlled by a few millionaires in each country."

The cheers echoed and re-echoed as they would for the months to come, wherever Franco went. By imperturbability, by shrewd manipulations, by defying "foreign" bogeys, Franco had won again. The opposition was silenced. Spain fell back into its comfortable obedience.

The Black Legend

Yellow and red are the colors of Spain, and they are appropriate.

The yellow calls to mind the gold of the Incas, the midsummer heat of Andalusia, the bright beaches of Benidorm, the molten passion of the gypsies dancing at the *ferias* of Seville. Yellow is the sunlight of Spain.

The red stands for courage: the blood-red that seeps from the torn neck muscles of the bull as he stands, wounded, panting, preparing to charge and charge again and die charging. Red is the violence of Spain.

Yellow and red make up the flag, but somehow, black should have been added, for no color more truly symbolizes Spain. Black is death, and death is at home in Spain. It may be the heritage of Arab fatalism after seven hundred years of occupation, but whatever the reason, the Spanish appear to fear death less than any Western people.

No traveler in the cities, towns, or little country *aldeas*, can miss the prevalence of black: the women in mourning who wear black year after year as a status symbol, the priests, the nuns, the somber bourgeois businessmen and bankers. In recent years, as conditions have begun to improve, color has been creeping back into the dress of the people, especially of the young, but black still predominates.

From the recesses of their history, the Spanish have fashioned their Black Legend, or *Leyenda Negra,* which imputes to a hostile world the responsibility for Spain's long troubles and decline: Spain's enemies, motivated by envy, malice, or miscomprehension, have created such a myth about Spanish fanaticism, cruelty, and inefficiency that it has come to be accepted abroad as gospel. If, therefore, there still lingers dislike of Franco beyond the Pyrenees, it proves the validity of this Black Legend. It is not Franco's fault but the foreigners'.

In olden times, so runs this convenient saga, it was the Elizabethan English, together with Spain's heretical Dutch subjects, who first caricatured Spain as a warren of brutal *conquistadores,* a dungeon of Catholic persecution, a land peopled solely by an illiterate nobility, a scheming clergy, and a starving peasantry. In later centuries, the Black Legend continues, fresh enemies have added their smears: the eighteenth-century French Encyclopedists; American colonists hungry for Spanish Florida and Louisiana; nineteenth-century liberals; Freemasons; Socialists; Jews; Protestants; and now—the Communists. All without exception have traduced Spain for ulterior motives, Spaniards insist.

This deep xenophobia is more than merely a national idiosyncrasy. Franco has turned it into a powerful political asset. It has saved him again and again, for by drawing around Spain an imaginary circle in the sand with his sword and proclaiming that all outside the ring are enemies, he has retained power since 1936. This portrait of a fortress under siege, a beleaguered redoubt, an *alcázar,* has held Spain together. The chief enemy has been Communism; if Communism had not existed, Franco would have had to invent it.

"We were the first European nation to fight Communism— and to win!" is Franco's proudest boast. It has been the doctrine and philosophy of his regime, its defiant self-justification. "The nation expressed its will by arms," say Franco's aides. "Spain ral-

lied to Franco and he led it to victory, but the enemy has only
been routed, not destroyed. Communism is still trying to creep
back in through the Demo-Christians, the Republicans, and the
Socialists; through Catholic Workers' Brotherhoods, through
films, books, reviews, through the press and radio." Spain is still
"mobilized" against Communism, they add. How can the Americans, the British, the Italians, the French continue to criticize
Franco when he is the original anti-Communist?

Whose economy, they ask, was wrecked and whose gold reserve
shipped to Russia by Communists? Which European nation outmaneuvered Hitler and defied the Wehrmacht to cross its territory? Which West European nation was cut off from U.S. trade
and aid after the war despite its anti-Communist record? To
whom did the United States turn when the Korean War broke
out and Europe's defenses were nil? The answer in each case is—
Spain.

These arguments—call them emotional or call them valid—are
basic to any discussion of Spanish foreign policy. Franco has
never conceded the least guilt about his wartime ties with Hitler
and Mussolini; or about his vague pledges to join the war against
Britain, to seize Gibraltar and grab French Morocco. Franco
epitomizes Talleyrand's adage: "Treason is a question of dates."

"It is not Spain that has shifted," he often tells his people.
"Spain has remained firm. It is the West that is coming to meet
us."

Whatever the truth in this claim, dislike of Franco is still
widely felt in Western democracies. It is chiefly emotional and
thus hard to combat because, except for liberal intellectuals or
fanatic leftists, few in the West know precisely why they dislike
Franco. Probably it is because Franco never plays up to foreign
opinion, never travels, detests Western-style democracy—and
openly says so. One could see Khrushchev in shirt sleeves and a
Panama hat, eating a hot dog and roaring with delight at an
American baseball game, but not Franco. Franco—short, pomp-
ous, and stiff—offends American egalitarianism.

David Low, the great British cartoonist, used to limn Franco as a ridiculous jack-in-the-box, his overseas cap tassel dangling over his Roman nose, his eyes and paunch bulging, yet the image was unfair. When relaxed, Franco is singularly attractive. The boredom of his many years in power sloughs off when he makes contact with a new visitor: the face relaxes, the reserve melts, the eyes—keen and penetrating—grow warm. Smiles, even laughter follow. But as the visit ends, one can see the mask being put on again. Franco can doff, but never discard, the chain mail.

Two qualities set Franco apart—patience and realism. Unlike most Spaniards, he says little, but watches, waits, and swings with the tide. And the hobgoblin of consistency seldom troubles him. For instance, in 1944, as World War II was drawing to a close, he coolly proposed to Churchill an alliance against the U.S.S.R.

"After [Europe's] terrific travail," he wrote, "those who have shown themselves strong and virile . . . [and] great in population and resources are England, Spain, and Germany. But once Germany is destroyed, England will have only one country left in Europe toward which she can turn her eyes—Spain. Once Russia has consolidated her [power] in Europe and Asia and once the United States has consolidated her position in the Atlantic and Pacific, thus becoming the most powerful nation in the universe, European interests will suffer their most dangerous crisis." His words have a curiously prophetic ring, given De Gaulle's current thesis.

Franco's offer was rejected, as he must have expected from Churchill, but he was no whit discomfited. He knew that in time the West vs. East rupture would ensue, and his chief task was to hold out until it did. It was to take six years until the Korean War proved him right.

After V-J Day, when the Allies turned on him, Franco rallied Spain as he might have rallied a beleaguered Spanish Foreign Legion garrison in the Rif Mountains. Iron discipline and propaganda were his tools. The enemy's campfires surround us, he proclaimed; any weakness will be punished, all dissent must be silenced, help is coming. His toughness succeeded. Those inside

Spain who loathed Franco had no force to expel him, and the contemptuous platitudes emanating from Western chancelleries did little to help them.

Day by day, Franco's counterpropaganda continued, and year by year his predictions of an East-West split were borne out. By 1950, the North Korean attack had altered world history, and, by 1951, a U.S. emissary, Admiral Forrest Sherman, had clasped hands with Franco, foreshadowing the defense agreements of 1953. In 1953, Franco also won from the Vatican a new Concordat and was voted into UNESCO, a prelude to full membership in the U.N. itself two years later.

The pariah of 1945 had come a long way through guile, patience, and realism.

Underlying Franco's devious foreign policy is a morbid craving for respectability. No statesman in modern times has been more universally condemned—by Communists and non-Communists alike—and Franco is weary of censure. So are his people. This wounded pride has helped bind the Caudillo and the Spaniards together; for even when the clouds were darkest, Franco's refusal to bow to foreign pressures, whether from Stalin, Hitler, Roosevelt, or Truman, gave the Spaniards the boost they needed. They might grumble about dictatorship at home—but at least it was Spanish dictatorship. All supported Franco's defiance of dictation from abroad.

The best way to follow Franco's zigzag foreign policy is to link successive incidents like so many beads onto a string. The beads may vary in color and value but the string remains the same: Franco's determination to boost Spain's name and role in world affairs. He flirted with Hitler and Mussolini; he congratulated Japan's Admiral Tojo on the aftermath of Pearl Harbor; he berated Churchill throughout the war, then offered him an anti-Soviet alliance; he reviled Truman, then later accepted Truman's aid—he will sup with the devil himself if it will help Spain. Every move is calculated.

In his postwar "wilderness" years, Franco cultivated the Arabs, citing Spain's role as a bridge between Christianity and Islam, which flattered both sides and, in 1955, brought Spain the Arab votes to back her membership in the U.N. Likewise, he has sought friendly ties with the Latin Americans, in part for their U.N. votes, but mainly to furnish Spain a wider forum for activity. Friendship with Portugal has been held aloft as the third pillar of Franco's foreign policy, not only because Portugal is Spain's Iberian ally, but because Salazar is Franco's closest ideological crony. The two Catholic dictators rule their lands in basically the same way.

Spain's current economic comeback has boosted her out of the Arab, Latin American, and Portuguese orbits into more rewarding ties with the United States and Western Europe. Washington is now Franco's chief defense partner and arms supplier. Western Europe's doctrinaire hostility to Franco is dying, and the Common Market countries, plus Britain, have become Spain's chief trading partners. Even the lure of increased trade with the Iron Curtain countries now flickers fitfully at the end of a long tunnel. Franco has played his cards shrewdly.

Often he engages in what appear to be petulant disputes with his neighbors, but underneath there is a coldly realistic purpose. Gibraltar is a case in point.

Gibraltar

Gibraltar is not a necessity to Spain—strategic, economic, or political. It is a *banderilla:* it goads Spain's pride. It was wrenched from Spain originally in 711 by Tariq,* the advance man for the Arab occupation, and it has been rewon and lost repeatedly through the centuries. In 1704, it was seized by an Anglo-Dutch fleet led by the British Admiral Rooke; and although the Spanish tried to recapture it in 1705, in 1762, and during a four-year siege (1789–93), the Union Jack still flies over the "Rock." This, of course, gives Franco a splendid publicity issue.

Franco repeatedly foiled Hitler's plans to seize Gibraltar dur-

* Hence, Jebel-al-Tariq, Mount of Tariq, or Gibraltar.

234

ing World War II; after the war, the Gibraltar issue lay dormant until 1950, when a visit by Prince Philip, Duke of Edinburgh, highlighted the British Government's long-range plan to make Gibraltar self-governing. The Spanish immediately saw that a "free" Gibraltar would never willingly return to Spain. With each succeeding grant of self-rule by London, the Spanish choler has grown. Britain has no "right" to give the Gibraltarians self-rule, says Madrid: In the 1713 Treaty of Utrecht, Spain ceded to England only the "military use" of Gibraltar and not "sovereignty." If the British relinquish control, the Spanish have first option to fill the vacuum.

The tension over Gibraltar rose to a new pitch during the visit of Queen Elizabeth II at the end of her world tour in 1954. Franco had nothing, personally, against the young monarch who had ascended the throne the year before and for whom he felt a characteristically Spanish chivalry, but her visit seemed a deliberate act of defiance by her government.

On Franco's orders, the Falange pulled out all the stops. The British "rape" of Gibraltar in 1704 was recalled in flamboyant detail and Spain's historians heaped coals of fire on "perfidious Albion." The forays of Morgan and other pirates against Spain's treasure galleons, even Henry VIII's treatment of Catherine of Aragon were all evoked. Gibraltar was held up as an example of British perfidy, and when the royal visit ended, Franco forbade Spaniards to visit Gibraltar.* The ban persists to this day and Spain periodically revives its claims to Gibraltar in the U.N.

The tiny British colony covers two and a half acres. It has a permanent population of 25,000, most of whom are of Italian, Maltese, or Moroccan descent, plus a sprinkling of Mediterranean Jews and 200 Pakistanis with British passports. Legally, Gibraltar is a Crown Colony, under the Colonial Office. However, it elects its own ruling Legislative Council, although the

---

* Because of Spain's need for sterling, however, he has never prevented 10,000 Spanish workers from entering Gibraltar every morning to work, returning to Spain each night.

Governor, usually a retired general, retains veto power over finance, defense, and foreign relations (for example, with Spain). Great Britain spends about £5 million yearly to maintain the naval shipyards and military forces on the "Rock," and this guarantees the colony's economy.

"If Her Majesty's Government ever stopped its defense spending, we would go broke," a prominent Gibraltarian told me not long ago. The sun was setting over the mountains beyond Algeciras, across the bay in Spain, as we sat talking on the terrace of the famous old Rock Hotel. Below us, in Gibraltar Harbor, Royal Navy warships lay at anchor close to Soviet tankers and whaling ships en route between the Black Sea and the South Atlantic, and my friend told me that every day of the year one or more Soviet ships enter or leave Gibraltar. Slowly, as night fell, locally owned launches, painted gray-black and lying low in the water, began nosing out into the Strait on their smuggling adventures.

"Smuggling probably nets up to $3 million a year," said my friend. "Most of it consists of Japanese transistor radios, watches, cigarettes—things that are light and easy to handle. Once outside of Gibraltar, they're out of our jurisdiction. They rendezvous in the Mediterranean at night and offload onto other ships. It is fantastically well organized. Now and then, a boat is seized by Spanish Customs but never before it has returned at least 300 per cent profit on the original investment."

"Don't the Spanish ever get tough?" I asked.

"They're in it up to their necks!" he laughed. "Nobody loses except when some outsider tries to muscle in—or welches on a deal. Then there's trouble, shooting and all that, but Spain doesn't really care. The government leases the monopoly of tobacco to some millionaire, and it's up to him to worry about illegal competition."*

* Spanish sources say that during the past four years, the Spanish Customs have captured forty smugglers' launches operating from Gibraltar, while another twenty have been seized by France, Italy, Algeria, and Morocco. In December, 1964, they say, British warships closed in to protect two launches that were chased back to Gibraltar by Spanish coast-guard ships.

Gibraltar's lucrative smuggling appears doomed, however, for the western Mediterranean is prosperous, and demand for smuggled cigarettes, watches, and transistor radios is declining as such items become available from Cádiz to Sardinia—and especially in Morocco, Algeria, and Tunisia. The requisite payoff to police and Customs guards, to fences, boatmen, truckers, tipsters, and bodyguards, moreover, sharply cuts profits.

Franco holds a club over Gibraltar: Spanish labor. The colony's ship repair yards and construction industry need manpower, and Spain can best provide it. On the other hand, the 8,000 to 9,000 Spanish day laborers earn an average of £7 weekly —almost as much as a Spanish civil servant earns in a month—and Franco profits by letting them retain one-fifth of their pay in sterling while taking the remaining four-fifths in exchange for pesetas. Gibraltar thus is a vital source of foreign currency for Franco. It also benefits the local Spanish population. The local Spanish Customs guards do not seriously impede returning Spanish workers from bringing back under their shirts, pants, or blouses, cigarettes, small radios, and other luxuries, which sell for high prices along the tourist-thronged coast of Marbella, Torremolinos, and Malaga.

"Spain gets about £3 million ($8.4 million) in foreign currency from Gibraltar every year," said one Gibraltar official. "Franco is too shrewd to kill the goose that lays so many eggs."

Gibraltar also has a political nuisance-value for Spain. Franco's perennial claims at the U.N., which stress that Gibraltar is Europe's "last colony," bring him some sympathy from the Afro-Asian bloc. They divert anticolonialist attention from Franco's own tiny African territories and give him the satisfaction of swimming with a major U.N. faction.

One day, when Franco is gone, Spain will probably be admitted to NATO, or to its successor, and Gibraltar may become a condominium flying the British, Spanish, and NATO flags. This will salve Spain's pride, without forcing the 25,000 non-Spanish Gibraltarians to pass under Spanish rule. Sir Joshua Hassan, the elected Mayor of Gibraltar, warned the U.N. Special

Committee on Colonialism in September, 1964, that his fellow citizens wanted friendly relations with Spain but insisted on retaining their British citizenship, their autonomy, their own laws, their religious freedoms, and their lucrative trade.

With the decline of Tangier since Moroccan independence, Gibraltar is booming. Thousands of tourists fly from England to Gibraltar every summer, fanning out along the southern Spanish coast, and neither the British nor the Gibraltarians want to jeopardize this rich traffic. The Spanish, however, are quixotic. Their own tourism is growing so fast that they can afford to throttle Gibraltar. Moreover, this is an easy answer to the doctrinaire hostility of Harold Wilson's Labour Government.

Young Gibraltar businessmen are beginning to realize that their economy can never flourish in the face of Spanish hostility, and discreet soundings are already being made in Madrid and elsewhere. Some day, a formula for friendly coexistence will have to be found, for, as Franco quipped in 1958: "Gibraltar is not worth a war. It is a rotten fruit that will fall sooner or later."

Morocco

Since Morocco's independence in 1956, Spain has been slightly embarrassed about her claims to Gibraltar—and for a reason. On Morocco's Mediterranean coast lie two Spanish "Gibraltars": the city-states, or *presidios*, of Melilla and Ceuta, which have belonged to Spain since 1497 and 1580, respectively. Each city consists of one or two acres of land inhabited by 60,000 to 80,000 Spaniards and a permanent Moorish population of 3,000 to 4,000. Both *presidios* are armed garrisons into which the Spanish have withdrawn what remains of the 100,000-man army that once garrisoned the old Spanish protectorate during and after World War II. Ceuta is self-sufficient, but Melilla's water supply lies in Moroccan territory in the hills above the city, an easy target in event of trouble.

At present, relations are improving, but Spain and Morocco have a long history of conflict. Most recently, in the winter of

1957–58, they came to blows over Ifni, a little-known pocket of Spanish sovereignty on Morocco's Atlantic coast, which Morocco tried to snatch.

As early as 1860, Spain won from the Sultan of Morocco the right to Ifni as a fishing port "in perpetuity," and in 1934, the Spanish Republican Government chose Ifni as a convenient exile for right-wing political prisoners, thus rousing the hamlet from its sleep. Slowly the town grew, until today it has about 4,000 inhabitants, including Spanish fishermen, traders, and the army garrison. Another 8,000 Moorish nomads live in the surrounding desert. Sidi Ifni, the provincial seat, lies along the Atlantic beaches, and all around it, scrub stretches over parched rolling land.

Moroccan independence began to alter Ifni's peaceful rhythm. In the summer of 1957, Morocco's Foreign Minister, Ahmed Balafrej, began pressure on Spain for its return. The Moroccans believed that Spain was decadent and in no position to hold out, but the Spanish dug their heels in. Castiella met Balafrej at Tangier on September 15, 1957, for a series of inconclusive talks. Tension steadily grew. Franco, meanwhile, had begun receiving French intelligence reports that indicated that a thousand armed Moorish "irregulars" had already started filtering south from Tangier through the former French zone into southern Morocco near Ifni.

These reports marked a new turn in Spanish-French relations. Rivals in Africa for centuries, the French and Spanish only began their cautious *rapprochement* after surrendering their respective protectorates. It seemed obvious to each that Morocco would try to play one off against the other, and that, therefore, cooperation was essential to protect their substantial commercial investments and European populations. France, in 1957, still had a colony of 250,000 civilians plus military air bases in Morocco; Spain, 100,000 civilians and 60,000 troops.

Ironically, the Moorish "irregulars" gathering around Ifni were the remnant of a 3,000-man force armed and trained by

Lieutenant General Rafael García-Valiño, former High Commissioner, to harass the French; 2,000 of them had been incorporated into the new Royal Moroccan Army, but the remaining 1,000—dregs of the cities—had been bribed by Moroccan politicians to work their way south, where they were promised fighting and looting at Spain's expense.

The French reports of guerrilla movements began to alarm Franco's generals, who now urged a punitive raid from Villa Cisneros, the Spanish base in the southern Sahara, to scatter the Moors before they could attack Ifni. Franco, however, procrastinated.

He, too, had spent long years in Morocco and knew the Arab respect for force. Yet his much-touted Arab policy was at stake. Arab votes had won Franco a seat in the United Nations, and Arab friendship gave Spain a new prestige. Furthermore, he had continued to back King Mohamed V after the French had exiled that independence-minded Moroccan sovereign to Madagascar in 1953. Mohamed V was now back on the throne and at that moment on a goodwill visit to Washington. Franco wanted neither the censure of the United States, which was supplying him arms, nor of the Arab League. He hesitated—permitting his general staff to draw up plans but no more—and suddenly the Moorish irregulars struck at sleepy Ifni. The date was November 23, 1957, the time 5:00 A.M. The Moors had calculated that the Spanish would be off guard—and they were right.

Despite the presence of 1,500 Spanish troops in Sidi Ifni itself, the "Moroccan Liberation Army," led by a local bravo named Ben Hammun, penetrated the barbed-wire defenses, stole past the Spanish sentries, and came within an ace of seizing an important arms dump on the beach. At the last moment, they were detected and beaten off, but meanwhile, all along the perimeters of the territory, Spanish outposts were falling, one after the other. Within hours, a large Moroccan force was besieging Sidi Ifni itself.

As the first reports reached Spain, Franco's Minister of Infor-

mation and Tourism, Arias Salgado, slapped an immediate censorship on the news, and slowly confusion grew. For three weeks,
the Spanish people and the world outside received its news of the
Ifni clash exclusively from Rabat. Understandably, the news was
100 per cent pro-Moroccan.

Franco, who had been touring northern Spain when the attack
occurred, hurried back to Madrid, and soon his very presence
restored calm. Troop reinforcements were ordered from Andalusia and from the Canaries to beleaguered Ifni. Old Junkers and
Heinkel bombers and World War II Messerschmitt fighters were
pressed into service, and eventually began cruising the bright
sky over the African enclave to seek out attacking Moorish bands
in the desert scrub. A severe storm broke, and for five days no
supply planes could land, but the 1912 cruiser "Canarias" somehow managed to land 5,000 troops in the breakers, whence they
struggled onto the beaches. Despite Spain's occupancy of Ifni for
ninety-seven years, there was no pier or dock. Ammunition,
medical supplies, and food had to be ferried in whaleboats
through rolling breakers and lugged up the beaches on the backs
of native laborers or Spanish soldiers.*

Rabat radio continued day after day to denounce Spain for
bombing its "defenseless civilians," as the Spanish began sending
paratroop patrols from Sidi Ifni by foot to relieve the outlying
garrisons. At last, tales of heroic exploits began to appear in the
Spanish press, for even Arias Salgado could no longer pretend
that nothing was happening. Spain's Army Minister Barroso and
the army generals were smarting, indignant over the attack, over
Franco's procrastination, and especially over widespread criticism
of the Army's unreadiness.

After intense army pressure, Franco agreed to let three foreign
newspaper correspondents fly to Ifni. Two—Eric Ollivier of
Figaro and Gilbert Graziani of *Paris Match*—were French, for
Franco wanted French support in Morocco, and the third was an

---

* A pier has since been built of hollow concrete blocks towed individually from
the Canary Islands, 200 miles away.

American: myself. No Spanish reporters were allowed into Ifni, however, for weeks.

Within seven days—by December 1, 1957—the Moroccan irregulars had been driven off, and the Spanish Army, on Franco's orders, began abandoning the province's 1,200 square miles of scrub, pulling back into a tight little perimeter around the seaside village of Sidi Ifni itself. Gradually, as world attention began to focus on Ifni, Rabat realized that its gamble had failed. Soon it began protesting its innocence. No longer was the attack hailed as a "patriotic" movement against Spanish colonialism. Rabat now disavowed the "Liberation Army." King Mohamed V hurried home from Washington and the embarrassed Crown Prince Muley Hassan, Commander in Chief of the Moroccan Army in his father's absence, put out peace feelers to the Spanish Ambassador. Gradually, the "irregulars" withdrew from Spanish soil.

Any doubts as to Rabat's complicity were dispelled by a series of colorful dispatches from Thomas F. Brady of *The New York Times,* who had spent ten days with the "unofficial" Moroccan advisers accompanying the "Liberation" forces.

As a stalemate set in, Franco crowded 8,000 troops into the fishing port. Artillery pieces sat atop the surrounding heights, black-bereted paratroops patrolled the streets, Spanish Messerschmitts cruised the skies, and the yellow-plaster officer's casino rang with gaiety and laughter, as Spanish Foreign Legion officers with shiny black boots, spurs, and swagger sticks joked and drank with comrades from the Ifni *Tiradores* (Rifles) in red fezzes. The fighting was over and there was nothing to do now but drink and chat, bathe in the sea, or, in the evenings, visit the dark-eyed damsels imported by a solicitous Army Quartermaster Corps from the Canaries for the troops' nonspiritual needs.

Meanwhile, in Madrid's Army Ministry, a former palace of the Dukes of Alba, young staff officers tiptoed busily, papers in hand, over luxurious carpets, past marble busts of mustachioed generals. Army Minister Barroso sat surrounded by Goya paintings, contemplating the army reports with a heavy heart. A general of the old school, floridly courteous, he gazed lugubriously across his ornate desk and shook his head. Communism, he told me, was steadily creeping across North Africa, outflanking NATO and the United States. The Ifni assault was another typical Communist maneuver aimed at crippling Spain: Czech arms had been found on Moorish prisoners. Would the West not see the light? Was Spain to be left to fight Communism alone in Africa? Already Spain had lost 230 men, killed and wounded, in the Ifni fighting, and the cost to the Spanish treasury was about $250,000 each day—a steep price for a nation whose reserves were at rock bottom. Barroso was deeply affronted by Washington's refusal to let Spain use U.S.–donated arms in the Ifni fray.

After weeks of tension, a new Moroccan-Spanish clash erupted, this time in the Spanish Sahara south of Ifni. On January 14, 1958, after all-day fighting near El Aiun, a new Moroccan band, the "Saharan Liberation Army," fled, leaving 241 dead. Spanish casualties were given as 51 dead and wounded. For Franco, this was the breaking point. The pro-Arab policy was now scrapped, and he agreed to immediate Spanish-French punitive measures.

On February 10, Spanish and French troops launched joint mopping-up operations where the Spanish Sahara, Morocco, southern Algeria, and Mauretania meet. It was the first time since the 1925–26 Rif rebellion that the two European rivals had cooperated so closely. The combined air-and-ground attacks began successfully, but soon bad weather intervened. Details of the "mop-up" are still restricted, but Spain, with 10,000 soldiers in the Spanish Sahara, is known to have provided the manpower; France, the aircraft and the direction. Spanish paratroopers, for instance, were flown to bases in French Mauretania, whence they set out in jeep columns to catch the Moorish bands in the flank.

Three French ground columns swept into the Spanish Sahara from the desert fortresses of Tindouf, Fort Trinquet, and Fort Gouraud—all sites of valuable iron ore and copper deposits, which the French and the Arabs were both hoping some day to exploit.

Within sixteen days, the "irregulars" had been chased hundreds of miles back into Morocco, for the Spanish had killed the raiders' camels and pack animals, and without these the guerrillas were helpless.

The joint Spanish-French desert mop-up had significant after-effects. It sobered the Moroccan Government and indicated that Spain, though slow to react, was not so "decadent" as some African politicians believed. It also brought home to Franco the need for better relations with France. As a final snub to Morocco, Franco disbanded his colorful Moorish bodyguard dating from the Civil War, and ordered Castiella to prepare a new "pro-European" policy.

Ever since, despite cabinet intrigues and setbacks, Castiella has pursued a policy of integration with the West. He is a burly, square-shouldered, square-featured Basque, tireless, shy, lacking in humor—and utterly loyal to Franco. A technician rather than a politician, Castiella represents the type of administrator who must steer Spain through the shoals after Franco dies. He is at heart a Monarchist, like most of Spain's diplomats, but first and foremost he is a *regimenista,* a man of the regime, cautious and slow, yet purposeful. His pro-Western policy has been aided by his veteran collaborator José María Areilza, Conde de Motrico, one of the shrewdest envoys in Spain's service. Motrico won some $2 billion in U.S. aid for Spain while serving as Ambassador in Washington from 1953 to 1959.

Dissimilar in appearance, mental process, and style, the plodding Castiella and the rapierlike Motrico have proved an adroit team in a field strewn with emotional dislike of all dictatorships and of Franco's in particular. Between them, they have improved Spain's reputation surprisingly, and if Franco is less disliked abroad than before, he owes much to these two.

The men Franco trusts are those who fought with or who served him in the Civil War, and Castiella and Motrico are no exceptions. The former, a twenty-eight-year-old lawyer when the war broke out, reached Franco's lines late. He decided on a bold maneuver to attract Franco's attention. Teaming up with

Areilza, a fellow Basque of unusual mental agility, he set to work on a book, and in 1941 the two published a massive tome setting forth Spain's claims not only to Gibraltar but to large parts of the French empire in Africa. Today, *Reivindicaciones de España (Spain's Claims)* makes droll reading. It has disappeared, understandably, from Spain's bookshops, and neither the Foreign Minister nor the former Ambassador to Washington and Paris particularly cares to discuss it. Two or three lines suffice to give an idea of its theme:

> The old British leopard will be torn from its Gibraltarian lair and the French threat from Algeria will no longer impose itself on a nation such as ours, freshly revived. Here is the first portion of our future empire. Spain needs colonies, not merely land . . . such as Oran . . . nor native kingdoms . . . such as Morocco. No, Spain must have her role in the redistribution of Africa, in that fated redivision of the black continent which must surely follow any readjustment in the life of Europe.

The book brought both men to Franco's attention and set their feet on the ladder of promotion. Castiella, for example, volunteered in 1942 as a private in the Blue Division, served on the Russian front, and was decorated by Hitler for heroism in the Ukraine.

On returning to Spain in 1943, he helped found the Institute for Political Studies, a crucible for Falangist ideology, and directed it for five years. In 1948, he was named Ambassador to Peru, the most "Spanish" of the Latin American nations, and traditionally a steppingstone to higher office. Three years later, with the mild improvement in Spain's international relations, Franco sought to name Castiella ambassador to London but Prime Minister Attlee, remembering *Spain's Claims,* declared the burly Basque *persona non grata.* Attlee had served briefly with the International Brigades in the Spanish Civil War and his memory was long.

"Franco considers this an insult to Spain," said a Madrid politician at the time. "You'll see. Castiella will end up as Foreign Minister.

He was right. Franco sent to London Miguel Primo de Rivera, a brother of the martyred Falangist and an affable man-about-town, and Castiella was sent to the Vatican, where he negotiated the new Concordat. In his seven years at the Holy See, he matured from a neo-Falangist to a statesman.

As Foreign Minister since 1957, he has been skillfully reweaving the torn strands of Spanish ties with the West; and while he has stumbled occasionally, he has earned both the respect of his Western colleagues and Franco's confidence. His tenure has been noteworthy for his policy of *rapprochement* with the West and by his unremitting efforts to end the maltreatment of Spain's Protestants, eliminating a principal source of foreign criticism.

Castiella faced his first serious test in mid-1959, for by then Spain tottered on the brink of financial collapse. Franco's wage increases of 1956 had set off an inflationary spiral, and living costs were soaring. The peseta, pegged artificially at 42 to the dollar, had fallen to 60 on the black market. Spain's currency reserves were $200 million in 1955, but by 1959, there was a $4 million deficit. Spanish ambassadors overseas had even begun paying their staffs and their food bills out of their own pockets.

Spain's economic plight had long worried the United States Ambassador, John Davis Lodge, and the head of his economic mission, Richard S. Aldrich. Their aides, as well as experts of the World Bank, the International Monetary Fund, the Organization for European Economic Cooperation (OEEC) in Paris, and Wall Street banks had been urging a sweeping overhaul. The United States had already poured in $1 billion to rebuild Spain's economy and now pressed for reforms with increasing insistence.

As always, though, Franco had procrastinated. A military commander to the core, he had once told an associate that he could "order" prices to stand still just as he ordered soldiers. Franco, moreover, distrusted foreign-imposed reforms. Reforms might antagonize the bankers and industrialists whose backing he needed, and he feared, too, that reforms might open the door to foreign efforts to ease him from power. Thanks to Castiella and Motrico, and to the orthodox economists of Opus Dei, however, Franco finally moved.

In mid-July, 1959, the new reforms—the most sweeping in Spanish history—were announced, and they elicited approval abroad. Spain now was admitted as a full member into the OEEC and the International Monetary Fund, and private American banks jointly offered $418 million in loans to help Spain carry through her "economic stabilization" program.

Eisenhower's Visit

Meanwhile, with the economic crisis safely past, Castiella and Motrico were now planning a political coup. Castiella flew to London to meet President Eisenhower, who was on a brief visit to the United Kingdom.

Castiella had, in fact, come to invite Eisenhower to Spain. The invitation was the brainchild of Motrico, who had discovered in Washington that the American President was planning a world tour that autumn. If the American Chief Executive could be persuaded to stop in Spain, it would be a prime political plum for Franco. No American President had ever visited Spain.

Shrewdly, Castiella reminded Eisenhower that the $400 million chain of American bases on Spanish soil had never been officially "inspected." If Eisenhower was planning to visit eleven countries, surely a few hours could be spared to inspect the U.S. bases in Spain. Such a visit would create tremendous good will in the Spanish public, he emphasized.

Eisenhower and his aides were in a quandary. The world tour was still in the planning stage. Could the U.S. afford to bypass Spain? On the other hand, might not a visit to Franco stir liberal protests at home and abroad? As Eisenhower wrestled with the problem, Castiella flew triumphantly back to Franco to report nibbles on the line.

By November, 1959, Eisenhower had reluctantly agreed to visit Spain, although with characteristic caution, he agreed only to stop in Madrid for a few hours. Nonetheless, under the baton of Arias Salgado, the Spanish press now began paeans of praise to Franco's coup. At last, it exulted, the West had begun to realize the "unfairness and uselessness" of its past hostility.

"We may not be a great military or economic power," observed *Ya,* "but no one can discount our mission as a bridge between Europe and Africa and Latin America and our unshakable brotherhood with [the Philippines] the sole Asian country of Christian, Western culture."

On the afternoon of December 21, 1959, Eisenhower landed at the SAC base at Torrejon, thirteen miles outside Madrid. There to greet him was Franco in full-dress uniform with all his cabinet. The Spanish flag flew over the $120 million "joint" installation, but Franco had never deigned to set foot on Torrejon. Now, because the President of the United States had come to call, the Spanish Chief of State could also inspect Torrejon without loss of dignity.

Eisenhower descended the ramp and shook Franco's hand somewhat stiffly, then, standing bareheaded in the wind, he read a brief statement inviting Spain to "join" the U.S. and to work for a world "free from aggression, from hunger and disease, and also from war and the threat of war." Tactfully, he praised Spain as "one of the ancestors of the Americas," then hurriedly inspected a mixed honor guard and climbed into Franco's Rolls Royce for the twenty-minute drive to Madrid. The initial encounter was coldly correct—nothing more.

As the cavalcade entered the Spanish capital, thousands of men, women, and children crowded the streets. Trucks parked inconspicuously in side streets attested to the Falangists' zeal in rounding up their loyal adherents. Yet there also were many thousands of curious onlookers. The cavalcade swept into sight, and suddenly the cheers went up: "Ee-kay ("Ike"), Ee-kay, Ee-kay!!" There he was, as the Spanish had seen him in magazines and newsreels; the famous wide grin, the soft felt hat waved over his head as he stood next to Franco, one hand on the guardrail. The President turned right and left, taking everything in, showing good humor despite the strain of traveling 22,000 miles through eleven countries.

The cheers grew louder, and Franco, standing beside Eisenhower in the brooding winter evening, smiled contentedly. As the cavalcade swung off the broad tree-lined Castellana, turning right at the Cibeles fountain up the Alcalá, Franco pointed up to a floodlit balcony where Señora de Franco, her daughter and son-in-law, and Franco's small grandchildren were waiting. Eisenhower lifted his hat in a gallant gesture that brought cheers from thousands, for here was not only the President of the United States, but a new friend with old-world manners. And this appealed to the Spaniards.

Later that evening, at a glittering state banquet in the Oriente Palace, the leader of the West found himself opposite Franco at the banquet table. Franco had placed at his own right the sparkling Francesca, wife of Ambassador John Davis Lodge, and Señora de Franco at Eisenhower's right. In an overhead gallery, a Spanish military string band struggled manfully through the "Yellow Rose of Texas," for the Spanish had been told it was an Eisenhower favorite. Nothing had been left to chance. Silence fell, as the Caudillo, glittering with decorations, stood and raised his glass to Mrs. Eisenhower, the "distinguished lady who, far from here, awaits you at home." All drank to the First Lady, who had remained in Washington. Then, in an unprecedented public tribute, Franco thanked the American nation.

"Our relations are reaching the point of maturity and understanding," he said, as Spanish generals and admirals, cardinals, archbishops, dignitaries, and even the liveried footmen listened intently. "We are well aware that we owe the peace we enjoy and the preservation of Western Europe against falling under the

Communist yoke to your energy and generosity, and that of your country. We cannot forget how magnificently [your] country accepts the sacrifices imposed by destiny, nor the friendly and sincere generosity with which it has helped Spain."

This was rare coming from the man whose tightly ruled press had long refrained from making but the most passing reference to American aid. Franco and the entire assembly rose and stood silently as the band played "The Star-Spangled Banner," and those near Franco saw tears in his eyes. For the much-criticized dictator, this was a memorable moment.

The next morning, Eisenhower rose early. From his window in the Moncloa Palace, he could see over the Castilian plain to the snow-tipped peaks of the Guadarrama range, thirty miles away. It was a fine, sunny winter day, and, escorted by Ambassador Lodge, Undersecretary Robert Murphy, Embassy Counselor William Fraleigh, and his son, Major John Eisenhower, the President now introduced Franco to the typically American custom of the breakfast conference.

For Franco, a breakfast conference was something he had never savored and very probably never will again. Followed by Castiella, Areilza, and Jaime de Piniés, an English-speaking diplomat, the Caudillo joined his American guests in the Pardo dining room. Eisenhower's breakfast fare was a two-inch thick steak flown from Kansas City by the Spanish Government, served along with coffee, jam, and toast. For the Spanish, there were the traditional cold meats, sweet cakes, and *cafe au lait*. A leaden silence hung over the formal, oak-trimmed room until Murphy, a veteran of thirty years' diplomacy, essayed a mild joke to break the ice, and Ambassador Lodge tried to plunge through the line with hearty cordiality. The silence only deepened. Franco was ill at ease. Eisenhower now tried his own hand with a Texan joke.

Slowly, the ice began to melt. Franco recounted his exploits at partridge shooting, and the jokes began to fly about the table. Suddenly, a story occurred to the Caudillo. He had a little yarn about generals, he said, which seemed appropriate. During the Battle of Waterloo, he began, a young French major fell wounded in the midst of a charge. He was borne to the rear, placed on an operating table, and the surgeons were beginning to extract a bullet from his brain, when one of Napoleon's couriers galloped up with a battlefield order promoting the young major to general. Only half-conscious, the hero struggled off the table and insisted on finding and mounting his horse.

"You can't go! We haven't finished removing the bullet from your brain," protested the surgeons. "Now that I'm a general," retorted the hero, galloping away, "I don't need my brains any more!"

The effect of the tale on Eisenhower has been lost to history, but as the laughter died away, Eisenhower plunged into a review of his world tour and of the trend of international affairs. He was "precise, clear, and in absolute command of his subject," said a Spanish participant admiringly.

By ten o'clock, the talks ended. U.S. Air Force helicopters stood on the green lawns near Franco's palace, and Eisenhower, Franco, and their aides piled in. Seven and a half minutes later, they dropped gently onto the Tarmac at Torrejon.

Now came handshakes all around, compliments from the President for Ambassador Lodge and for Major General Stanley J. "Moose" Donovan, the U.S. military chief in Spain. Castiella stood wreathed in smiles, and Areilza, due to return as Eisenhower's guest on the plane to Washington, glowed with triumph. Finally, the President came to Franco, and the crowd, Spanish and foreign, including television newsreel cameramen and reporters, watched intently. Grinning broadly, Eisenhower threw his arms about Franco in a traditional Spanish *abrazo*. The photographers leaped to record it. It is one of the most human photographs ever taken of Eisenhower or Franco. Franco's expression, as he gazes with appreciation and real emotion into Eisenhower's face reveals a side of the dictator seldom captured on film.

"Merry Christmas and a Happy New Year!" Eisenhower cried

251

as he mounted the steps. He asked an interpreter to thank the Spanish crowds who had so lustily cheered "Ee-kay"—"which," added the President, "I understand is Spanish for my nickname."

The "Columbine" lifted quickly and was gone, but the Spaniards' memory of Eisenhower remained. In eighteen hours. Franco, the onetime outcast, had been elevated from a stiff handshake to a demonstrative embrace from the President of the United States.

The German Bases

Early in 1960, the Spanish Government had one of its periodic fits of annoyance with the foreign press. This time the culprit was Cyrus L. Sulzberger, the able foreign-affairs columnist of *The New York Times,* who had disclosed in Paris that Spain was planning to give West Germany military "facilities" (bases) on Spanish soil. Alerted by Sulzberger's scoop, the foreign press had begun violently denouncing "reviving Nazism" and the dangers of renewed German-Spanish military ties so soon after World War II. Embarrassed, Madrid and Bonn backed and filled, but the truth came out.

Apparently, five months earlier, Bonn's Foreign Minister von Brentano had confidentially asked Castiella for "fall-back" facilities—supply dumps and base hospitals—as part of Bonn's contingency planning in event of war. Brentano had not suggested training German troops in Spain but had intimated that West Germany's fledgling air force might take advantage of Spain's clear weather for flight training. Eager to please, Castiella had promised to take it up with Franco but had cautiously extracted Von Brentano's promise to clear it first with the United States, Britain, and France. As an afterthought, Castiella had also asked that another NATO member—Portugal—be notified, and Von Brentano, for his part, had proposed that the scheme be mentioned to Paul-Henri Spaak, the Secretary General of NATO. Castiella knew that veteran Belgian Socialist's old hatred of Franco but he could hardly demur.

The West German military "facilities" deal was a classic example of bungling. Despite Von Brentano's promise to consult the Americans, British, French, and Portuguese, the German military opted for secrecy. One German staff officer at SHAPE, however, had already mentioned the plan casually to General Lauris Norstad, then Supreme Allied Commander, who saw the dangers and urged the Germans to drop it. Instead, they ignored his advice. Meanwhile, Castiella, while visiting Paris, had mentioned the plan to Livingston Merchant, a ranking State Department official, who, in turn, informed Eisenhower; but apparently the President had failed to take it sufficiently seriously to raise it with Franco when he saw him a few days later.

The Germans sent a five-man military team to Madrid in civilian clothes in early January, led by a brigadier general. In retrospect, it would be hard to conceive of anything more clumsy or more certain to revive World War II memories. On February 22, Sulzberger's story broke, and soon Franco's enemies were ringing all the alarms. Madrid frantically issued clarifications and denials. Bonn continued to look stonily ahead, and Franco blamed the Black Legend for the outcry. Nevertheless, Sulzberger's column was the death knell of German bases in Spain for many years to come.

Salan and the OAS

While Franco and Castiella were blowing on fingers badly singed by the West German bases deal, Franco's Naziphile brother-in-law, Serrano Suñer, was acting as midwife at the birth of the French Fascist OAS (Organisation Armée Secrète) in Spain.

Serrano, long fallen from power, still nursed extremist dreams. He believed that Spain and France had a "Christian, civilizing mission" among the Arabs. France had settled Algeria in 1830, and French genius had made the desert bloom. Spain had contributed to this Christian civilization through its colony of 60,-000 Spaniards in and around Oran, in western Algeria. De Gaulle was threatening to abandon Algeria, and to Serrano as well as to many other Spaniards, De Gaulle's policy of self-determination was criminal treason. They foresaw chaos in Algeria if the French withdrew. They feared that the Algerians would help the Moroccans to seize Melilla and Ceuta, Ifni, and the Spanish Sahara, and wrench away Spain's last footholds in Africa. Communism would infect the Arab masses and—as in 711—Spain would find the enemy on her doorstep. Serrano's philosophy fitted perfectly with the doctrine of *Algérie Française,* whose leaders found Spain an ideal base for clandestine operations.

The leader of the OAS conspiracy was General Raoul Salan, Commander in Chief in Algeria until De Gaulle dismissed him in 1959. After months of brooding, Salan dodged De Gaulle's police and slipped over the border into Spain in October, 1960.

Serrano was to become Salan's chief courier and his financier, until, on a sunny April day six months later, Salan flew on a Spanish airplane to join the generals' *Putsch* in Algiers. From there, his trail was to lead through senseless, brutal killings to a cell in a French prison, where he still sits.

That autumn, however, Serrano Suñer was the man Salan needed. They had met many years before, when the General had periodically visited a sister living in Spain whose property adjoined Serrano's. The two neo-Fascists often rode together, and soon their similar right-wing political beliefs ripened into friendship. Serrano saw in Salan a chance to get back into the shady international politics from which Franco had long barred him, and thus to undercut the august brother-in-law toward whom he felt a bitterness equal only to Salan's bitterness for De Gaulle. Serrano and Franco had broken years before, and neither saw the other.

How much Franco knew of Salan's conspiracy is hard to say. He certainly knew something. Franco admired De Gaulle as a general, an authoritarian, a European, and a Catholic. Yet De Gaulle had sworn to keep Algeria French, and now he seemed to be abandoning his promise. This was dangerous, for an independent Algeria could open the doors to Communism. Franco detested his brother-in-law Serrano, but their views over Africa coincided. Characteristically, Franco trimmed his sails. He gave orders that Salan was to be treated as an honored guest.

Salan, meanwhile, settled in a quiet Madrid hotel where, to his embarrassment, the giddy young Duchess of Alba and other socialites began to lionize him. Salan had more serious fish to fry. He had a revolution to plan, and he and his grim co-conspirators had no liking for the social spotlight or for the reporters hanging around the lobby. After a spell, Salan moved north to San Sebastián on the coast, where he walked, read, retired to bed early, and soon fell back into the obscurity he desired.

During this winter of 1960–61, several noisy but less dangerous French "ultras" had also fled to Spain. One was Pierre Lagaillarde, the bearded rabble-rouser from Algiers. Another was Marcel Ronda, small, dark, and half-Spanish. They had been met at the Atocha railway station by hordes of Spanish and foreign reporters and had settled in the luxurious Fénix Hotel where, draped in bath towels and racing from room to room to answer the never-ceasing telephone calls, they basked in the limelight.

After several days of lurid publicity, Roland de Margerie, the French Ambassador, drew Castiella's attention to the spectacle, and soon the headline-hunters, nudged by the Spanish authorities and short of funds, retired to a back-street apartment with a Spanish detective-escort and orders to keep quiet. Lagaillarde still haunted the night spots, his beard and leopard-spotted paratroop attire drawing reporters and girl tourists like flies. More and more "ultras," meanwhile, were slipping into Spain as the weeks passed, and Salan's plot gathered speed.

By spring, preparations for the Algerian *Putsch* were well along, and Salan gave his posse of Spanish detectives the slip. Using techniques learned in thirty years of secret service work,* he changed cars at a prearranged crossroads and disappeared. For

* De Gaulle once remarked: *"Le pauvre Salan.* He's spent thirty years in the Deuxième Bureau and now can't live without conspiring."

forty-eight hours, all Spain knew he was hiding at Serrano Suñer's country home, but the regime insisted he was "lost."

Eventually, he reappeared in Madrid, bland, unruffled, once more dodging photographers, refusing interviews, this time settling back in the comfortable routine of the Princesa Hotel opposite the Alba's home. Salan resumed his apparently idle life, and the reporters drifted away, little suspecting what was brewing.

Finally, in mid-March, 1961, under Salan's direction, twenty French "ultras" met in the heart of Madrid to create the OAS. Besides Salan there were Jean-Jacques Susini, the fanatical twenty-six-year-old Algerian student organizer; Colonel Yves Godard, the paratrooper; Joseph Ortiz, the Algiers *cafetier*-Fascist; Colonel Charles Lacheroy, the psychological warfare addict; and many others from Algeria, from French Army units in West Germany and France, and even from inside the French Government and from French big business. The military plotters met with Salan in the Hotel Princesa; the civilians under Susini in the 35-story Torre de Madrid, the highest office building in south Europe, which, ironically, gazes down on a statue of Don Quixote.

It is too much to believe that by now Franco was unaware of Salan's activities. The Spanish police are experienced and well armed with funds and spies. Their normal quarry, however, consists of the left, not the right; Communists, not neo-Fascists. Salan was, moreover, a master of intrigue, as were the fanatics around him, and they covered their tracks. The Spanish detectives, after months of sitting in hotel lobbies and tailing a well-known general who went only for brief walks or to dine with influential friends, gradually lost interest. They began to nod just as Salan was preparing for action. His move caught them sound asleep.

Early in the morning of Saturday, April 22, the long-simmering anti-De Gaulle *Putsch* burst forth in Algiers. General Challe, the commander in chief, was joined by General Jouhaud and General Zeller, and an open revolt against De Gaulle was declared. Where now was Salan?

The Spaniards, too, were wondering, for once more Salan had given them the slip. Too late, the wheels of the Spanish police began to revolve. As Castiella sat reading a French novel in his palatial residence, the French Ambassador hurried to see him. Quick and nervous in speech and manner, the brilliant De Margerie had been awakened by Paris at four in the morning with news of the *Putsch*. On the "highest" authority—De Gaulle or Foreign Minister Couve de Murville—he had been asked to have the Spanish Government prevent Salan's leaving Spain at all costs, for obviously Salan would try to reach Algeria and there imperil De Gaulle's task of re-establishing authority over the French Army. The situation was critical.

Castiella immediately placed a long-distance call to Franco, who was touring Andalusia, but Franco was unavailable. Castiella spoke with Alonso Vega, Minister of Interior, who had just learned of the *Putsch* himself, through a French inspector on duty with the Madrid police. Castiella also learned from Alonso Vega that Salan already had "disappeared."

For twenty-four hours, the search continued. With all the resources at their disposal, the Spanish police proved unable—or unwilling—to locate the celebrated French intriguer.

The next day (Sunday) at noon, a private Spanish airplane, chartered for an apparently innocuous flight to Mallorca, taxied slowly out to the end of a runway at Madrid's busy Barajas Airport. At the controls was a Spanish Air Force lieutenant colonel. The plane reached the runway's end, turned, and braked. As the motors revved, a car drew up and two men in civilian clothes hurriedly climbed aboard. The plane took off and an hour later passed over the Valencia tower.

Now a curious incident occurred. Though the weather was perfectly clear, the pilot radioed Valencia that winds were "too strong" to permit him to reach Mallorca, so he would land instead at Algiers. Back from Valencia came the formal order: "Do not proceed to Algiers. On orders of the Foreign Ministry, no aircraft are to leave Spain for Algeria without special permission." Nevertheless, the Spanish military pilot flew on, and an hour later landed Salan and an aide at Maison Blanche Airport outside Algiers. Salan had defied Castiella, with the complicity of high Spanish Air Ministry officials, in a plane piloted by one of Spain's top air force pilots, and was able to reach a territory in open rebellion against De Gaulle.

In Madrid, officials now alternated between embarrassment and offended dignity.

"When Castiella is most embarrassed, he seems most self-assured," commented one European diplomat caustically. It was true. Castiella was chagrined, but he had to put on a bold front. The world press quickly denounced Franco's "complicity," and Cyrus L. Sulzberger reported De Gaulle's fury and the damage to French-Spanish relations. As in the German-bases deal, the lack of Spanish cabinet coordination and the cynical maneuvering of Franco's henchmen revived accusations of "Fascist" influence in Spain.

Scalded by the foreign press, Castiella, who had avoided all contact with *The New York Times* for a full year, summoned me to see him three times in four days. Ramblingly, he told me what had happened, wandering into byways about the Black Legend, about Castro's Cuba, and about the incessant efforts of "Masons and Marxists" to blacken Spain's good name and "drive wedges between Spain and France." Placing a hand on his heart, he vowed that Franco had known nothing of Salan's departure. It was ridiculous, he asserted, to claim that Franco had been playing Serrano Suñer's game.

"If there is one man in Spain whom Franco detests," he said, "it is Serrano Suñer. The two barely speak. Serrano Suñer has done everything conceivable against Franco."

Who, then, I asked, *had* organized Salan's escape? What had the police uncovered? Was Serrano Suñer the culprit? What were the facts?

The Foreign Minister heaved himself from a velvet-covered divan, strode heavily across Aubusson carpets to a study where, through an open door, I could hear him ask for the Director

General of Security, Colonel Arias Navarro. Several minutes later he returned, embarrassed, yet smiling fixedly.

"They know nothing," he confessed, as I showed my astonishment. "They seem to have lost interest now that Salan is gone."

"But what about the Spanish pilot?" I asked. "Has he nothing to say?"

"He was arrested but refuses to speak," replied Castiella, swallowing. "Of course," he added with heavy humor, "we might torture him—but think of the international outcry!"

The facts, of course, were never revealed. The pilot's trial was repeatedly postponed and will never be held. Franco has no desire to irritate his Air Ministry.

In Algiers, the *Putsch* failed; Challe and Zeller surrendered, but Salan (and Jouhaud) escaped in the night to organize the OAS blood bath that broke out months later. Meanwhile, Salan faded from Spain's attention, and De Margerie had the duty of transmitting Franco's "congratulations" to De Gaulle on quelling the revolt. For months, Castiella avoided De Margerie's eye, but Franco carried on as if nothing had happened.

Kennedy and Spain

Not long after, Franco held another of his periodic border conferences with his old friend Salazar, for the international situation confronting the two dictators was far from satisfactory. A young "liberal" Catholic, John F. Kennedy, had recently become President of the United States; a revolutionary movement called DRIL (Directorio Revolucionario Ibérico de Liberación) was conspiring openly against the two Iberian regimes; the Congo was in chaos; and rebellion was spreading to Angola. Inside Spain and Portugal, meanwhile, opposition movements were increasingly active, and the Roman Catholic Church itself was beginning, cautiously, to disassociate itself from both aging regimes.

The election of John F. Kennedy had disturbed Franco and Salazar. For years, they had both accepted the common illusion that American Catholics were a financially affluent but politically frustrated minority. Now an American Catholic had won the most powerful elective office on earth—but what sort of Catholic was he? Since 99.9 per cent of all Spaniards were Catholics, the mere fact of being a Catholic was no automatic key to Franco's heart. Even the popes were viewed by many Spanish prelates as dangerously progressive, and here was a young Catholic President who was avowedly "liberal." Kennedy's campaign promises to observe the constitutional separation of Church and State had annoyed the Spanish hierarchy, while discreet soundings of conservative American colleagues had confirmed their fears that Kennedy was first a politician and second an obedient son of the Church. To the Spanish regime, he was more dangerous by far than a right-wing Protestant.

Kennedy had begun to appoint liberals to high office—Adlai Stevenson as Ambassador to the United Nations, Chester Bowles as Undersecretary of State, G. Mennen Williams as Assistant Secretary of State for Africa, among others. Franco's cable of congratulations to the new President had gone unanswered for a full month, and Franco began to sense the winds of change in Washington.

Meanwhile, in Madrid, the end of the Eisenhower era brought Franco another loss. American Ambassador John Davis Lodge, one of the most energetic, though controversial, envoys ever to grace the post, was leaving. Few Americans spoke better Spanish or loved Spain more sincerely than Lodge. A scion of a family noted for its public servants, Lodge was tall, handsome, endowed with a fine voice, energetic—and brilliantly backed by his wife, the talented Francesca Braggiotti.

An objective review of Lodge's ambassadorship must evoke both praise and criticism. Franco's critics felt that Lodge's policy was solely to keep Franco happy and to insure the use of the bases. They nicknamed him the Pentagon's ambassador, considered him less concerned with traditional American support for democracy than with military expediency. His Spanish friends, they also complained, comprised principally aristocrats eager to freeload at the Embassy table and bask in the ambassadorial prestige, whereas Spaniards suspected of being anti-Franco were blackballed from Embassy functions. Leading intellectuals, such as Pedro Laín Entralgo, Julián Marías, José Luis López Aranguren, Enrique Tierno Galvan, Manuel Giménez Fernández, and, before his death, the great humanist-savant Gregorio Marañón, were seldom if ever seen at the American Embassy. They would have come if they had been asked—and their influence among the rising generations of Spain was important. Lodge had the warmth, the stature, and the command of Spanish to attract such men, but he was not sufficiently curious to plumb the intricacies of Spanish politics. He viewed his role differently.

"Must we always try to reform the rest of the world when there is so much to be done right in our own country?" he would often answer critics of Franco's system.

His concept of his role was uncomplicated. He played it like a successful American politician, keeping the constituents happy. Franco and the regime were his "constituents," and unless they were happy, American policy in Spain would fail. Spain, in Lodge's view, was a nation emerging from civil war and from twenty years' isolation and Franco was a phenomenon cast up by Spain's own historic evolution. Franco was not perfect, but he was necessary until Spain could stand on its own feet. U.S. aid admittedly helped keep the Franco regime in power, but what was the alternative? To cut off aid?

Would cutting off aid hurt the dictator, backed by the army, police, Church, and business interests, or would it hurt the masses recovering from years of poverty and international ill will, he would ask. The "tough" techniques, Lodge noted, had already been tried in 1946, and Franco had emerged stronger than before.

He pursued his way unruffled, giving the regime no pretext to complain that he was "meddling" with subversives. He traveled widely, made many speeches, formed many friendships, and no non-Spaniard sang Spanish songs with greater gusto. His wife helped raise funds for Spanish charities, started a seeing-eye-dog training program for the blind, and three days a week ran dancing classes for Spanish and American wives. To this day, the peasants in a hamlet near Madrid sit nightly before a television set bought with dancing class fees collected through the energy of "la Señora embajadora."

Africa

Early in 1961, Franco began quietly putting his African house in order. It was none too soon.

The Algerian war was pitting the French against both Arabs and Africans; the Congo crisis had set African against white; and now Spain, with two small territories in the heart of black Africa, decided that the time had come for a radical overhaul. She would make her possessions into show windows. And if that failed to satisfy African nationalism, she would grant them independence.

In June, when the Cortes held its plenary session, observers noticed the publicity surrounding the appearance of Spain's first three Negro *procuradores*. For the first time, Spanish Negroes had knelt on velvet cushions to take their oaths as lawmakers with rank equal to that of the 600-odd white legislators. They were Don Wilwardo Jones Niger, Don Felipe Esono Nsue, and Don Carlos Cabrera James, all courtly, polished, Spanish-speaking Negroes. Along with them came three white deputies to compose the six-man legislative delegation from Spain's Guinean provinces in West Africa. The Guinean territory is now lavishly subsidized by Madrid and largely self-ruling.

In centuries gone by, Spain claimed most of the West African coast, but in the nineteenth-century colonial race Britain, France, and Germany nibbled much away. All that is left now consists of two postage-stamp provinces where the red and yellow banner flies over jungle vegetation. One is the island of Fernando Poo, off Nigeria. The other is Río Muni, a jungle enclave of 200,000

Africans on the mainland, hemmed in between the newly independent African republics of Cameroun and Gabon.

Río Muni and Fernando Poo are each enchanting. The Spanish and African cultures seem to blend smoothly, resulting in bright little towns that dot the lovely jungle land and bear such names as Valladolid de los Bimbiles or Sevilla de Niefang. The mayors and town councilors are drawn predominantly from among the white Spanish planters, but Negroes are being prepared, and Madrid keeps a close eye on the natives' welfare by means of young volunteer administrators handpicked from the armed forces or the Guardia Civil.

The Spanish natives seem friendly and happy. On market days, the towns are filled with color and noise. African mothers carefully select European canned goods or bolts of bright cloth, their sleeping babies slung in sashes over their backs. The men, in khaki pants and shirts, sit or stand around in bunches, jawing, laughing, and arguing. Spanish-trained African constables in white or khaki shorts keep a wary eye on law and order, and at day's end they can be seen gently shepherding tipsy natives onto homebound buses.

Catholic schools and hospitals have been built throughout the province, and at Mikomeseng stands one of the largest leprosariums in Africa. Each Guinea native is now required to take a free blood test every six months and this measure has reduced the leper population in recent years from 4,000 to 600. In a few more years, leprosy will have been wiped out. Mikomeseng, 50 miles from Dr. Albert Schweitzer's famous hospital at Lambaréné, in West Gabon, is gradually putting itself out of business.

Fernando Poo, the island province, raises cacao while Río Muni specializes in jungle hardwoods. Elephants and gorillas still roam Río Muni; the gorillas frequently invade native villages to gorge on their favorite delicacy, banana shoots. The gorilla population is protected by law, but elephant hunting with a Spanish guide is permitted, and a license costs only 1,000 pesetas ($17).

Dirt roads wind through the jungle, sometimes ending at a

hilltop mansion where young Spaniards supervise the lumbering and rubber plantations with a feudal comfort reminiscent of America's ante-bellum South. There are few more delightful experiences than to sit on the verandah of a Spanish Guinea *estancia,* waited on by smiling Africans in spotless white, and watching the sun disappear behind hills blue in the evening mist. Evening breezes waft through the louvers in the walls, and all around is silence.

On every side, the jungle undulates away over the horizon— and the Atlantic Ocean roars endlessly nearby. The host speaks. There—he waves his hand—lies the former French Gabon. In that direction—another wave—lie the Cameroons. There are still no fixed boundaries, and one can follow the elephant for days from one country to another without seeing a human being. The natives are peaceful. There have been one or two minor differences with the Cameroons since their independence, but Gabon, which enfolds Río Muni on two sides, is a good neighbor. The Gabonese regard their kin with envy because native living standards in Spanish Guinea are at least 35 per cent higher than in either of the neighboring African republics.

Because of its isolation, Spanish Guinea was long a fief of the Spanish Navy, which normally provided governors general. In 1959, the two colonies were raised to "provinces" with the same system of administration as Spanish home provinces.*

Fernando Poo contains about 4,000 Spanish whites, 16,000 Spanish African *bubis,* and 35,000 Nigerian plantation hands, or *braceros,* imported every year on 2-year contracts. One can circumnavigate Fernando Poo in an hour in the governor general's helicopter. Like Ascension and St. Helena, it is a mountain peak in a chain that stretches southwest into the Atlantic. The capital, Santa Isabel, is a bustling little city with palm-shaded plazas, African policemen in shorts, and a Cathedral square reminiscent of Andalusia. In the evenings, one can hear the Nigerian workers

* In October, 1964, Franco further Africanized the Guinea territories by appointing Africans as civil governors, or administrative chiefs, of Río Muni and Fernando Poo.

singing Welsh missionary hymns across the harbor as local planters on the terrace of the Club Nautico (Yacht Club) play cards
and sip whiskies-and-soda as they might in Malaga or Alicante.
The planters are well-off, for the regime buys cacao at high prices
and lets them import American trucks and other machinery at
only 10 per cent duty—compared with 90 per cent or more in
peninsular Spain.

Salaries for whites in Guinea are at least three times those in
Spain, and many young men come out with their brides, planning to stay only a year or two, fall in love with the climate, the
equatorial beauty, and the peace, and stay on. Fevers and other
tropical diseases have long since been eliminated.

Above Santa Isabel tower fresh green peaks where the governor
general, his staff, and the wealthy Spaniards repair during the
hot summer months. Friesian and Jersey cattle can be seen cropping the emerald grass, scattering madly as the helicopter flies
low. "There is the Duke of Ifantado's home," shouts the pilot
over the motor's roar, pointing to a handsome wood and stone
residence among fields. "Some say it really belongs to Don Juan
the Pretender."

Along the coast are small clearings, the native villages, each
with its wooden church and open plaza. Every Spanish conquista-
dor in history must have laid out new towns in the same way.
Along the roads, rows of small concrete houses confront each
other. These belong to the *bubis,* Spain's native capitalists. Protected by a paternalistic regime, the easygoing *bubis* rent their
land to Spanish whites or to Nigerians and sit back, eventually
building themselves waterproof, snakeproof, insectproof houses
with their rents. They furnish the houses with refrigerators,
stock the refrigerators with beer—and enjoy life. A few break
through their congenital insouciance and rise in business, law, or
government—but not many.

Don Wilwardo Jones, the African Mayor of Santa Isabel, is
one who has risen high. Grave and slow-spoken, his voice deep
and his skin black as ebony, he receives visitors in his high-

ceilinged office with the aplomb of a rajah. A ceiling fan circles slowly overhead, and a crucifix hangs on the whitewashed wall.

"We Spanish Africans have complete equality with the Europeans here," he says in fluent Castilian. "How far we rise depends on ourselves. There is no racial bar. More and more Africans are joining the government service and rising to positions of authority. There is little discontent. Now and then, some of the Nigerians stir up trouble, or one of our own people behaves foolishly, but everywhere in Guinea the situation is calm. We want nothing better than to remain Spanish."

I ask about his un-Spanish name, Jones.

"My grandfather was a slave in Sierra Leone," he replies with a smile. "He got his freedom and came to Nigeria for a better job. My father eventually came here, and I was born here. I consider myself 100 per cent Spanish."

Cuba and Angola

In the spring of 1961, two events provoked widespread criticism in Spain of the Kennedy Administration. One was the Bay of Pigs fiasco; the other, the native uprising in Angola, which cost a thousand white Portuguese lives in the first twenty-four hours. The Bay of Pigs touched an especially raw nerve.

Cuba has not only been Spain's first, and richest New World colony—a staging post for Columbus, Cortes, Pizarro, Nuñez de Balboa, Cabeza de Vaca, and the other great conquistadores—but it had been wrenched away from Spain in 1898, by what most Spaniards still regard as naked American aggression. Cuba has an emotional hold on Spain that time has never dimmed. Not only do Spaniards still retain sizable investments in Cuba, there are at least 50,000 Spanish citizens living on the island, and despite Fidel Castro, the Spanish regarded themselves as the natural interlocutors between the outside world and the Cubans.

Officially, Castro's Communism is deplored, but emotionally millions of Spaniards, especially the youth, felt a perverse sympathy for Castro. This bravo of pure Spanish blood (his father

was born in Galicia) not only overthrew the venal Batista, but
has defied the American "colossus." The image of the flamboyant, bearded, cigar-smoking Fidel aroused a certain quixotism
in the Spanish subconscious.

The Bay of Pigs was condemned by Spaniards whether they
were pro-Castro or anti-Castro. It created pro-Castro sympathy
among the young, while those who fulminated against "Castroism" now condemned Washington for having unleashed a
wave of fresh Communist repression throughout the unhappy
island.

The native uprising in Portuguese Angola, on the other hand,
although not blamed directly on Washington, was imputed to
America's anticolonialist support of the Afro-Asians. Franco's
press pointed out that on March 15, the day the revolt broke out,
Ambassador Adlai Stevenson had voted with the U.S.S.R. delegate in the Security Council to condemn Portugal for colonial
maladministration. From Portugal came reports that captured
rebels had cried out hysterically, "We have the United States and
Russia on our side!" Spanish-Portuguese irritation with the
United States steadily increased, and by the autumn of 1961,
Franco and Salazar had decided on a state visit by Portugal's
President, Admiral Americo Thomaz, as a warning to the West
not to take the Iberian countries for granted.

As the taciturn Portuguese dignitary arrived for a four-day
visit, Franco's press hailed Portugal's "valiant" stand at the U.N.
and condemned the "cynical abandonment" of Portugal by its
NATO allies, the United States and Britain. Spain and South
Africa alone had voted for Portugal a week earlier when eighty-
three members of the Trusteeship Committee had censured
Portugal for refusing to submit reports on her overseas administration. By contrast, the United States had supported an Afro-
Asian demand for a "Committee of Seven" to probe Angolan
conditions.

Rising Iberian irritation toward the United Nations and toward the United States, too, began now to concern Washington,

and Kennedy's new Secretary of State, Dean Rusk, hurried off to Madrid after attending NATO meetings in Paris. John Foster Dulles had always visited Madrid after NATO meetings to brief Franco, but this was the first visit by the new Democratic Secretary of State.

Rusk arrived in Madrid on December 16—almost two years after Eisenhower had raised Spanish-American relations to their friendliest level. Well briefed by the U.S. Chargé d'Affaires, Robert McBride, Rusk made a tactful reference to the "triangular" relationship among the United States, Spain, and Latin America. This gesture, the first of its kind from the Kennedy Administration, slightly mollified Spanish sensitivity.

Franco told Rusk that Portugal would stand firm in Africa. Fresh from his conversations with Thomaz, Franco warned the U.S. Secretary of State that pressure on Portugal would not force her to quit Angola but would only make her dig her heels in harder.

There were disturbing reports of an imminent Indian attack on Portuguese Goa, Franco said; would United States Ambassador John K. Galbraith in New Delhi prevent Nehru and Defense Minister Krishna Menon from overrunning the tiny pocket of Portuguese civilization? What about India's vaunted neutralism? Gandhian nonviolence? Nehru's advocacy of peaceful negotiations?

Franco left Rusk in no doubt that Spanish and Portuguese opinion was increasingly incensed over what appeared to be a double standard: one for colonial powers; another for the Afro-Asians.

Fate now intervened to strain U.S.–Spanish ties once again. Within twenty-four hours of Rusk's visit, 17,000 Indian troops, supported by Canberra jet bombers and destroyers, swarmed into the three tiny Portuguese enclaves, Goa, Damão, and Diu, ending four centuries of Portuguese "presence" in India.

The Spanish press outdid itself in bitterness that Christmas Eve. Instead of cozy Yuletide messages, Madrid's dailies heaped coals of fire on Western "cowardice, timidity, and weakness."

"Goa, Katanga, and Dutch New Guinea: three names for one face [aggression]" ran a headline in *Ya*. "One must link all these sad episodes: Katanga and Goa now; Dutch New Guinea certainly tomorrow; Berlin, Cuba, Budapest yesterday."

ABC referred to the "unburied corpse" of the United Nations, while *Arriba* denounced the Security Council's failure to condemn India as an indication of the "weakness, renunciation, and cowardice" that had gripped the West.

The Common Market

By early 1962, Franco was approaching a political crossroads: whether or not to link Spain with the Common Market. The risks were great. What if The Six publicly rebuffed him?

The cabinet wrestled in an agony of indecision, and Army Minister Barroso told friends that no fewer than fifteen successive meetings had been devoted to the pros and cons of Spain's motive. It was, as he put it, "a calculated adventure." Some ministers had vehemently opposed the idea, fearing it might mean more "foreign interference," but ultimately the "Europeanists" had prevailed.

Fully 40 per cent of Spain's exports, for instance, had gone to Common Market countries in 1961, and as much as 29 per cent of her imports had come from the Big Six. Britain (Spain's chief customer) had applied for admission, and in time the remaining EFTA countries would probably apply too. One of them, Greece, had already requested a fifteen-year "association" as preparation for eventual full membership in the Common Market. If Greece could take the plunge, why not Spain?

Franco's indecision ended in January, 1962, when the Common Market's decision to adopt a common agricultural policy tipped the scale. Now Spain was truly caught "between the sword and the wall." As a predominantly agricultural country, Spain would never be able to compete with Italy. Spain must join—or be squeezed out.

On February 9, in a letter to Couve de Murville, Castiella requested negotiations to examine the "possible attachment" of Spain to the European Economic Community. Spain's request was based on her "territorial contiguity" with the six-nation community, and on the contribution her geographic position could mean for "European cohesion." He noted that "the ties uniting Spain with the [Latin] American countries could be a positive contribution" toward solving the problems between Latin America and the Community.

Two years were to pass before Franco's application was even accepted by The Six, and then it was with marked reluctance. The European Socialists, led by the Belgian Foreign Minister Spaak and by the Italian Vice Premier Nenni (an ex-Commissar in the International Brigades) tried to reject Franco, but counterpressure from Couve de Murville and from Schroeder of West Germany turned the tide. By the autumn of 1964, Spanish–Common Market talks were under way.

With his application to join the Common Market, Franco had finally cast his lot with Western Europe. The day of "splendid" isolation was over; the xenophobic, hostile, brooding suspicion of everything foreign had been relegated to the attic.

Franco's relations have improved with Britain,* his best customer; with West Germany; with the Benelux countries; but most of all with De Gaulle, whose authoritarianism, control over labor and parliament, and political independence from the United States are all to Franco's liking. The time is not yet ripe for a meeting between Franco and De Gaulle but the two heads of state have quietly given their governments authorization to coordinate economic, industrial, social, and military policies.

De Gaulle's Finance Minister, Giscard d'Estaing, visited Madrid twice in 1963 to arrange a $150 million credit to Spain, while Armed Forces Minister Pierre Messmer and the chief of the French Navy, Admiral Georges Cabanier, flew down to plan military collaboration. Franco has granted De Gaulle space- and

* That is, until the advent of the Labour Government in October, 1964.

missile-tracking facilities in the Canary Islands, and is allowing French air and naval units to use the Canaries for refueling.

In May, 1964, Couve de Murville paid a formal three-day visit to Madrid, the first by any French foreign minister in thirty-two years. Correspondents who asked him whether a "Paris-Madrid-Rabat" axis was in the making were brushed off, but the idea was not without foundation. De Gaulle wants to forge a French-led community of European and Arab nations in the western Mediterranean.

France has agreed to help Spain build a nuclear power station near the Catalonian frontier, using natural Spanish uranium and taking 40 per cent of the power for industry in southern France. Other planned joint ventures include a natural gas pipeline from the French oil fields in Algeria across Morocco and Spain to France; bridges and motorways across the Pyrenean border; and a French-financed petroleum refinery near Barcelona. Spain is now France's sixth ranking trade partner.

In the political field, too, Paris and Madrid seem to be marching in step. Both have an interest in the stability of the Maghrib: Tunisia, Algeria, and Morocco. Morocco's King Hassan II flew to Madrid after seeing De Gaulle in June, 1963, and closeted himself for a ninety-minute interview with Franco. Spain has since indicated a willingness to discuss the cession of Ifni and the Spanish Sahara in return for guarantees to Ceuta and Melilla.

Along with his wooing of the Arabs and Africans, Franco has also been moving to achieve his own "accommodation" with the U.S.S.R. and its satellites. Spanish–Iron Curtain trade amounts to $50 million yearly, a drop in the bucket compared with Spain's $2 billion annual trade turnover, but nonetheless these contacts have brought a new politeness. Franco not only signed the Moscow nuclear-test-ban treaty in 1962, he also sent aid to the Yugoslav victims of the earthquake at Skoplje that summer, thus tacitly forgiving Tito's key role as a Commissar in the Spanish Civil War.

The Soviet Union has persistently sought a *détente* with

Franco. In recent years, there have been mounting contacts in Paris between Ambassador Vinogradov and Spanish Ambassadors Casa Rojas and, later, Motrico. The Caudillo, however, warned the Soviets of his price when he told the Stuttgart newspaper *Christ und Welt* in May, 1964, that relations could never be normal as long as Moscow "continues to be a center for Communist agitation in other countries and Spain is a priority object of that activity. In any case," he added, "the return of the [518 tons of] Spanish gold now in Russia would be indispensable."

Relations with Latin America

Friendship with Latin America remains a pillar of Franco's foreign policy, even though Spain's insistence on her right to trade and to retain political contacts with Castro has been misunderstood and criticized in the United States. The link between the right-wing Catholic Franco and the left-wing Communist Castro has been denounced as cynical, or sinister, or both. It is none of these. It is a combination of typical Spanish reactions: stubborn resistance to foreign pressure, a desire to protect the Spanish minority in Cuba and to foment good relations with all former colonies, regardless of their political coloration. From the right-wing Stroessner in Paraguay to the left-wing Castro, Franco intends to be on friendly terms with all.

This policy of Hispanity, or *Hispanidad,* is relatively new, yet it forms one of the main pillars of Spanish foreign policy, along with friendship for Portugal, for the Arabs, and for the United States. Since its inception at the start of World War II, and despite its early Fascist coloration, the policy of Hispanity has paid off. Thanks largely to Latin American support, Spain was finally admitted to full United Nations membership in 1955, and now, on most issues that concern her—Gibraltar, for instance —Spain can count on virtually all of the twenty votes in the Latin American bloc. Spain, in turn, voices the interests of the Latin Americans in European assemblies such as the OECD, and generally acts as their European political bridgehead. This newly found amity with the former colonies is in marked contrast to the past, which has been stormy.

The American and French revolutions had sparked the flames of discontent in Spanish America, and the Napoleonic invasion of Spain in 1808 had sent them roaring up into a conflagration. The flight of the Spanish Borbóns, the military juntas that sprang up to fight the French, the wild exultation set off by the liberal Cortes of Cádiz in 1812, and, finally, Napoleon's surrender three years later, all gave rise to hopes for enlightened rule in the colonies. It was not to be. The restoration of the worthless Fernando VII led to black reaction and brutal reprisals. Not only in Spain but especially in the colonies, all traces of liberalism were savagely suppressed. Yet the officers sent out from Spain to the New World to suppress liberalism carried the germs of liberalism with them. Many who had fought Napoleon's tyranny now turned their swords against Spain's tyranny.

By 1824, revolt after revolt had swept the Spanish colonies. Bolívar, San Martín, O'Higgins, Sucre, and Miranda had become world figures, and Spain's American empire—except for Cuba and Puerto Rico—had come to an end.

For nearly seventy-five years, until the beginning of this century, relations between Spain and the ex-colonies remained strained. Slowly, the tide began to turn, as signs of rampant U.S. expansion—the annexation of Texas, the Mexican War of 1846, and the acquisition of New Mexico and California—not only fostered suspicion of U.S. intentions, but sympathy for Spain. Few today could deny that but for the Civil War the southern boundaries of the United States would lie far below the Rio Grande.

The climax of Latin American suspicion of our "manifest destiny" came in 1898, when the weak McKinley Administration, goaded by the Hearst and Pulitzer chains, demanded of Congress permission to intervene against Spain in Cuba—although Spain had already agreed to all U.S. demands. The American victory and later domination of Spain's last colonies—Cuba, the Philippines, Guam, and Puerto Rico—added to the Latin Americans' mistrust. The mother country from whom they had torn away angrily was now humiliated, despoiled, and more to be pitied than feared.

Gradually, as the twentieth century began, Latin American sympathy for Spain rose, culminating in the successful 1929 Seville fair, which Primo de Rivera staged as a tribute to the former colonies. Not for a hundred years had the bonds been so warm, but they were short-lived. The collapse of the monarchy in 1931, and the social and economic disasters of the Second Republic led straight to Franco's military rebellion. Opinion in Latin America split violently between those who saw in Franco a Catholic savior of his country and those who saw a mountebank caricature of Hitler or Mussolini. The Latin American states began to choose sides. Guatemala and El Salvador became the first countries in the world to recognize Franco. The date was November 8, 1936—less than four months after the rising. They were followed by Hitler's Germany and Mussolini's Italy on November 18, and by Nicaragua on November 27. By April, 1939, when the United States finally recognized Franco, virtually all the Latin American states had done so.

Within six months, World War II had commenced, and now the latent Nazi-Fascist influences in Franco's movement burst out in a hysteria of imperial arrogance. Spain, it was predicted, would share in the spoils of the Axis victories and partake in the "redistribution" of Britain's and France's colonial empires. Self-mesmerized by Falangist nonsense, Franco created—one month before Pearl Harbor—the Council of Hispanity. Composed of Spanish envoys to Latin America plus intellectuals and churchmen at home (as well as the Spanish Consul General in the Philippines), the new organization was attached to the Foreign Ministry led by Serrano Suñer. Its overt mission was to strengthen Spain's prestige and its contacts in Latin America; its covert mission, to promote Nazi, Fascist, and even Japanese subversion and to sabotage the increasingly warm Latin American–United

States defense ties promoted by Roosevelt's Good Neighbor policy. Throughout World War II, Franco's Council, run by the Andalusian Falangist Manuel Halcón, struggled with meager success to countervail Allied influence in Latin America, but, by the war's end, Spain's prestige in the Southern Hemisphere had fallen to a new low. Every Latin American country—except Argentina under Perón—sided with the United States against the Axis. Virtually all criticized Franco's Axis ties.

Many Latin American republics joined in condemning Franco after the war. Mexico permitted the Spanish Republic Cortes-in-exile to meet in Mexico City in August, 1945, and its sessions were attended by observers from ten nations. Panama and Guatemala broke off relations with Spain; the Cuban House of Representatives publicly expressed hope that the Spanish people would soon "recover their liberty" and oust Franco; and shortly after, both Cuba and Bolivia also withdrew recognition.

Beset on every side, Franco now weeded the more notorious Falangists from his cabinet and junked the Council of Hispanity. In its place, he created an Institute of Hispanic Culture to concentrate on promoting Spanish culture in Latin America. The year 1946 marked the nadir of Franco's political fortunes, for he had defied world opinion and ordered several Republican opponents publicly executed. The outcry, fully exploited by the Soviet bloc, beat on Spain with hurricane force.

Panama demanded a United Nations investigation of Spain's conduct, and the Western Big Three (the United States, Great Britain, and France) denounced Franco publicly. In April, at Poland's insistence, Spain was accused of building "atom bombs" at Ocaña, a tranquil hamlet an hour south of Madrid, and the Security Council voted to investigate this "threat" to world peace. That an impoverished nation like Spain, exhausted by three years of civil war plus six years of world war isolation, could in 1945 have even designed, let alone built, an atom bomb, was patent nonsense. Yet so strong was world feeling that the United Nations seriously accepted the charges.

Franco, characteristically, refused the U.N.'s demands to investigate, and world opinion boiled over. On December 12, 1946, the General Assembly voted to bar Spain from its ranks, threatened sanctions, and called on all U.N. members to withdraw their chiefs of mission.

Behind the scenes, Perón was cautiously offering his hand to his Spanish colleague. Perón's own electoral victory earlier in 1946 had come about largely through Argentine popular resentment of U.S. Ambassador Spruille Braden's blustering intervention in the Argentine elections. With his victory, Perón was in a position to assist any fellow-victim of American moral disapproval. He concluded a trade agreement with Spain, and two years later, in 1948, came the Perón-Franco protocol to provide Spain with vital wheat on credit. The rich daughter was now maintaining the indigent, unpopular mother. To this day, there are many in Spain who recall how Perón's wheat ships saved Franco from food riots, and this explains why Perón has been granted political asylum in Spain for the last eight years.

From 1945 to 1950, isolated and bankrupt, Franco managed to hang on, and slowly the Latin American governments began restoring normal diplomatic ties. During 1948, for instance, Argentina, Costa Rica, the Dominican Republic, Ecuador, El Salvador, Paraguay, and Peru all returned their ambassadors, and an American envoy warned friends in the U.S. that

> Franco Spain is entering the arena with flying flags and rumbling drums and screaming trumpets, organizing that Iberian movement which the Franco press promised during the Spanish War . . . to "liberate our racial brothers from Yankee imperialism." They are putting out a beautiful magazine on fine paper, remarkably illustrated with old prints, paintings, pictures of Spain and colonial Chile. They are inviting as guests of the Franco government newspapermen, doctors, teachers, and even government officials. . . . We [the U.S.] have all but retired from the field.

Even more important, Latin American influence on behalf of Spain began to make itself felt in the U.N. Franco skillfully cultivated the U.N.'s two main voting blocs—the Latin Americans and the Arabs—and the campaign paid off. By early 1950, Secretary Acheson had admitted the failure of the cold-shoulder policy, and that autumn, the U.N. reversed its 1946 denunciation. The outbreak of the Korean War and Spain's geographic value to Western defense turned the tide.

The Spanish in Latin America, on the other hand, still remain centers of anti-Franco agitation. Most of them are emigrés who fled Spain after Franco's victory, and whose political influence—especially in Mexico and Venezuela—is still great. Yet, as in Paris and Toulouse (the two other chief centers of Socialist-Republican opposition), the old clenched-fist antipathy to Franco is dwindling. The emigrés in Latin America have settled into jobs, reared their families, and many have prospered. Spain's economic revival has awakened their interest, and this has begun to turn into a grudging admiration for the "old country," if not necessarily for Franco.

Spain's two postwar Foreign Ministers, Martín-Artajo and Castiella, have furthermore cultivated emigré good will, emphasizing Franco's offers of political amnesty to all willing to return and abstain from political activity. His envoys in Washington—Motrico, Garrigues, and now Merry del Val (appointed in May, 1964)—have also urged a reconciliation through the OAS (Organization of American States), to which Franco recently gave a bust of the sixteenth-century Spanish theologian-jurist Francisco de Vitoria.

During his tenure (1945–56), Martín-Artajo used the annual October 12th "Day of the Race" celebrations for a ringing appeal to Latin American (and Philippine) good will, stressing the ties of blood, language, religion, and culture, but always playing down any suspicion of Spanish hegemony. By 1953, however, his annual speeches began hinting at the desirability of "common" political action. That year, Franco had scored two diplomatic triumphs—the Vatican Concordat and the U.S.–Spanish defense agreements—and could risk to take a more vigorous line. In 1954,

Martín-Artajo even urged Hispanic "super-nationality" or double nationality and called for reciprocal tariff agreements, for an Ibero-American payments union, and for bigger and better trade fairs.

To suggest that such appeals set the chancelleries of Latin America agog would obviously be an exaggeration. Yet, they did create an awakening interest. Mario Amadeo, a former Argentine Foreign Minister, while visiting Spain that summer, told an audience at Zaragoza that the Hispanic peoples should assert their "due role" in preserving world peace. José Antonio Mora, the Uruguayan Secretary General of the OAS, affirmed at Salamanca in 1964 that Spain is "part of us." Far from seeking to separate from Spain, he said, Latin America is seeking bonds that unite and essentials that bind the two regions. He praised the historic University of Salamanca as the model for the great majority of Latin American universities.

While a deep-seated suspicion of Franco exists among Latin American intellectuals, workers, and students (as it does in Spain itself), Spain's comeback is being closely watched. The 1957 cabinet reshuffle, which brought the Opus Dei "technocrats" to prominence; the 1959 economic reforms; the hardening of the peseta; the tourist boom; the rise of Spain's gold and dollar reserves to an unprecedented $1.5 billion; and recent cautious advances in social legislation have stirred Latin American interest. More than 14,000 Latin American students, for instance, are now studying in Spain, including 1,000 Puerto Ricans who, for reasons of language, lower costs, or environment, have preferred Spain's medical schools to those in the United States.

Meanwhile, the Institute of Hispanic Culture, headed by Gregorio Marañón Moya, is promoting cultural activities over the length and breadth of Latin America. Most Spanish ambassadors in Latin America are men of letters in their own right, and in the Spanish diplomatic service an assignment to Latin America is now a prerequisite to promotion.

Of all the ties between Spain and her ex-colonies, the ties of religion are probably the most enduring. Here the Spanish Church is continuing its traditional paramountcy. There are some 18,000 Spanish priests or brothers of various religious orders and 15,000 Spanish nuns working among the 200 million Catholics of Latin America.

It is in trade, however, that Spain is making her most effective approach to Latin America.* More and more Latin American buyers are visiting Spanish trade fairs, drawn both by the annual 11 to 15 per cent rise in Spain's industrial output and by the successful start of the Four Year Development Plan. Spain's modern ship-building industry is filling Latin American orders, including coastal vessels for Cuba, and there is also growing interest in Spanish books, canned foods, bicycles, textiles, chemical products, and other manufactured goods. Spain's trade with Latin America now runs at around $250 million yearly—$180 million in imports and $70 million in exports—about 7 per cent of her world trade. The target figure is 10 per cent, but owing to a recent boost in Spain's exports to other markets nearer home—the Common Market and the Arab states, particularly—Latin America's share is less than was planned. Nonetheless, Latin American businessmen welcome Spain's support of their interests in the OECD and look forward to the day—perhaps ten years from now—when Spain can become their bridgehead in the European Common Market.

Spain's future remains a chief topic of interest for many Latin Americans, as for Spaniards themselves. Opinion in a continent of nearly 200 million varies widely, but a leading Latin American statesman remarked recently in Washington that a Monarchist restoration in Spain might be viewed favorably by Latin America. "England, Holland, and Denmark are all monarchies, and true democracy exists there," he pointed out. "It all depends on whether democratic institutions are allowed to function again in Spain. That is what really matters to Latin Americans."

* On March 30, 1965, Spain loaned $20 million in U.S. currency to the Inter-American Development Bank for development projects in Latin America—her first loan to the Alliance for Progress program.

Spain has already negotiated treaties of friendship with eight Latin American states; cultural agreements with four more; emigration and social security pacts with another two; and individual "double-nationality" treaties with Chile, Peru, Paraguay, Guatemala, Nicaragua, and Bolivia. Since Evita Perón's much-publicized visit to Franco in 1947, the Caudillo has received Ricardo Arias of Panama in 1953, the late Dominican dictator Trujillo in 1954, Brazil's Kubitschek in 1956, and Argentina's Frondizi in 1960. He sent his own former Foreign Minister, Martín-Artajo, around Latin America in 1953, his current Commerce Minister, Ullastres, on a similar swing in 1961, and Castiella to Central America in 1962.

Only Mexico, with its revolutionary background, still refuses diplomatic recognition of Franco. Ex-President Cárdenas is widely viewed as Franco's die-hard critic. Yet even his influence is diminishing. Mexico allows Franco to maintain a liaison office in Mexico City, and growing numbers of Mexicans are touring Spain. One of the gayest sights in Madrid last spring was a posse of Mexican *chorros,* or cowboys, in western saddles, silver-trimmed chaps, and huge cartwheel sombreros, prancing and pirouetting their horses down the highway from Franco's Pardo Palace, where the Caudillo had cordially reviewed them. Wherever they rode throughout Spain, they drew enthusiastic crowds.

Above all, the old specter of U.S.–Spanish rivalry throughout Latin America seems buried, although Cuba still occasionally bedevils Spanish–U.S. relations. One incident took place in the spring of 1964, when Spain was preparing to deliver coastal fishing vessels to Cuba as part of a Cuban-Spanish trade agreement totaling around $12 million yearly. The State Department, under White House and Congressional pressure, announced that aid to five (out of nineteen) nations trading with Cuba would be cut or frozen. One of the five singled out for "punishment" was Spain; the others were Great Britain, France, Yugoslavia, and Morocco. Had the American gesture been effective, it might have been easier to ignore Spain's protests, but Spain was receiving little "aid," anyway. It was a blunder, characterized by *The Times* of London as "legislative impatience" and by *The New York Times* as an example of conducting foreign policy from "weakness, not strength."

"In the case of Britain, France, and Yugoslavia," noted *The New York Times*, "the cut in military aid is the merest tap on the wrist. In the case of Spain and Morocco, whose aid total will be frozen, more is potentially at stake, but not enough to force these countries to give up their trade with Cuba. Greece and Japan are inexplicably left unpunished."

Max Frankel, *The New York Times*' diplomatic correspondent, citing the "continuous failure" of the U.S.–sponsored trade embargo on Cuba, also noted the "number of statements and motions that [the Johnson Administration] came to regret."

The outcry forced the State Department to back down, and within a week the threat of punishment for Spain had been dropped.

Slowly, the diplomatic temperature returned to normal, and by May, Franco's new Ambassador to Washington, the Marqués Merry del Val, on presenting his credentials, heard President Johnson express warm thanks for the "good wishes of General Franco"—a reference the late President Kennedy would have avoided. Johnson, no doctrinaire hater, stressed U.S.–Spanish cultural and historic ties, and the "remarkable economic and social progress made under Franco."

Slowly, but successfully, Franco was continuing what the *Economist* once called his "crabwise sidle" back to respectability.

U.S.–Spanish Defense Ties

On the evening of September 26, 1963, three men stood sipping champagne in the office of the U.S. delegation at the United Nations in New York. One was Secretary of State Dean Rusk, tall and massive, yet carrying his bulk with surprising ease. Another was Spain's Foreign Minister, Fernando María Castiella, a square-shouldered, square-handed Basque, a tough bargainer, and very proud of his Texan grandmother. The third was Spain's Ambassador in Washington, Antonio Garrigues, whose romantic looks do not prepare people for his knife-sharp legal mind.

Their mood was hardly festive. Rather, it was one of fatigue and relief. A year's prolonged, often bitter, negotiation had ended minutes before, and the three had signed a new U.S.–Spanish agreement, extending for five years America's right to air and naval bases in Spain.

The main point of the agreement was the continuing U.S. control of Rota, the great naval base near Cádiz, on which the U.S. had spent more than $250 million and which was rapidly becoming the major Mediterranean base for the Polaris submarines. Each of these great underwater vessels carried sixteen nuclear missiles, each missile capable of destroying an enemy city 2,500 miles away. With the use of Rota guaranteed for another five years, U.S. strategic control over the Mediterranean and eastern Atlantic remained unassailable. American press comment was generally favorable.

The New Bedford, Massachusetts, *Standard-Times* termed the U.S. bases in Spain of "supreme importance" in view of the recent withdrawal of the Jupiter missile from the Mediterranean. It was paradoxical, the newspaper said, to lavish aid on Indonesia, "rich in every resource," while Spain, "our steadfast ally, with much of its land barren [sits] way below the salt."

The New Orleans *States-Item* insisted that the new agreement should cause "relief" in Western circles, while its colleague in New Orleans, the *Times-Picayune,* praised "quiet, responsible diplomacy." The first U.S.–Spanish pacts, in 1953, had been between "landlord and tenant," it said; the 1963 version was between "defense cooperators."

The Philadelphia *Inquirer* hailed the new agreements as a "matter for quiet rejoicing," and noted that although there had been disturbing reports that Franco was going to hold out for "fantastic demands—he didn't."

Two of the leading U.S. newspapers, however, took diametrically opposite viewpoints. *The New York Times,* alluding to widespread political criticism, "not to say abhorrence," of Franco's regime, claimed that in real terms Franco seems to have got "nothing." *The Washington Post* insisted that the "shrewd" Caudillo had got what he most wanted: "a new status as a partner." Franco, it declared, was now a "virtual ally" of the U.S. and had won a "new degree of international prestige."

It is ironic that the United States should be the nation most responsible for reviving Spain's prestige, for no nation had done more to erode it. Soon after the American Revolution (aided and financed in part by the liberal-minded Charles III of Spain), American settlers gradually dislodged the Spanish from Florida, the Gulf Coast, and Spain's huge holdings west of the Mississippi. In the nineteenth century, the U.S. conquered what is now Texas, Arizona, New Mexico, and California. The American victory over Spain in 1898 not only stripped a decadent empire of Cuba, the Philippines, Guam, and Puerto Rico but exposed the rot at home, thus animating the celebrated "generation of '98" whose poets, writers, and philosophers excoriated the Spanish ruling oligarchy.

Most Americans ignored Spain in the first third of this century. When the victory bells ceased pealing for Admiral Dewey and Theodore Roosevelt, Spain was virtually forgotten. The fall of King Alfonso XIII in 1931 brought a ripple of interest, but it was not until a cabal of rebellious generals launched Spain into a full-scale Civil War on July 18, 1936, that American interest focused on the Iberian peninsula. Then, for the next three years, American opinion divided sharply between those who viewed Franco as Spain's Christian defender and those who saw him as a squalid offshoot of Nazism. Paradoxically, by winning the Civil War, Franco hung the millstone of American disapproval around Spain's neck. His ties with Hitler in World War II confirmed American hostility.

In 1945, despite more urgent problems, the United States sought to root out Franco by the technique of high moral disapproval. At Potsdam, Truman, Stalin, and (more reluctantly) Churchill agreed to bar Franco from the United Nations because of the "origins, nature, record, and close association" of his regime with the Axis. Between 1948 and 1952, approximately $16 billion in U.S. Marshall Plan aid was poured into Europe, but not a penny went to Spain.*

Time and Communist aggression, however, were working for Franco. As Stalin's appetite grew, American military experts became convinced that Spain's position at the mouth of the Mediterranean was too vital to ignore.

General Alfred M. Gruenther, at the time director of the Pentagon's Joint Staff, recognized, for instance, the strategic value

---

* Technically, it was the European recipients themselves who decided on allocations and thus barred Spain from aid. Nonetheless, when Representative Alvin O'Konski (R., Wisconsin) persuaded the House of Representatives to vote Spain's inclusion, President Truman objected, and the Senate backed him.

of Spain's geography—but, always, the military advantages of Spain were outweighed by the political disadvantages. The United States had no qualms about alliances with Chiang Kai-shek, Syngman Rhee, and other right-wing dictators—but Franco remained a pariah.

Chance often influences world affairs, however, and it was chance that led to the appointment of Lieutenant Commander John Fitzpatrick, USN, as Assistant Naval Attaché in Madrid in 1947. This appointment was significant because Fitzpatrick was the son-in-law of Admiral Forrest Sherman, the future Chief of Naval Operations and architect of U.S.–Spanish defense ties.

During 1947, Mrs. Sherman began to visit her daughter and son-in-law in Madrid, coming to know Spanish hospitality and Spanish officials, and reflecting her impressions to her husband. Few high American officials had any knowledge of Spain or its people in 1947, and Sherman was grateful for the courtesy and kindness shown his family in the Spanish capital.

His favorable opinion was strengthened the following year, when he was named commander in chief of the U.S. Sixth Fleet and, in effect, a roving American ambassador in the Mediterranean. The 60,000 sailors and marines aboard the huge Forrestal-class carriers, the escorting cruisers, the destroyers, the tenders, the submarines, and the air squadrons provided a rich market for Mediterranean merchants, and Sixth Fleet visits to Mediterranean ports were economically important. In addition, several Mediterranean nations—including Spain—were periodically invited to send units to the Sixth Fleet for training and maneuvers. When Sherman returned to Washington in 1949, to become Chief of Naval Operations, his visits to Spain and his contacts with Spanish officials had made him a firm proponent of U.S.–Spanish defense ties.

The Communist attack on Korea in June, 1950, and the danger of a Soviet attack on defenseless Western Europe brought urgent demands in Congress for a crash rearmament program. Six months later, at a hastily convened meeting in Brussels, the

United States and its allies agreed to pool troops and resources in Europe under the supreme command of Eisenhower, and shortly after, Admiral Sherman, who had attended the parley, flew to London to confer with his friend Admiral Robert B. Carney, the commander of all U.S. naval forces in northern Europe and the lower Mediterranean.

Sherman and Carney quickly agreed on the need for bases in Spain. Sherman toyed briefly with the idea of sending Carney to Spain in civilian clothes to make soundings, but the idea was abandoned. Carney was already being considered as Eisenhower's deputy for NATO's Mediterranean flank and any such visit, if discovered, would have violent repercussions. Sherman returned to Washington, certain that he alone could bring the Spanish project to fruition.

After a full year of high-level argument. President Truman gave way. "I don't like Franco and I never will," he told Sherman after long soul-searching, "but I won't let my personal feelings override the convictions of you military men."

On July 14, 1951, Admiral Sherman, his wife, Fitzpatrick, and a few aides took off for Spain in the CNO's new DC6-B. Four and a half centuries earlier, an admiral of Spain had sailed for the New World. Now an American admiral was returning the compliment.

Two days later, on July 16, U.S.–Spanish agreement was reached "in principle." Franco received Sherman, Ambassador Stanton Griffis, and Fitzpatrick in the Pardo Palace, but "neither Franco nor Sherman discussed details," Fitzpatrick recalls. "They talked about the need to improve U.S.–Spanish relations in view of world conditions, and they agreed. They left the question of bases and military or economic aid to later negotiations."

Franco was "exceedingly cordial," and invited Admiral and Mrs. Sherman and their aides to be his guests at the traditional July 18 garden party at LaGranja Palace, which marks the start of the Spanish summer. The next day, Sherman flew to Paris to see Eisenhower at SHAPE, and on July 21 went on to Naples to see Carney. One day later, he died of a heart attack.

He and Franco had reached agreement in two hours, yet it was to take their governments two years to settle the details. There were many reasons why. To begin with, Washington had no precise idea what it wanted in Spain or how to negotiate with Spaniards. The United States was accustomed to dealing with wartime allies, with conquered enemies such as Germany, Italy, and Japan, or with Latin American clients. Spain, impoverished but proud, was a puzzle.

The United States believed, correctly, that by proffering aid it was doing Franco a favor but, incorrectly, that it could automatically "rent" bases from him. Franco had no bases to "rent"; he had only bases to share, provided the Americans would build, equip, and man them and help put Spain on its feet in the process.

The United States was hypersensitive over its role as champion of democracy and embarrassed to be seen dealing with Franco. There were many in the U.S. Government who flatly opposed any tie with Franco; others dreamed of ensnaring the dictator in the coils of U.S. aid, thus shoving him off stage. Franco learned soon of these schemes, and they fortified his Gallegan suspiciousness of U.S. intentions.

The NATO allies also objected to any U.S. tie with Franco, in whom they saw the legatee of Hitler and Mussolini. By some somersault of logic, no objection was raised to NATO membership for Portugal, whose courtly, white-haired dictator, Dr. Antonio Oliveira de Salazar, jailed his critics, stifled free speech, and suppressed trade unions no less ruthlessly than Franco. Yet Franco's name and his personality seemed to goad Americans. As one State Department official observed, "We'll never get close to Spain until Franco changes his name."

If there were doubts along the Potomac, there were also doubts along the Manzanares—the turgid little stream that trickles through Madrid. A virulent, doctrinaire anti-Americanism infected many of Franco's generals, bishops, and bureaucrats, and Franco, who had fostered anti-Americanism before and during World War II, knew it only too well. He was now suddenly asking the Spanish people to ally themselves with a "decadent" democracy that he had so long vilified. It required preparation. To have ordered his officials merely to obey him would have proved useless, for no one excels the Spaniard in mulish obstruction. Nor was this Franco's technique of rule: he preferred always to let time bear the burden along for him. Time alone could prepare the terrain.

That autumn of 1951, the Pentagon picked Major General James Spry, an aviator with Latin American experience, to lead a small military survey team to Spain. As word of Spry's mission began to circulate in the Pentagon, the air force, the army, the navy, and even the marine corps began climbing on the bandwagon. Spry's survey team soon grew to ninety.

The Spanish, now seeing so big a Pentagon contingent arrive in Madrid, automatically assumed that it had come to "negotiate," but their optimism soon gave way to chagrin when Spry explained that he and his party had come merely to look around. The Spanish, traditional masters of bureaucracy, had finally met their match.

Spry's mission remained in Spain six weeks, seeing everything it wanted, being accorded every facility. When it flew home with no promises made, the Spanish draped themselves in their dignity, resentful and suspicious. It was to take two years and two months before the U.S.–Spanish base agreements were signed, and by then, the Korean War was over.

What did the United States and Spain agree to on September 26, 1953?

The United States received permission to build and use for ten years "joint" air bases at Torrejon, near Madrid; at Zaragoza and at Móron de la Frontera; a major air supply depot near Seville; a naval and naval-air base at Rota on the Bay of Cádiz; seven radar sites; and twenty-three other military installations

ranging from microwave communication stations and naval ammunition dumps at El Ferrol and Cartagena to a 485-mile jet
fuel pipeline running from Rota through Móron and Torrejon
to Zaragoza.*

This vast complex cost approximately $500 million to build
and equip and required 12,000 U.S. servicemen (accompanied
by 25,000 wives and children) to man. Under the 1953 agreement, it would be available for a ten-year period, followed by
two automatic five-year extensions, provided neither government
renounced the agreements. If one or the other did, six months
were provided for renegotiation. If negotiations failed, a further
year was provided for the "orderly" withdrawal of U.S. person-
nel and equipment. The United States thus was guaranteed occupancy of its Spanish bases at least until March, 1965.

In return, the U.S. agreed to provide Franco with $350 mil-
lion in arms (later raised to nearly $600 million) plus "defense
support"—a euphemism for economic aid. By 1963, Franco had
received nearly $2 billion in various types of aid.

To coat the pill for Congress and liberal U.S. sentiment, the
Washington-Madrid link was designated an "executive agreement" rather than a military alliance, since it did not specify the
mutual obligation of the two governments in case of war. Franco,
at Washington's urging, agreed to balance his budget, encourage competition, and assist the U.S. Government in "observing and reporting on labor conditions" in Spain, and also to
cooperate with the United States in the strategic embargo on
trade with the Communist world.† The United States, in turn,
justified its economic aid to Franco on the grounds that "individual liberty, free institutions, and genuine independence," as
well as defense in Spain, depended on a "sound" economy.

The United States committed itself only to defend its own

* The pipeline was crucial, for the SAC B-47 fleets stationed in Spain consumed in an afternoon as much fuel as the entire Spanish railway system could
transport in a month.

† This gave the United States the right to station a labor attaché in Madrid
and establish contacts with the politically volatile labor element in Spain.

bases in wartime; not Spanish soil or the Spanish people. More-over, it did not bind itself to "consult" Spain on major changes in weapons or strategy, even if they affected the Spanish bases. Thus, in 1953, the United States was in the fullest sense a "boarder." Ten years later, when the agreements came up for re-newal, the Soviet Union had its own nuclear capacity, and Franco no longer wanted a boarder—he wanted an ally.

Looking back, the $500 million base-building program had a beneficial effect on Spain's economy. Although at least 70 per cent of all materials required for the bases were imported from the United States, the acquisition of the remaining 30 per cent spurred Spanish producers and imparted valuable techniques. At the height of the program, in 1957–58, the U.S. contractors* had 5,000 Spaniards employed directly, and another 15,000 in-directly, through Spanish subcontractors. When the bases were completed, Spain acquired $30 million worth of American con-struction equipment free.

At first, the xenophobic Spaniards regarded the promised inva-sion of American servicemen dourly, fearing an immediate rise in prices and drop in morals. The Church threw up its hands at the prospect of well-paid Protestants proselytizing needy Catho-lics while generals, civil governors, and Falangists brooded over the probable dissemination of liberal democratic ideas among the controlled masses. U.S. forces, however, were well disci-plined, and the U.S. commanders were handpicked.

Major General August W. Kissner, head of the military mis-sion in Madrid, ordered tight discipline and trouble-makers found themselves on the next plane home. U.S. uniforms were worn on the bases only—never in the Spanish streets. There were occasional rapes, bar brawls, and attacks on taxi drivers, but as the months passed and the American servicemen settled down, the combination of U.S. discipline and Spanish friendliness be-gan to work. Americans finishing their duty began to ask for re-assignment to Spain and, as base housing caught up with demand,

---

* The consortium known as Brown-Raymond-Walsh.

U.S. service families found themselves as happy in Spain as at any post in Europe.

The thorney religious problem proved less serious than expected. At each base, the senior American chaplain was a Catholic, responsible for liaison with local Spanish Catholic authorities, and so friendly did relations become that even Protestant chaplains soon found themselves invited with their Catholic colleagues to the homes of local Spanish prelates.

"I don't know who was converting whom," said one Protestant chaplain returning from dinner with a Spanish bishop, "but we had a wonderful time!"

This liaison smoothed over issues arising from mixed marriages between young Protestant or Jewish servicemen with local Spanish Catholic girls. Eventually, hundreds of marriages took place. In each case, the prospective groom was "vetted" by the U.S. base chaplains and given religious instruction to avoid complications with the overwhelmingly Catholic population.

In the early years, lack of suitable housing and recreation facilities posed problems. The Pentagon, hoping to avoid the much criticized "golden ghettoes" of France and West Germany, had hoped to blend its service families into the Spanish economy, but Spanish standards of plumbing, light, heat, and furnishings were not up to the tastes of young American wives away from home for the first time and at sea in the Spanish tongue. In time, military "Levittowns" sprang up around the bases, and morale improved.

"About 5 per cent of our people want to live among the Spaniards, speak their language, and get to know them," said one U.S. base commander. "The other 95 per cent want American schools, American hospitals, American movies, American food, and American recreation. Once they have these, they like Spain.

The Pentagon grew well content with its Spanish bases as the 1950's turned into the 1960's. There were no left-wing demonstrations in Spain, no Aldermaston marchers, no demagogues scribbling "U.S. Go Home" on the walls. Nor did workers strike in Spain. Washington, beset by crises in NATO, in Southeast Asia, in Korea, in Latin America, and elsewhere, began to take Spain for granted, and the belief grew that Franco had been "paid" enough to ensure compliance. This, however, was a serious misapprehension. Franco thought that he had excellent reasons for demanding a new and better agreement in 1963.

It is difficult to appreciate Franco's almost pathological need for respectability.

Apart from prestige, Franco also wanted American protection. The world strategic situation had altered strikingly since 1953. Then, the United States had had an atomic monopoly; by 1963, Russia too had ICBM's.

Ten years of collaboration with U.S. experts had opened the Spanish eyes to the problems of nuclear war, and Spanish generals had come to see that Soviet missiles could destroy the cities of Spain. Since 1953, the stabilizing influence of British and French power in the Mediterranean had been declining, and along North Africa there were now a series of nationalist Arab states, all politically unstable. Tunisia, Algeria, and Morocco were especially prey to leftist agitation. Morocco's attack on Spanish Ifni in the winter of 1957–58 had left deep scars. And Soviet-donated MIG's were already sitting on Moroccan airfields, ten minutes' flying time from southern Spain.

There was, furthermore, the nightly Communist radio propaganda from Prague and Moscow, interspersing news with hints of nuclear retaliation. This propaganda was beginning to tell, and there were now few Spaniards unaware of the fact that the mighty SAC base at Torrejon lay only thirteen miles from Madrid, a prime target in case of war.

These, then, were Franco's politico-strategic problems as the initial ten-year base period drew to a close: the need for prestige, Spain's defenselessness against Soviet attack, and the sinister effect of Communist propaganda. There was another problem, however, of cardinal importance: the insistence of the armed forces on new arms. This, as much as anything, spurred Franco to act.

By 1960, with an eye on 1963, the Spanish had begun to assume that the Pentagon would again pay a stiff price. The three fighting services, therefore, compiled a massive Pentagon "shopping list." Visions of plums danced before their eyes as Spain's generals and admirals conjured up new motorized divisions and ground-to-air weapons systems for the army; "baby" aircraft carriers and guided missile destroyers for the navy; squadrons of costly new F-102, F-104, or F-5 jet fighters for the air force. To compound the confusion, each Spanish service began privately lobbying with its U.S. counterpart in the Joint U.S. Military Advisory Group (JUSMAG) in Madrid.

By 1961, the Spanish requirements list had swollen to a staggering $500 million. It was, in fact, so excessive that it was slashed by Major General Joseph Caldara, USAF, JUSMAG chief at the time, who implored Captain General Muñoz Grandes to force the quarreling Spanish services to coordinate their priorities and squeeze the water out of their demands before submitting them to the Pentagon. But for all his rank and gruff honesty, the grizzled old warrior would or could do nothing. Draping himself in Castilian dignity, he declared that Spain's military needs had been cut to their irreducible minimum and any suggestions to cut them further would constitute "interference" in Spain's affairs!

So it happened that a still grossly inflated $250 million request for arms was forwarded to the Pentagon in June, 1961, and, as Caldara had warned, ended up in a pigeonhole. Not only was the U.S. gold drain already alarming the Kennedy Administration; Congressional and public opinion was turning against foreign aid.

Now, for the first time, the ugly words "Spanish blackmail" began circulating in Washington's halls. It was not, in fact, blackmail as much as a characteristically exaggerated Spanish belief in her own strategic importance and in the fighting capacities of her men. It was what the Spanish call *pundonor,* a sense of magnificent, if unreal, self-assurance. The United States would find no truer allies against Communism, the Spanish insisted, so it was not charity but justice that Spanish forces should be as well armed by the United States as, say, the armies of Chiang Kai-shek, Diem, or Sukarno.

Franco's opening move came on October 1, 1961, the twenty-fifth anniversary of his seizure of power. He timed it shrewdly. The diplomatic corps was invited to Burgos to observe a two-hour military review where U.S. M-47 tanks manned by swarthy, black-bereted Spanish tank crews clanked down the streets; Spanish infantry marched proudly past or sat at rigid attention in U.S.–built troop carriers; while overhead, Spanish pilots in U.S. F-86's screamed low over the rooftops, before fanning out over the flat Castilian mesa.

Franco issued his preliminary warning to the United States in characteristically vague style. After the parade, he told a rally of his army chiefs that the time was approaching for a *renovación* of the 1953 agreements. Four-fifths of the initial ten-year period had already elapsed, and world strategic conditions had changed.

His warning appeared next day in American and European newspapers, but if it made any impression in Washington it was not evident. Fifteen more months were to pass while Washington waited to see if Franco was serious.

Nine months later came the first signs of Spanish stirring. Mariano Iturralde, Spain's caretaker ambassador in Washington, had died unexpectedly, and, at Castiella's urging, Franco now named Antonio Garrigues to replace him.

Garrigues' appointment was a surprise, for the new envoy was no Franquista. He had even served the Republic as a high official in the Ministry of Justice. Politically, he was, if anything, a liberal Monarchist, with ties to the Church, to the legal profession, and to business circles. His family was prominent, one brother, Joaquín, being a liberal professor of law, and another, Emilio, a prominent diplomat. The Garrigues clan was in no sense linked with the regime, and one of Garrigues' nephews had even been arrested on suspicion of anti-Franco political activities.

Garrigues' legal prowess had won him a host of top-flight American clients, including IBM, Hilton, Westinghouse, RCA, Standard Oil, and the Chase Manhattan Bank. If any Spaniard knew the American mind, it was Garrigues, and it was his knowledge of American methods, his contacts in Wall Street, and his political independence that had led Castiella to sponsor his appointment. That Franco accepted Garrigues was proof of his desire for an understanding with the United States.

There was also a personal reason for his selection. Fate had given him a curious link with the Kennedy family.

In the spring of 1939, as the Spanish Civil War was drawing to its close, Madrid lay encircled by Franco's troops. The Republican Government had fled to Valencia, 300 miles to the east, leaving only a narrow corridor linking it with the capital. As Franco's pressure grew, Madrid swarmed with Communist, Socialist, and Anarchist bands clashing with each other and hunting down suspected Franco sympathizers. In this grim atmosphere, Garrigues, his wife, and his children waited for deliverance.

One day, a young American who had managed to slip in through the Valencia corridor appeared in Madrid with a letter of introduction. He was Joseph P. Kennedy, Jr., a recent graduate of Harvard.

Soon after Kennedy's arrival, he, Garrigues, and two Spanish friends were driving up the winding "S" Street in the heart of the capital when their car was halted by an armed patrol. Covered by rifles, Kennedy, Garrigues, and the other two passengers were ordered to face a wall, their arms raised, while their papers were examined.

"We all carried various documents in those days," Garrigues recalled recently. "The problem was which set to produce. You never knew which faction was stopping you—Communist, Anarchist, or Socialist—and all were ready to shoot you on sight."

Young Kennedy's American passport apparently impressed the

militiamen. They examined it, held it up, murmured among themselves, and finally let the party go. Twenty-two years later, on presenting his credentials to John F. Kennedy, Garrigues told him the story, and a bond developed between the two men, for the President revered his late brother.

In July, 1962, Garrigues settled into the unfamiliar routine of Washington but with neither written instructions nor clear-cut negotiating authority from Franco and only fifteen months until the deadline. Two developments were taking place meanwhile, each destined to strain relations with Spain. One was the use of the Polaris submarine, now America's chief strategic weapon. The other was "Off-Set," a Pentagon formula for making foreign allies pay for U.S. arms.

Polaris had come of age by 1962, and the value of SAC's bomber fleets and bases in Spain was diminishing. The Spanish bases would be useful for ten more years for aerial refueling, for radar early warning, for dispersal, and for ferrying troops to the Middle East or Africa. Yet the Spanish knew that Rota was the apple of the Pentagon's eye, for the U.S. had spent $250 million or more to make it one of the most powerful submarine bases in the world.

Rota, on the Atlantic side of the Straits of Gibraltar, had long supplanted Gibraltar as the key to the Mediterranean. U.S. naval bases inside the Mediterranean might lie exposed to Soviet missile attack, but Rota lay sufficiently far away for protection. In war, U.S. aircraft and vessels operating from Rota could hunt down Soviet submarines throughout the eastern Atlantic, while the base's huge repair depot would save U.S. aircraft carriers a week or more spent in crossing the Atlantic to U.S. home ports.

There was, however, one major catch. While the Polaris submarine was unquestionably the most deadly weapons system ever devised, it was also political poison. No nation wanted Polaris subs in its ports, not merely for fear of accidents but to avoid left-wing propaganda. The sight of Polaris submarines in Holy Loch, Scotland, even the mere proposal to base Polaris in Japanese ports had been the signal for angry demonstrations. Politically wobbly NATO allies like Greece, Turkey, and Italy had begged Washington not to send Polaris to their harbors.

Franco had no desire to give the Communists food for propaganda without a *quid pro quo* from the United States. He demanded to be "consulted" in advance before the U.S. sent Polaris subs to Rota; but he misjudged Washington. Fearing a fuss, the Pentagon decided to slip Polaris subs into Rota by legal doubletalk.

Thus, as Garrigues was taking up his post in Washington, Muñoz Grandes received an apparently innocuous U.S. request to be allowed to dredge Rota harbor for the "safe berthing" of the Forrestal-class carriers. As an afterthought, the U.S. request, signed by General Caldara, added that Polaris subs might eventually be sent into Rota. No date was specified, and the Polaris issue was deliberately obscured by the query about dredging.

Muñoz Grandes' answer exceeded the Pentagon's fondest hopes. *"Doy autorización*—I give my authorization" for the dredging, the old warrior replied. Then, scenting no trouble, he added that he saw no objection in principle to the entry of Polaris subs but said that when the time came, the two governments should work out the details by "consultation."

For the Pentagon, this letter was "consultation" enough. If Spain's Vice President raised no objections, why kick the embers alive? Unfortunately, as it turned out, Muñoz Grandes had tossed off his authorization without consulting his own Foreign Minister. This, of course, was normal in Spain. Castiella was fifteen years his junior and had once served under him as a volunteer in the Blue Division. Military affairs were handled solely by military men. What did civilians know about bases?

The Pentagon's lack of candor with the Spanish Government was to lead to long and bitter arguments. There was little justification for the sleight of hand. In the years since 1953, Franco had never sought to hamper U.S. military operations in Spain. Over each U.S. base flew the Spanish flag, and each had nominal "joint" U.S. and Spanish commanders; but once these minor norms were accepted, the U.S. had had total freedom of operation. Spain had never, for instance, objected to the stationing of U.S. nuclear weapons on her soil, as had France.

Spanish cooperation had been admirable. No questions about nuclear arms were asked. Time and again, Franco had kept his word, and during the 1958 Lebanon landings, after France and Italy had refused U.S. requests to allow troop-carrier planes to refuel at their fields, Spain had agreed instantly when asked.

"That's what they're there for, isn't it?" Muñoz Grandes had growled when Major General Stanley J. Donovan, the JUSMAG chief, had come to him with the Pentagon's urgent request.

Meanwhile, the "Off-Set" issue was beginning to simmer. As its name implied, it was a device to offset America's gold loss by pressuring aid recipients to buy $2 billion worth of U.S. arms in the course of the coming five years. The scheme, devised in the Pentagon, had been enthusiastically welcomed at the highest levels.

The fanfare was dazzling, but collecting the money was not so easy. Japan and Italy were both on the Off-Set list and it was decided now that Spain, which was asking for $250 million in arms, could also be pressured into signing. Accordingly, William P. Bundy, then Deputy Assistant Secretary of Defense for International Security Affairs, was sent to Madrid as head of an Off-Set mission.

Bundy, an older brother of the White House's McGeorge Bundy, was one of the Pentagon's ablest young officials. Cool and perceptive, he might have worked wonders elsewhere, but his mission to Spain was poorly timed and poorly prepared. He was escorted, moreover, by a band of Off-Set promoters whose insensitivity to foreign mentalities in general was exceeded only by their indifference to Spain's in particular.

On January 11, 1963, he sat down in the Spanish Foreign Ministry, the lovely old Palacio Santa Cruz—a onetime prison for errant nobles—and proposed that Spain buy $85 million worth of arms for each of the next three years. By mischance, Bundy had not been taken to call on Muñoz Grandes, but was steered instead to the Foreign Undersecretary, Pedro Cortina, a jurist much given to legal metaphysics but with little power and less knowledge of defense. Cortina, hearing Bundy's dictum, almost gagged. Taking refuge in Castilian prolixity, he proceeded for an hour or more to lecture Bundy and his team on a variety of irrelevancies ranging from Spanish history to Communist subversion in North Africa. Added up, it amounted to a resounding "no."

Spain had no intention of providing U.S. bases free and spending $250 million of her hard-earned reserves on American arms, asserted Cortina. Her $1.2 billion in gold and dollar reserves was vital backing for the peseta, not a sign of opulence. Moreover, he continued, as the bevy of Spanish generals and admirals around him nodded obediently, the United States had already "promised" Spain $250 million in arms.

Now it was Bundy's turn. He quickly trumped Cortina's ace by producing a Spanish letter conceding that the United States had even exceeded its contractual arms obligations to Spain under the 1953 agreements. The U.S. military mission had *advised* the Spanish forces on their future needs, Bundy agreed, but this did not mean the United States was picking up the check a second time.

To break the deadlock, he hinted that the United States might give $75 million in arms if the Spanish would buy $175 million; but still it was no sale. Bundy and his Off-Set enthusiasts returned to Washington with empty hands, and Franco, convinced now that the U.S. meant to stall, grew irritated.

On January 14, 1963, Foreign Minister Castiella notified U.S. Ambassador Robert Woodward that Spain now demanded formal renegotiation of the 1953 agreements before the expiration date, September 26. Franco had thrown down the gauntlet.

Meanwhile, in Washington, the Off-Set team was angry. What was Franco up to? After consideration, the next step was decided. McNamara's chief assistant, Deputy Defense Secretary Roswell

Gilpatric was about to make Off-Set visits to Tokyo and Bonn, and Madrid was now added to his itinerary. His rank, thought the Pentagon, would quell Spanish obduracy, but again Washington misread the auguries. Again the Pentagon was sending a first-class emissary on a second-class mission.

On the day of his departure, Gilpatric was guest of honor at a luncheon in the Spanish Embassy and heard his host, Garrigues, note pointedly that Spain no longer intended to be "regarded and treated as a second-class associate from whom . . . one takes what one needs while excluding her from gatherings where decisions are made and policies outlined." Spain, he went on, "does not agree to be quarantined anymore."

Nevertheless, the Pentagon cabled Madrid that Gilpatric would arrive in a fortnight "to sign" the Off-Set proposal offered by Bundy and already refused. To Gilpatric's chagrin, on arriving in Tokyo next day, he found a reply from Madrid announcing tersely that the three cabinet ministers he wished to see would be away "hunting with Franco." If he still insisted on coming, he could see the prolix, but powerless, Cortina. Gilpatric tartly canceled his visit, and the press promptly speculated about a fresh crisis in U.S.–Spanish relations.

What had happened was characteristically Spanish. Incredible as it may sound, no one in Madrid seemed to know precisely who Gilpatric was—despite his rank. Inundated by the hordes of "deputy secretaries" who had flocked through Madrid in recent years, the Franco cabinet had not really ascertained Gilpatric's role as McNamara's chief deputy. Moreover, the truant cabinet ministers—Muñoz Grandes, Castiella, and Finance Minister Navarro Rubio—had had no intention of being pressured hurriedly by Washington. When Franco invited them to go shooting with him, they leaped at the opportunity. On such trips, the Caudillo was always relaxed, and one could catch his ear for pet projects.

Gilpatric thus avoided Spain on his way home, and on the Senate floor such fiery lawmakers as Wayne Morse of Oregon charged that Spain had "rebuffed and insulted" a U.S. official.

By now it was March, 1963, and three of the precious nine months had passed. Yet Madrid seemed paralyzed. When Woodward would ask Castiella what specific points Spain wished to renegotiate before September, the Foreign Minister would reply that the "military" were still pondering the problem.

In fact, the renewal issue was stuck flat on the mudbanks of indecision. No one from Franco down had any concrete ideas as to what to ask for or how to get it, and it was fast becoming apparent that Washington intended to stand pat and hold out for automatic renewal.

Public opinion in the United States, meanwhile, was running strongly against foreign aid—especially aid to Spain. The Clay Report on Foreign Aid, for instance, asserted on March 20, 1963, that economic and military aid already given to "certain countries in exchange for bases" seemed excessive and should be cut "especially [to] Spain which [is] already more than adequately compensated."

Garrigues, brooding night after night in his tapestried Washington office on 16th Street, now saw that Madrid's insouciant partridge-shooting ways were ill-tuned to success. The more he pondered, the more he realized that a completely new approach was essential. He poured out his ideas in a forty-page memorandum to Franco.

What Garrigues urged on the dictator was what no one else in Spain would have dared urge, and what no other man could have persuaded Franco to accept. It was nothing less than the exclusion of the all-powerful Spanish military from the negotiations, concentration of responsibility in Garrigues' own hands, and *carte blanche* to make the best deal he could. Never in twenty-five years had Franco delegated such authority over foreign negotiations; never certainly to a liberal Monarchist. He weighed the memorandum, called Garrigues back to Spain to discuss his ideas in person, and eventually accepted them *in toto*.

Garrigues insisted that Spain must create a moral negotiating basis and not merely hold out its hat; must seek an alliance, or at least get U.S. military guarantees. Perhaps then military and economic aid would follow. If these terms were refused, Spain could at least terminate the U.S. base rights with dignity.

Throughout all Garrigues' arguments ran the same thread: Only in step with the United States could Spain continue her recovery, insure her internal stability, and restore her civil liberties. Only in concert with the United States and other Western powers could Spain avoid the risk of a savage power struggle when Franco died. Garrigues' problem was not only to convince Franco, however; it was also to convince Washington.

Before flying home, Garrigues set up appointments in Washington with everyone who might help: Secretaries Rusk, McNamara, and Dillon; Senate Foreign Relations Committee Chairman Fulbright; Presidential Adviser McGeorge Bundy; Air Force Chief of Staff LeMay; Assistant Secretary of State for Europe William R. Tyler; and many others. On every hand he found sympathy, but little help. Spain could expect little aid, he was told; even less, an alliance.

The State Department seemed a major obstacle, for while the Pentagon saw the advantages of ties with Spain, the State Department seemed to stress the disadvantages. Assistant Secretary Tyler, for instance, knew and admired Spanish culture and spoke Spanish well, but he knew that many European nations were still emotionally hostile to Franco. Illogical though these dislikes might seem in 1962, they were facts, and international relations were based on facts.

As Tyler pointed out, Spain had acquired $1.2 billion in gold and convertible currency reserves and could hardly plead poverty. As for an alliance, it would be impossible to persuade the Senate that Spain had a better claim to automatic protection in event of war than several other friendly nations. In short, there was nothing to "renegotiate," and Spain should accept an automatic prolongation of the agreements on September 26.

Garrigues' hopes slumped. The weeks of strain, the endless conferences in an atmosphere of polite but unyielding resistance, the long nights of writing began to show. He had to struggle to keep his temper in check and, in one celebrated conference in the State Department, he let it rip. Spain would go it alone, he stormed; the United States could pack up and go! Some believe that his outburst was devised to shock Washington. His strategy worked, but that night he returned to his embassy more weary than ever. It was the low point of the negotiations; it was late April—with only five months left.

The wheel of fate, however, had begun to turn. A few days later, Secretary McNamara called Garrigues to the Pentagon, and together with Gilpatric and Paul Nitze they weighed the situation in detail. This conference seems to have marked a psychological turning point, for Garrigues now learned that the Defense Department needed its bases in Spain for ten more years.

Progress continued. On May 3, shortly before his departure, Garrigues was urgently summoned to the White House, where he found President Kennedy in conference with Tyler. The President evidently had been warned of Garrigues' pessimism and had decided to take a hand in the matter before a rupture occurred.

Exerting his celebrated charm, Kennedy assured the Spanish envoy that there was no real problem between their two countries. The United States wanted close ties with Spain, he said, and intended to do what it could, but Spain had to recognize the political facts of life. An alliance was out of the question; neither was there much hope of appreciable military or economic aid. The President would see what could be done, however, to help meet Spain's needs.

Then Mrs. Lincoln, his secretary, entered to notify President Kennedy of an urgent telephone call, and as Kennedy excused himself, he paused in the doorway and remarked to Garrigues with a broad smile, "Bill Tyler's my man on this Spanish question and he has my full confidence. Why don't you and he just go ahead and sign the new agreement in my office before I get back?"

304

Tyler knew the young President's jocular humor but the European envoy, accustomed to the meticulous protocol of his own land, looked shocked. Nonetheless, the ice had been broken.

A fortnight later, Garrigues was back, armed with the first *written* instructions from Franco a Spanish envoy to the United States had ever had. Garrigues also had a letter from Castiella, naming him Spain's sole negotiator and formally asking Rusk for early negotiations. Rusk at last agreed to negotiate once Spain's requests were listed, and Garrigues plunged into work. It was now June. Three months remained.

He analyzed every U.S. treaty commitment around the world. With his Counselor, Nuño Aguirre de Cárcer, he pored over the texts of the treaties establishing NATO, CENTO, SEATO, and especially the U.S. treaties with the Philippines and Japan.

The U.S. bilateral treaty with Japan finally became his model. It included a provision for "consultation" on changes in weapons or strategy, which both the Pentagon and State Department had stoutly resisted but which the Japanese had eventually won. This was what Garrigues decided to obtain for Spain. Through "consultation," Spain would become a partner; later, perhaps, an ally. His ideas now took shape.

In June, Kennedy flew to Europe, and on his return, Tyler was sent to Moscow for the nuclear-test-ban treaty negotiations. In his absence, U. Alexis Johnson, Deputy Undersecretary for Political Affairs, took over supervision of the Spanish talks, and it was to Johnson that Garrigues finally presented the result of his labors on July 22, 1963. This took the form of a sixty-page memorandum, setting forth the type of guarantees Spain expected, and pointing out the hardship forced on Spain by her exclusion from NATO. Garrigues insisted it was up to the "imagination" of the United States to meet Spain's needs within the limits of American law and Congressional sentiment. This subtlety was not wholly welcome to the preoccupied State Department but at last, twenty months after Franco's murmur of discontent at Burgos, Spain was putting her demands on paper.

Five weeks passed as the government agencies pondered, and finally, on August 30, Undersecretary Johnson called Garrigues to his office and handed him the U.S. counteroffer. It came in two parts.

Part I was a joint statement in which the United States agreed that a threat to Spain (as distinct from the bases), would be a matter for "common concern." This was a major advance. It agreed, too, that the U.S.–Spanish defense ties would henceforth become part of the "security arrangements for the Atlantic and Mediterranean areas." This was neither an alliance nor even a mutual defense treaty, but it was more than Spain had had in 1953.

Part II proposed setting up in Madrid a permanent Joint Consultative Committee to discuss, at least once monthly, "mutual" defense problems. The United States would name as one co-chairman the chief of its JUSMAG and Spain, an officer of equivalent rank.*

If these proposals were acceptable as a negotiating basis, said Johnson, the United States might furnish Spain with limited military and financial aid; but this was as far as it could go.

It was already the end of August, and Garrigues realized that Franco would be in the north of Spain or at sea on his yacht, while the cabinet would be scattered. He cabled the American proposals and was ordered to fly home once more. Castiella was awaiting him at San Sebastián, and after a quick discussion the two men set off by car along the winding coastal road to Meirás, in Galicia, where Franco received them in his summer villa. There the Caudillo and four key advisors—Castiella, Muñoz Grandes, Navy Minister Nieto Antúnez, and Garrigues—plunged into a prolonged discussion.

Muñoz Grandes denounced the American concessions as neg-

---

* While many Americans regarded the new committee as mere window dressing, the Spanish won a significant, if little noticed, point: either nation could summon a special meeting, in Madrid or Washington, to be attended by "foreign, or other ministers, or *other high officials* [author's italics]," and to some this seemed to give Franco the right, if ever menaced by a foreign or domestic crisis, to demand a face-to-face meeting with the President of the United States.

ligible, and Nieto Antúnez, too, was critical. But the civilians, Castiella and Garrigues, insisted that the U.S. offer should not be rejected, that it was the best obtainable. As the hours passed, Franco finally inclined to their point of view.

Now it was urgent that the cabinet be gathered. On September 19, Franco gave his assembled ministers a forty-five-minute résumé of the American political climate. When he had finished, Garrigues was asked to speak—a rare honor. Opposition still flared. The military were still discontent, and the Opus Dei group considered the American offer derisory. Several ministers demanded a flat "no" to Washington and suggested that feelers be put out to De Gaulle, but once more Franco's realism tipped the scales. That night, Garrigues caught the plane back to Washington, the cabinet approval in his pocket.

One week remained. He began to race the clock as every hour new problems seemed to crop up. Castiella was due to attend the United Nations General Assembly meeting in New York and wanted to sign the accords before the watchful gaze of 111 nations.

Franco's insistence on prior "consultation" over major changes in weapons or strategy almost caused a breakdown. The Spanish had Polaris in mind, but even though Japan had already won this concession, the Pentagon and State Department continued to hold out. At last, the Spanish contented themselves with a U.S. "gentlemen's agreement" to consult.

Castiella arrived in New York, where he, Rusk, and Garrigues went into a final session. Rusk made a final offer: "matching aid." Spain's $250 million request would be cut to $150 million; the United States would provide $100 million—but Spain would have to buy $50 million herself. Castiella accepted it. As for economic aid, Treasury Secretary Dillon would agree only to Export-Import Bank loans (at 5.75 per cent interest) up to $100 million over the "next few years." This was all the aid Spain could hope for, but the United States and Spain were now on more nearly equal terms. The agreement was signed as the clock raced toward the deadline.

In the twenty-three months since Franco's vague warning at Burgos, Spain's hopes had often appeared bleak, but thanks to Garrigues* advocacy and Kennedy's good will, Spain had gained more than anyone might have foreseen.

Both nations had shown common sense. By recognizing belatedly Spain's desire for prestige, the United States had turned the 1953 "tenant-landlord" agreement into a defense partnership, if not a full alliance.

As *The Washington Post* had observed, Franco was now a "virtual ally" with a "new degree of international prestige."

---

* In May, 1964, his task in Washington completed, Garrigues was transferred to become envoy to the Holy See, a post as challenging and, for him personally, more congenial.

10

Economic Recovery

"Spain," noted the *Economist* in 1963, "is in a perfect whirlpool of reforms: banking, taxes, general accountancy, and the like."

The term is no exaggeration. In recent years, new laws, new projects, new plans, new reforms have followed in bewildering array and while—as always in Spain—there has been more talk than action, Spain's recovery has been dramatic. Some call it the "Spanish miracle."

Spain has begun to balance her budgets, has introduced tax and other reforms, has freed 70 per cent of her foreign trade from controls, and has seen her initial efforts praised by the prestigious eighteenth-nation OECD* as "very successful." The peseta is now one of the world's hard currencies; and while inflation still tugs, personal consumption and industrial output are steadily rising, and foreign investors see Spain as the "last untapped market" in Europe.

The great unknown remains, of course, who or what will succeed Franco; this no one can answer. However, the framework of reforms now being constructed will both buttress and guide

---

* Organization for Economic Cooperation and Development; a successor to the OEEC, which was created as a consortium of original Marshall Plan recipient countries.

any successor, and this fact has evidently impressed hardheaded foreign businessmen. In 1964, nearly $300 million in foreign capital flowed into Spain.

In Madrid, Barcelona, Seville, and other Spanish cities, streets nowadays are crowded with a better-dressed, better-shod, better-fed citizenry that has more money to spend than at any period of modern Spanish history. New factories are competing for space in the suburbs with vast low-cost housing developments as the population continues to grow.

The tourist industry is remaking the country's face. Along the Mediterranean, from Port Bou to Huelva, hotels, apartment buildings, villas, chalets, cinemas, restaurants, bowling alleys, and "urbanizations" are proliferating. New buildings swarm with workmen in rope-soled sandals and berets, singing or whistling as they plaster and hammer. New gasoline stations dot the main roads, and new trucks race buses. Not everything has changed, and often the huge vehicles must grind to a halt behind some slow-plodding cart as the driver casts black looks at a farmer asleep over the reins.

Still, for a country poised at the brink of bankruptcy in mid-1959,* Spain has made a heartening recovery. Her financial reserves have changed from a deficit of $4 million to $1.5 billion. The peseta won the *Financial Times's* "Oscar" for stability in 1962. Tourism, the largest single money-earner, grew 21 per cent in 1961; 16 per cent in 1962; 22 per cent in 1963; 28.8 per cent in 1964. In 1964, 14 million tourists deposited $1 billion in Spain's coffers.

Foreign capital, some of it admittedly "hot" money from Goa, Cuba, Macao, Panama, or the Middle East, has been flowing into Spain at an increasing rate. Before 1958, there was virtually no foreign capital: now the total is estimated at $700 million. These are positive indications for a country long caricatured as decadent, lazy, and corrupt.

The new ferment is noticeable everywhere except the country-

* Spain then had $63 million in gold and hard currencies; $67 million in debts.

side, which still lags a half century behind. Even the country-side, however, is changing as youth pours off the land, drawn to the cities for jobs and higher wages. In the past five years, half a million farm workers have quit agriculture for jobs in industry or service occupations, and the regime hopes that in the next four years another 340,000 will follow. The day of starvation wages is not yet over, but it is doomed. The expansion of economic activity, the pull of emigration, and especially the increase of the minimum daily wage to 60 pesetas at the beginning of 1963, led to what the OECD called "significant" new wage increases.

The rising pressure for higher wages, the emigration of 65,000 to 100,000 young workers yearly, and the persistent strikes in the northern coal mines and industrial belt all show that a silent revolution is taking place. Spain is awakening from a long sleep.

Why this transformation? There are many answers: internal peace, Europe's postwar boom, U.S. aid, tourism, the native dynamism of the Spanish people, and the new post-Civil War generation.

A quarter century of enforced peace has had a sobering effect on a people notorious for their restlessness.

Moreover, Europe's postwar boom, spurred by the Marshall Plan, has spilt over the Pyrenees, providing Spanish economists with a blueprint for recovery. The successful French Four-Year Plans, for instance, have been carefully studied.

American aid, too, must be given its due for having bought time, and thus stability, and for having given the Spanish people a psychological spur to reform. Frequently, the charge is heard that the U.S. military base-building program caused more inflation than it cured, but this is nonsense. Between the first American aid shipments in 1954 and the end of the program in 1962, nonmilitary American aid to Spain in all forms totaled $1.2 billion. Of this, 31.8 per cent consisted of foodstuffs, which saved the regime vital foreign currency; 32.8 per cent comprised raw materials to help Spain's idle factories get going; and 35.4 per cent consisted of capital equipment, machinery, and the like.

American aid never exceeded $200 million in any year, less than 2 per cent of the Spanish gross national product in 1955, for instance. Its value lay in its timeliness. It provided one-third of all of Spain's imports in the early years and freed Franco's regime from paralysis. Needless to say, no other nation furnished assistance in these crucial years, and if today Spain's economy is a healthy toddler, it is only fair to assert that without U.S. help it might have remained stillborn. Yet American aid has not, as sometimes claimed, been "responsible" for Spain's recovery.

A decisive factor has been the natural intelligence and energy of the Spaniards, now showing what they can do when controls are eased. The most important single stimulus has been the rise of the new post-Civil War generation, now reaching positions of leadership. This has had a profound sociological effect. Spain is less bitter, less absorbed by its past, and more concerned with its future. Suspicion of the foreigner is passing. Young Spaniards, though still barred by Franco from politics, are becoming absorbed by jobs, education, technical training, homes, social security, consumer goods, recreation, and holidays. This has inevitably brought a new materialism, yet personal standards of morality remain surprisingly high and the incidence of juvenile delinquency low. The family and the Church still play major roles.

Only time will tell whether a quarter century of enforced peace has altered the Spanish character. Some observers believe that it has not; that revolution will stalk the land on the morrow of Franco's death. Others, including myself, profoundly disagree. Political predictions are idiots' delight, but the Spaniard of the 1960's is not the Spaniard of the 1930's, or even of the 1940's.

Franco's ban on politics has deflected the Spanish energy into business and commerce, and this in turn has fostered a new conservatism. Each year, more new wealth is being created, and much of it eventually trickles down to the new middle class, to the workers, even to the peasantry.

Meat consumption, a key index of better times, increased 27 per cent per capita between 1955 and 1961. In 1953, not a car was built in Spain; in 1962, 74,500 were built. Television sales have jumped in five years from an annual 39,400 to 250,000. More than 100,000 refrigerators were built during the first nine months of 1963, compared with 30,000 during the year before; more than 97,000 washing machines, compared with 47,000. Electric output is *doubling* every seven years, owing to rising demand.

On a midsummer Sunday night in 1962, I sat with a Spanish friend at the luxurious Puerto de Hierro Golf Club outside Madrid. Beyond the golf course, in the gathering gloom, stretched the main highway to the north.

"Watch that road," said my host. "There's the story of Spain today."

Over the brow of the hill came a solid stream of headlights. My friend and I dined, returned, and still they came. Vespa and Lambretta motor scooters threaded in and out, but the bulk of the traffic consisted of little Spanish-built *SEAT*'s, Spanish-built Citroëns, Spanish-built Renaults. This was the new bourgeoisie of Spain returning from its Sunday outing.

"Five years ago, you might have sat all night and not seen a hundred cars," said my host. "Now it takes them hours to pass. If anyone wants to know what's happening in Spain—there's the answer."

The Four-Year Development Plan

On January 1, 1964, the Spanish Government launched its new four-year Plan de Desarrollo Económico y Social (Economic and Social Development Program). Not only was it the first attempt ever at long-range growth planning in Spain, but possibly the most important single factor in Spanish history since the Civil War.

El Plan, as it is known, sets growth targets—obligatory for state enterprises but, as in France, merely indicative for private enterprise. Private investment is expected to follow where the government bulldozer has first cleared off the scrub, and this already is happening. The Plan creates seven industrial growth and development zones* to which both Spanish and foreign investment is to be attracted by a variety of incentives: cash grants up to 20 per cent of a plant's cost; 95 per cent tax reductions; duty-free import of equipment; and officially guaranteed credit facilities. Already, some 700 applications have been submitted to the government, involving an estimated 80,000 new jobs. Early in 1964, lines of would-be investors, Spanish and foreign, could be seen queueing outside state offices to obtain options on low-cost industrial sites before the deadline.

El Plan calls for an over-all four-year investment of roughly $14 billion; $5.6 billion in governmental funds, the rest private. The emphasis will be two-thirds on "economic" development and the remainder on "social" projects: homes, schools, job training, and the like.

The aim is a 6 per cent annual rise in the gross national product†— a target only slightly higher than the 5 per cent growth of recent years. Annual income per person is expected to rise to $462 by 1967,‡ and the average income per member of the "active" population (between sixteen and sixty-five) from the present $810 to more than $1,000.

Spending priorities will be: transport (24.6 per cent), agriculture and irrigation (20.3 per cent), housing and urbanization (19.5 per cent), financing the state's industrial sector (17.1 per cent), and educational-vocational training (6.8 per cent). Almost 90 per cent of the program thus will go to five key sectors.

The regime plans, among other things, to repair 6,000 miles of roads, build 120 miles of throughways, and renew 2,000 miles of track. It plans to move 340,000 surplus workers off the land into industry and services, double the number of tractors to 200,-000, consolidate 2 million acres into economically sensible units,

---

* Valladolid, Burgos, Zaragoza, Vigo, La Coruña, Seville, and Huelva.

† The nation's total output of goods and services.

‡ Recent reports say that it is already nearing the $500 mark—ahead of schedule.

reforest 1.2 million more acres, and irrigate another 750,000, as well as extending soil preservation measures to 750,000 more.

It plans, furthermore, to build 720,000 low-cost apartments (620,000 of them state-subsidized) and 16,000 new primary-school classrooms; to place 75,000 more pupils in secondary schools, 107,000 more youths in vocational training. Four new technical colleges are to be built and the school-leaving age raised from twelve to fourteen.

New goals, new hopes, new ideas abound. For the statistically minded, it should be noted that by 1967 the Franco regime foresees an annual increase of 5.5 per cent in national consumption, 11 per cent in imports, 10 per cent in exports, and the creation of a million new jobs. Above all, the regime wants to attract foreign capital, and it is beginning to succeed. Since May, 1963, the barriers have been lifted, and foreigners now may invest in all sectors of Spain's economy (except defense, utilities, and public information), and repatriate freely their capital, profits, and dividends.

One hundred fifty U.S. firms are already doing business in Spain, and U.S. private investment has risen steadily. Nearly $300 million (40 per cent of the estimated foreign investment in Spain) today is American.

El Plan incorporates recommendations made in 1963 by a World Bank mission led by the British economist Sir Hugh Ellis-Rees. Not only has it become a milestone in Spain's history, it may prove the touchstone of Franco's success. If Spain remains stable after his death, his sins may be forgiven and forgotten.

The economic plan is too new to gauge: it is only a start.* It still arouses heated controversy between its sponsors, who see it as the straight and narrow path to salvation, and the Falangists, monopolists, and speculators, who decry it as a maneuver of "international capitalists," foreign competitors, and visionary pinks.

---

* Performance statistics covering the first half of 1964 indicate that the plan is succeeding, despite strikes and inflationary tendencies. In that period, the individual worker's hourly productivity reportedly rose 10.2 per cent, his wages 11.4 per cent.

It is neither of these. It is the product of twenty years' trial and error after a terrible civil war, followed by World War II and by isolation. It represents the junking of the Hitler doctrine of subordinating economics to politics.

These facts help explain what obstacles Franco has surmounted and why he has often acted as he has.

Spain's economy after World War II was not only starved of foreign trade but, still worse, strangled by controls. The Falangist doctrine was negative: Everything was forbidden that was not specifically permitted. Those with power won monopolies and killed off competition. The regime fixed all prices, set all wages, froze industry, and hobbled all imports to "protect" the home market. Labor was forbidden to strike and employers forbidden to dismiss labor. Spain obviously stagnated—except in the black market, in which a new generation of Spanish businessmen cut their eyeteeth.

In economics, as in love and war, the Spanish are extremists, and from the stagnation of the 1940's the pendulum began to swing to the inflationary boom of the 1950's. The acumen of the Spanish entrepreneur, sharpened by years of black-marketeering, began to transform the national scene. Everyone began to scramble, and now began the dramatic sprawl of Franco's Instituto Nacional de Industria (INI).

Conceived in 1941, and sold to Franco by Juan Antonio Suanzes, a brilliant naval engineer and lifelong crony, INI was the state's chosen instrument for overnight industrialization via the printing press. It was operation bootstrap: painless, and guaranteed to "free" Franco from foreign suppliers. Franco, of course, gave Suanzes his enthusiastic blessing.

By the mid-1950's, INI had swollen to an industrial octopus capitalized at more than $1 billion and controlling 70 plants throughout the nation. Criticism that it was squandering public funds on showy but uneconomic projects, such as the Aviles steelworks or the Puertollano shale-oil refinery, that it was concealing huge losses and competing unfairly with private industry, were ignored. Suanzes, backed by Franco, moved INI in where private enterprise could not or would not go, and no one dared gainsay him.

The regime now began to reap the whirlwind of inflation. Demand and deficit spending marched hand in hand. Between 1951 and 1959, the national income rose 400 per cent (in current pesetas) each year, although in fact, the real income rose also at least 50 per cent. Private banks, however, were forced to buy state bonds and then permitted to pledge them to the Bank of Spain at 10 or 15 per cent less than face value. The Bank of Spain issued more paper money. Speculators began making fortunes and corruption became rampant. One cabinet minister spent his last night in office, in 1957, signing dozens of lucrative import licenses for his friends. To keep up with rising prices, virtually everyone worked fourteen hours daily at two jobs and the national result was lowered efficiency.

Overnight, in February, 1957, men of a new school appeared at the helm: orthodox, austere, discreet. These were the technocrats whose sudden rise to power and whose intimate ties with Opus Dei aroused passionate debate. As *The New York Times'* Paul Hofmann wrote some time later, "the technocrats were in their forties, managerial types who look rather out of place in Madrid's majestic and somnolent citadels of bureaucracy. . . . The planners and their young aides work longer hours than most Spaniards and there is a dash of asceticism in their dedication that is not too popular with many of their countrymen."

The foremost of the ascetic new planners was Alberto Ullastres, a little-known Catalan professor of economics who suddenly became Commerce Minister. Another was Mariano Navarro Rubio, a bland, somewhat unctuous former director of the Banco Popular (the Opus Dei bank) who now became Finance Minister. A third was Laureano López Rodó, a slim, cool, thirty-seven-year-old professor of administrative law whose treatise on reforms, printed in a magazine early in 1956, had first brought him to Franco's attention. López Rodó now became Technical Secretary

General (second-ranking official) of the Presidency, the Prime Minister's office, and from this vantage point began to prune Spain's archaic bureaucracy and draft the nation's economic future.

It was inevitable that more Spaniards would join forces against Opus Dei than would support the overdue reforms. The affiliation of Ullastres, Navarro Rubio, López Rodó, and their young aides with Opus was enough to start outraged whispers of a "white masonry" taking over the state. This charge is still being heard in many sectors of Spain today.

Crisis

Even with Franco's backing, however, López Rodó and his technocrats could not tame the inflationary tempest overnight. By 1958, prices were rising faster than either output or demand, and rich Spaniards were buying foreign currencies or gold to salt away in Switzerland. The peseta was dropping ominously: the official rate was 42 to the dollar; on the black market it was already selling at 60.

By mid-1959, Spain stood at the abyss of bankruptcy. Cabinet ministers could be heard wondering where the gasoline for their Cadillacs would come from.

The crisis had long been foreseen both by Spanish and foreign experts. At the start of 1959, for instance, Alejandro de Araoz, a respected industrialist, had warned the regime: "We have exhausted our gold reserve. . . . We have spent more than we have earned . . . we have invested and pledged more than we have saved . . . except for hydroelectric projects and new dams, scarcely any other class of wealth has been created."

The United States Economic Mission, headed by Richard S. Aldrich, had urged the regime repeatedly to end deficit spending, to cut back military expenditure, to set a realistic rate for the peseta, to scrap controls and liberalize trade. The regime had turned a deaf ear.

Spanish bankers and businessmen had urged less intervention

in business, but their voices, too, had been ignored. Franco, while sensing that his technocrats and the other orthodox advisers all were right, still could not bring himself to rein in such political cronies as Suanzes, whose INI gulped down one-seventh of the budget every year, or the generals who spent one-third of the budget; or the avaricious in-laws; or the flatterers and the sycophants. Caught in a squeeze, Franco, as usual, temporized.

The crisis, however, would not temporize. By June, 1959, Spain's foreign reserves were gone, prices were climbing, and vital imports grinding to a halt. Disaster loomed and Franco finally capitulated. Ironically, it was the hated foreigners who saved him. Wall Street, Paris, London, and the OEEC bailed him out, but on strict conditions. Spain had to join the OEEC, adopt its recommendations, and put her house in order. This meant drastic reforms which, in turn, meant violent criticism and perhaps even agitation among the masses, for it was the low-paid masses who would bear the brunt. But there was no alternative. Time was running out. It was a grim, ugly moment. Franco turned wearily, angrily to the Opus Dei ministers, waiting for his decision: reform—or drift.

"Hagan lo que les de la gana," he snapped. "Do as you want."

He had crossed his Rubicon.

Reactivation and Recovery

"These [stabilization] decisions," noted the International Bank for Reconstruction and Development later,* "were significant . . . politically and economically . . . [they] marked the end of economic isolation and cleared the way for a freer economy, based on international trade and economic cooperation with other countries."

From mid-1959, the old galleon of Spain ceased yawing to every passing wind. By late 1960, speculation and black-marketeering had begun to diminish and prices were leveling off. Exports of

* *The Economic Development of Spain* (Baltimore, Md.: Johns Hopkins Press, 1963; London: Oxford University Press, 1963).

steel, textiles, and ships were rising, stimulated by the U.S. steel strike, the reorganization of Britain's Lancashire textile industry, and world demand for shipping. Imports had again begun to mount, for private trade had now been 50 per cent liberalized, and Ullastres promised that 75 per cent would be freed in time. Most important of all, the peseta began to harden.

With "stabilization" achieved, the next step was "reactivation," for the abrupt end of inflation had gripped the business world in panic. Ullastres, Navarro Rubio, López Rodó, and the other technocrats now turned to the serious task, and from 1960 on, their policies followed those already successfully adopted in France. Slowly, business began to pick up, output increased, and profits rose, but as always in Spain, wages lagged far behind, and in 1962 Asturian coal strikers showed plainly the need for sweeping labor reforms.

At the height of the strikes, in July, 1962, Franco moved. He dropped three Falangist members from his cabinet, named Muñoz Grandes Vice Premier to ensure law and order, and assigned a brilliant young Opus Dei protégé, the thirty-nine-year-old Gregorio López Bravo, to the key Ministry of Industry. Now, with Ullastres at Commerce, Navarro Rubio at Finance, López Rodó as Commissioner of the Four-Year Plan, and López Bravo at Industry, reforms could be implemented. The path might be rocky, but no one could claim that Franco had not given his Opus Dei "Europeans" their chance.

Half a year later, on New Year's Day, 1963, Franco raised the national minimum wage for male Spaniards of eighteen or more from 36 to 60 pesetas ($1) for an eight-hour day, and while a few critics grumbled that this benefited merely the worst-paid 15 per cent of the farm workers and ducked real Sindical reform, it was at least a step in the right direction.

Meanwhile, a 500-page economic survey prepared at Spain's request by the World Bank had been submitted to Franco and on the advice of López Rodó, Ullastres, and Navarro Rubio, its recommendations were accepted. With characteristic pride,

Franco insisted that all references to Spain's past economic errors be deleted, and the World Bank agreed nonetheless, its survey was of major importance as the forerunner of the well-publicized new Four-Year Development Plan.

Throughout 1963, López Rodó toiled with a staff of forty-two young technicians to prepare the first Four-Year Plan; by the end of the year, it comprised thirty-one fat volumes.

Not only was such detailed economic planning in itself revolutionary in Spain, but López Rodó's methods also were unique. Instead of merely issuing decrees to be ignored, the new Commissioner began to consult everyone concerned. Cool, courteous, neither shouting nor dictating, he heard everyone who could proffer objections or suggestions, yet managed to keep the tiller in his own hands.

More than 1,200 Spaniards were named to 22 "vertical" consultative committees authorized to evaluate growth targets for as many sectors of the nation's economic life. In addition, "horizontal" groups were formed to study such problems as labor, productivity, finance, commerce, regional development, and economic flexibility, which were common to all. The "vertical" committees and the "horizontal" study groups were taken directly from French planning experience.

Naturally, opposition arose. Suanzes, for instance, fought a desperate rear-guard action to keep his 9 billion peseta ($150 million) yearly budget for INI, but slowly López Rodó began to deflate even Suanzes. By late 1963, acknowledging defeat, Suanzes finally resigned and was created a marqués by Franco as consolation. Yet the opposition was far from dead. Rich profiteers snorted that El Plan was a vision conceived by theoreticians with no business training, while the Falangists, still eager for labor popularity, shrilled that José Antonio's social program had been crushed under the juggernaut of "technocracy."

By the end of 1963, however, business was on the rise and Navarro Rubio could tell the Cortes that foreign capital investment that year alone had reached a record $159 million compared with $99 million the preceding year. The first ten months of 1963 also witnessed the greatest expansion of private credit in Spain's history, running to $1.3 billion, compared with $1.1 billion during the same period of 1962.

Yet, once again prices began to edge up. The building boom along the tourist-packed Mediterranean coast was causing serious bottlenecks in labor and materials, and trucks setting out from Malaga with workmen for projects at Torremolinos an hour away were being stopped en route by builders or foremen offering the men bribes to get off to work for them. So tight had the building labor market become that contractors were flying peasants from inland Spain to Mallorca, teaching them masonry or bricklaying on the work site, and paying them bonus wages. The pendulum was swinging from one extreme to the other again, but now, unlike the past, Franco's technocrats were watching the dials. For the first time, there were rudimentary fiscal controls.

Spanish firms needing money, for instance, could now turn to the stock exchange, offering their issues to foreign investors, and American, British, French, and Swiss investors responded. In the first nine months of 1963, according to one bank, foreign buying of Spanish stocks reached $46.3 million—double the rate of the previous year. Most of the buying centered on real estate, building and construction, service industries, foodstuffs, and investment trusts.

By late 1963, American business investment in Spain was also increasing. Chrysler announced plans to spend $16 million to acquire 35 per cent of the Barreiros truck firm and intimated it would start building the Dodge Dart in Spanish factories during 1965. General Motors and Ford were reported scouting the land. Sears Roebuck invested $4 million in a wholly-owned Spanish subsidiary and was reported planning stores in Madrid and Barcelona.

U.S. Steel was reported buying $12 million worth of stock in Altos Hornos de Vizcaya, Spain's largest private steel works, with an option to acquire up to 25 per cent of the total shares over the next ten years, while American Cyanamid bought control of the Spanish Laboratorios Reunidos. Ralston Purina also negotiated a lucrative agreement with the prosperous Spanish Gallina Blanca poultry feeds group.

The bulk of U.S. investment lay in manufacturing or petroleum, but there were some signs of diversification. One hundred and fifty American firms were doing—or preparing to do—business in Spain, among them U.S. Rubber, Dunlop, Firestone, Goodyear, General Electric, Standard Electric, Westinghouse, Hilton, Babcock & Wilcox, Chase Manhattan, National City Bank, Dow Chemical, Monsanto, Phillips Petroleum, Gulf Oil, ESSO, Merrill Lynch, and others. European firms, too, were joining the parade to Spain and, as one American banker observed, "Spain is the last mass market in Europe left to be cracked."

The Danger Spots

There are, of course, danger signals still.

Spanish exports, for instance, are sluggish: $496 million in 1959; $726 million in 1960; $710 million in 1961; $734 million in 1962; $736 million in 1963; and $950 million in 1964. This is a lackluster performance for a country luxuriating in a billion-dollar yearly trade gap. In 1963 alone, Spain bought three times what she sold.

In addition, inflationary pressures, restive labor, agricultural and industrial obsolescence* also threaten an economy "dangerously perched," as the *Economist* recently said, on tourism and remittances. A setback in the Common Market could force thousands of Spanish workers out of European jobs, cutting their remittances home overnight, while a crisis in Spain—Franco's death or a struggle for the succession—could scare off millions of tourists.

"Tourism is essential for our future balance of payments," In-

* Eighty-two per cent of all Spanish companies are reported to have fewer than ten workers.

formation and Tourism Minister Fraga conceded early in 1964. "It pays . . . two-thirds of the deficit anticipated in our commerce." So optimistic are the Spanish over the golden goose of tourism, however, that they are already counting on 17 million tourists by 1967.

This lingering doctrinaire dislike of the ogre Franco seems jejune after nearly thirty years, for Spain's trade with the Common Market countries cannot be based on like or dislike. Between 1959 and 1962, Common Market exports to Spain jumped 130 per cent, from $177 million to $408 million. In the same period, Common Market exports inside the community rose only 70 per cent and to the rest of the outside world, only 35 per cent.

The EEC buys heavily from Spain. In 1962, nearly 40 per cent of Spain's exports went to Common Market countries and their value totaled $295 million. By 1963, the value had risen to $371 million. These are facts; and it seems self-evident that a country with nearly 31 million people, with a rising standard of living, with reserves of $1.5 billion, and with an economy expanding at the rate of 5 per cent yearly is an interesting economic proposition.

The lingering hostility of Europe's Socialists, however idealistically motivated, does not hurt Franco, it hurts the Spanish people; it does not weaken Franco's grip on power, it merely tightens it. The force in Spain that can best eliminate Francoism peacefully consists of the "Europeans" in high office who are trying to get Spain back into the mainstream of European life and who, having reformed her economy, hope to reform her political structure as well. This is a slow, uphill struggle, and political face-making, such as Prime Minister Wilson's peevish gesture of canceling Anglo-Spanish naval maneuvers the day after assuming office, will not hasten but, if anything, retard Spain's emancipation. Such gestures encourage the latent Spanish xenophobia that is Franco's major weapon.

Apart from foreign hostility, inflation is another difficulty which arises, paradoxically, from better conditions in Spain. With a gross national product up from $9.5 billion to $13.8 billion in the past five years, this is not surprising. Many Spaniards are now making money and want more of everything. The new generation is "conspicuously unascetic," as Paul Hofmann recently noted. "This generation is frankly impatient to share the good life of other Western Europeans," he wrote in *The New York Times.* "They want autos, affluent vacations like those enjoyed by the millions of tourists who invade Spain from spring to autumn, modern household appliances, smart clothes, and better food. If they lack the cash they buy on the installment plan."

There is, in addition, a psychological factor behind this demand for gaiety, color, luxury, weekend villas, backyard swimming pools, yachts, red sports cars, and sumptuous homes. Not only have the Spanish people long been deprived of comfort, they have been deprived still longer of glamour. The Spanish people, frankly, are bored.

Ergo the growing adulation of movie stars, bullfighters, society gadabouts, glamor, ease, and laughter. *Ergo* the bright new *boutiques* in Madrid and other cities, the glossy restaurants, the "get it quick" atmosphere. It is little wonder that inflation strains at the leash.

Agricultural stagnation is another major problem. So arid is the land, so harsh the climate, so ill-paid the farmers, and so deeply rooted the neglect that 40 per cent of Spain's population produces only 25 per cent of the nation's revenues. The average income for a farmer-owner and family is $300 yearly, yet two-thirds of Spain's farmland is owned by such farmers.

Historically, Spain's countryside has been split between the tiny *minifundias,* the uneconomic plots in the north divided and subdivided with each generation until they almost disappear;* and the *latifundias,* the vast rolling estates of the south, used for bull-breeding or olive-growing and usually owned by absentee

* A classic example is the farm in Galicia of thirty-odd square meters, one tree, and three owners.

325

aristocrats. In 1951, for example, a French periodical reported that seven grandees still owned nearly 658,000 acres.

These enormous and often neglected estates sometimes comprise a third or even a half of an entire province. Ten years ago, another survey showed that there were still ten thousand *latifundias* averaging 1,500 acres each, whereas the average farm in Spain comprised only 2.1 acres.

As in all feudal countries, the landlords have consistently blocked land reforms, and Spanish landowners are as entrenched today under Franco as they were under the Borbón dynasty before 1931. Should a monarchy follow Franco, the demand for land reform will confront it with one of its gravest crises. Some progress toward land reform has been made in recent years—but at snail's pace.

"In some areas of the countryside," noted a U.S. Congressional Investigating Subcommittee in 1963, "prosperous small farms and . . . communities [testify] to the success of the Spanish land reform. . . ." However, it continued, "many villages, towns, and sections of large cities display poverty and stagnation. . . . Land reform and irrigation projects have directly affected less than 5 per cent of Spain's agricultural population."

There has, on the other hand, been some success in consolidating the *minifundias*. The Land Consolidation Service succeeded, with U.S. aid between 1953 and 1962, in amalgamating 900,000 acres, which represents only about one-thirtieth of the tillable acreage of Spain. Progress in this program is based on voluntary cooperation and is therefore slow, for the LCS can step in only when a municipality votes by a 60 per cent majority to invite it.

Another government service, the National Colonization Institute, aided by $50 million in U.S. counterpart funds, reports having cleared 250,000 acres, placed 850,000 acres under irrigation, reparcelled 223,000 acres, built 15,600 homes, and resettled 46,000 peasants.

Irrigation remains Spain's chief need, but in the last ten years, says the government, 1.8 million acres have been irrigated, bringing the total to almost 4.5 million (10 per cent of the country's nonarid surface). Reforestation—dear to Franco's heart—has also advanced. Since 1941, when Franco founded his Patrimonio Nacional, 4.1 million acres have been seeded—an average of 250,000 acres yearly, and probably the greatest number in Europe.

Of all Spain's economic woes, labor unrest remains the greatest threat, but no account of contemporary Spain could ignore the economic concessions granted labor in recent years. Free trade unions, freely chosen delegates, freedom of speech, freedom to strike, freedom from harassment, freedom of political association—these, of course, are still missing.

However, job security, wages and conditions, education, health and social security benefits, recreation and holiday facilities, plus vocational training, have gradually improved. In 1958, for instance, a liberalized collective bargaining law led to 2,465 new wage agreements in the next four years involving 840,559 firms and 4,334,166 workers: virtually half of Spain's labor force. In 1962, the year of the first Asturian strikes, wages rose by an average of 20 per cent, as Ullastres told *The Times* of London in a recent interview. A *Fortune* survey of 1963 reported that miners' pay in Asturias had been upped 30 per cent after the 1962 walkouts. Already technicians in key industries—chemicals, to name but one—earn an average of $5,800 and will probably be earning about $13,000 by 1967. These are high wages in Spain.

The term "wage" is sometimes misinterpreted, for in Spain it refers only to the legal minimum—not to the actual take-home pay, which includes family bonuses, labor mutual bonuses, and other extras, such as the "blue-envelope" incentive pay passed by management under the table to hang on to skilled workers. The Spanish worker also benefits from social security. The list of obligatory state-run social security schemes is impressive: health, maternity, old age, sickness, working accident, domestic service, family, unemployment, agrarian, and scholarship. Even a voluntary retirement program is now being developed.

Housing for workers also has burgeoned. Since 1940, the regime claims to have built, or helped build, 1,280,000 workers' homes—206,600 of them in 1963.

New worker-training schemes are beginning. Three-quarters of all Spaniards still receive no vocational training after the age of twelve, and the ratio between skilled (or semiskilled) workers and nonskilled is 1:4. By 1967, however, the regime hopes to cut this to 1:2. In February, 1964, for instance, it announced a new $45 million program to train 800,000 men and youths in industrial skills.

Few would claim that Spain's labor problems are diminishing; in fact, they are growing, for the backlog of apathy and neglect is enormous, and the population is increasing. Yet, social and tax reforms could do much to placate labor. The problem lies not so much in collecting more taxes but in shifting the burden from indirect taxes, which press hardest on the poor, to direct taxes, which mainly affect the rich. Between 1958 and 1962, for example, tax revenues in Spain increased 71 per cent; yet while the proportion of direct taxation rose 41 per cent, the proportion of indirect taxation rose nearly 82 per cent.

The need for a fairer distribution of income was graphically demonstrated by a study published in 1962 by Professor Perpiñá y Grau. In that year, he revealed, approximately 30,000 families had incomes exceeding $8,500; in Spain, this amounts to real wealth. The rest of the national income, however, was distributed as follows:

Approximate Number of Families	Approximate Per Cent of Population	Approximate Income
100,000	1.5	$5,000 or more
1,000,000	15.0	$1,661–$4,800
1,800,000	27.0	$1,001–$1,660
1,800,000	27.0	$ 501–$1,000
1,500,000	22.0	$ 500 or less
460,000	7.0	No fixed income

These are sobering statistics, and Americans, reminded recently that one-fifth of their own compatriots still live on less than $3,500 yearly, will be able to evaluate them without false condescension.

With El Plan, Spain has turned a historic corner and seems to be heading for a new stability. If the succession is peaceful, Franco will be immortalized. If Spain relapses into anarchy, he will be swept to oblivion. At the moment, the signs point to a peaceful succession and to increased prosperity.

"The prospects for the growth of the Spanish economy are very favorable," declared the World Bank in 1963. "With suitable policies . . . an annual growth rate of 5 per cent per capita should be possible over an extended period."

This was the statistical viewpoint. There was another: the socio-political.

"By creating a base of well-being," wrote López Rodó, "liberty is enriched, and only on such a base can man make his choice with dignity. Misery annuls any possible liberty."

"He Even Speaks Spanish!"—
The Monarchy

On Saturday, April 14, 1962, the white, gaff-rigged yacht "Sal-tillo" limped into the Spanish port of Huelva. Two days out of Estoril, Portugal, it had developed engine trouble, and the skipper had radioed ahead for help. This request created an unusual flurry among the port authorities. They bore the radio message to the naval commandant; the commandant called the mayor; and the mayor notified the civil governor. Surrounded by aides, the governor shouted into his receiver and demanded an urgent long-distance call to the Interior Ministry in Madrid. Told that there would be at least a four-hour delay, he shouted all the louder.

In the meantime, a giant of a man in a blue sweater, denims, sneakers, and a yachting cap had disembarked and was walking down Huelva's main street, followed by six sailing companions. The stranger towered over the others, and he frequently broke into laughter as if he were delighted to find himself on Spanish soil. His dark brown eyes took in every detail of the town: its docks, wharves, and taverns; its unhurried citizenry lounging under the palms. He spoke in rapid Spanish, now and again

331

breaking into fluent English when he addressed one of his six companions. They treated him with deference tempered by the easygoing familiarity of men thrown together for long periods at sea.

After strolling about the town for some time, the yachting party settled at a café and had just ordered drinks, when a nervous official hurried up, followed by a tight-faced officer from the Guardia Civil. Scanning the newcomers' faces, the official addressing the leader of the group bowed and stammered: *"Majestad—*Your Majesty."

He had, in fact, correctly identified the skipper of "Saltillo": His Royal Highness Don Juan de Borbón y Battenberg, Count of Barcelona, son of the late King Alfonso XIII, and to most Spanish Monarchists the lawful "King John III" of Spain. In Spanish usage, he was "Don Juan."

The official expressed the honor felt by the Ayuntamiento (City Hall) at having so illustrious a personage in their midst. Would "His Majesty" be so kind as to accept the city's invitation to a glass of wine? Don Juan expressed his thanks and set off with his companions, preceded by the local official, flanked by the Guardia Civil officer, and followed by the usual knot of idlers, who realized now that something was afoot.

By then, word had reached Franco in Madrid that his political rival, the Pretender, had disembarked on Spanish soil, requesting mechanical assistance for his yacht. What were the authorities to do? How was he to be treated? How should he be addressed? How long could he stay? Back came Franco's orders: accord the Count of Barcelona every courtesy and every assistance. He could stay as long as necessary. He was to be treated as a royal personage.

So it came about that thirty-one years to the day after the late King Alfonso XIII had abandoned his throne and fled Spain, his legal heir, Juan, found himself dining on Spanish soil, surrounded by local dignitaries addressing him as "Majesty" and joining in a hastily arranged banquet. Don Juan was the soul of joviality, raising his glass in repeated toasts, as the evening wore on.

He and his companions, including a retired British admiral, were en route to Athens, where his son, Prince Juan Carlos, was soon to marry the Greek Princess Sophie. The toasts redoubled as everyone present vied in proposing the health, happiness, and prosperity of the young couple. Waiters hurried to and fro with the heady wines of Malaga, and tongues began to loosen. Many indeed who drank to the coming royal wedding seemed to be drinking to the return of the monarchy. But despite their exuberance, all kept a check on their tongues. All knew that in a few hours Don Juan would be gone and Franco would be studying the secret reports his informers were already preparing for him.

Next morning, Palm Sunday, Don Juan attended Mass at the historic monastery of La Rabida, from which Columbus had sailed in 1492 on his first voyage for Don Juan's ancestors, Isabella and Ferdinand. After Mass, he strolled in the bright sunshine among the throngs, shaking hands and chatting with fishermen, tradesmen, shopkeepers, and peasants. At first suspicious or reserved, they gradually relaxed as the strapping royal sailor spoke to them in their own idiom.

Soon the "Saltillo's" engine was ready, and the moment had come to weigh anchor. As the yacht headed slowly out into the Gibraltar Straits, Don Juan could be seen at the tiller, waving.

"Es un buen tio . . . A good fellow," muttered a laborer in old overalls and a black beret, as his mates nodded. "Imagine! He even speaks Spanish!"

It might seem strange that Spaniards should marvel that the Pretender to the Spanish throne can speak Spanish—but it is a precise indication of what Franco wants. Franco wants Don Juan to be unknown in Spain. His censors have effaced Don Juan's character, his ideas, his background. A new generation has now grown up that knows nothing of the monarchy—except its mistakes. Yet, paradoxically, Franco turned Spain back into a monarchy in 1947. He has been grooming Prince Juan Carlos, Don Juan's son, for the throne, and every indication is that a monarchy will succeed Franco. The off-and-on relations between Franco and Don Juan, nevertheless, tell the recent history of Spain.

The Law of Succession

Foreign visitors, especially Americans, who ask Franco about the future are invariably referred to the 1947 Law of Succession.

The Law of Succession is a masterpiece of obfuscation; the Spanish mind at its most meticulously vague. It makes Spain a kingdom without a king; it tranquilizes the power blocs; and it leaves Franco in sole control. It even refutes those critics who call Franco a dictator, for he points to this law as his constitutional mandate.

Franco submitted the Succession Law to the nation on July 6, 1947, and it was approved by an 82 per cent majority—a result that was scarcely surprising, as the voters had the choice either to vote "yes," or, by voting "no," to waste their votes. Out of 17,178,812 electors, the records show that 14,145,163 voted "yes"; 722,656 "no"; 351,744 ballots were invalidated.

The Succession Law permits Franco to exclude from the succession anyone he dislikes; to name as his successor anyone he likes; and even to change his mind. Spain is a "Catholic, social, and representative . . . kingdom," but the Jefatura, or supreme leadership, is entrusted *by name* to Franco with no time limit. Should the leadership fall vacant through his death or incapacity, a three-man Regency Council* automatically assumes power for three days. Then it must call into joint session the cabinet and the Consejo del Reino. These two organs must choose Franco's successor by a two-thirds vote.

* This Regency Council has as members the President of the Cortes, now Esteban Marqués de Bilbao; the senior Roman Catholic prelate in the Cortes, now Dr. Marcelino Olaechea; and the senior military officer in the Consejo del Reino, at present, the Vice President of the Government, Captain General Agustín Muñoz Grandes.

334

The successor must be a Spanish male "of royal lineage," at least thirty, and a Catholic. He must swear to uphold not only the six Fundamental Laws, but also Franco's twelve "Principles of the Movement."

Should no royal candidate be acceptable, the Consejo del Reino and the cabinet can jointly name a regent of "prestige, capacity, and potential usefulness" to the nation. The final choice must be approved by the Cortes within eight days.

The Consejo del Reino

In 1959, in a rare interview granted the Sindicalist newspaper *Pueblo,* Franco stressed the importance of the Consejo del Reino (Council of the Realm), and did so again in 1961, in a speech to the Cortes. The Council is the key factor in the Law of Succession, he said, and it is a "reflection of the forces" to which all nations turn in moments of crisis.

Franco created the Consejo del Reino on December 30, 1948, as the highest consultative body in Spain. It now comprises thirteen dignitaries whose average age is sixty-eight* and whose only function to date has been to appear every January 6 at the Pardo Palace, incline respectfully before Franco, and hear its President, the elderly Esteban Marqués de Bilbao, give another of his celebrated adulatory perorations. The process terminated, Franco murmurs a few words of thanks, proffers his councillors a glass

* As of January, 1965, the roster of the Consejo del Reino read: President, Esteban Marqués de Bilbao, 86, President of the Cortes. Members, Dr. Marcelino Olaechea, 76, Archbishop of Valencia, senior prelate in the Cortes; Captain General Agustín Muñoz Grandes, 69, Vice President of the Government; Lieutenant General Rafael García-Valiño, 66, senior active Lieutenant General; a vacancy, owing to the death last year of the incumbent, Conde de Vallellano, President of the Council of State; José Castán Tobeñas, 76, President of the Supreme Court; Marqués de Lozoya, 72, President of the Spanish Institute; Pedro Lamata, 53, elected by the Sindical bloc in the Cortes; Marqués de Castell-Florite, 59, elected by the local administration bloc in the Cortes; Enrique Gutiérrez Ríos, 49, elected by the university rectors' bloc in the Cortes; Eduardo López Palop, 75, elected by the professional colleges' bloc; José Luis de Arrese, 60, named personally by Franco from among the *procuradores* in the Cortes; Admiral Salvador Moreno Fernández, 78, named personally by Franco; and Lieutenant General Carlos Asenio Cabanillas, 69, named personally by Franco.

335

of sherry, and soon after, they all return to their respective pre-occupations.

Theoretically, the Council comprises a cross section of political power. In addition to representatives of the army, the Church, the Monarchists, and the judiciary, there are four members representing the Sindicates, local administration, university rectors, and professional colleges. Three more are named by Franco personally. It is significant that there is no official representative of the Falange. In fact, it is one of the Falange's chief complaints that Franco has never given it a permanent seat in this constitutional body. Most observers believe that the Consejo del Reino will flush down the drain of history when Franco dies, but others are not so sure. The Spaniard is legalistic to a fault, and Franco has always sought to cloak his regime in the toga of legality. The Consejo could easily become the "smoke-filled room" of Spanish politics when Franco dies, for its members have been meticulously chosen to represent the most influential sectors—if not the most influential men—of the regime. If Franco purges it of its deadwood, it may even play a vital role in the future. If the monarchy returns, it is virtually certain that some such privy council will have to take up its position near the monarch. Assuming that a monarchy will succeed Franco, what kind of monarchy will it be? This is Franco's dilemma. Like many Spaniards, Franco knows better what he dislikes than what he likes, and he equally dislikes traditional monarchies and liberal republics.

"We broke with an atheistic, antinational, bitterly sectarian republic in the final throes of dissolution," he declared at the opening of a low-cost housing estate on July 17, 1962. "We also . . . discarded and condemned . . . a liberal, inefficient, parliamentary system based on courtiers!"

A year earlier, Franco had denounced Spain's traditional monarchies in the Cortes.

"What use was our old monarchy with its constitution and all its history when it lost the support of the nation?" he demanded, as the Falangists cheered and the Monarchists glowered. The "crusade" had not been fought merely to effect a "simple restoration." His regime was the beginning of a fundamental process of remolding Spain, and future political legitimacy would be based on continuity. His "supreme magistracy" was not transitory. He was no "umpire," no "bridge" across an abyss of chaos and anarchy.

"The Law of Succession has been solemnly backed by the . . . people," he proclaimed. No one disputed this except "meager bands of political meddlers" who "deliberately exaggerate the power of my personality to pretend that when I die the law will become meaningless."

Don Juan

Who is Don Juan? Is he a royal yachtsman, dozing through the years in torpid Estoril, out of touch with reality and forgotten by the Spanish people? Or is he, as his admirers insist, a patriot, steeled by adversity, a student of world affairs, a modern-minded Catholic, the one man around whom the Spanish nation could unite after Franco? Will he succeed Franco? Or will Franco choose his son, Prince Juan Carlos? Or will he bypass them both?

These are the questions haunting Spain, and no one knows the answers; possibly not even Franco. The dictator wants no rival while he lives, yet neither does he want chaos when he dies. He hopes to go down in history as the man who saved Spain from Communism, nursed her to health through discipline, and made her walk again. This image would go up in smoke if after Franco's death Spain relapsed into the familiar cycle of weak government, public discontent, political demonstrations, street riots, and civil war.

The search for a successor is complex. It might be easier were Prince Juan Carlos not twenty-seven but thirty—constitutionally old enough to ascend the throne now, under Franco's tutelage. But he is politically immature, a pawn in the power struggle, and Franco privately referred to him not long ago as "good, charming—and timid."

Don Juan, on the other hand, is fifty-two and ready to move. "I keep a bag permanently packed," he tells friends. There is little likelihood that he will be called to the throne during Franco's lifetime, for he disapproves of Franco and Franco disapproves of him. Yet Franco needs him because he represents Spain's legitimacy. Furthermore, Franco prefers an amateur opponent, and Don Juan is no urgent threat. Older, wiser, and heavier after years in exile, Don Juan no longer dreams of driving Franco from power but only of succeeding him, and thus relations between the dictator and the pretender have become calmly correct. Letters pass between them periodically via trusted emissaries, and each wishes the other good health or sends congratulations on their respective saints' days. Franco invariably addresses Don Juan as "Your Highness," while the Pretender limits himself to the polite but cool "General." Neither is in a hurry.

On June 20, 1913, guns boomed at the royal palace of San Ildefonso to welcome the birth of a third son to King Alfonso XIII and his English-born wife, Queen Victoria Eugenia. With the laborious protocol so beloved in Spain, the child was baptized Juan Carlos Teresa Silverio Alfonso de Borbón y Battenberg, honoring the saint whose day it was, but also the many royal godparents. From his dashing father, the King, twelfth in Spain's Borbón line, "Juani" inherited charm, courage, and a fine memory. From his mother, Queen Victoria's granddaughter, came his robust physique and love of the sea.

His older brothers, Alfonso and Jaime, loved the brilliant uniforms and bright swords of the army, but the summers spent by the sea at San Sebastián and the sight of the warships lying majestically offshore soon set Juan's heart on a naval career. Early photographs show him in a sailor suit with his father, with mustachioed Spanish aides in German-type helmets standing proudly around. The education of royal children in those days seemed endless. There were four languages to learn: there was an English governess with whom Juan and his brothers and sisters conversed daily in English; a French nurse; their Austrian-born grandmother, Queen Maria Cristina, always spoke to them in German; while their father addressed them in faultless, slightly lisping Castilian. Juan, to his delight, was entered in the naval academy at Cádiz on his sixteenth birthday, and it was there a year later—on April 14, 1931—that he was urgently summoned to the telephone.

"His Majesty, your father, is leaving Spain," he heard his father's secretary saying from Madrid. "You are to leave immediately and join him. Do the best you can. That is all I can say." There was a click, then silence. H.R.H. Infante Juan's days in Spain were over.

There was no time for questions. That same night, loyal officers spirited him across the bay to Gibraltar, where he was received by the British governor. Two days later, he caught a passing liner to Genoa, and after an overnight train ride to Paris, he joined his family in Fontainebleau.

"How good is your English?" his father asked. Juan said that it was rusty, but could be improved. Two weeks later, the Spanish-English princeling found himself enrolled, thanks to "Uncle George" (King George V), at Dartmouth, a cadet in the British Navy. His naval training was now to continue in less revolutionary surroundings.

These were the happiest years of his life. "Prince John of Spain," R.N., was soon commissioned a midshipman and assigned to sea. He asked to be spared duty with the Mediterranean fleet, which touched periodically at Spanish ports and was ordered to the Far Eastern squadron. One of his cherished memories is of a parade in sweltering Bombay, when he rode a charger in full-dress naval uniform as honorary aide to the Viceroy. A tattoo on his muscular left arm still recalls the carefree bonhomie of his days in the Royal Navy.

Fate, however, was to change the pattern of his life, for his ailing oldest brother, Alfonso, Prince of Asturias, decided to renounce his rights to marry (morganatically) a Cuban girl he had met in Switzerland. Ignoring his family's entreaties, the Prince of Asturias ceded his heritage on June 11, 1933, and ten days later Jaime, Juan's next older brother, a deaf-mute from birth, renounced the rights that had now devolved on him. Sub-Lieutenant Prince John of Spain, R.N., while tiger-hunting near Bombay, learned by cable that he had become heir to the Spanish throne and Prince of Asturias.

The new honor brought little immediate change, for Britain's Navy took royal sprigs for granted. What mattered was how well an officer laid down his salvos or held his liquor. The throne seemed very far away to Juan that summer of 1933, when his squadron was on the Indian Ocean.

On August 12, 1934, his younger brother Gonzalo, then eighteen, crashed in an automobile accident in Austria and bled to death within hours. He was a victim of hemophilia, a hereditary disease that prevents normal clotting of the blood. It was the first but not the last bereavement in Don Juan's life.

Hemophilia is often called the "royal disease" because of its prevalence in royal families. It is transmitted through the female line, seldom afflicting women, but cropping out with unpredictable and usually fatal effect among men. Queen Victoria (Don Juan's great-grandmother) is said to have transmitted the malady to her son Prince Leopold (who bled to death) and through her daughters, Princess Alix, who married Nicolas II of Russia, and Princess Beatrice, who married Don Juan's grandfather, to the royal houses of Romanov and Borbón.* Don Juan himself is free from hemophilia and so is his son Juan Carlos.

Heartsick over the death of his brother, whom he adored, Juan remained with the navy, but soon suffered another blow.

---

* Alfonso, Juan's oldest brother, who took the historic title of Count of Covadonga on his morganatic marriage, perished in Miami in 1938, the victim of hemophilia following a car crash.

Early in 1935, he passed the stiff examinations in naval gunnery
and navigation qualifying him for promotion to lieutenant and
returned eagerly to Portsmouth, where the destroyer H.M.S.
"Winchester" lay awaiting his command. As he unpacked, a
petty officer appeared with the request that he call on the Admiral Commandant at his home. This was an unusual invitation
for a junior officer, however royal, and the twenty-two-year-old
sub-lieutenant straightened his uniform with care. Arriving at
the Admiral's quarters, he was greeted politely and asked to be
seated. The Admiral poured two drinks, then paused, as if struggling with his thoughts.

"I have been charged by Their Lordships of Admiralty," he
said, "to inquire whether you would consider relinquishing
Spanish nationality and becoming a British subject. As you may
know, recent naval regulations introduced by the past Labour
Government* make it impossible to confer command of a British warship on a non-British officer. I rather fear that unless you
are prepared to become a British subject, we must ask you to
leave the navy."

Struggling to hide his dismay, Prince John reminded the Admiral that he was now heir to the Spanish throne—a royal duty
he could never renounce. He had been born a Spaniard, and he
would die a Spaniard. Prince John's naval career had come to an
end a second time.

Before leaving England, he went to Windsor to tell "Uncle
George" what had happened. He still recalls the sailor King's
massive fist thudding down on his desk and the silver inkwells
and photographs dancing as he cursed the "bloody Socialists"
and their "damn meddling." Not even the King of England,
however, could alter the laws. All he could do was to confer on
his Spanish nephew the rank of honorary Lieutenant, R.N.

"I am the oldest honorary lieutenant still in the Royal Navy,"
Don Juan chuckles to this day.

Juan was now to turn to the cloistered halls of learning, the

* The short-lived Labour Government of 1929, headed by Ramsay MacDonald.

responsibilities of parenthood, and the poison-cup atmosphere of Spanish politics.

At the suggestion of his father, now living in Rome, he entered Florence University and began intensive studies in law, history, political science, and economics. He completed in four months courses normally requiring two years, but he was adrift and lonely.

He began to consider marriage because his family, his friends, and the Monarchists who still trooped to Rome to bow before the exiled Alfonso all urged the heir apparent to wed and safeguard the dynasty. That winter, at the wedding of his sister Beatriz, he met the blonde Infanta María de las Mercedes, Princess of Borbón-Sicily-Orleáns, a granddaughter of the last (Carlist) King of Naples and a distant cousin. The attraction that sprang up between them quickly won the approval of King Alfonso, who perceived that the match would link the rival Alfonsist and Carlist branches and thus strengthen Juan's right to the throne.

On October 12, 1935, the Day of Hispanidad and the anniversary of Columbus' discovery of America, Juan de Borbón-Battenberg and María de las Mercedes were married in a wedding that became the social event of the year. Spanish Monarchists, led by Antonio Goicoechea, leader of the Monarchist underground movement in Spain, flocked to Rome to reaffirm their allegiance to Alfonso XIII and swear fealty to his heir, Juan.

A six-month honeymoon took the newlyweds around the world, via India, Ceylon, Japan, and along the California coast on a sentimental tour of Spanish missions. Finally, they settled in Cannes in the summer of 1936, to await the birth of their first child. But again fate was to intervene. The smoldering flames of civil war now burst out in Spain on July 18. Glued to the radio, Don Juan waited until his first child, a daughter Pilar, was safely delivered and then drove off with a handful of Spanish friends to volunteer against the "reds."

Under the alias "Juan López," he slipped across the Pyrenees and headed south with his companions for Somosierra, near Madrid, where the fighting was already heavy. The volunteers passed without incident through Burgos, General Mola's headquarters, and near Somosierra stopped for a meal at the *parador* at Aranda de Duero. In the group were his cousin the Infante José Eugenio de Baviera, the late Conde de Ruiseñada, Eugenio Vegas Latapié, Luis María Zunzunegui, the Marqués de Eliseda, and Captain Jorge Vigón (now Franco's Public Works Minister).

As they ate hurriedly, Vigón was summoned to the telephone. He returned stricken. Their entry had been betrayed to Mola and Mola had ordered Vigón to escort Don Juan back to the French border and out of Spain. At that moment, a Guardia Civil lieutenant approached the group, and, addressing "Juan López" as *"Vuestra Alteza . . .* Your Highness," confirmed Mola's order. He offered to wait outside until the Prince and his friends had finished eating. Don Juan raised his glass to the "crusade," rose, and drove back through the night to France, to his wife and daughter—into an exile that has not yet ended.

Several weeks later, he again sought to volunteer and on December 7, 1936, he wrote Franco, by then head of the insurgents, offering to serve aboard the cruiser "Baleares," the only major fleet unit in the Nationalist navy. Franco's answer was courteous but negative. The "singularity" of Don Juan's status would make his serving in the rebel forces impossible, he explained. The "enthusiasms" of some and the "officiousness" of others would create command problems. Much as he wished to, he could not accede to the "dictates of his soldier's heart."

"The place you hold in the dynastic line and the obligations that derive from it," he concluded, "impose on all . . . and demand of you . . . sacrifices for the nation."

Before the Civil War ended, Don Juan had moved to Rome to be close to his ailing father, and there, in January, 1941, Alfonso XIII abdicated the royal rights he had never relinquished on fleeing Spain. As death approached, he designated Juan as his heir "without any discussion whatsoever as to his legitimate right." This duty accomplished, the onetime playboy monarch died peacefully.

By 1942, leading Monarchists became increasingly alarmed over the rise of Axis influence. Serrano Suñer and his Falangists were openly pressing Franco to enter the war on Hitler's side. To sabotage their schemes, the Monarchists began to organize a clandestine network linked to Don Juan, who had moved to Lausanne after his father's death.

Some were Anglophiles by family, education, or business ties; some hated Hitler ideologically; but all had fought "Communism" in the Civil War to restore the monarchy, not to install Franco as dictator. Among them were the late General Alfredo Kindelán, a tall, dignified aristocrat who had commanded Franco's Civil War aviation forces; José María Areilza, Conde de Motrico; Eugenio Vegas Latapié; López Oliván; the elderly Conde de los Andes; Don Juan's cousin, Infante Alfonso d'Orleáns-Borbón; the rotund, clever Pedro Sáinz Rodríguez; and José María Gil Robles. Fearing Spain's entry into the war, they used their influence and contacts to pass back and forth through Nazi-occupied France to meet Don Juan in Lausanne.

Don Juan shared their anti-Hitler sentiments, and slowly his duty became plain. On November 11, 1942, he issued his first public appeal as the legitimate heir to the throne. In an interview in the *Journal de Genève,* he warned Franco to keep Spain out of the war and offered his "sword as a Spanish soldier," should the Axis power dare to invade his country.

His timing was significant. The Allies had just landed in North Africa, and Eisenhower's untested American armies were strung out along a thin rail line from Casablanca past Spanish Morocco where Franco had 100,000 troops.

History consists of "ifs," and Don Juan's proclamation has long since been forgotten, but if Franco's army had moved to aid Rommel at that moment, Operation Torch—and the course of World War II—might have taken a different turn.

The next royal defiance came at the end of the war. On March 19, 1945, Don Juan called on the Spanish people to oust Franco.

"Spaniards!" he proclaimed from the shores of Lake Leman, "the only instrument capable of bringing about reconciliation is the traditional monarchy. Following my father's death, I lost no time in disapproving the policy pursued by General Franco. I do not raise the banner of rebellion nor incite anyone to sedition, but I remind those who support the present regime of their immense responsibility in helping prolong a situation that is leading the nation to irreparable disaster."

Don Juan was alone in Switzerland and Franco in Madrid, backed by a powerful army. The Lausanne *manifiesto* failed dismally. A few loyal Monarchists—the Duke of Alba, serving as Franco's wartime Ambassador in London, Casa Tilly, Goyoaga, and a few others—resigned their government posts, but the majority sat tight. They did not think the time ripe for heroics.

The sole effect of the *manifiesto* was to sharpen Franco's resentment against the Monarchists and to deprive Spain of a key envoy. Alba, a descendant of the Stuarts and a lifelong friend of Churchill, might have wielded powerful influence on Spain's behalf in the immediate postwar years. Churchill later conceded that he had agreed at Potsdam to bar Spain from the United Nations mainly as a concession to Stalin, to give the new charter "generous and friendly aid and support." Alba's sagacity and contacts might have induced Churchill, possibly even Roosevelt, to treat Spain more generously. But after such Spaniards as Alba had resigned, the world saw only Franco when it looked at Spain.

V-E Day produced a wave of autointoxication among the Monarchists. They assumed that foreign dislike would sweep Franco away and sweep the throne—and themselves—back. Each sign of Allied disapproval was secretly hailed as another nail in Franco's coffin, and when, at the end of 1945, Franco began to replace his more notorious Falangists with moderate Catholics, the Monarchists told themselves that their hour was near.

Gil Robles began secret negotiations in Paris and London

345

with Indalecio Prieto, head of the exiled Socialists, and the contacts stretched on through 1946. In the background, lending help and counsel, was Salvador de Madariaga, whose long residence at Oxford had brought him into contact with many British political leaders, including Ernest Bevin, the new Labour Foreign Secretary. Thanks to Madariaga, Bevin agreed to hear the Gil Robles–Prieto proposals once they were ripe, and, in fact, had their plans ever come to fruition, had some program of action ever been adopted and carried out, Franco's power might well have been challenged. The British Prime Minister, Attlee, detested Franco, as did most of his Labour colleagues, and in 1946 Britain held a commanding position among the new Socialist-oriented governments of Western Europe.

But as always in Spanish politics, months passed in inconclusive bickering, and the opportunity was lost. Bevin's interest gradually flagged, and the Labour Party turned to more immediate problems.

Franco, however, had caught wind of the conspiracy and now began to form the idea of a succession law. In Spain, his army chiefs were pressing for a less obvious military dictatorship; for some façade that would give Spain a better image. Their pleas were transformed by Franco to suit his own purpose. The generals wanted respectability. He would give it to them. The Monarchists wanted a monarchy. He would give them one. The world called him a dictator. He would prove his national backing.

By March, 1947, Franco had drafted the Law of Succession. On his orders, a trusted aide, Navy Captain Carrero Blanco, bore it privately to Don Juan, who had moved to Estoril in nearby Portugal, to be on hand. At once, Don Juan realized that he was trapped. Spain was to be a monarchy, but he was not to be its monarch. Stung to fury, he could do nothing but issue another scathing denunciation.

The new law, he proclaimed, was utterly opposed to the laws that, throughout history, had regulated the succession to the throne. The "hostility with which the country sees itself threatened from abroad springs largely from the presence . . . of Franco who . . . now wishes to extend his dictatorship for life." He could not "assent" to acts that infringed "not only the rights of the Crown but the spiritual heritage" of Spain.

His assent—or lack of it—changed nothing. He was being told, not asked. Now, the Falangist press in Spain outdid itself in abuse. The pretender was called a plotter, a traitor, a Freemason, even an "Englishman." Financial reprisals were employed to punish him. The royal properties in Spain were sequestered, and the moderate income Franco had permitted the widowed Queen Mother Eugenia Victoria in Switzerland was slashed.

Don Juan's opposition to the Law of Succession must be attributed to his "absolute ignorance" of conditions in Spain and to the "deception and maneuvering" of his advisers, noted Franco with icy contempt. As the campaign grew, the Monarchists began to see the writing on the wall. Soon they had relapsed into silence. Don Juan's star had waned.

The Villa Giralda

From the railway station near the beach at Estoril, up past the ornate but characterless Palácio Hotel, the yellowing old casino, and sleepy villas on emerald lawns, runs the road to the Villa Giralda. There, on a hilltop overlooking the Atlantic, stands Don Juan's house; a white two-story villa fronted by a balcony on which he, his wife, and their children appear to greet visiting deputations of loyal Spaniards.

Don Juan is not officially exiled from Spain; he is self-exiled. He can enter and leave Spain and occasionally does, coming ashore from a yacht or pausing between airplanes at Barajas Airport, where a few friends drive out to greet him and exchange news. But there must be no demonstrations, and there is always a police officer hovering in the background. As long as Franco lives, there will be no permanent place in Spain for the Pretender.

Don Juan's move from Lausanne to Estoril in 1946 has long

been a bone of contention. At the time, it seemed wise. Franco's prestige was low, Allied pressure was growing, and it was agreed that the Pretender should be near at hand.

"You will be in Madrid in two months," one leading Monarchist exulted at the time. It was an example of the daydreaming that has characterized Monarchist thinking and left Franco in power.

Yet, in some ways, the Pretender's move to Estoril has been convenient. The Portuguese resort lies but an hour's flight from Madrid, an overnight trip by car or train. The Pretender is thus accessible to all Spaniards, rich or poor. Many call on him, including even charabancs of Spanish tourists. Franco knows who the visitors are, for his embassy in Lisbon is a useful watchtower. Yet the more realistic Monarchists lament the years spent in Portugal's luxuriant stagnation. Estoril is like a graveyard: its lawns are clipped, its hedges trimmed, but the air hangs lifeless, and nothing breaks the silence but the click of the roulette wheel or the shuffling of cards in the millionaires' villas.

"I've often thought of moving," Don Juan tells friends, "but where? After all these years, you can't easily ask your wife and family to pack up and move. Here, I'm in contact with Spain. My phones are tapped, but whatever happens in the Puerta del Sol (Madrid's Times Square) I know within ten minutes."

Protocol at the Villa Giralda is informal, yet the staff never forgets the royal status of the sun-tanned sailor who lives there: King Juan III of Spain, King of Aragon, King of Castile, King of Jerusalem, King of the Two Sicilies, King of Gibraltar, King of the East and West Indies, King of the Oceanic Countries, Archduke of Austria, Duke of Burgundy, Duke of Brabant and Duke of Milan, Count of Barcelona, Count of Flanders, Count of the Tyrol, and a Cavalier of the Golden Fleece. His preferred title, Count of Barcelona, is a gesture toward the Catalan capital, a city of 2 million inhabitants, and a flourishing port at a time when Madrid was a hamlet.

He is physically impressive, this man who may yet ascend the throne. He stands six feet three and holds himself erect. The eyes are keen, brown, and crinkle with good humor.

"Franco will never restore the monarchy in his lifetime," he tells callers calmly. His words carry no bitterness—only resignation.

Spain needs a constitutional monarchy, he says, to bind up the nation's wounds and preserve its traditions. A monarchy of the British, Scandinavian, or Dutch model could restore civil liberties without abandoning law and order; allow evolution without revolution. If such a monarchy does not succeed Franco quickly, Spain will revert to another right-wing dictatorship or gravitate to Castroism.

He is nonetheless sanguine, because he believes that the Spanish will accept a constitutional monarchy, which would restore Spain's prestige abroad and might even open the doors to NATO and to the Common Market.

Don Juan has had long years in exile to ponder not only his father's mistakes, but also his own. He admits that he has made mistakes, and it is clear that the day of the ringing anti-Franco *pronunciamientos* is over. The keynote now is caution. His critics call this caution as bad as—if not worse than—Franco's immobilism, but Don Juan points out that Franco controls the censorship and that every word he utters is distorted in Spain. If he pledges that he will rule as a "constitutional" king, the very word "constitutional" takes on a pejorative ring—like the word "liberal." Both have come to imply bickering, parliamentary deadlocks, occult maneuverings, civil chaos, anticlericalism, and antimilitarism.

The term "social justice" is currently in vogue in Spain, but whenever Don Juan urges social justice, or freedom of the press, or trade union freedom, the Falange bays "treason." The Pretender is, in effect, muzzled: if he urges education reforms, the Church sees its monopoly threatened; if he urges fiscal reforms, the bankers cry "Socialism"; if he urges land reforms, the landowners murmur that he has fallen prey to Marxism.

349

Gradually, he has lapsed into a leaden silence. Even his occasional appeals to faith and unity have become bloodless after the nervous editing by his councilors. His image in Spain has all but disappeared. This suits Franco well, but it is unfortunate, for Don Juan has an image of his own.

"He is not brilliant, but he is wise," said a Spanish observer. "He has seen a lot. He listens to everyone, yet he knows his own mind. He has few illusions, but he has courage. He would make a good king."

Don Juan's Anglo-Saxon heritage and his many years abroad have reinforced his natural belief in democracy; yet in order to gain the army's support, he has had to obscure his political ideas in public, leaving such vital issues as universal suffrage, free elections, political parties, freedom of the press, speech, and association as well as social and economic reforms to the future. He has democratic ideas, but he believes it would be political suicide to proclaim them now. If ever he returns, he will dismantle the Francoist machinery with caution.

"Much that has grown up under Franco will be of permanent use to Spain," he says. "It can't be tossed away. Many of the younger men high in the regime have no connection with the Civil War. Spain needs them. And the older officials cannot be dismissed abruptly—only slowly and decorously."

During the 1962 Asturian strikes I asked one leader what the workers thought about a monarchy after Franco. "The monarchy might be all right for people up here," he said, lifting his hand above his head, "but what about the people down here?" He looked at me intently, his hand a foot above the floor. Not hostility but indifference seems to be their general reaction. Knowing this, Don Juan has lately begun to make cautious contacts with intellectuals and labor leaders.

"I asked some intellectuals for ideas on the monarchy," he told me not long ago, "and I got back a sixty-page memorandum from Professor José Luis Aranguren alone. He wrote that he was no *cortesano* (courtier), but that he was happy to respond to my invitation."

But Don Juan still refuses to engage in clandestine deals with the anti-Franco opposition. Even Gil Robles has been dropped from the Royal Privy Council because of his involvement in the Munich affair. Don Juan is skeptical, moreover, of the opposition's airy claims of mass support. "If I am as popular at home as these gentlemen say," he often inquires, "why am I still in exile?"

The First Two Meetings

To date, Franco and Don Juan have held three meetings, at six-year intervals (1948, 1954, 1960). Each time, the main topic has been the education of Don Juan's sons, Juan Carlos and, until his death, the little "Alfonsito."*

It is not clear who first proposed that Don Juan's sons be educated in Spain, but there were advantages for both the Pretender and the dictator in this arrangement.

At the first meeting, Don Juan told Franco that "I wanted my sons brought up in their own country and not called foreigners as I had been. I know my own people, and I did not want my boys penalized because of their birth. I wanted them educated in Spain as Spaniards—whatever the regime." Franco agreed "without great enthusiasm" says Don Juan, but warned that the arrangement would mean "no change in the political situation." The Pretender, egged on by his advisers, had hoped to use his sons as a lever for recognition of his own rights. But Franco held the whip hand.

"I was too pliant, too conciliatory," Don Juan says, but it is hard to see what else he could have done in 1948. As he had feared, many Monarchists, comfortable in their Madrid palaces or country estates, protested that he had sold out; that the Princes would be reared in Falangist doctrines; that the monarchy was tarnished.

* The younger son, Infante Alfonso, died in 1956 in a gun accident at his home in Estoril.

But Franco had also gambled when he met Don Juan publicly and agreed to educate the Princes in Spain. The Falangists, seeing a threat to their position, vented their ire on the Monarchists inside Spain. Don Juan recalls that "Franco was still hounding my supporters in 1948, but the fact that he was willing to meet me at all showed he could not do without the monarchy."

Franco could not do without the monarchy—but he *could* do without the monarch.

The second meeting took place in December, 1954, at Las Cabezas, the lavish country estate of the late millionaire shipowner Juan-Claudio, Conde de Ruiseñada. Much had happened in the meantime. The U.S.–Spanish defense treaties and the Concordat had been signed, foreign aid was beginning to pour into Spain—and Franco was politically stronger.

Ruiseñada was a lifelong Monarchist who had fought for Franco in the Civil War and had long sought to win him over to the royalist cause. He was the guiding spirit of the "collaborators," those Monarchists who saw no hope of ousting Franco and who felt that Spain's interests would better be served by reconciliation. Franco might name Don Juan his successor if the Pretender was loyal, Ruiseñada contended, but if the Monarchists continued to oppose him, Franco might choose as his successor a regent or even a rival Carlist claimant.

To propagate his views, Ruiseñada had founded the Amigos de Maeztu (Friends of Maeztu), a private club named for a turn-of-the-century Anglo-Basque intellectual who had combined admiration for British style with ultra-Catholic orthodoxy and an intellectual absolutism bordering on Fascism.

Ruiseñada was one of the few Spaniards with prewar contacts in the banks of London, Paris, and Wall Street. Astute and cultivated, his wealth and Civil War record had won him Franco's trust. His open Monarchist sympathies gave him unrivaled access to Don Juan. He thus played a key role in Spanish politics. The meeting he now arranged was intended not only to settle Prince Juan Carlos' military training in Spain but also to give Don Juan a chance to protest against the Falangist persecution. No one else in Spain would dare to criticize the Falange to Franco's face.

In November, 1954, Franco had authorized the first municipal elections in years, and the Monarchists had put up four candidates in Monarchist strongholds in Madrid. To their indignation, Franco and his entire cabinet had ostentatiously left Madrid a week before the election, and the Falangists, taking this as a cue, had begun a campaign of harassment and intimidation that had shocked even the cynical Spaniards. Falangist gangs broke up Monarchist election meetings, ripped Monarchist posters off the hustings, harassed Monarchist voters, and turned Franco's "authentic" representation into a farce. The judges and officials had only shrugged or turned away.

Franco, sensing the coming complaints, took the offensive from the start and tried to keep the Pretender off balance by confining the talks exclusively to Juan Carlos' education.

"I'll put him through the army, navy, and air force academies," Franco proposed, "then after one or two years in a university, I'll put him beside me to see how government works."

Don Juan agreed to the three service academies but insisted he did not want his son sent later to a Spanish university. He wanted him given special training instead for the throne, but finally the two men decided to drop the subject until the time drew nearer. Both agreed, however, that Juan Carlos would enter the army academy at Zaragoza a few weeks later in early 1955. Now Don Juan turned to his own political complaints.

The time had come, he said, to tell Spain when and how the monarchy was to be restored. Since World War II, the people had been awaiting the end of the dictatorship and the establishment of a democratic regime. Time was passing. He bluntly criticized Franco's censorship, police brutality, administrative corruption, and government incompetence, and he urged Franco to divest himself of some of his powers as a move toward reforms. No king who succeeded could hope to wield the same dictatorial powers, he warned.

The Pretender urged Franco to adopt a five-point political program including (1) liberty of the press; (2) independence of the judiciary; (3) social justice through redistribution of public spending; (4) Sindical freedom to prevent the workers' turning to "extremism" and, (5) "authentic" political and social representation outside the totalitarian Falange party.

Franco heard his pleas for reform in silence.

"I do not find the burden of rule heavy," he replied coldly. "Spain is easy to govern."

Another six years were to pass before the slow orbit of Spanish politics brought Don Juan and Franco together for their third meeting. During those six years, major changes had taken place in the world, in Spain, and in the Monarchist movement too. Yet the succession remained unclear, and many Spaniards had begun to rig a private lifeline to Don Juan. Opus Dei was one example. Its two chief publicists, Rafael Calvo Serer and Florentino Pérez Embid, became frequent visitors at Estoril. The Carlists, too, were keeping an eye to windward, and late in 1957, forty-six of them, headed by Aráuz de Robles, had called on Don Juan, bending their knees and kissing his hand as their lawful king. Don Juan donned the Carlists' red *boina* (beret), placed a white *boina* on his wife's head, and invited the delegation to lunch.

Not long after, an incident involving Franco's wife, Doña Carmen, had set political tongues wagging. Stopping in Lisbon en route to a holiday in Madeira in May, 1958, Doña Carmen had found an invitation to tea with the royal family at Villa Giralda. Escorted by her suite, including Castiella, his wife, and the wife of Interior Minister Alonso Vega, Señora de Franco had entered the royal home-in-exile and had dropped Don Juan and Doña Maria a deep curtsy, addressing them both as *"Majestad."*

Her aides, regardless of their sentiments, had had no alternative but to follow suit. Soon, all Spain was buzzing with rumors about the political significance of the deference shown the Pretender by the dictator's consort.

That same spring, Franco allowed Juan Carlos, now a naval cadet, to sail with his classmates on the training ship "Juan Sebastian Elcano" for a visit to the United States and approved Motrico's plans for a banquet at the Washington Embassy, visits to Annapolis and West Point, calls on Eisenhower and Dulles, and a luncheon with representatives of *The New York Times*. These signs of Franco's good will toward his son so heartened Don Juan that he, too, seized the occasion to sail across the Atlantic on his yacht and meet Juan Carlos in New York.

Yet Franco's benevolence had no political content. While weekending in Connecticut, Don Juan was awakened by an urgent telephone call from Estoril. He was told that Franco had just promulgated the "Twelve Principles of the Movement" in the Cortes. Should Don Juan not hurry back? Warily, the Pretender asked what Franco had said, and with each succeeding sentence, his heart sank.

It was the same old political potpourri; something for the Monarchists, something for the Falangists, everything for Franco. Don Juan hung up the telephone. There was no reason to hurry back.

The Provisional Government

That autumn, after his return to Estoril, several opposition groups made Don Juan a new proposal. They would work for his restoration, eschewing any alternative, regency or republic, if Don Juan would agree in advance to a "provisional government" of two years when Franco died. This provisional government would redress grievances, punish malefactors, dismantle the remnants of Francoism—in short, put Spain on the road to recovery and prepare it for Don Juan's return. The *Lugarteniente,* or

355

head of such a transitional regime, would be his cousin, H.R.H. Infante General Alfonso d'Orléans y Borbón.

Infante Alfonso is not only Spain's senior military aviator but one of the most remarkable Spaniards alive. Still active and hale at seventy-nine, he lives on his estates near Jerez de la Frontera. Born a double first cousin of Alfonso XIII, he descends from Louis Philippe, last "King of the French," and from Isabella II of Spain.

As a military pilot, he flew in the 1925–26 Spanish-French pacification of the Rif, and was decorated. On April 14, 1931, he accompanied Alfonso XIII into exile. Finding himself stranded penniless in Paris, he cabled Henry Ford, whom he knew slightly, asking him for a job. Back came a laconic order to report to the Ford plant in Asnières, and the next day "Mr. Orleans," aged forty-four, was given a broom and set to sweeping floors.

Within four years, he had risen to be confidential assistant to senior Ford executives, in Europe and in the United States. One of his more intriguing assignments was to evaluate the likelihood of an Italian invasion of Abyssinia in 1935. He set to work analyzing the political and military factors in both countries, the climate, terrain, and even the tidal conditions of Ethiopia so astutely that Ford shipped and sold large numbers of trucks to both sides just before hostilities began, and the Infante received his first bonus.* Another dramatic assignment was a study of the operations of Al Capone's gang in Cook County, Illinois, where Ford was trying to sell taxis. To this day, he can reminisce about Capone's empire of 4,000 gunmen with firsthand knowledge.

At the start of the Civil War, he returned to Spain, offering his services to Franco as a step toward restoring the monarchy. He knew every military chieftain in Spain, including Franco, intimately. Yet as Franco's grip tightened, the Infante, like other Monarchists, became disillusioned. He began to organize against

---

* Out of it he bought for his wife, the Infanta Beatriz—a granddaughter both of Queen Victoria of England and of the Czar of Russia—her first new dress in four years.

Franco, and after World War II, when it looked as if Franco might be forced from power, he agreed to become Don Juan's chief delegate in Spain. He threw himself wholeheartedly into the task, putting his Ford-trained talent at the monarchy's service, organizing a network of 3,500 reliable Monarchists across the country, and even keeping a card index of Monarchist "shadow cabinets," should Franco fall. But soon Franco cracked down. Don Juan was persuaded that his cousin was "too active." Infante Alfonso was stripped of his aviation command and ordered to retire to his estates, raise sherry, and keep away from politics.

Don Juan's rejection of the proposed provisional government headed by his cousin caused little surprise and only faint protests. Soon, however, a new ferment was stirring, called Unión Española.

On January 29, 1959, a hawk-visaged young Monarchist openly challenged Franco's rule during a banquet in a Madrid hotel. This was the historic Menfis dinner in honor of Joaquín Satrustegui, the young society lawyer who had founded the militant Liberal Monarchist movement Unión Española two years earlier. The banquet was a thinly disguised defiance of Franco.

The ninety or more Spaniards who gathered in the Menfis dining room that night were scarcely revolutionaries. Most were rich and well connected. They included lawyers, bankers, teachers, sportsmen, industrialists, a general or two—all men of substance and position. There was Gil Robles. There were Jaime Miralles and Fernando Álvarez de Miranda, both socially prominent; Antonio Menchaca, a hothead famed for his exploits in Franco's Civil War navy. There was the law professor Enrique Tierno Galvan, one of Franco's bitter critics and increasingly influential in university circles. With his silvery hair and mild manner, Tierno seemed inoffensive. It was hard to place him in any political category. He was a Socialist, yet attracted by Satrustegui's boldness.

After dinner, a hush fell over the assemblage. Satrustegui, remaining seated, read a fifteen-page indictment of the juridic "illegality" of Franco's regime. Couched in sober legal prose, it avoided personal attacks but was nonetheless an act of singular daring. Point by point, it assailed "one-man rule" and soon shouts of *muy bien* could be heard on all sides. When Satrustegui finished, the banquet party broke into applause and cheers.

The Menfis dinner has passed into history but the reactions have not. It did Franco little visible harm, but it marked a new stage in Monarchist activity, and it was the most outspoken semi-public denunciation of the regime. Arias Salgado's censors sought to smother the news, but it was known throughout Spain within twenty-four hours. Satrustegui and his friends were heavily fined and warned that a repetition would mean prison.

Yet in Estoril, Satrustegui's attack only irritated Don Juan and his privy council. In their view, it was a purposeless provocation of Franco, and they feared that the dictator would now order reprisals against Monarchist "plotting." The hour called, not for declamations around a banquet table, they complained, but for cautious approximation to Franco and, above all, no angering of the potent army chiefs.

Satrustegui has remained a militantly unrepentant thorn in Franco's side. Lean, and slightly lame, he thrives on battle. His forte is closely reasoned denunciation of the "illegality" of Franco's reign plus unswerving nonviolent opposition at every turn. Fines, persecution, a year spent in exile in the Canary Islands (for his attendance at Munich in 1962) have not cowed him. Persecution confirms his charge that Spain is a "police" state.

"We have been living twenty-five years under total personal rule, which," he tells visitors, "was originally conceded for a concrete task in exceptional circumstances. Few Spaniards thought it would last so long." He insists that the regime must start preparing at once for an "orderly" transfer to a monarchy under Don Juan, and that such a monarchy must be "absolutely contemporary, up to date, capable of representing all Spaniards with adequate guarantees for the orderly restoration of their liberties."

Such liberties would include free association, "authentic" representation of the people, freedom to strike, freedom of collective bargaining, an independent judiciary, and replacement of censorship by a press law. His Unión Española proposes outlawing Communism as well as "all other totalitarian" systems, and advocates a strong executive free from "continuing, mandatory" interference by the Cortes. When the monarchy has been restored, Satrustegui says, Unión Española will demand a national referendum to approve, or disapprove, Franco's Fundamental Laws.

Unlike the medieval-minded Carlists, who shudder at the thought of political parties, Unión Española foresees the inevitable revival of parties and even hints at cooperation with left-of-center moderate groups like the Socialists. Unique among Monarchist factions, it is well disposed toward labor.

"We are certain that the monarchy will consider the [cooperation of] workers' organizations absolutely indispensable," its program states. Also, unlike most Monarchist cliques, it hopes that Spanish Socialism will know how to adopt that "European configuration," which has enabled it to "form the government in so many monarchies."

In Franco Spain, where Socialism is tantamount to Communism, such views have tarred Satrustegui and his Unión Española as "left wing." Not only Franco but also rival political blocs such as Opus Dei and the Carlists have warned Don Juan to shun Unión Española, and Don Juan has complied. Satrustegui remains an unknown factor in Spanish politics: brave, lucid, articulate, yet perhaps too quixotic for his own good. Whatever the future, he is likely to be heard of once Franco is gone.

Almost a year after the Menfis dinner, Juan Carlos completed his four years in Franco's military academies. The question now arose of his higher education. While he had matured consider-

359

ably, he was, as one instructor put it, "no older than his actual age (twenty-one)." He had the tastes of aristocratic young Spaniards: sports, parties, jazz records, fast cars, and dancing. Convivial and democratic, he was popular with his fellow cadets. He had worked hard, had dodged publicity, and had qualified as a jet pilot in the Spanish Air Force. No other Spaniard had won commissions in all three services, and the service chiefs were proud of him. But when Juan Carlos returned to Estoril for the 1959–60 Christmas holidays, tension began to mount between the Villa Giralda and the Pardo.

Don Juan, supported by many followers, now took the line that a *nueva etapa* (new phase) had begun in Juan Carlos' life, necessitating another meeting with Franco. Using his son as a lever, he would again try to get Franco's recognition that he, Don Juan, was still first in line to the throne. Juan Carlos' long years in Spain had focused world attention on the boy, rather than the father, and it was inevitable, perhaps, that despite all the devotion existing between the two, the father would grow restive. Don Juan decided to demand recognition of Juan Carlos as "Prince of Asturias." The title is politically important, for unlike the British title Prince of Wales, which is conferred on the heir apparent at the pleasure of the sovereign, the title Prince of Asturias is *automatically* assumed by the heir to the Spanish throne. Since 1933, Juan Carlos had been recognized by Spanish legitimists as Prince of Asturias, but not by Franco. Now, Don Juan was preparing for a "tougher" line with Franco and intended to delay Juan Carlos' return to Spain until a new interview was arranged.

In preparation for his third confrontation, Don Juan shook up his moribund Consejo Privado. This council had been created as a brain trust in 1944, when the scent of Allied victory had begun rallying to Don Juan such disparate supporters as Gil Robles, who admired British and American democracy, and Carlist chiefs who wanted a return to the days of Philip II. The Council's usefulness had been debatable, yet by the late 1950's, its membership had swollen to nearly fifty grandees and generals, bankers and landowners, lawyers, intellectuals, ex-Falangists, Opus Dei priests, poets, publishers, diplomats, and even a psychiatrist.

Some claimed to represent geographical regions, others the Demo-Christian masses; some Opus Dei, others the Carlists. All quarreled ceaselessly and succeeded only in reducing their advice to Don Juan to the lowest common denominator—passivity.

Yet Don Juan believed that he needed a royalist organization in Spain, and largely on the suggestion of his Opus Dei aides, he decided in early 1960 to shake up the Council by giving it a new leader and a seven-man Permanente, or inner executive body. The Council chief, Lieutenant General Alfredo Kindelán, was ill and aging, so José María Pemán, the Andalusian poet, was now named to replace him as president of the Council.* The new Permanente, meanwhile, created four committees, for legal, financial, propaganda, and intelligence-gathering functions, and the Opus Dei activists Calvo Serer and Pérez Embid assumed key roles.

Many Monarchists scoffed that this was all daydreaming, but Opus and its adherents insisted that the time had come for hard-headed planning and organization, for the creation of a Monarchist network to gather funds, to disseminate propaganda, and to enlarge the chain of Monarchist Circulos Balmes in the larger cities. Soon a Monarchist newssheet, the *Boletín del Secretariado del Consejo Privado de SAR el Conde de Barcelona*, began finding its way once each fortnight, by hand or in plain envelopes sent through the mails, to 3,000 Monarchist sympathizers, some high in Franco's regime.

The Third Meeting

The third meeting was preceded by a welter of confusion typical of Iberian politics. By mid-March, 1960, Madrid's political circles were seething with rumors of another Franco–Don Juan meeting; rumors that "well-informed" sources confirmed, denied,

---

* Still riven by jealousies, the Council has once again lapsed into torpor. Don Juan's key agent in Spain now is the veteran Monarchist Jesús Pabón.

reaffirmed, redenied, ridiculed, and confirmed again. Days before the rumored date—March 22—foreign journalists, television and newsreel cameramen, magazine writers, and radio reporters had begun pouring into the moated border fortress of Ciudad Rodrigo, on the Portuguese frontier. Hurriedly renting balconies and other strategic points, they set up their cameras, strung up lights, and began arranging radio, telephone, and teletype circuits to Paris, London, New York, and other capitals.

Somehow, Franco's "secret" plans to meet Don Juan had leaked out, but no one could say how. Franco had selected the border town not only for its isolation but to prevent Don Juan from promenading inside Spain, since the Caudillo wanted no publicity. However, to his indignation he learned that not only were foreign reporters pouring into Ciudad Rodrigo, but even the excited Spanish press had begun to arrive, while local Spanish officials, not to be outdone, started to erect flags and bunting. Everyone anticipated a major political development. Angry and embarrassed, Franco sent a courier to Don Juan, asking to postpone the meeting at least a week and then to move it to a less spectacular arena. Once more, the isolated Las Cabezas was chosen. Ruiseñada had died in 1958, but his son, the Marqués de Comillas, now willingly played host.

At the meeting, Franco made it clear that he wanted Juan Carlos to return to continue his higher education in Spain, and to sugar the pill, he offered to arrange special courses for him at Madrid University, to give him a state residence and honors due his rank. But agreement on Juan Carlos' higher education in Spain was only one of Don Juan's reasons for this meeting. More important, he was hoping to smoke out Franco's political intentions; to force him to listen to criticism of his regime; and, above all, to show the world that Don Juan and not Juan Carlos was the head of the dynasty. In his pocket was a draft communiqué, which stated that Juan Carlos' continuing presence in Spain in no way "prejudiced" Don Juan's own claims. The communiqué was to be the price Franco had to pay for Don Juan's concession to let his son return to Spain.

Franco once again tried to be "cordial," Don Juan told friends later, but succeeded only in being "cold and very reserved." This is easy to understand, since the Pretender now fired off salvo after salvo against Franco's "corrupt" and "inefficient" government; against his "impossible" administrative system; against Arias Salgado and his policy of stifling news favorable to the monarchy while giving free rein to anti-Monarchist scurrility.

In 1954, charged Don Juan, Franco had agreed to permit "constructive" Monarchist propaganda, but the promise had not been kept. At this point, Franco is said to have twisted in his chair, protesting that Don Juan was *"muy duro—very hard"* on Arias Salgado, who, he said, was "trying to do his best."

A heated argument now broke out over the rival Consejos— Franco's Consejo del Reino and Don Juan's Consejo Privado. Don Juan labeled Franco's Consejo del Reino a collection of elderly nonentities who could render no service should Don Juan suddenly have to ascend the throne, and Franco is said to have conceded that he should devote some thought to appointing younger men.

Now it was Franco's turn to take the offensive. He had learned of the recent reorganization of Don Juan's Consejo Privado, and he wanted to know why Don Juan needed "political" advice anyway? What purpose did the Consejo Privado serve, beside intrigue? Don Juan had surrounded himself with the same "dukes and marquises" who had brought past monarchies into discredit.

For an hour, Franco poured scorn on Don Juan's privy councilors. Don Juan is said to have retorted that advisers such as Gil Robles and José María Pemán were *"muy noble"* patriots, every bit as representative of the best in Spain as such Franco ministers as Arias Salgado or Carrero Blanco. "Is it a matter of national concern that you have chosen the Conde de Casa Loja, a man with a title, to be head of your own civil household?" he asked. Franco stirred without replying.

The day wore on, but neither yielded. In discussing Spain, Franco repeatedly referred to "them" and "us," as if the Civil War were still raging and Spain were still split into hostile halves. When he expressed his flat opposition to any revival of political parties, Don Juan coldly asked whether Spain was to be saddled forever with "one bad political party"—the Falange. Franco permitted himself the ghost of a smile.

At the day's end, Don Juan played his trump: the communiqué. He handed it to Franco, who read it, flushed with anger, and refused to sign it. Without a communiqué, Don Juan said, Prince Juan Carlos would not return to Spain. The Pretender and the dictator sat eyeing each other, neither giving way. But it was growing late, and Franco, visibly irritated, was tiring.

"Deme el comunicado . . . Give me the communiqué," he growled at last. He scrawled his signature hastily onto the two copies, handed one to Don Juan and shoved the other in his pocket. He would release his copy to the press that night on his return to Madrid, he said.

At that point, an incident occurred that gives a penetrating insight into Franco's character. Without warning, he said, "I have brought Vigón and Rubio with me. They are outside. They have asked to be presented to you. Do you agree?"

Lieutenant General Jorge Vigón, the Minister of Public Works, was not only the leading Monarchist in the cabinet but a lifelong friend of Don Juan. Rubio, the Minister of Education, on the other hand, was a Falangist and reputedly an arch-Republican, whom Don Juan had never met.* He assented immediately, and Franco touched a bell. What happened remains one of the most embarrassing moments in Don Juan's life.

As the elderly Vigón entered, Don Juan rose, and the two friends embraced in the warm Spanish *abrazo*. Rubio followed, bowing stiffly to Don Juan and shaking his hand somewhat perfunctorily. Don Juan resumed his seat. Franco, however, re-

---

* After the interview, Rubio was said to have told friends, "I may not be a Monarchist, but I am now 100 per cent pro Don Juan de Borbón."

mained seated and refused even to acknowledge the presence of his two ministers. The minutes passed in silence.

Don Juan wondered whether he should invite the ministers to be seated, but reflecting that they were Franco's aides, brought by Franco, he refrained. Finally, as the silence became unbearable, he looked up and said: "Gentlemen, General Franco and I have agreed that in the interests of Spain my son will return to Madrid to continue his education. We have agreed to work for perfect understanding and mutual cordiality from now on."

Vigón beamed while Rubio stiffly replied: "Since the Caudillo has decreed that Spain is a kingdom, we pledge our complete cooperation."

Silence descended once more, and a clock could be heard ticking in a faraway room. From time to time, Don Juan tried to start a general conversation, but Franco remained cold and aloof. For an hour, the dictator left his two cabinet ministers standing like footmen.

Next morning, Don Juan and his friends avidly scanned the Madrid newspapers, only to find that they had been outmaneuvered again. On the front pages was the communiqué—significantly altered by Franco. It read:

> On the twenty-ninth, at the Palace of Las Cabezas [Cáceres province], His Excellency the Chief of State and His Royal Highness the Count of Barcelona met. During the interview, which was conducted with great cordiality, matters of importance to the life of the nation were discussed in which both participants [*interlocutores*] concurred.
>
> Among the ideas reviewed was that of the new and final stage of Prince Juan Carlos' civil studies. Agreement was reached on . . . organization of these studies, which the Prince must now carry out inside our country in intimate and constant contact with Spanish university life.
>
> In view of groundless interpretations that have arisen, especially abroad, as a result of the Prince's presence in Spain, His Excel-

365

lency, the Chief of State, and H.R.H. the Count of Barcelona announce that his presence is due to reasons of education and to national sentiment, since it is fitting that Prince Juan Carlos be educated in the atmosphere of his own country and since (in accordance with the Law of Succession) this does not prejudice the question of succession or the normal transmission of dynastic obligations and responsibilities.

The interview ended with the reinforced conviction that cordiality and good understanding are important for the future of Spain and for the consolidation and continuation of the benefits of peace and for the achievements of the National Movement.

Four major changes had been made in the text accepted by Franco the evening before:

1. Franco had changed Don Juan's *"ambas personalidades"* ("both personages") to *"ambas interlocutores,"* ("participants"), eliminating any suggestion that Don Juan was an equal.

2. He had eliminated the title "Prince of Asturias" in reference to Juan Carlos.

3. He had inserted a tribute to the "achievements of the National Movement," a reference that Don Juan had always avoided.

4. Most galling of all, he had inserted "in accordance with the Law of Succession," leaving Don Juan's royal status as unclear as before.

Nevertheless, one of the shrewdest European ambassadors in Madrid cabled his government that the interview had marked a "turning point" in Spanish history. The Monarchists tried hard to give it the appearance of victory, but a few days later, Carrero Blanco assured me that the interview had merely been a "new phase" in the slow unfolding of the Caudillo's plans. Nothing had changed. Despite Don Juan's pleas, there would be no increased Monarchist propaganda, for, as he put it, "the wrong people" would begin propagandizing.

"Why, there are even *liberals* among the Monarchists!" he exclaimed, his black, bushy eyebrows rising in indignation.

Did this mean that Franco would never restore the monarchy?

"Not at all," he answered blandly. "The only possible guarantee of continuity in what we have achieved is the monarchy. Juan Carlos will be king one day. If anything suddenly happens to Franco, he will have to ascend the throne."

"What about Don Juan?" I asked. "Is he not first in line?"

Carrero paused for a minute before answering. Then, almost reproachfully, he replied:

"Ya es viejo—He is already old."

Juan Carlos finally returned to Spain in April, 1960, and began a rigorous study program of law, political science, history, and economics. His arrival at Madrid University created some excitement among the students, the girls especially, but the word had gone out that there were to be no demonstrations, and the press stayed away.

Franco gave him the little Zarzuela Palace, not far from his creamed-colored Pardo, and surrounded him with army, navy, and air force aides. Some observers noted that the prince's chief tutor was Father Federico Suárez Verdaguer, an eminent historian and ranking member of Opus Dei.

Unsuspected even by Franco, a new drama was now beginning to unfold. At the far end of the Mediterranean, Queen Frederika of Greece had taken an interest in Juan Carlos. He was six feet tall, well built, with blond, wavy hair—and he was a suitable match for her daughter, Princess Sophie. And Greece and Spain had much in common: the same timelessness; the same sun and soil; the same Mediterranean shores; the same olive groves; and warm-hearted, strong peasants. Juan Carlos was invited to Athens for holidays and soon found himself teaching Spanish to Sophie.

Don Juan and Doña María knew vaguely of their son's interest in the Greek princess, but he had flirted with many girls. They had known of his fondness for blonde Maria Gabriella, daughter of their neighbor-in-exile, Umberto of Italy. But Gabriella was too worldly for Juan Carlos, to the core a Spanish male with very decided views about women's role in life. When on September 13, 1961, the King and Queen of Greece announced the betrothal of their daughter to Juan Carlos, Don Juan and Doña María had little advance warning; they barely had time to arrive from Estoril for the announcement made at the Queen Mother's home in Lausanne.

The betrothal was well received in Spain. The Monarchists had been urging that Juan Carlos marry to safeguard the dynasty, but the Pretender had protested that a twenty-three-year-old should have a few more years to sow his wild oats before settling down. But no one was more surprised to hear of the engagement than Franco, who was fishing aboard his yacht "Azor" when an aide hurried to his swivel chair on the quarter-deck.

"The Count of Barcelona is calling by radio telephone from Lausanne, Excellency. He says it is urgent."

Franco rushed to his cabin. Now another one of those comic dramas took place that occasionally make Spanish politics a delight. The radio-telephone connection passed from Lausanne via Geneva, Paris, and Madrid to San Sebastián, and from there to the yacht. Needless to say, the sound quality was terrible. Franco could faintly hear Don Juan shouting something about a wedding; that a letter was on its way. Suddenly, it dawned on Franco that this was a historic moment.

"Hold the phone, Alteza," he shouted. Don Juan, in Lausanne, held the receiver for five minutes, ten minutes, fifteen minutes. After eighteen minutes, he thrust it angrily into the hands of his secretary, Padilla, and crossed the room to pour himself a drink. Warned by Padilla's agitated face, he hurried back to hear Franco reading a long congratulatory peroration. The Caudillo had been composing it laboriously while Don Juan was holding the phone. It took five minutes to read. This was no perfunctory "give the children my love" message; this was high history, and Franco, a true Spaniard, was ready to lay aside the fishing line for the pen when history beckoned.

When Juan Carlos called on Franco a few weeks later to inform him of his engagement, the Generalissimo gazed up at the tall young lieutenant with a long, penetrating look.

"Are you pleased with your fiancée?" he asked, and added enigmatically, "You know, you don't *have* to marry a princess."

At any other time, the Monarchists would have rejoiced in any embarrassment to Franco, such as the Asturian strikes. But in the spring of 1962, their minds were on the wedding that was to take place in Athens on May 14. Arias Salgado censored both the strikes and the wedding preparations with equal ferocity, and only after heated Monarchist protests did Franco order him to announce a national subscription to present Juan Carlos and Sophie with a wedding gift from the nation.

The wedding threatened to split the Monarchists even more than did Arias' maneuverings. One grandee responsible for seating arrangements threw up his hands in horror as he described the fierce intriguing for invitations.

Before Juan Carlos left, Franco slipped over his head the glittering collar of Carlos III, an honor reserved for reigning sovereigns and told him he would send a "decorous" representative of the regime to the wedding. A few days later, Navy Minister Admiral Felipe Abarzuza and his English wife sailed aboard the veteran cruiser "Canarias," which was gaily decorated for the occasion. Now page after page of Spain's newspapers were devoted to pictures of Juan Carlos, Sophie, Queen Mother Victoria Eugenia, even Doña María. But the one and only picture of Don Juan appeared on the day of the wedding—on page 78 of the "royal" issue of *ABC*.

In July, 1962, Francisco Franco, in black-and-white sport shoes and a summer suit, received me at his summer home on the Galician coast. The Caudillo's face was tanned from the ocean air and he was in good spirits. His eyes frequently strayed through the huge windows over trimmed emerald lawns to the Atlantic he so loves. The drawing room was cluttered with gewgaws: elephant

369

tusks and porcelain parrots on the mantelpiece; wagon wheels skillfully carved into coffee tables.

He talked quietly of the transformation taking place in Spain. Periodically it was necessary to *"perfeccionar—perfect"* the machinery of government; tighten up here, and ease a little there. Men grew tired and had to be replaced. The strikes had been fomented by "foreign Communists," and he added with a laugh, "our police tried to lay their hands on them, but unsuccessfully."

What about Spain's future, I asked. Had the time come to start preparing public opinion for a monarchy? Would Don Juan return while Franco lived?

"No," replied Franco, shaking his head gently. "He cannot return. The wrong people would start maneuvering."

Did Franco recognize Don Juan as chief claimant to the throne?

"No, he has no special recognition. The Law of Succession provides for either a king or regent. There is always Don Jaime."

This reference to Don Juan's deaf-mute brother, who had twice renounced his claims, was startling, yet Franco spoke without a trace of irony. What about Don Jaime's two categoric renunciations, I asked.

"They do not affect his son Alfonso," Franco replied. "There is also . . ."—he hesitated, as if trying to recall the name—"Don Hugo."

It was clear that the name of the young French son of the elderly Carlist pretender was not on the tip of his tongue.

"Whoever will be king," Franco went on, "must know the country and be identified with its institutions. And," he added, pointedly, "he must be loved by the country."

Epilogue

Little has changed.

Juan Carlos and Sophie have taken up residence near Madrid under Franco's watchful eye. But while they occasionally take part in state ceremonies or identify themselves with charitable good works, their lives are circumscribed and their circle of friends restricted. Literally, they are gilded birds in Franco's cage.

In late 1963, when their first child—a girl—was born, Don Juan flew to Madrid for the christening. Franco greeted him cordially, but both men eschewed politics, and the Pretender withdrew discreetly from Madrid every night to the country place of a grandee.

Inexorably, however, the pressures are growing. Part of the cabinet wants Franco to place Juan Carlos directly on the throne in 1968, when the Prince will be thirty and Franco himself seventy-five. Others, including the top generals, favor a monarchy under Don Juan as the only safe alternative to another republic, with its partisan passions and agitation involving Communists, Socialists, and a demagogic Falange.

Don Juan himself has consistently refused all hints that he abdicate in favor of his son, holding that such a tactic would defraud millions of Spaniards who regard him as the only possible clean break with Francoism. Yet, for this very reason, it is clear that Franco would prefer the son, Juan Carlos, as a symbol of "continuity." He told a ranking Spanish visitor recently that he would never ask Don Juan to abdicate his right; he would "expect" him to know what was best for his country.

To a large degree, the future of Spain rests in the father-son relationship. Jointly, they can wield a decisive influence over the future, for they alone embody tradition and legitimacy after nearly thirty years of dictatorship and isolation. So far, all efforts to split them have failed. *Ciegamente leal,* blindly loyal, is how Don Juan describes his son; *siempre contigo,* always with you, is how Juan Carlos ends letters to his father. He insists Don Juan is more than his father; he is his king.

Moreover, by standing together, they can overshadow Franco's "nuisance" claimants: the French-born Hugo (Carlos) de Bourbon-Parme and young Alfonso de Borbón-Dampierre, son of Don Juan's deaf-mute brother, Jaime.

Hugo, following his marriage to the ambitious Irene of Holland, was promptly nicknamed "Orange Juice" (Hugo of Orange, or, Jugo de Naranja) by Madrid's wits, and while he added Carlos to his name to lure Carlist support, an icy editorial in *ABC* soon showed that Franco was shooting down this trial balloon before political hot air carried it too far.

Similarly, the Falange, always eager to discomfit Don Juan, has been trying to lionize his restive nephew "Alfonsito," a Madrid bank clerk, but without conspicuous success. Franco wants just enough confusion in Spain; never too much.

Meanwhile, the new generations are pressing for reforms, and Franco's policy of suppressing most news of the monarchy has, paradoxically, spurred the interest of young Spain in a republic again. It is the army and the moneyed interests who prefer a monarchy as the safest transition.

Franco, as usual, is waiting, watching, waiting. Time is carrying away his cronies, and now Muñoz Grandes is seriously ill. Meanwhile, Nieto Antúnez and Carrero Blanco have begun pressing Franco to dust off the Organic Law, which creates the office of a prime minister, and submit it to a national referendum. There is now increasing evidence Franco will do so—not because he has the least intention of yielding total power, but merely to play for time.

"Franco will use the national referendum merely as a symbol of popular support," said a shrewd Spanish observer not long ago. "Then he will put the Organic Law back in its pigeonhole and go on ruling quietly till he dies. He has not the slightest intention of sharing power with anyone, so long as there is breath in him."

Index

Index

Index

Index

Index